PADRE PIO OF PIETRELCINA

LETTERS

VOL. II

CORRESPONDENCE WITH RAFFAELINA CERASE, NOBLEWOMAN

(1914-1915)

Edited by Melchiorre of Pobladura
and Alessandro of Ripabottoni

* * *

English Version

edited by
Father Gerardo Di Flumeri O.F.M. Cap.

Editions
«Padre Pio da Pietrelcina»
Our Lady of Grace Friary
71013 SAN GIOVANNI ROTONDO (FG) - ITALY
2002

First Edition 1987
Second Edition 1997
Third Edition 2002

Nihil obstat

Fr. CRISPINO DI FLUMERI
Min. Prov. O.F.M. Cap.

Foggia, 15 January 1975.

Imprimatur

† GIUSEPPE LENOTTI, Bishop

Foggia, 25 January 1975.

Original title of this book: *Epistolario II. Corrispondenza con la nobildonna Raffaelina Cerase (1914-1915),* San Giovanni Rotondo 1975.

Translated by Mary F. Ingoldsby

ISBN 88-499-0001-5

CONTENTS

PREFACE TO THE ENGLISH EDITION

San Giovanni Rotondo,
23 September 1986.

I am happy to present the second volume of letters of the Servant of God Padre Pio of Pietrelcina to the vast English speaking public.

This volume contains the correspondence that the Padre had with Raffaelina Cerase, a noblewoman of Foggia. She had received a Christian education and was on the road to spiritual perfection when she had the grace of meeting the Padre towards the end of her life, to be prepared by him to meet the Spouse in love and suffering.

But this noblewoman of Foggia did not only benefit spiritually from the Padre. She was also the fortunate instrument used by Providence to make the Servant of God return permanently to the friary. She also prophesied his admirable apostolic ministry. "Padre," she said to Padre Agostino, "make him go back to the friary and make him hear confessions because he will do a lot of good."

According to the explicit testimony of Padre Agostino, she had offered her life to the Lord for the Padre's return to the friary and for his ministry: "I can affirm that that holy soul had sacrificed herself for Padre Pio so that he would return permanently to the friary and do a lot of good for souls through the medium of the confessional." And Raffaelina Cerase died of cancer on 25 March 1916, assisted by her spiritual father.

This then, in brief, is the soul to whom Padre Pio wrote his letters in the years 1914-1915, while he still lived in his native town retained by a mysterious illness.

These letters teach with certainty the ways of God, on the basis of reliable mystical doctrine and solid biblical information. They are therefore a proof of the Padre's cultural grounding and that he is not an improvised spiritual director, but an enlightened guide of souls, sustained by an enviable theological, ascetic-mystical and biblical training.

The principles that guided me in the preparation of the edition of this second volume are the same that guided me in the publication of the first.

The translation is based on the Italian edition of 1975, but the quotations of the first volume do not refer to the Italian edition, but to the English one of 1980. It could not be otherwise for a book addressed to English speaking readers.

The biblical quotations are taken from the *Revised Standard Version, Catholic Edition (London).* Therefore the Psalm numbers follow the Hebrew version and not the Greek. Sometimes, when the meaning moves away from the original, I have noted it by putting Vg., in parenthesis, to indicate that the translation follows the text of the Vulgate.

I need hardly say that I corrected a few errors that nevertheless escaped the painstaking Italian editors, especially in the biblical quotations.

I wish to thank Miss Mary Ingoldsby from Ireland for the translation of this second volume, that has been done, as the first, with great diligence and exceptional skill. And I also thank all those who have helped me in preparing this edition.

On 22 July 1914, Raffaelina Cerase wrote to Padre Pio: "yours words, your assurances give me joy, light and peace."

May this volume kindle "joy, light and peace" in the souls of all the readers.

FR. GERARDO DI FLUMERI
O.F.M.Cap.

INTRODUCTION

Those who take up this volume will certainly want to know something about the authors, origin, vicissitudes, and content of the letters it contains. We intend to satisfy this lawful expectation with a few brief introductory notes which, for the sake of clarity, will be dealt with under the following headings:

I Authors of the letters.
II The letters.
III Spiritual direction: methodology, pedagogics, etc.
IV Conclusion: assessment.

I Authors of the Letters

Our readers are sufficiently familiar with the beloved figure of Padre Pio to dispense us from dwelling here on his spiritual biography even in briefest outline.[1] We intend, on the other hand, to present in greater detail the other correspondent, to illustrate with due care the relationship which

[1] Cf. Padre Pio of Pietrelcina, *Letters, Vol. I, Correspondence with his Spiritual Directors* (1910-1922), edited by Melchiorre of Pobladura and Alessandro of Ripabottoni. English Version edited by Father Gerardo Di Flumeri, San Giovanni Rotondo, 1980, 2nd edition 1985.

existed between the two persons concerned, in order to be in a position to investigate and evaluate the teaching contained in these letters of spiritual direction.

1. *Raffaelina Cerase: biographical notes*

Raffaella or Raffaelina (known to her family and friends as Lellina)[2] was born in Foggia on 1 November 1868, of wealthy and aristocratic parents, Michele Cerase and Maria Barisani. As a child she was sent to the Carmelite convent in Lucera, in which community she had an aunt on her mother's side who died in the odour of sanctity in 1903. She had another aunt who became a cloistered nun in the Convent of the Most Holy Redeemer in Foggia, where she died on 7 December 1913 (22-7-1914).[3]

In the letter which Raffaelina sent to Padre Pio on 31 October we find the following details of her own life: "Up to seven years of age (until 1875) in a convent; from 7 to 21 (until 1889) the world, the world, the world (Father, you must be horrified—not even my Easter duty); from 21 up to the present, nothing but sins. I was blind and deaf and wicked. To obtain a grace... at 21 years of age (1889) I made for the first time the 15 Saturdays to our beautiful and dear Mother of Pompeii. This was the first link in the holy chain which unites me with Jesus and it was all due to my good Mother."

Her "conversion" therefore began in 1889 and during the years which followed it was developed and consolidated

---

[2] See the warm and perspicaçious account of her spiritual life by Padre Benedetto of San Marco in Lamis, O.F.M. Cap.: *Raffaelina Cerase of the Foggia aristocracy, Franciscan tertiary, a hidden treasure*, Barletta (Bari), 1917.

[3] The figures in brackets throughout this introduction indicate the dates of the letters contained in the present volume.

on the difficult upward path to perfection which led her to join the Franciscan Third Order and become an active member of the women's branch of Catholic Action.

Gifted with intelligence and a lively imagination, Raffaelina became well versed in literature, for she was an avid reader of books written in brisk and elegant style.

> "I always prefer the modern free-and-easy style," she wrote to Padre Pio. "I read a great many old-fashioned books years ago, but I have no use for them now."
>
> "Free-and-easy and pleasing... this is the type of book I would like to have on hand at all times. A heavy and abstruse style of writing, even in articles, makes no appeal to me" (22-7-1914).

Misfortune struck her when three of her brothers died one after the other prior to 1892 and in each case her love led her to assist them in their sufferings. She was also to assist her sister Anna who died on 20 March 1909. While still quite young she saw her mother pass to her eternal rest (26-1-1889) and likewise her father whom she adored (6-10-1904).

After her father's death she suffered deeply as a result of a disagreement with her brother Matteo, who died on 10 October 1924, and because of strained relations with other relatives over money matters. These conflicts kept her away from her own home for a full seven years, from 1907 to 1914, during which time she lived with her sister Giovina in a rented house.

It was towards the end of this period, as will be seen, that Raffaelina began to correspond with Padre Pio, through Padre Agostino of San Marco in Lamis. She attributed largely to Padre Pio's prayers the restoration of peace in her family in January 1915, a fact which filled her with joy, after many previous attempts had proved futile.

She always lived with her elder sister Giovina (who died in October 1931), to whom she was united by a deep and tender love. She used to refer to her as "my second mother," "my most unhappy sister" and "my saintly sister."

Both sisters were in bad health and in the attempt to recover they undertook journeys which in the end became a real Calvary for them.

Towards the end of June 1914 they went to Savona, where they stayed in a convent with great profit for their spiritual life (17-6-1914). As they were close to France, they intended going to Lourdes and were encouraged in this by Padre Pio. They would have fulfilled their desire had it not been for the outbreak of World War I which made it advisable to return to Foggia after they had visited a few cities in Northern Italy. In September of that year they were able to return to their own home. Here they obtained permission to have a private chapel, which was inaugurated in March 1915.

In the continual search for remedies for their delicate health, from 1895 onwards they went every year to Casamicciola, a health resort on the island of Ischia. In 1915, with Padre Pio's approval, they remained there from 26 July to 25 August. It was during this period that Raffaelina became aware of the first symptoms of a tumour. Reluctant to place herself in the hands of doctors and desiring to hide her illness from her sister, she sought Padre Pio's advice. On 7 September he ordered her to submit to a medical examination without further delay. Meanwhile, on 25 August, she had left for Bologna, where her sister Giovina was to have "further medical examinations." Padre Pio informed Padre Agostino with due discretion of the seriousness of Raffaelina's condition.[4]

In Bologna on 22 September the doctor examined her and pronounced the dreaded verdict. She had a tumour which would have to be removed immediately! Padre Pio followed

[4] *Letters, Vol. I*, Nos. 285, 292, 293.

anxiously the course of her illness. On 11 October Giovina informed him that the operation had been successful and Raffaelina herself reassured him a week later. Padre Pio answered on 21 October: "Your last letter, which I had awaited with indescribable anxiety."

At long last, on 25 October, Raffaelina was able to return home to Foggia. A few weeks later Padre Pio was called up once more to the army and on 6 December had to report to Naples. Both Raffaelina and Padre Pio's own spiritual directors wanted to use this opportunity of his absence from Pietrelcina to bring him back for good to community life. Their attempt on this occasion was not successful, but their plan was to meet with success some time later, at the time and in the manner willed by God. On the morning of 17 February 1916 Padre Pio moved to St. Anne's Friary in Foggia and that same day went to the Cerase home for the first time. Thus, after almost three years of spiritual direction by correspondence, they actually met and were able to have a long conversation on the matters which meant so much to them.

Raffaelina's illness obliged her to remain in bed. Padre Pio visited her every day and remained there for long spiritual colloquies. Padre Benedetto and Padre Agostino, delighted to have brought Padre Pio back to the friary with the excuse of spiritual assistance to this privileged soul, continued to follow closely and with deep interest the course of Raffaelina's illness.[5]

On 27 February 1916 Padre Pio wrote to Padre Agostino: "The poor invalid is in a very bad way. Pray and get other prayers for this poor patient."[6] In point of fact, things grew worse from day to day. Padre Pio administered the Last Sacraments to the sick woman and on 25 March, assisted by him, she breathed her last.

---

[5] *Letters, Vol. I*, Nos. 329, 324, 330.
[6] *Ibid.*, No. 325.

That same day Padre Pio wrote to Padre Agostino to give him the sad news:

> "*Let us exult in the Lord with tears!* This morning at four o'clock we gained another intercessor at the throne of the Most High. Raffaellina has just finished the course, she has celebrated her nuptials with her divine Spouse. She fell asleep in the Lord with a smile of contempt for this world. Lucky soul!
>
> "I leave you to imagine what is going on within me. For the past 16 days, since the Lord was pleased to manifest to me and to herself what was to happen this morning, I had been preparing myself for this divine will.
>
> "I envy her choice and may it please God through the intercession of this elect soul to grant also to me the repose of the just. I am weary of life, dear Father; I detest this world as much as a soul belonging to Jesus can detest sin."[7]

Again, on 7 April: "I went to see Giovina yesterday. I found her up and about and very resigned, thanks be to God!"[8]

After a month or a little more, Padre Pio complained to Padre Agostino about some people who were praying for him the wrong way round, that is to say, instead of praying as he desired, that he might leave this world, they prayed that the Lord might keep him there as long as possible:

> "My dear Father, how many other souls there are who, with the pretext of piety, still obstinately persist in asking Jesus not to allow me to depart. These are my real enemies and may God have mercy on them! I cannot bring myself to forgive those who possess eternal happiness[9] and who also resist me. To me

---

[7] *Letters, Vol. I*, No. 334.
[8] *Ibid.*, No. 335.
[9] "In one of her conversations with Padre Pio, Raffaelina was heard to exclaim: 'Father, allow me to die and to go to Jesus before you do, for I'll be mindful of you when I'm up there!' Padre Pio remained in Foggia. When I passed through Foggia on my way to join the army, I found him in

these are the real traitors. I cannot help looking on them as such, for they have perjured themselves before my God. My Jesus, use mercy towards them all!"[10]

2. *Relations with Padre Pio*

The spiritual relationship between Raffaelina Cerase and Padre Pio passed through three phases:

(a) indirect acquaintance through Padre Agostino;

(b) direct spiritual correspondence;

(c) personal acquaintance.

(a) *First phase: 22 June 1913 to 13 March 1914.*

Padre Agostino made the acquaintance of the Cerase sisters, Raffaelina and Giovina, in Foggia about the year 1911 and he recommended them for the first time to Padre Pio's prayers on 22 June 1913, without mentioning them by name[11]. On 26 June Padre Pio answered him, assuring him that he was "praying constantly for those two holy people."[12] On 2 August, after he had "recommended the matter a number of times to the Lord" he wrote a long letter to Padre Agostino on the subject of vainglory, "so as to put them on their guard against such a powerful enemy."[13]

In ignorance as to what Padre Pio thought and had written, Padre Agostino, in a letter dated 3 August, asked him

---

bed with his usual ailment. In reply to a question of mine he said in confidence with regard to Raffaelina: 'How cruel she is. She comes to tell me now that she can do nothing for me. I'll just have to be resigned.'" AGOSTINO DA SAN MARCO IN LAMIS, *Diario*, edited by Padre Gerardo Di Flumeri, San Giovanni Rotondo, 1971, p. 52.

[10] *Letters, Vol. I*, No. 338.

[11] Cf. *Ibid.*, No. 135.

[12] *Ibid.*, No. 137.

[13] *Ibid.*, Nos. 142-143.

for news of "those two people in Foggia."[14] This letter crossed Padre Pio's which Padre Agostino at once copied and sent on to Raffaelina, adding: "I merely repeat what I told you verbally, namely, that I have never said anything to our Padre Pio about the kind of life you two live, much less have I mentioned your name and social position. God alone has revealed to this beloved son the state of your souls."[15]

On 11 August Padre Agostino gave Padre Pio the sad news that the husband of Mrs. Maria Zicari Cairelli, a niece of the Cerase sisters, had committed suicide and in their name he asked for prayers for this soul. "This blow," replied Padre Pio on the 17th, "is a very harsh trial for his family and still more for those two angelic creatures, but may it contribute to the greater perfection of them all."[16] Padre Agostino copied this letter and sent it on to Giovina, with the following addition: "It is superfluous for me to ask you and Raffaelina to be so good as to keep to yourselves what Padre Pio has written. The saints are not canonized until they are dead" (21-8-1913).

This great misfortune had painful consequences in the suicide's family. When Padre Pio heard this, he asked Padre Agostino to "assure those two people that I never forget them before the Lord"[17] and when he learned that Padre Agostino was about to visit Foggia, he added on 24 October:

> "When you see those two people, convey to them first of all my gratitude for the prayers they are offering to the Lord for me and ask them to go on praying so that my soul may no longer be unfaithful to its God. Continue to impress on them, moreover, how important it is for them to avoid being

---

[14] *Ibid.*, No. 144.

[15] All the letters which Padre Agostino wrote to Raffaelina and which we quote from now on are kept in the records of the Capuchin friary in San Giovanni Rotondo.

[16] *Letters, Vol. I*, Nos. 145-146.

[17] *Ibid.*, No. 150.

upset by the vicissitudes of this life, for these things always tend to contract the heart rather than opening it up to trust in God."[18]

Padre Agostino continued to act as intermediary.

"Early this month," he wrote to the Cerase sisters (21-11-1913), "I visited Padre Pio and remained there for three days. Naturally I spoke about your spiritual and temporal needs. He told me that he could not forget your souls in the Lord's presence, that you were to be resigned in the hands of the good God, for all will turn out for His glory and your own salvation. All this in a general way. At all events, I'll write again to the *santarello* (little saint) regarding all that you told me in your last letter."

The very next day, 22 November, he outlined to Padre Pio the complicated problem of their home, but on the 26th Padre Pio replied that in regard to that "affair" he had nothing to say in the name of the Lord.[19]

The letter he wrote to Padre Agostino on 19 December 1913 shows clearly how interested Padre Pio was in Raffaelina's spiritual progress:

> "May He allow a little heavenly dew to come down into the hearts of those afflicted souls! For the moment I have nothing to suggest to them, but can only say that their lot is enviable."

There follows a shrewd diagnosis of the state of their souls.[20]

Padre Agostino, as a faithful executor, promised to inform the two people concerned of what the *santarello* had said[21] and next day (22-12-1913) he hastened to do so.

---

[18] *Ibid.*, No. 154.
[19] Cf. *Letters, Vol. I*, No. 162.
[20] Cf. *ibid.*, Nos. 168, p. 493 ss.
[21] Cf. *ibid.*, No. 170.

In the meantime, the "affair" of their home, which they had been obliged to leave six years previously, became almost an obsession.[22] On 16 January 1914 Padre Agostino told the two sisters: "I wrote and rewrote to Padre Pio for a definitive answer on that matter... Yesterday[23] the little saint replied, but always in the same vein. He does not know what to say... I enclose a copy of what he has written", and he then copied the text of Padre Pio's letter of 26 November 1913[24].

In response to repeated requests from Padre Agostino, Padre Pio wrote on 15 March 1914:

> "I am not allowed to say anything about those holy people. All I can say is that they should keep calm and make every effort to love the Lord with ever-increasing love and without any trace of self-interest. This love is what will lead them to the highest peak of perfection. They must not forget to pray for the one who loves them with a holy love."[25]

The problem of their home was still unsolved, but this proved to be a favourable moment for the beginning of direct personal correspondence between Padre Pio and Raffaelina.

(b) *Second phase: personal relationship by direct correspondence.*

While the troublesome business concerning their home became more acute and crucial, direct personal relations began between Padre Pio and Raffaelina, giving rise to spiritual direction in the true sense of the term. We are unable to say when exactly this began and who took the initiative.

---

[22] Cf. *Letters, Vol. I*, Nos. 170-171-172.

[23] This letter written by Padre Pio is dated 10 January 1914. Cf. *Letters, Vol. I*, No. 172.

[24] *Letters, Vol. I*, No. 163.

[25] *Ibid.*, No. 180.

On 19 February 1914 Padre Agostino, who had perhaps discussed the matter with Padre Pio, seemingly in response to a gentle hint on the part of the Cerase sisters, wrote:

> "Raffaelina may write directly to Padre Pio (and there is no need for my permission), either c/o myself of else addressing the letters to Padre Pio Cappuccino, Pietrelcina (Benevento). The latter method would be quicker and safer and I feel sure that the *santarello*, always with the Lord's permission, of course, would also reply directly. I advise this course...
>
> "P.S. I have written twice to Padre Pio[26] and he has replied telling me that he prays constantly for that affair. I am awaiting another reply at present."

On 20 March he informed Padre Pio that before long he would receive directly a letter from "one of those two ladies", that he felt this was God's will and therefore asked him to reply without delay to all such letters[27].

Raffaelina lost no time in availing herself of this permission and on 24 March she wrote the first letter, to which she received a reply on the 29th.

Padre Agostino was not informed immediately, for on 5 April he wrote to the Cerase sisters as follows:

> "Did Raffaelina write to the little saint? Did she receive an answer? I am in the dark so far. I'll write to him one of these days. It consoles me to think that he prays constantly for us."

On 7 April he asked Padre Pio if "that lady in Foggia" had written and if he had answered her[28].

This silence was certainly not due to any hidden motive

---

[26] From San Giovanni Rotondo on 2 and 14 February. Cf. *Letters, Vol. I*, Nos. 176, 178.

[27] *Letters, Vol. I*, No. 182.

[28] *Ibid.*, No. 186.

on the part of Padre Pio or Raffaelina. Padre Agostino was always aware of the letters which passed between them and he himself was often Raffaelina's spokesman, as can be seen from his correspondence with Padre Pio[29].

Padre Agostino was perfectly right when he said that "these two understood each other very well."[30] Nevertheless, tense and painful moments were not lacking for either of them. This is only human. It seems useful to mention the painful episodes which were not caused by doctrinal principles or by argument about directives but by factors which had nothing to do with spiritual counselling and were involuntary on the part of both. Difficulties and misunderstandings were always peacefully and satisfactorily overcome even though such things sometimes endangered the relationship between the two correspondents and threatened to interrupt Padre Pio's guidance of this soul.

"You have cooled off considerably in your correspondence" (11-5-1915). Early in January 1915 when Raffaelina was passing through a period of keen spiritual suffering and her director was doing all he could to sustain her, there was some friction between them which caused both to suffer more than a little. There was a danger that he might ask her to return the letters and discontinue his spiritual direction.

In a letter which we do not possess, Padre Pio dispensed Raffaelina from doing him the favour he had asked, namely, passing on a letter of his to a servant in the Cerase home, Francesca by name. At the same time he warned Raffaelina to keep the correspondence in order, as he intended asking her to return the letters on the first occasion that presented itself.

We have been unable to trace this letter or to discover

[29] Cf. *Letters, Vol. I,* Nos. 190, 193, 203, 215, 218, 231, 233, 263, 265.
[30] Cf. Agostino da San Marco in Lamis, *Diario*, *cit.*, p. 200.

the exact date on which it was written. In a letter dated 31 January 1915 Raffaelina states that she received it the previous day. However, the two letters written previously by Padre Pio are dated respectively 23 January (received before the 26th) and 30 January, and the latter could not have reached Foggia on the same day. Moreover, his letter of the 30th does not deal with the matters which caused Raffaelina such deep anguish. Perhaps the missing letter was destroyed by Raffaelina herself as desired and advised by Padre Pio (14-2-1915) along with the accompanying note. At all events, the regrettable incident served to clarify and strengthen further the bonds which united them in the pursuit of holiness.

Nevertheless, this spiritual direction did not proceed altogether smoothly. At times it was upset by misunderstandings and perhaps by excessive sensitiveness, which can easily be explained by the far from easy circumstances under which it was carried on.

After a period of silence on the part of Raffaelina, Padre Pio complained somewhat resentfully on 11 May:

> "For a great many days now the Lord has deprived me of your correspondence. I cannot explain this and it worries me exceedingly. To tell the truth, for some time past I have noticed a great cooling off in your letters...
>
> "If you want to break off relations with me, please let me know in all sincerity. I want to and must know all."

Fortunately this letter crossed another of Raffaelina's, written on the 10th, to which Padre Pio replied on the 13th: "I am extremely glad, after a long and negligent silence on your part, to have had the divine grace to see once more your much-loved and precious handwriting." However, he did not withdraw his previous reproaches, but saw fit to draw Raffaelina's attention once more to the diabolical snares which were at the root of her failure to write.

Padre Pio was probably unaware of the consequences

of this rather impulsive and severe language, but the reaction of the recipient was immediate and quite frank and sincere:

> "What delightful reprimands! Certain expressions of yours grieve me very much and make me weep. 'If you want to break off relations with me, please tell me so and be sincere on this point also. I want to and must know all.' It is the devil who suggests all this to you—forgive me and allow me to tell you so—he knows well how to make fun of you."

Then she becomes calmer and more cheerful; she explains the spiritual and material difficulties involved in writing to him and ends:

> "As far as I am concerned, you will always find unalterable, unchangeable filial trust in revealing to you my interior state, in informing you of the circumstances which have helped to change it, more or less."

Padre Pio explains himself, but holds firmly to his own point of view:

> "You tell me that certain expressions I used were suggested to me by the devil. May the Lord look on you with merciful eyes. He knows who placed those questions on my lips. It is evident, however, that you are always wide of the mark and continue to behave as a quite capricious and unmanageable child. Instead of deserving reproof, for me you are an object of compassion. I asked you such a question, not because you could, through your own fault, have considered interrupting our correspondence, for I hadn't the remotest notion of such a thing, but because I feared the devil might have suggested something of the kind to you. Judge for yourself, now, who was the true author of that question. May Jesus forgive you! You are accustomed to look at things from one side only, and hence you are very often mistaken in your judgment" (23-5-1915).

"I am not jealous by any means when you seek counsel elsewhere with regard to your spiritual problems" (25-5-1915). Padre Benedetto's intervention was also the cause of a brief storm. At times the human element, the character of the person concerned and his or her own way of looking at things, emerged in this eminently supernatural matter of spiritual direction.

We consider that one of the reasons for the friction already described may have been the fact that Padre Pio suspected that the Provincial, Padre Benedetto, intended to use Raffaelina as a means to bring him back to community life.

In her letter of 20 May 1915, already quoted, Raffaelina told her director about a long spiritual conversation she had had on the 14th of the month with Padre Benedetto, who had gone to say Mass in her private chapel:

> "We had a fairly long spiritual colloquy... Later, as usual, I wondered had I done well or not in speaking about myself... Speak to me on this point and do not forget it."

Padre Pio replied on 23 May:

> "I am very pleased that you opened your heart to Father Provincial on such a suitable occasion. Don't be worried; I am not jealous by any means when you seek counsel on spiritual matters from learned and enlightened persons... You acted well and you deceived neither yourself nor him... I should just like to know how he found you spiritually and if either of you spoke about me. Be sincere as regards this matter which is so important for you and for me, and the Lord will love you more dearly. Don't be distressed if you cannot have me close to you to enable you to run more swiftly in the Lord's paths."

Frankly and sincerely Raffaelina replied:

> "You ask me if we spoke about you during our spiritual

colloquy. How could we fail to do so? I was the first to mention your name. We spoke about our spiritual correspondence, about which he was already informed and of which he approved. You ask me how he found me spiritually, but what can I tell you on this score? He said that my story was the same as that of many others, etc., etc.. My dear Father, by word of mouth I could tell you all, absolutely all, but this is not possible in writing; the pen is insufficient, inadequate. Come here and I'll have very many things to tell you. I'll tell you everything, all that you want and think you ought to know" (5-6-1915).

By no means satisfied, Padre Pio insisted:

"May I ask you not to be so reticent with regard to your spiritual colloquy with Father Provincial. I want to know all about it from you also, especially his opinion of your spiritual state. Make an effort to obey and the Lord will help you also in this respect" (8-6-1916).

Raffaelina answered him:

"I would very willingly obey you and tell you all about the spiritual conversation I had with Father Provincial, but I am unable to do so. Forgive my ignorance and make allowances for me. Do you call this reticence? Reticence with you? Allow me to tell you that you do not know me yet" (23-6-1915).

Convinced that the contrary was the case, Padre Pio confirmed what he had already written:

"I want you to know that as long as you refuse to answer fully the questions I put to you in my second-last letter, I'll be obliged, to my immense sorrow, to make you feel the effects of my silence" (25-6-1915).

"*You continue to afflict me by your silence*" (12-7-1915). When the difficult situation was about to become more serious still, Raffaelina turned to Padre Agostino for help and the latter in his turn intervened with Padre Pio to clarify matters and find a solution:

"I have received from Raffaelina the last letter you sent me," he wrote on 29 June 1915. "My infinite thanks for your news and may Jesus be blessed!

"Raffaelina showed me the last three letters you wrote to her and told me how upset she is by your threat to keep silence if she does not tell you everything about her conversation with the Provincial.

"The poor soul says she has done everything possible to obey you and that her conscience does not reproach her about anything. I myself looked into the matter and I find it quite simple and by no means alarming. I advise you for the moment to calm your anxiety in this regard. When I get back to San Marco (la Catola) I'll have a talk with the Provincial about it and then let you know everything. In the meantime I can tell you what the Provincial said to me about that soul with whom he had had a spiritual conversation. He pronounced judgment in exactly the same way as you did yourself, that is to say, he found she was undergoing a purgation of the soul, etc. Raffaelina will write to you today, although I told her not to worry as I myself intended to write to you about this matter."[31]

The matter did not end here and Padre Agostino wrote again to Padre Pio to set his mind at rest:

"I spoke to the Provincial about that soul (Raffaelina), so dear to Jesus and whom you know so well. As a matter of fact the Provincial does not remember the entire conversation he had with her (so you can imagine whether the person concerned will be able to recall it!). He told me that the whole topic of conversation was, of course, the state of that soul who is undergoing a passive purgation. The poor creature is suffering a great deal, cannot be consoled and is only sustained by the thought of God.

---

[31] From Foggia, 29 June 1915. *Letters, Vol. I*, No. 266.

"In view of these facts I consider it useless for you to worry if she cannot remember everything in detail and tell you all. In this way you are adding to her sufferings. Please calm your fears, therefore.

"Perhaps I too am mistaken in my opinion, but as this is not deliberate, Jesus will not blame me for it. Don't you think so? I believe that all of us agree in our judgment of that soul, myself, yourself and the Provincial, so what can you expect from the soul herself? For my own part I ask you to calm yourself, because the poor creature has done and is doing all she can and Jesus is therefore satisfied with her."[32]

It would appear, however, that Padre Pio was disinclined to forget the episode or change his attitude, for on 12 July Raffaelina wrote to him as follows:

"Meanwhile you continue to make me feel the effects of your silence (your own exact words). Very well! The confessor scolds me, you continue to sulk, you keep silent and remain indifferent to my sufferings, leaving me to struggle and weep all on my own."

"*For some time past I have found you very different towards me*" (23-9-1915). Padre Pio did not spare his reprimands even though they wounded deeply Raffaelina's delicate feminine and spiritual sensitiveness, as may be seen from some of her vivacious and immediate reactions. His language was frank and demanding. For example: for some time there had been symptoms of the disease which was to undermine little by little Raffaelina's existence, but she had not said a word about this to her director. At the first mention of her illness Padre Pio replied on 7 September 1915:

"Your behaviour up to the present with regard to this new illness (cancer) hurts me more than a little...

---

[32] From San Marco la Catola, 10 July 1915: *Letters, Vol. I,* No. 269.

"I don't intend to rebuke you, but I am certainly displeased with you. Please take note that I want you to have a medical examination without further delay...

"If you refuse to obey it will be very painful for me to be obliged to deal with you and I won't know how to do so any longer. Obey me, then, and be at peace.

"Moreover, you have already consulted too many doctors without waiting for the consent and opinion of the one to whom God has entrusted you."

This reproof did not fail to produce an echo and the reaction was immediate and vivacious:

"For some time past I have found your attitude very changed towards me. I find you severe—almost rough and at times quite harsh... I may be mistaken, but to me, accustomed to your gentleness, what is merely justice appears to be strictness...

"You reproach me, but up to the present Jesus has not allowed me to have a doctor examine me unknown to Giovina—and what fault of mine is this? You intend to hold me responsible for something I could not and should not do for the sake of my poor sick sister. You must agree with me here. The saints sometimes argue with heaven...

"I would like to have the happiness of seeing you and opening the infinite recesses of my wretched conscience to you in the confessional. Answer me fully on this point" (23-9-1915).

The fencing-match continued:

"I cannot hide from you, Raffaelina, my great bewilderment at your complaints that I have been very different in my attitude towards you for some time past, that you have found me severe, almost rough and sometimes quite harsh. On the one hand, I admire and appreciate your frankness, but for the sake of truth I cannot refrain from raising my voice to inform you that you are mistaken again this time as always. What you attribute to the light is merely due to your own eyes.

> "Unfortunately, by this time I ought to have made you begin to feel the effects of what you attribute to me, but this is not necessary for the moment. We'll meet in Foggia and settle our accounts there. Meanwhile, be at peace" (28-9-1915).

The "poor tertiary" Raffaelina, anxious, curious and in submissive tones wrote:

> "You tell me, and rightly, that for some time past you ought to have made me feel the effects of your severity. Why is this? I beg you, Father, to tell me frankly. You intend to settle accounts with me in Foggia, but what accounts, holy Father? Don't be reluctant to tell me, I implore you" (3-10-1915).

Padre Pio changed his tone, but without giving up his method of direction:

> "I ask you not to worry about what you have done in God's sight with regard to your excellent sister, Giovina. The Lord has accepted only too fully our joint offerings and he has accepted them in a very different manner from what we intended. What pains me, however, is the fact that you only thought of informing me on this matter when you had already acted. In order to avoid being deceived in actions which appear holy, you ought, on the contrary, to seek the opinion of the one who has charge of you. Do you understand? Hence, what you have not done in the past you must do now and thus make up for all the rest.
>
> "Don't tell me this time also that I am too demanding in a matter which to an ignorant person would appear negligible. Jesus who reads the depths of the heart knows whether or not I am too pretentious in this" (4-11-1915).

In this rather unpleasant atmosphere in which they carried on their correspondence from September to November 1915, the question of his return to community life loomed, giving rise to somewhat anxious behaviour on the part of Padre Pio. His spiritual directors, unknown to him, considered it advisable to use Raffaelina in order to obtain, at last, what they had tried unsuccessfully for several years to achieve. As will be seen in the paragraphs which follow, tensions, misunderstandings and doubts arose which threatened to jeopardize everything and to cause a cooling-off in the spiritual relationship which had now existed for almost two years.

(c) *Third phase: personal meeting between the protagonists.*

We have seen how the relationship between Padre Pio and Raffaelina began by correspondence, continued for almost a year without their having met and was intensified by a more frequent exchange of letters for almost two years. We shall now see how Padre Pio and Raffaelina came to know each other personally, a direct relationship which lasted little more than a month, from 17 February to 25 March 1916.

Towards the middle of 1914 Raffaelina expressed repeatedly the desire to go to confession to Padre Pio, as she was sure this would stimulate her to run more swiftly in the Lord's ways. On the other hand, her director discerned in this attitude a lack of trust and abandonment to his written instruction:

> "I can assure you that you are not at fault. However, I perceive in you a lack of docility since you fail to be convinced by my assurances. Do you not see that it is the devil who wants to make you lose at all costs that trust and abandonment towards the one who is your spiritual guide? Moreover, when all is said and done, this is a real waste of time and prevents you from advancing rapidly. I cannot spare you this time from a gentle brotherly reproof" (21-6-1914).

As she found it more and more difficult to explain herself and to catch a photographic glimpse, as it were, of her state of soul, Raffaelina demanded from her director at least the promise that they would meet one day: "You have forgotten to tell me whether I'll be able to speak to you one day... The pen is unable to explain in the same way as the tongue" (7-12-1914). Padre Pio was aware of this by experience and he hoped the desired meeting would take place, although he said nothing as to when and where it might be:

> "You ask me if the Lord will grant us the grace to meet one day face to face to tell each other many things concerning Jesus, things that the pen cannot put on paper. I don't know what I would not do to satisfy you in this respect, but my condition prevents me absolutely from doing so at present. I am confident, however, that our joint desire will be fulfilled one day which I hope is not far away" (29-12-1914).

Raffaelina cheered up on receiving this breath of hope, but time passed and seemed to betray her longing. At last, on 7 February 1915, she wrote to him: "We expect you in May and let our desire hasten this holy and blessed day full of spiritual joy. Amen."

When May arrived Raffaelina hoped for a miracle which would bring her director to live in Foggia city so that he might fulfil more perfectly his task of sanctifying her: "If you were to remain at the friary in Foggia (only a miracle could bring this to pass), who knows if this unworthy, perverse and great sinner might not become a saint?" (20-5-1915).

Raffaelina's mystical life made it more and more difficult for her to explain herself and she was convinced that certain impressions and expressions on the part of her spiritual director were due precisely to the fact that she failed to explain herself adequately in writing and from a distance. She therefore wrote to Padre Pio on 23 September 1915: "I should like to have the happiness of seeing you and opening the infinite recesses of my wretched conscience to you in the confessional. Answer me fully on this point."

Evidently the situation had become increasingly tense when Padre Pio took up the challenge, as it were, to write to her clearly, though not at great length, on 28 September, pledging himself to visit her: "We'll meet in Foggia and settle our accounts there. Meanwhile, be at peace."

Raffaelina's illness and the serious operation she underwent at the beginning of October delayed the desired meeting and reversed the position, for the possibility was broached of a trip on the part of Raffaelina to Pietrelcina. On 11 October her sister Giovina wrote to Padre Pio from Bologna: "We hope to be sufficiently well to pay you a visit in order to thank you personally for your genuine interest in our existence which is beset by continual troubles and trials."

Unfortunately the trip to Pietrelcina did not take place, to Raffaelina's deep regret. On 2 November, rejoicing on account of an approaching visit of Padre Agostino, she wrote to Padre Pio: "I have so many things to tell him! If I could only speak to you in this way! But Jesus will not grant me this grace because I am so very wicked! What must I do to move Jesus to consent to this? Advise me what to do and do not forget it."

It seemed as if Providence was to open up the way. On 6 December of that same year 1915 Padre Pio was called up again to the army and went to Naples, intending to pass through Foggia before returning to his own town. "Pray," he wrote on 13 December to Raffaelina, "and don't fail to do so in charity. If Our Lord grants me this grace, it won't be long before we meet."

In reality there were several people who wanted to bring about this meeting and allow these two to become acquainted. Both Padre Agostino and Padre Benedetto hoped to avail of Padre Pio's call to the army in order to bring him back for good to conventual life. With this end in view, they attempted a stratagem, with Raffaelina's aid.

On 14 December Padre Agostino revealed to her his intention of going personally to Naples to bring Padre Pio to Foggia as soon as he was set free from military service, warning her to keep the matter quite secret: "I'll bring him there, in any event. Once he is on the spot it will be up to you to keep him there until death... All of us will be very happy if we can bring this about! (14-12-1915). He informed her that he was writing at the same time to Padre Pio, but without even mentioning the proposed plan. All he said to him was: "All the souls belonging to Jesus are praying for you... I wrote at once to Raffaelina so that she herself and all the others of whom you know might make the same novenas."[33]

Prevented from going to Naples himself, he wrote again to Raffaelina on 17 December to tell her the task had been entrusted to Padre Luigi of Avellino:

> "Let us hope and pray that Jesus will permit this. But if He doesn't permit it now, He will have to do so before long and you must be the intercessor with the Heart of Jesus Christ. You must not only pray, but by writing to Padre Pio induce him to go there at least for a few days. We ourselves will look after things from that time on. May everything be carried out to the glory of God and for the salvation of souls."

This programme was not put into effect, for events very soon came to a head. Raffaelina had done her utmost to recommend Padre Pio's case to influential people, but before these could intervene he was discharged and he left at once for Pietrelcina. From there he wrote on 20 December to inform Padre Agostino[34] who, already notified from Naples,

---

[33] From San Marco la Catola, 14 December 1915: *Letters, Vol. I*, No. 302.

[34] *Letters, Vol. I*, No. 304.

wrote on the same day to Padre Pio rejoicing at the news of his discharge but unaware of his hurried journey: "May Jesus also console Raffaelina, who has nobody who understands her so well and with whom you will be able to have a better understanding verbally."[35] He was not yet aware that the attempt to bring about a meeting and a verbal understanding between them had gone up in smoke!

On 21 December Padre Agostino wrote to Raffaelina and in expressing his sympathy on the death of Francesca, continued:

> "I am glad to know that to you, too, Padre Pio has mentioned his desire to return and precisely to Foggia. Well, then, may I tell you once again that you yourself must be the interceding angel—I have said this to the Provincial also—it is you who must induce our beloved son to come and to remain there, after you have pestered Jesus about it. Don't tell me you are a wretched little creature. I assure you in Jesus' name that God wants you to do as I say and that is sufficient. Your charity will be acceptable to His divine Heart.
>
> "Padre Pio has sent me a postcard of the same kind. I sent him my best wishes by letter and renewed my recommendations to him to pray and continue to pray for this other grace (the first was his liberation from the army) which we must obtain, for it is a question of God's glory and the salvation of many souls.
>
> "Therefore in every letter you write to the *santarello* you must not forget to repeat this wish of ours which is also his own. Jesus has already granted him the grace of liberation from this last trial precisely for this reason."

While Padre Agostino was writing this letter, Padre Pio informed Raffaelina directly of the ups and downs which had ended in his discharge from the army and his hasty return to Pietrelcina:

> "It was my intention, Raffaelina, on my return trip from Naples to travel as far as Foggia in order to come to see you

[35] *Ibid.*, No. 305.

personally and to thank you all. But the Lord arranged things differently. I should undoubtedly have been unable to reach Foggia without endangering my life. Let us hope in the Lord, then, that He will keep this fresh consolation for me until a more suitable occasion presents itself, before I am called to His embrace" (21-12-1915).

Padre Pio was therefore unaware of Padre Agostino's scheme to which Padre Benedetto was a party and in which Raffaelina also shared, with a view to bringing him back to community life when he ended his term in the army. However, some news of this had leaked out. In point of fact, Padre Pio wrote from Pietrelcina on 30 December (last letter in the present volume):

"I want you to tell me how you can say that it is the will of Jesus for me to settle in Foggia. Please be quite sincere in this regard and tell me everything. I want you to know, moreover, that the fact of being obliged to live outside the cloister saddens my whole life. I have never relied on my own judgment in this matter. I have explained my case to learned persons who are enlightened as to God's ways and they have replied that in view of my exceptional position and taking everything into consideration, I cannot venture to live in the cloister without directly attempting suicide."

Unfortunately we are not in a position to throw further light on this whole matter, as Raffaelina's last letter is dated 15 December. But from Padre Pio's letter of 30 December it appears obvious that he was replying to one from Raffaelina in which, perhaps, she told him that it was God's will for him to settle in Foggia, or else she had said so to Padre Agostino who had then told Padre Pio.

Meanwhile Padre Agostino continued to insist with Raffaelina that she must really be the "interceding angel." On 7 January 1916 he asked her if "our little saint had said nothing to her regarding his return to his community." It is probable that as a result of Padre Agostino's insistence in a further and very strong letter dated 12 January, Raffaelina sent him a copy of Padre Pio's letter of 30 December addressed to her. In point of fact, Padre Agostino wrote to Padre Pio on 16 January:

> "I wrote to Raffaelina a few days ago to have some news about *your return*. This holy daughter of Jesus sent me your letter of 30 December. This surprised me when I learned that your continued stay outside the cloister is approved by learned persons enlightened with regard to God's ways. Tell me, my son, who are these people?"[36]

Padre Pio, counselled by prudence, replied only partially to this explicit question: "What I wrote to that person in Foggia is true, but it is not lawful for me to mention names here in writing. If we get a chance to meet, I'll tell you everything."[37]

On 31 January Padre Agostino wrote once more to Padre Pio and informed him that Raffaelina, who was ill, was most anxious to have him hear her confession. He considered she deserved this, which Padre Pio himself had promised her, while both the Provincial and Padre Agostino would be very happy about it.[38]

On 3 February, in reply to Padre Agostino, Padre Pio said he was "sorry to be unable for the moment to satisfy the pious desire of that poor soul, which is also my own desire," because a "heavy dose of influenza" prevented him. He hoped as soon as he felt "a little better", to go there, possibly accompanied by someone else.

Padre Agostino had no sooner received this consoling news than he informed Raffaelina.[39] On 13 February he

---

[36] *Letters, Vol. I,* No. 313.

[37] From Pietrelcina, end of January 1916: *Letters, Vol. I*, No. 315.

[38] From San Marco la Catola, 31 January 1916: cf. *Letters, Vol. I*, No. 317.

[39] From the same, 5 February 1916: *ibid.*, No. 319.

went personally to see her and found her quite ill but "very comforted on hearing that Jesus grants her the grace of your visit when you come here. I therefore hope", wrote Padre Agostino, "that Jesus will give you the strength to travel."[40]

Padre Agostino busied himself personally about arrangements for the greatly-desired trip and at last on 17 February Padre Pio arrived in Foggia and was installed in St. Anne's Friary.

Up to the day of Raffaelina's death, Padre Pio went to see her every day, where he had "long spiritual conversations" with her and sometimes said Mass in the private chapel in her home. At the same time he was in constant touch with his directors and kept them informed on the progress of the illness which was to end her life on 25 March 1916.

II The Letters

1. *Their origin and preservation*

The correspondence between Padre Pio and Raffaelina extends over a period of about 20 months. It begins with a letter from Raffaelina on 24 March 1914 and ends with Padre Pio's letter of 30 December 1915.

The entire collection contains 97 letters, all of them originals, 56 of which were written by Padre Pio and 41 by Raffaelina. We believe that the collection we have is complete.

Raffaelina guarded jealously the secret of her correspondence with Padre Pio and precisely to avoid the danger of discovery she did not pass on to a young seamstress named Anna a letter which her director had enclosed for the latter:

> "At all events, I think I am right to guard my spiritual secret carefully. None but Rosa and another holy and discreet per-

[40] *Ibid.*, No. 322.

> son (this orphan's teacher whom I mentioned to you in another letter) share it with me...
>
> "Oh! My poor letters! May Jesus permit them to be seen by no other eyes but yours, for you alone are my counsellor" (26-12-1914).

She not only desired that her letters should not be read by others, but even wanted them to be destroyed either as soon as they had been carefully read by her director (20-4-1914) or at least after she died:

> "When you hear of my death, I want you to do something which is very important for me. My poor letters are written for you alone, they contain all that concerns my conscience and also family matters. To you alone I confide all, so I ask you to burn them. In this regard, set my mind at rest, reassure me, reply to me" (15-12-1914).

By return post he answered her:

> "As regard your letters, you mustn't worry about what is to happen to them. You have no further rights in this respect. All will be done as God wills. Be at peace, then, on this score, and let vain fears about your letters be far from your mind" (17-12-1914).

Despite this reassuring reply, sometimes when she had written very freely about her deepest feelings, she asked that the letters be destroyed: "I want you to tear up this letter as soon as you have read it. It is incoherent, disjointed and blameworthy and it deserves to be destroyed like the one who has written it. Will you satisfy me in this? Tell me that you will" (21/25-2-1915).

On 20 May 1915, speaking to her director about the uncertainties of the war and the danger of his being called up for military service also, she added: "No matter what happens I strongly urge you to think of my poor correspondence and to entrust it to nobody but your saintly father (Padre Agostino); this I beg of you." On 5 June she insisted once more that if he went to the army he was to "let me know beforehand for fear that my letters might fall into the hands of who knows who. I can be sure of this, can't I? Let me have a word on the subject that will set my mind completely at rest." This time also she received the desired assurance three days later, namely, on 8 June: "Don't have any fear with regard to your letters. Whatever the Lord may have disposed in my regard, they will be in good hands. Let there be no more talk about them."

There is no further word on the subject in their letters. The "good hands" of which he was thinking at the time were certainly those of Padre Agostino, and in point of fact, the letters arrived in his hands, although we cannot say how or when.

On 28 July 1917 Padre Agostino wrote to Padre Pio: "Giovina wrote to me once, telling me that she would like to have some more of her sister's letters. What do you say to this?[1] (Question without a reply, at least with no written reply.)

We know, on the other hand, that after Raffaelina's death, the letters which Padre Pio had written to her were handed over to Padre Agostino by her sister. "In the chest assigned for my use," he wrote in his *Diary*, "there is a bundle of letters in which Padre Pio replied to the young lady who, before she died, told her sister Giovina to hand them over to me. The letters, I repeat, are in this chest. I have been able to read a few of them[3]."

---

[1] *Letters, Vol. I*, No. 412.
[2] Cf. *Diario, cit.*, p. 200.
[3] Raffaelina's letters have been published in *La voce di Padre Pio* from 1972 onwards.

2. *Raffaelina's letters*

"*My poor letters.*". From the very outset she assured her director that she was writing to him "quite simply, in a free-and-easy manner" (24-3-1914), and she repeated many times: "I set down for you my poor ideas, my many needs, always in very simple fashion" (8-8-1914). "These poor writings of mine, set down quite simply, without head or tail" (20-4-1914) etc.

She considered her letters "silly" (27-5-1914), "muddled" (17-4-1914), "incoherent and disjointed" (21/25-2-1915) and referred to "my poor letters" (15-12-1914) and "my extremely poor pen" (7-12-1914). Again, she wrote: "Forgive me and absolve me for the blunders of all kinds contained in my awful letters"(22-7-1914); "I wonder what you will say to these poor writings of mine, silly and incoherent as they are. You who are so good will make allowances for me and forgive me" (15-12-1914).

The reader will recognize the evident exaggeration in these and other similar phrases. Nevertheless, it must be admitted that Raffaelina did not stop to consider literary values when writing about her inner life. She manifested her feelings rapidly and the words poured from her pen like water bubbling from a spring. She multiplied epithets and synonyms and at times her adjectives and verbs tumbled over one another like the waves of a stormy sea.

We give just a few examples:

> "Some of the expressions you use... astonish me, confuse me, overwhelm me and cast me down into the depths" (22-7-1914).
>
> "All that you know about me is misery, earth and mud. Whereas what I want to know from you is light, virtue, love, holiness, perfection; tears, throbbings, colloquies, ecstasy, union, transformation in immense charity" (15-12-1914).

"*My pen is never satisfied.*" Although she writes with such abundance of words, she complains of the difficulty she has in expressing feelings and ideas which she wants to manifest to her director:

> "You have forgotten to tell me whether I'll have a chance to speak to you one day. My very poor pen is never satisfied. It would never stop and yet this is nothing in comparison to what my tongue would have to tell you. The pen cannot and does not know how to explain itself as the tongue would—it is impossible. Allow me to hope...
>
> "I am quite right in saying that my poor pen cannot stop. It runs on and on to tell everything to good Padre Pio, but it is never, never satisfied" (7-12-1914).

Evidently this difficulty is due especially to the impossibility of disclosing all the anguish of the most painful spiritual trial through which she is passing:

> "Nothing rouses me, nothing attracts me, nothing distracts me. I find everything boring and even to write to you is very difficult and burdensome, leaving me indifferent (this is something new and horrible which never happened before; for me to write used to be a spiritual feast)" (21/25-2-1915).

"*Modern and free-and-easy style.*" Although she never worried, much less remained a slave to elegance of form, she did not despise or underrate literary style. Indeed, in her choice of reading she preferred "the modern free-and-easy style" (22-7-1914). Without intending to produce a literary work, when she lets her pen run freely she gives us fresh, vivid, almost poetical descriptions which can be witty and facetious.

Raffaelina's letters are not "poor letters," even though they yield more to the logic of feelings than of grammar and are marked by a punctuation all her own, which sometimes makes them seem like telegraph letters, frequently interspersed with dashes.

Her style is clearcut, vivid, effective, effervescent, suffocated by the anxiety of a soul that has too much to say and without a breathing space. When she intends to be "very brief" her "pen runs on and on and won't be denied" when she is writing "to good Padre Pio."

Just as in her reading, so too in what she writes, Raffaelina has no time for "heavy and abstruse" expressions. We have ample material from which to choose in order to illustrate this point. Her letters give genuine proof of this and reflect her soul which is thirsting for God. She "dashes them off" according to circumstances and to her interior and exterior needs, without the slightest notion of writing in an elegant style. But they show forth, on the other hand, an original and spontaneous style and manner of thinking.

Here is a sample:

"After stopping in Florence for a day-and-a-half, with God's help we arrived at six o'clock on Saturday in this holy place in Savona where we have lodgings.

"This is a school run by Sisters who also keep a boarding-house for ladies. It is beautifully situated, with marvellous views of the sea, hills and luxurious vegetation. The silence and quiet, the tranquillity of nature reach the body and speak to the soul. Here one's spirit is delighted and rests serenely, completely removed from all the annoyances of life—it rejoices and continues to rejoice between these holy walls, surrounded by virginal souls dedicated to God by the three solemn vows, pious, beautiful and holy souls.

"In the dear little church, in the galleries, refectory and gardens, in the vast corridors, I see continually these people who really love Jesus and sacrifice themselves for Him: Sisters, oblates, postulants, pupils, all of these speak to me of Him and unknown to themselves, silently and severely, they reproach me for my indolence and condemn my selfish, easy-going, empty and useless life.

"This is an infinite grace which Jesus has granted me through you. If I am not converted now, in this holy retreat, I'll never be converted" (8-7-1914).

"*The good father and the wretched tertiary.*" We intend to deal elsewhere with some aspects of their mutual esteem, but we merely list here the titles by which Raffaelina referred to her director:

> "good father" (17-6-1914; 23-9-1915); "holy father" (1-9-1914; 26-6-1915); "good, good, good holy father" (15-9-1914); "my good, holy, holy father" (8-10-1914); "my good, good, holy, holy father" (21-10-1914); "my poor, good father", "holy father", "good father" (31-10-1914); "worthy minister and friend", "holy father" (7-12-1914); "minister and friend of the Bridegroom", "holy father", "teacher of love" (15-12-1914); "my holy advocate", "the saintly Padre Pio" (25-3-1915); "my good father", "holy father", "good father" (14-4-1915); "my holy father, my good father, my generous father", "holy hero of virtue", etc.

Her firm belief in her own spiritual wretchedness stands out against the great esteem she had for her director, to the extent of not wanting to sign her own name to her letters but using phrases savouring of humility, such as:

> "a poor Franciscan tertiary"; "this bad woman who is a tertiary only in name" (8-7-1914); "a troublesome tertiary" (8-4-1914); "a stubborn sheep" (20-4-1914).

3. *Padre Pio's letters*

"*Do not deprive me of your correspondence.*" As if to facilitate the really difficult task of manifesting in writing the changes in her state of soul, her anxieties, her difficulties and aspirations, Padre Pio earnestly exhorted Raffaelina to be punctual in giving an account of her conscience. He made her understand how keenly he desired to have her news and he was pleased to allow this soul to know that God looked with favour on their continual spiritual correspondence. When Padre Pio had told her repeatedly that her letters were indispensable in order that he might guide her and that he sincerely desired them and suffered when their arrival was delayed, Raffaelina certainly could have no doubts on the subject:

> "Continue invariably to explain to me all your needs with complete trust and simplicity and you may be sure you are doing me a favour while at the same time pleasing Jesus" (31-5-1914).
>
> "Meanwhile do not deprive me of your correspondence, which is pleasing to Jesus" (15-6-1914).
>
> "Write to me frequently and open your heart to me without reticence or reserve" (6-9-1914).
>
> "Write to me often, and as soon as this reaches you send me a picture postcard" (10-10-1914).
>
> "In the meantime, write often, as this gives me very great pleasure" (4-11-1914).

Padre Pio made no secret of the fact that he himself drew great spiritual benefit from Raffaelina's letters and he asked her not to deny him this comfort and help in his own trials and difficulties.

> "Write to me often, I too am in need of relief in my present state. If you don't receive a reply, write again. During this Holy Week and in Easter week, it will be difficult for me to answer you" (30-3-1915).
>
> "Write to me very often to give me a present of invariably good news about Giovina's state and your own" (4-8-1915).
>
> "I certainly don't mean to dispense you from writing to me frequently and at length, for the simple reason of my spiritual desolation, for this would mean a further torment for me and would add suffering to suffering" (7-9-1915).

They accuse each other very frankly of writing only short letters and of delays in replying:

> "I don't know who suggested that expression to you: that I find your letters tiresome. I hope it is the last time this is mentioned and I should be inclined to impose on you a rigorous precept to write to me every time you can, were I not aware that such an order would upset you. Don't give me another chance to have recourse to this harsh measure" (14-7-1915).
>
> "You tell me to read your letters a second time so as not to deprive you of an answer to some of the things you ask me. I do this many times, but what can you expect? Even if I read them 50 times, when I'm writing I only remember what Jesus wants me to remember. There you are! It's too bad, but may the Lord's will be done" (23-5-1915).
>
> "The Lord has deprived me of your correspondence now for a great many days and I am very worried on this account" (11-5-1915).
>
> "I am extremely glad of the divine grace of having been able, after a long and careless silence on your part, to see once more your gracious and very precious handwriting" (13-5-1915).
>
> "I am replying at once to your last letter, which I awaited anxiously, with indescribable emotion. I thank you, my child, on Jesus' behalf, for the sacrifice you have made in giving me news of yourself... In the meantime, don't be stingy with this news" (21-10-1915).
>
> "Write me a long letter and tell me everything you want and you will give me immense pleasure" (13-12-1915).
>
> "Write me a long letter at home, if you want to do something I'll deeply appreciate" (17-12-1915).

"I am consumed by the desire to write you a long letter" (31-5-1914). Padre Pio wrote 56 letters to Raffaelina and we believe none of these are missing, with the exception of a note dated 30 January 1915.

From this batch of letters are excluded those which Padre Pio wrote to Padre Agostino, intended for the Cerase sisters, and which appear in the first volume of his *Letters*.

Padre Pio took on this further labour most willingly and regretted his inability to devote more time to it, to be unable to write more frequently and at greater length, as he would have wished. His weak health and his apostolic work created difficulties in this respect:

"I am obliged to end here and you may be sure that I am consumed by the desire to write you a really long letter, something I am unable to do as I have been really ill for the past few days. It seems as if the Lord intends to make me pay for the health I enjoyed some years ago, as I used it so badly. But may the hand which strikes me in this way be for ever blessed" (31-5-1914).

"I must end here, Raffaelina, for my strength will not permit me to continue. In the meantime, when you do not find your wishes answered and satisfied, please read my letters over again, as I feel they contain everything" (25-3-1915).

At all events, whether his letters were short or long, what mattered to him was that they should be understood materially and spiritually:

"Whenever you find in my letters things which you do not sufficiently understand, please ask me for an explanation, and I say this once and for all. I don't want to work in vain and fail to obtain the result intended by Jesus" (23-10-1914).

Raffaelina reassured him in this respect:

"I understand all your most beautiful teachings and holy lectures. You explain yourself wonderfully well... I can read your handwriting quite well, so don't worry" (31-10-1914).

Padre Pio, for his own part, was most diligent in counselling by correspondence and prepared his answers conscientiously by study and prayer. He did not depend on the inspiration of the moment, much less approach this responsible task in the manner of one who tackles some bureaucratic procedure inherent in his duties or profession. He did not write his letters straight off, but made a rough draft, which he sometimes corrected and changed, as can be seen from four exercise books which he kept and which are labelled A.B.C.D. However, the drafts do not contain any substantial differences when compared to the final version of his letters.

"*Your beautiful teachings*" (31-10-1914). Padre Pio's counselling was solid and substantial. His teachings were clear and usually tested by experience. Some of the letters may be considered as genuine monographical studies, synthetic, original, personal and practical in their application.

Take, for instance, the letter he wrote on 23 October 1914, in which he expounded some very clear and important ideas on the subject of the "heavenly wisdom" required by the soul that aims at perfection and on the nature and implications of the concept of "Christian perfection."

On other occasions he dwelt on problems and subjects which the circumstances demanded and which he developed in logical fashion, almost invariably on the basis of Sacred Scripture, especially St. Paul, who was his favourite author. Thus in his letter of 4 November 1914 he dealt extensively with the annihilation of Jesus and the power of his name. In another letter he developed the theme: "What ought to be the life of one who lives in the spirit of Jesus." Speaking of this letter, which is undoubtedly one of the more pondered and fully developed, he himself said: "I am aware that my manner of speaking is not, unfortunately, what it ought to be. It is quite harsh and tiresome, and precisely on this account I am afraid that I may not make my meaning clear. However, I fix my gaze on the One who moves me to speak and who is the source of wisdom and I earnestly hope that all will redound to His glory" (16-11-1914).

His teaching was distinguished by its concreteness and drew inspiration from the traditional practices of Christian piety. In this respect the daily programme he proposed to Raffaelina on 17 December 1914 is revealing: Here are the main items of this programme: (a) arrange two periods to be devoted to meditation; (b) do not lose sight of the presence of God during any action whatsoever; (c) do not undertake and conclude any task without raising your mind to God to ask His help and to thank Him; (d) renew your pure intention frequently; (e) pray before and after dinner; (f) examine your conscience before going to bed; (g) offer your night's rest to the Lord.

In his letter of 23 February 1915, at Raffaelina's request, he paused to comment on verses 23-24 of the first chapter of St. Paul to the Philippians, that is to say, on the Apostle's twofold desire to live and to die. Aware of the delicate nature of this subject, he did not present his hypotheses or his judgments as the only true ones and twice he added: "always subject to a better interpretation and to the judgment of the Church, in which I declare my intention to live and die."

It is not our intention here to exaggerate the exegetical originality of his comments on St. Paul, even though they are not lacking in personal considerations. What is more important is to stress the personal experience on which his ideas rest. Interesting in particular is his application of "for me to live is Christ" and "to die is gain."

In this context he also introduced an interpretation of the *Our Father*: "give us this day our daily bread," which according to Padre Pio is the Eucharist, of which he speaks magnificently. He also interpreted the invocation "Thy will be done on earth as it is in heaven" (23-2-1915).

A final remark. Not only did the director counsel, encourage and reasure; he wished the soul he was directing to realize why he offered these counsels and reassurances. His pedagogical method here is important also as proof of what he himself had learned by personal experience and from his reading. His letter of 9 January 1915 is most interesting from this point of view. It expounds clearly and precisely the origin of purgation of the senses and of the spirit, it deals equally clearly with acquired and infused contemplation, with the specific nature of each and also with the degrees through which the soul has already passed on its spiritual journey and those through which it still has to pass. In this entire diagnosis it is easy to discern the reflection of personal experience.

Echoes and results. To Raffaelina Padre Pio's letters were "beautiful teachings, holy lectures" (31-10-1914). It is no wonder, then, that she wanted to receive them frequently and at greatest possible length:

> "When you can do so without tiring yourself, write me a long letter; instruct me, scold me when I deserve it and punish me" (22-7-1914).
>
> "Don't worry if you cannot answer me at once, for I don't want you to tire yourself on my account. Write to me at your own convenience, when you can, but please don't delay so very long as to change my expectation into anxiety and then to agitation" (20-4-1914).

She was grateful to the Lord for allowing Padre Pio to write to her "with that angelic charity worthy of a son of St. Francis" (27-5-1914), a charity which encourages and tells her:

> "Write to me frequently and open your heart to me without reticence or reserve" (15-9-1914).

She reassured her spiritual father:

> "I can read your handwriting quite well; don't worry. I should like to be able to interpret equally well your intimate loving colloquies with Jesus, your delightful conversations, His daily visits to you and those of our good heavenly Mother and your Guardian Angel" (31-10-1914).

She told him frankly that she did not pray for his flight to heaven—as he ardently desired—because:

> "If you were dead I should not hear your words on this earth, your living, warm, persuasive, charitable words close at hand, which bring comfort in sorrow, encourage me in the struggle and spur me on to strong and genuine virtue" (7-2-1915).

We can therefore understand why Raffaelina was, as it were, greedy for those letters which she invariably awaited as beneficial dew on parched desert land:

> "Write me a long letter soon; tell me everything quite frankly and openly; don't be unwilling to manifest your feelings" (23-9-1915).
>
> "I intended to imitate the painful brevity of a great many of your letters (especially recent ones). I resolve to do this but I don't succeed and it is only when I come to the end that I realize I have been too lengthy and tiresome. You will object: so many long letters and to what purpose? You are quite right, good Father, but I cannot resign myself to your brevity, which is a sure sign of your indifference and neglect, etc., etc., although I am convinced that I deserve nothing else" (12-7-1915).

Mutual trust. A considerable amount of human affection emerges from the correspondence. For the moment we merely mention: (i) the closing phrases and signature; (ii) the names he applied to the one he was counselling.

(i) Padre Pio signed himself:

"Your poor Fra Pio, your unworthy servant and brother, your most affectionate servant and brother, your humble servant, your most unworthy servant, your servant, your poor servant."

"I am all yours; I take leave of you in the Lord's holy embrace, I leave you in the holy embrace of Jesus, my love to you all in Christ, I bless you with fatherly tenderness".

(ii) Some of the titles he used to stress the spiritual relationship with her soul referred to himself, others referred to the Lord:

For him Raffaelina was: "My dear" (19-5-1914; 15-6-1914; 28-7-1914, etc.); "My very dear Raffaelina" (29-12-1914; 20-4-1915); "My good Raffaelina" (12-12-1914); "My sister" (19-5-1914; 31-5-1914, etc.); "Beloved sister" (29-3-1914; 15-6-1914, etc.); "My daughter" (7-9-1915); "My beloved daughter" (8-10-1915); "Beloved child of my heart" (14-10-1915).

For Jesus Raffaelina was: "daughter" or "beloved daughter of Jesus" (11-4-1914; 19-5-1914; 31-5-1914, etc.); "spouse of Jesus" (25-10-1914; 17-12-1914); "little spouse of Jesus" (22-12-1914; 29-12-1914; 4-2-1915).

For the Father: "Beloved daughter of the heavenly Father" (17-12-1914; 9-1-1915; etc); "most faithful servant of the Lord" (16-11-1914).

4. *Method followed in this edition*

In preparing the publication of these letters we have followed the same principles which we observed in editing Padre Pio's correspondence with his spiritual directors.

The completed text of each letter is given, copied directly from the original letters which have been preserved up to the present.

To facilitate reading, however, we have followed the punctuation rules in use today, which causes variations in the use of capital letters.

Each letter bears a serial number, according to chronological order, as this makes it easier to follow the development and incidence of the counsel given and the reactions of the recipient. This order makes it unnecessary to repeat the name of writer and addressee, which are obvious at first sight.

A brief and concise summary of each letter is given, divided according to the numbered paragraphs in the text, for greater facility on the part of the reader.

Finally, there are some brief footnotes to explain events which have sometimes been barely mentioned, to identify persons and to complete quotations from Sacred Scripture or from some other source.

III Spiritual direction

In a future volume we hope to deal with the question of spiritual direction in Padre Pio's teaching and to consider it in all its vastness. In the present volume we give a synthesis of the accurate investigation carried out by Padre Gerardo Di Flumeri with exclusive regard to Padre Pio's correspondence with Raffaelina.

This is the substance of a paper read by the author during the First Meeting on the Spirituality of Padre Pio.[1] Rather than publishing the entire paper, we deem it sufficient to reproduce the headings with the more meaningful texts.

1. Necessity

In the first place we must mention that Padre Pio held spiritual direction in great esteem. He saw the need for it from

[1] The paper summarized here appears on pp. 267-305 of the *Acts of the First Congress on Padre Pio's Spirituality* (San Giovanni Rotondo, 1-6 May 1972). Edited by Padre Gerardo Di Flumeri, San Giovanni Rotondo, 1978.

two points of view: from the point of view of the person to be directed, he was convinced that the farther this person advanced on the path to perfection, the greater became his need of the director's help; from the director's point of view—and here Padre Pio's doctrine is rich and original—he felt that spiritual direction was a requirement of that apostolic spirit which should animate every priest. He made it clear that to him spiritual direction was a fruit of his supernatural charity.

2. Elements

When we analyze the 56 letters written by Padre Pio to Raffaelina, without claiming to treat the matter exhaustively, we can reduce the constituent elements of his direction to the following.

A relationship of supernatural affection. It has been said that a person finds it difficult to open up his heart completely to his director if the latter has not won his esteem, trust and affection. Padre Pio had the gift of knowing how to gain esteem and complete trust on the part of the one he directed. It is to be observed, however, that there was nothing natural in this relationship, that it had an eminently and exclusively supernatural character. Padre Pio pointed this out repeatedly to his disciple.

Participation in the affairs of his disciple. This supernatural character did not deprive Padre Pio's spiritual direction of that cordial affection which, on the human plane, gave greater credibility to his counselling. In point of fact, Padre Pio participated keenly and heartily in all Raffaelina's spiritual and temporal affairs, whether joyful or sad. In this connection we have some fine pages which show clearly the human character, the fatherly heart and affective charity of the director.

The action of the Holy Spirit. To draw attention to the action of the Holy Spirit who is invariably the only true teacher and counsellor of souls, to point out the progress of grace which works gently and silently in the hearts of the faithful, is a task which calls for insight, discernment and holiness. And Padre Pio did not neglect to the slightest degree this important element in the soul's progress towards perfection.

In that particular period of purgation of the senses during which the soul he was directing seemed to herself to be lost in the depths of night, in pitch darkness, the director made her understand the action of the Holy Spirit, the secret workings of grace and explained to her the ultimate purpose of that action on the part of the divine Bridegroom.

Disclosure of Satan's snares. Satan does not remain inactive. With his usual cunning he seeks every chance to render the action of grace ineffective, to throw the soul into a state of bewilderment and create confusion in the mind.

Discouraged by the inevitable difficulties encountered on the path towards perfection, Raffaelina felt sorry for herself, seeing nothing but pride and failures in her own life. On the other hand, flooded as she was with divine grace, she was invariably afraid of corresponding inadequately with all the grace she received. Padre Pio always intervened at the right moment and set everything in order so that the soul might proceed on its spiritual journey.

A frank and sincere character. We mention just one episode among many which can be found in the correspondence published here. Obliged to leave the family home to her brother, although it had been bequeathed to her, Raffaelina had been living for seven years in a rented house. However, she was looking out for a suitable place in which to live with her sister Giovina.

She made known her intention to her director and asked him to implore Jesus to reveal His will. Padre Pio, mindful only of the supreme spiritual good of his disciple, explained his point of view clearly, sincerely and frankly, but the disciple did not succeed in keeping calm on this occasion and she complained of the turn the affair had taken.

Her director's reply came immediately:

> "I cannot spare you this time from a gentle brotherly reproof...
>
> "May God forgive you, but this time you have made a big mistake. Take care in future not to fall into similar exaggerations" (21-6-1914).

3. Pedagogical method

On this subject also we confine ourselves to pointing out a few essential lines which illustrate the spiritual pedagogics developed by Padre Pio in the letters we present in this volume.

Psychological insight. Padre Pio knew how to adapt himself to the personal satisfaction of the soul under his guidance. He presented Christian perfection in a positive rather than a negative light and stimulated her self-love in such a way as to induce her to commit herself completely on the path to perfection.

Theological structure. We highlight two particular aspects in this regard. The first refers to development of the theological virtues. In this respect Padre Pio did not insist so much on principles to show that God was the centre of his spiritual direction; instead, he made every effort to develop grace in the soul under his guidance, to develop the three theological virtues of faith, hope and charity in order to steer her invariably towards these supernatural forces.

The second aspect to which we refer is the fact that under Padre Pio's guidance the development of the theological virtues took place in an atmosphere of Franciscan spirituality which found expression in certain moral virtues typical of every follower of the *Poverello* of Assisi. He strongly recommended the practice of these virtues.

Concreteness. His spiritual direction, well structured from the theological point of view and by his providential psychological insight, did not follow a merely abstract programme and a set of principles, but consisted in a concrete plan and practical application of those principles.

This practical sense induced Padre Pio primarily to show this soul the various steps to be taken on the way to perfection, giving her to understand that she would advance on this road little by little, gradually and laboriously according to God's plan. In the second place, in order to make sure of that journey, Padre Pio fostered in his disciple an intense spiritual life by suggesting and advising the use of ascetical practices which were undoubtedly traditional, but which beneath his pen and on his lips acquire quite a distinctive quality.

d. *Toward the summit*. We may say that in his letters Padre Pio presented Christian perfection as the noblest achievement that could be desired or fulfilled and consequently he demanded heroism from the soul under his guidance. Convinced that his disciple was called to the highest degree of perfection, he not only told her so quite clearly, but proposed to prepare her and accompany her continually until she reached the supreme goal of loving union with God. He was fully aware that he had been entrusted by God with the task of presenting her to the divine Bridegroom as a virgin chaste in mind and body.

His style. When we reflect on the teachings contained in this correspondence, we believe we may say that in his pedagogical method of guidance Padre Pio adopted a dignified, considerate and courteous manner, whether he advised or commanded, whether he reproved or encouraged, complained or rejoiced. This attitude induced him to respect the freedom of others even while making known his own divergent and contrary opinion. It also affected his literary style which was dignified and considerate in its mode of expression.

4. Effectiveness

At this point we must examine concretely the practical results of such spiritual guidance and the reasons for its undeniable effectiveness.

Two reference points. The effectiveness of Padre Pio's spiritual direction can undoubtedly be seen at one and the same time in its immediate effect, which was to console and restore peace and tranquillity to this soul, and in its ultimate effect which was to attain the goal of her vocation to holiness.

As regards peace and tranquillity of soul, it must be remembered that Raffaelina was passing through an acute spiritual crisis, that she was filled with uncertainty, doubts and anxieties. Matters were complicated still further by a whole series of circumstances (the illness of her sister Giovina, disagreement with her brother, suicide of her niece's husband, etc.) which took her breath away, interfered with her peace of soul and made matters worse from day to day. Padre Pio was the great craftsman who brought peace to this troubled and afflicted soul. Almost every letter of his contains repeated invitations to be consoled, to be calm and tranquil, invitations and exhortations which took effect, as Raffaelina herself, never disappointed in her expectations, recognized with a grateful heart.

From the point of view of its ultimate effect, which was to reach the goal of Christian perfection, this guidance was no less effective. Although we are unable to say just how high this privileged soul climbed on the mystical ladder, we can be certain that under Padre Pio's enlightened guidance she passed through the trial of sense purgation and through the still more painful trial of spiritual purgation.

Elements in the efficacy of this spiritual direction. - Dwelling briefly on these constituent elements which we have been able to glean from the correspondence, we shall mention just three of them:

1. *Sound doctrinal preparation.* It was primarily a matter of theological preparation firmly rooted in traditional doctrine, of an uncommon familiarity with the Bible, embodied especially in the teaching of his beloved apostle Paul, and of a genuine knowledge and experience of the ascetic-mystical life.

2. *A supernatural breath of holiness.* This emerges from all his letters and the soul he directed felt drawn towards the same ideal. In these introductory notes it is not possible to quote even a few of the more beautiful pages which speak to us of the supernatural world and its requirements, written by the director and also by the soul he was directing. We list just a few of the more meaningful themes: the desire to die, yearning for peace, love and suffering, the Eucharist, Our Lady, the Guardian Angel, the mystery of the Cross. At this point we have to consider the mystical experience of the director, which did not escape the attention of Raffaelina who found new evidence of it continually and was constantly stimulated by it.

3. *Special enlightenment.* Padre Pio was aware that he was passing on exhortations, advice, norms and doctrine which in most cases were not drawn from human effort but from divine impulses, from heavenly light, from revelations of the Lord. This is one of the more characteristic traits of his counselling and was perhaps the factor which more than any other accounted for the effectiveness of his action. This awareness gave him authority and made him speak with certainty, with what was at times the certainty of a professor.'

IV Conclusion

From what has been said so far the reader will undoubtedly have glimpsed the variety of orientations and suggestions, the wealth of doctrine and experience contained in the letters which passed between Padre Pio and this aristocratic lady, Raffaelina Cerase.

We earnestly hope that others will undertake the systematic treatment of at least some of these subjects, in the light of Padre Pio's teaching over so many years in the delicate and demanding field of spiritual direction, that they will deal with these matters in relation to the problems which arise today in the study of the theology of perfection.

This is a fascinating and inspiring subject, of undoubted value for the science of the spiritual life and the apostolate of spiritual direction. However, it is outside the range of the task we have undertaken in these brief introductory notes. Hence, as we come to the end of these notes which, we repeat, have been compiled as a presentation of the text rather than an assessment of its content, we confine ourselves to a few suggestions which may stimulate the experts to study and reflection.

1. The present collection of letters, like other works of its kind, is a source of primary importance for the progress of the theology of perfection considered from the ascetical and mystical viewpoint. In the light of what has been related and confirmed by experience, we see how divine grace accomplishes its transforming work through the enlightened action of spiritual directors, who represent the teaching authority of the Church, and the active and laborious cooperation of those generously committed to the acquisition of perfection, each according to his own state, in response to the universal vocation to holiness.

2. Spiritual teachers will discover new and practical ele-

ments in these pages which will confirm or rectify a number of principles in the science of perfection.

Spiritual directors will find a model to be imitated in carrying out with a sense of responsibility the delicate mission of guiding souls along the not always easy paths to holiness.

For their own part, those who are receiving direction will learn how to act at the decisive moments of their spiritual ascent, so that they may not oppose the Holy Spirit but collaborate effectively with the visible representatives of this same Spirit, who is and always will be the true and principal author of all genuine spiritual direction.

3. Lastly, Padre Pio's biographers will find in this correspondence a valuable addition to his spiritual heritage. It contains many autobiographical notes, personal experiences, trials he endured and overcame, etc. Everything is described or suggested by him without either emphasis or secondary motives, spontaneously, with no other purpose than to pour out in the presence of God his state of mind. We are allowed to see the man who thirsts for God, tormented by the desire to lose himself in Him alone. The phases of his spirituality already highlighted in his correspondence with his spiritual directors during the years 1913 to 1915 are further illustrated and confirmed here.

It seems to us that these simple outlines and brief considerations suffice to ensure a profitable reading of the correspondence we present.

THE EDITORS

San Giovanni Rotondo, 23 September 1974
Sixth Anniversary of Padre Pio's death.

LETTERS

1

Foggia, 24 March 1914.

The reason for this correspondence. Present state of the soul concerned. Relations with her sister. She asks his prayers. Postscript.

Alone with Jesus! Most Holy Spirit, help me!

Reverend Padre Pio,

Jesus has sent me to you and after having asked and obtained leave—spontaneously, fully and without limits—from my confessor and yours, I have decided to write to you.

Are you aware of all the needs of my soul? Your own most dear Father, in writing to you many times about me, was speaking as a saint, but I have to write to you as the sinner I am. For 50 days I have been confined to the house by illness, unable to receive Jesus, deprived of His presence for such a long time. Isn't this a true and well-deserved punishment for my bad Communions, distracted Masses, carelessly recited prayers and for my sins, sins of all description?

I am tortured by the past and the present; what does the future hold for me? I have done nothing so far for Jesus and I already have some white hairs. When am I going to make up my mind? I need a push and a big effort of my will. Tell Jesus, yes, tell Him that it is deep night within me and all around me. Am I acting rightly or wrongly? I don't know. Are my Confessions good or bad? I have no idea. Am I making progress along the path I have taken? I just don't know. It is invariably dark and I am aware of nothing but doubts, anxieties, distress and torment.

I am convinced, and it does not surprise me, that extreme wretchedness is my privilege, but it is malice that frightens me and prevents me being at peace. I know that this handful of filth does not deserve even a glance or the least remembrance before Jesus, but in your seraphic charity you must speak to Him about this wretched creature. Ask Him not to crush me, ask Him to make me die to myself and to everything, ask Him to let me occupy myself and concentrate entirely on Him and in Him. Tell Him to show me some way, the true way in which He wants to be served, for I am unable to choose it myself.

I am not alone, as you know. My life is bound up with someone very dear to me, my second mother, the only thread that binds me to this earth, so that in certain respects the storm involves both of us and affects each according to her nature. We are confidently awaiting the calm; will it come? Both of us await tranquillity of soul, peace for our thirsty, needy, prostrate souls exhausted by our continual struggles. We await this from our own Jesus, our All, and through you our intercessor.

Implore Jesus, I repeat, to the point of becoming tiresome, insist with Him and speak continually to Him. Tell Him that these two souls[1], especially my own, await His grace; these two rocks all alone in the world, these two leaves driven before the hurricane are waiting and hoping for His

[1] In the correspondence between Padre Pio and Padre Agostino, this is the manner in which reference is made to the sisters Raffaelina and Giovina Cerase.

hand to place them where He wants them to be. I hope, moreover, that Jesus will place His own cross between His mercy and my many sins and that He will forgive and bless me.

And you, too, Father, bless me in the Most Sacred Heart of Jesus, along with my unfortunate sister.

With deep respect I kiss your hand.

A poor Franciscan tertiary.

P.S. I am passing on to you a closed envelope[2] with the request to reply when you see fit and to send your answer likewise in a closed envelope inside your letter to me, which I would ask you to send by registered post.

I take the liberty of asking you to answer me. Pray very much for the conversion of myself and my sister.

Please make allowances for my simple, free-and-easy manner of expressing myself and forgive me.

Here is my address: Raffaella Cerase, Corso V.E., Palazzo Notari, Foggia.

---

[2] This envelope contained a letter from a priest asking Padre Pio's prayers and advice with regard to a seminarian who was still uncertain of his vocation. This letter and others which will be mentioned later have been kept for inclusion in the volume of Padre Pio's correspondence with priests and religious.

2

Pietrelcina. Passion Sunday, 29 March 1914.

He shares in her suffering. The state of suffering and anxiety which perturbs her is no punishment but a proof of love. Looking to the future with cheerful trust. Her illness is not a punishment. She must open her heart to the action of the Holy Spirit. Prayers for each other. Unconditional service.

J.M.J.D.F.C.

Beloved sister in Jesus Christ,

May the peace of Jesus Christ be in your heart.

I feel all your troubles as if they were my own. Knowing how upset you are, I am moved spontaneously to ask the Lord to command the enemy to desist somewhat from his fierce attack, or else to redouble your strength and enable you to endure the struggle with gracious resignation to His most holy will.

But while I am thus grieved and pray, I also feel a spiritual joy on account of Jesus' very particular love for you. The storm that rages around you and perturbs you is certainly a proof of this love. Don't think this is just my own personal conviction; it is God himself who tells us that temptation is a proof of the soul's union with Him: *My son, if you come forward to serve the Lord, prepare yourself for temptation*[1].

[1] Sir 2:1.

The fact of being harassed, therefore, means that you are in the Lord's service and the more fully you become the friend and intimate of God, the more you will have to endure temptation. Temptation is a most convincing proof that God is united with a soul: *I will be with him in trouble*[2]. All the disheartening thoughts that are running around in your mind, such as the idea that God may be punishing you for Communions and Confessions badly made and for all the other devotional practices carelessly performed, believe me, are nothing but temptations which you must drive far from you, for it is by no means true that in all these things you have offended God, since Jesus by His watchful grace has guarded you very well against all such offences.

When the soul grieves and is afraid of offending God, it does not offend Him and is very far from committing sin. Divine grace is with you continually and you are very dear to the Lord. Shadows and fears and convictions to the contrary are diabolical stratagems which you should despise in the name of Jesus. Do not listen to these temptations. The spirit of evil is busily engaged in trying to make you believe that your past life has been all strewn with sins.

Listen, rather, to me when I tell you, just as we are told by the Spouse of our souls, that your present state is an effect of your love for God and a proof of His incomparable love for you. Cast away those fears, dispel those shadows which the devil is increasing in your soul in order to torment you and drive you away, if possible, even from daily Communion.

Be consoled and rejoice in the knowledge that the heavenly Father permits these attacks of the devil, because His mercy makes you dear to Him and He wants to make you similar to His Only Begotten Son, who took upon Himself all

[2] Ps 91:15.

the iniquities of men and was subjected to terrible and unspeakable torment. May He therefore be thanked for treating you as one chosen to follow closely in the steps of Jesus up the Hill of Calvary. I myself observe with joy and deepest emotion this action of grace within you, O beloved sister of my heart.

I should be less happy if I did not see you so downcast, because I should then see the Lord bestowing less jewels upon you. Hence, in the holy charity of Jesus, while earnestly desiring your spiritual profit and your progress towards perfection, I rejoice more and more to see you in your present state. My joy is by no means foolish, for in the combat there is a crown to be won and the better the fight put up by the soul the more numerous the palms of victory. Don't you know how the apostle St. James exhorted his brethren to rejoice when they were harassed by various storms and numerous reverses? *Count it all joy, my brethren, when you meet various trials*[3].

Moreover, how can we fail to rejoice when we find ourselves involved in many combats, knowing as we do that every victory achieved has a corresponding degree of glory? May this thought of eternal bliss with Jesus and of being made similar to the Son of God encourage you and prevent you from yielding to the enemy's temptations. May you be urged onwards in this direction by the example of Jesus Christ of whom it is written: *One who in every respect has been tempted as we are, yet without sinning*[4], tempted to the point at which He could bear no more and cried out: *My God, why hast Thou forsaken me*[5]?

You say you are anxious about the future, but don't you know that the Lord is with you always and that our enemy

---

[3] Jas 1:2.
[4] Heb 4:15.
[5] Mt 27:46; Mk 15:34.

has no power over one who has resolved to belong entirely to Jesus? Moreover, isn't God good and faithful to the point of not permitting you to be tempted beyond your strength[6]?

Oh, beloved daughter of Jesus! If we were left to ourselves we should always be falling and never remain on our feet. Humble yourself, then, at the delightful thought that you are in the divine arms of Jesus, the best of fathers, like a little infant in its mother's arms, and sleep peacefully with the certainty that you are being guided towards the destination which will be to your greatest advantage. How can we be afraid to remain in such loving arms when our entire being is consecrated to God?

The fear which you say you have with regard to sins committed is illusory and a real torment brought about by the devil. Have you not, perhaps, confessed these sins? Of what, then, are you afraid? Once and for all, leave that miserable wretch to himself and open up your heart to a holy and unbounded trust in Jesus. Believe that He is not the cruel taskmaster depicted for you by that perpetrator of iniquity, but the Lamb who takes away the sins of the world[7], interceding for our salvation with ineffable groanings[8].

You complain that your poor health does not permit you to go to church and nourish yourself to the full on the Immaculate Flesh of the Son of God. You consider this to be a just punishment from the Most High for many Communions perhaps badly made. No, no, this too is a gesture of the ineffable charity of Jesus. He intends to take complete possession of your heart and desires it to be pierced with sorrow and love like His own.

It is also wrong to try to convince yourself that you have been cast off by Jesus. Oh! Trust in Him and do not be afraid,

---

6 Cf. 1 Cor 10:13.
7 Cf. Jn 1:29.
8 Cf. Heb 7:25.

for you have no reason whatever to fear. Our most tender Saviour has not forsaken you, but is showing His love for you and I have no adequate words by which to thank the Lord for His goodness in dealing with you and for protecting you so lovingly. The Evil One wants to persuade you that you are the victim of his attacks and are abandoned by God. Don't believe him, for he wants to deceive you. Despise him in the name of Jesus and His most holy Mother.

Never fall back on yourself alone, but place all your trust in God and don't be too eager to be set free from your present state. Let the Holy Spirit act within you. Give yourself up to all His transports and have no fear. He is so wise and gentle and discreet that He never brings about anything but good. How good this Holy Spirit, this Comforter, is to all, but how supremely good He is to those who seek Him!

Forgive me for being unable to continue, for my strength is running out. Before closing, though, I earnestly ask you and your saintly sister never to stop praying to our merciful Jesus for this rebellious, stiff-necked soul, so that he may not be unfaithful to God.

In my own small way I too never fail to present you to Jesus in my continual but very lukewarm prayers. Needless to say you may make use of my poor capacity when and in whatever manner suits you. Write to me every time you need to and you will always give me pleasure.

When you see Padre Agostino, please give him my kindest regards.

May Jesus bless you and comfort you and may He one day introduce you, along with your beloved sister, into the splendour of His immortal youth.

Your poor Fra Pio.

3

Foggia. Spy Wednesday, 8 April 1914.

Gratitude for his prompt and indulgent reply. The distressing problem of her home. She experiences a great void and is discouraged. Telling everything to Jesus. She asks for a little light. Full confidence in his guidance.

Jesus alone! Most Holy Spirit, help me!

Reverend Padre Pio,

Your charity in replying so promptly to my poor letter fills me with deep gratitude, a gratitude to which I am unable to give adequate expression, wretched as I am.

But in your goodness you understand and make allowances for all. Your charitable words encourage and urge me to write to you every time I feel the need to do so (for this my gratitude and thanks know no limits).

The need arises at present. For seven years we have been living in a rented house; for reasons which can easily be understood we were obliged to leave our own home which we ourselves had inherited. For the sake of peace we preferred to leave our brother[1] and his wife free in the old home.

---

[1] Matteo Cerase di Michele, who died on 10 October 1924 at the age of 77, whose wife Giovina Marianna, a native of Lucera, died in Foggia on 2 October 1921.

For six years we have been looking for a more suitable house than the present one, but so far Jesus has not wanted us to find one. A month from today, on 8 May, we have to reach the final decision. Where will Jesus send us? What will he arrange for us? How are we to act? What path should we take? Where are we to settle definitely for our spiritual benefit? All is darkness: doubts, uncertainty, ceaseless fears... how are we to know what is God's most holy will?

I turn to you, good Father. Pray to Jesus and entreat Him. He knows all. I know that I am an obstacle to His grace in my own home. May He humiliate me, forgive me and in the end convert me. I know that my life is nothing, an empty and useless life. How am I to reach the two great ideals, the two holy desires, the two sublime needs: God's glory and the good of souls? How can I reach them, how can I promote them and satisfy them? I don't know.

I feel a great void inside me and around me and this void is accompanied by a great sense of discouragement. I yearn and long for light, suffering, pardon and love. On Friday morning, the feast of the dolours of my good Mother of Sorrows, two months after the feast of the Purification, I received Holy Communion. Afterwards, closely united to Jesus, I placed the key of this poor and wretched heart of mine in His hands, or rather, I placed it among the swords which pierced the heart of His afflicted Mother, making an agreement that she should lend it to me each morning to open the door to Jesus alone.

Will my holy Mother listen to me? I don't know how to pray, how to be recollected; I lack absolutely the gift of meditation, the gift of God's presence. I see and feel other souls to be so good, while I myself am always so wretched and so very, very bad!

Tell Jesus all that I write to you and then make known to me what He says about me. Don't hide anything from me, correct me, instruct me, convert me.

My dear Father, I should like very much to speak to you. My poor pen is ineffectual and cannot compare with the spoken word. How many things this poor lost atom, groping in darkness and turmoil, would have to confess. Father, I expect a little light from you, from your charity, light to guide my steps, a holy impulse in this sluggish, stupid life of mine, a pure divine fire to warm my frozen heart.

Speak to Jesus for me, for I am unable to say anything to Him, and tell me frankly what He thinks of me. Ask and beg on my behalf, for He won't refuse you anything on the coming feast of His Resurrection. May all souls rise up to Him, my sister, my friend, all my relatives. Glory to God and *peace* on earth to men of good will, and also to those of bad will so that they may be converted to good, to virtue, to God, and all enjoy holy peace.

Among my relatives are two people who, because of money matters in the past, have refused even to greet us for three years, although they receive Holy Communion frequently. This causes me deep suffering. I have tried to obtain a reconciliation, but in vain. Pray that their hearts may turn towards us in holy peace.

At the solemn moment of the holy Resurrection, keep me in mind. I set down for your benefit my poor ideas, my many needs, always in a very simple way, inspired by my great confidence in you. Please forgive me. I try your patience too much; I am a tiresome tertiary; forgive me, make allowances for me and write to me. I anxiously await what Jesus reveals to you.

Kissing your hand respectfully, I beg your holy blessing for myself and my sister. Once again, in the Most Sacred Heart of Jesus,

A poor tertiary.

P.S. - The usual charity of a closed envelope[2].

My address: Raffaella Cerase, Palazzo Notari, Foggia.

---

[2] She is referring to the letter of thanks from the priest who had asked Padre Pio for prayers and advice with regard to the vocation of a seminarian. This letter bears no date. See p. 61, Note 2.

4

Pietrelcina. Holy Saturday, 11 April 1914.

Easter greetings. God demands purgation. The Lord will never leave her at Satan's mercy. God has adorned her with the gift of His holy love. The most effective apostolate. The question of the house. Their correspondence.

J.M.J.D.F.C.

Beloved daughter of Jesus Christ,

May Our Lord be always with you and make you holy.

In the first place, I want to wish you every happiness in the Lord during the Easter feasts, with the earnest hope that our beloved Redeemer may keep you always in His holy grace and invariably treat you as a chosen daughter.

You ask me to pray to the Lord that He may deign in His infinite goodness to manifest what He desires from you. Well, then, Jesus wants to toss and shake you, to thresh you like wheat in order that your spirit may be cleansed and purified as He wishes. Could grain be stored in the barn if it were not free from all husk or chaff? Could linen be stored in the owner's cupboard if it had not first been made quite spotless? So, too, must it be with the chosen soul.

I understand that temptations seem to stain rather than purify the soul, but this is not really the case. Let us hear what the saints have to say about it. For you it suffices to know what the great St. Francis de Sales says, namely, that temptations are like the soap which when spread on the laundry seems to soil but in reality cleanses it. It is well for you to pray continually to Jesus, however, that He may not allow you to be tempted, and I too, although very feebly, will pray for the same purpose.

Meanwhile you must by no means fear that the Lord will leave you at Satan's mercy. He is faithful and He never allows you to be tempted beyond your strength. He gives our enemy just as much power to torment you as serves His own fatherly plan for the sanctification of your soul and redounds to the greater glory of His divine Majesty. Hence you must be strong and cheerful in spirit, for the Lord is in the depths of your heart: He will fight along with you and for you. Who, then, will win the battle? Who is stronger than He is? Who will hold out against the King of the heavens? What is the creature, what is hell itself in front of the Lord?

Hold resolutely to the comforting thought that God is with you all the time and will never abandon you to Satan's attacks. You are downcast because you do not know how to pray, you complain that you do not possess the gift of holy meditation and the presence of God. On the contrary, I tell you that our merciful Lord, in spite of all your unworthiness, has adorned you with the gift of His holy love, the gift of charity. For this give glory to the most tender heavenly Father.

What are those continual laments of your soul, those holy and most delicate desires which frequently seem to make you faint? I mean to say, those desires to belong entirely to Jesus, to please Him in everything? What is that continual desire to see God's kingdom extended, that ceaseless longing to be set free from the bonds of this body in order to fly away to the bosom of the heavenly Father and be transformed into Him?

Tell me, are not all these impulses perhaps the effects of

that charity which Jesus has poured into your heart and which constitutes the happiness of the regions of the blessed? Is it, perhaps, within the power of wretched mortals like us to formulate similar desires? Certainly not. The human spirit without the flame of divine love tends to reach the level of the beast, while, on the other hand, charity, the love of God, raises it up so high that it can reach even to the throne of God.

Give thanks without ever growing weary for the liberality of such a good Father and ask Him to increase holy charity more and more in your heart.

All of us are not called by God to save souls and propagate His glory by the noble apostolate of preaching. Remember, moreover, that this is not the only means of achieving these two great ideals. One can promote God's glory and work for the salvation of souls by means of a truly Christian life, by praying without ceasing that "His kingdom come," that His name "be hallowed," that "we may not be led into temptation" and that He "deliver us from evil."

This is what you ought to do, offering yourself continually to the Lord for this purpose. Pray for the wicked, pray for the lukewarm, pray even for fervent souls, but pray especially for the supreme Pontiff, for all the spiritual and temporal needs of holy Church, our most tender mother. A special prayer also for all those who are working for the salvation of souls and for God's glory in the mission to many infidels and unbelievers.

I exhort you once more to devote yourself entirely and induce as many others as you can to devote themselves to the ends I have already explained to you. You may be perfectly sure that this is the highest form of apostolate that any one can carry on in the Church of God. Abide resolutely by this statement of mine, which is precisely what Jesus tells us, and treat with contempt all the suggestions to the contrary which the devil proposes to you.

You do well to desire the reconciliation between those

two people and you will do even better if you make efforts to bring it about. Let us pray confidently to the Lord that He may bring them to a better frame of mind by enlightening them and touching their hearts. Don't be unduly distressed about the matter, for the Lord, according to the great Doctor, St. Augustine, *allows the wicked to live on, either that they may change their ways or else that through Him the good may have a chance to practise patience.*[1]

As regards the question of the house, Jesus would be just as glad if you were to continue to live where you are at present. I believe I am not going against Jesus' will when I suggest that it would be better for you to find, if possible, a house closer to a parish church or to a convent. At all events, if this is not feasible, don't let it worry you. I tell you quite frankly that your anxiety about this wretched house is a bit excessive and I don't approve of it. May I ask you, then, to curb your anxiety about it unless you want to displease Jesus. It would be advisable for you to let the head of the family take care of the matter.

My illness obliges me to stop here. Write to me every time you feel the need to do so. I merely ask you not to blame me if I do not always reply at once, since my illness which is gradually wearing me out frequently makes this impossible.

If you see Padre Agostino in the course of the next few days, please convey to him my kind regards. I don't believe in sending the letters by registered post as they are entrusted to excellent hands.

Pray, pray for everyone.

Fra Pio.

---

[1] ST. AUGUSTINE, *Enarrationes in Psalm LIV*: PL, Vol. 36, Col. 630, No. 4.

5

Foggia, 20 April 1914.

His letters are "a real gift from heaven." Deprived again of sacramental Communion. Jesus "Spouse" and Mary "the good Mother." She thanks him on behalf of both herself and her sister. The affair of her home and family. "Your words do me so much good." "If only I could speak to you." She is, as it were, in a "labyrinth" from which she cannot escape. "Light, love and peace."

Jesus alone! Most Holy Spirit, help me!

Reverend Padre Pio,

Your letters are for me a real gift from heaven. How can I thank you for your fatherly charity towards me? How can I thank Jesus for the means He offers me for my conversion? Ungrateful and unfaithful as I am, though, I do not yet listen to Him. I fail to correspond, I don't yet follow Him.

Once again, as you know already, I am deprived of Him. The bad weather conspires to my spiritual detriment. Tell Jesus that I want Him always, every morning, at all costs.

I know how bad I am, but without Him I shall be much worse. Ask Him to grant me solitude with Him, interior silence, deep recollection, continual union with His adorable Heart. His intentions, His purposes, His feelings are mine: what a paradise it is to think and speak and act according to His most holy will!

Speak to Him at length about me, good Father. Tell Him that my tongue does not dare to call Him Spouse, because I am too unworthy and it would be too great a presumption on my part. I call Him Father, Brother, Friend; occasionally, with a great effort, I call Him Spouse. On the other hand, although I don't know why, I invariably call His most holy Mother my own good Mother. The Mother of Sorrows is my confidante, my counsellor, my teacher and my powerful advocate.

Thank Jesus on my behalf for all the spiritual aids He obtains for me and ask Him to make me use them for my good, or else to break off, cut off, put an end to everything in and around me. He knows all. Thank Him on my behalf for everything. Tell Him in the greatest confidence about my perpetual worry: my sister approaches the holy table two or three times a year. May Jesus grant her peace of soul, at last, by transferring her to different surroundings, to a place more in keeping with her impressionable nature which has been exceedingly upset by conflicts, disillusionment and continual tears—otherwise she will always remain as she is.

You rebuke me for being too concerned about the house. I am aware of it, but if you only knew, good Father, or rather, you already know, the awful storm through which we are passing precisely on account of this house. Our brother does not want to recognize his obligations and we ourselves, jammed between the door and the wall, struggling in the midst of disputes and upsets of all descriptions, don't know what decision to take for God's glory and for the good and peace of our souls.

Ask Jesus to sort out this complicated tangle, for pity's sake to calm the storm that is raging at present, otherwise endless sins will result. Here I end as regards myself. I don't want to be selfish by presenting to Jesus merely my own needs; I also want to commend to Him, through you, the many necessities of those around me.

So many troubles around us, holy Father! My spiritual friend, who has been in my home for 25 years[1], has an aged father, a younger sister whose only concern is to get married, and a sick brother, a strange man, married only in a registry office.

A family of six, first cousins of ours and all of them old, pushed around from one place to another, have waited for years for decent employment. This is a harrowing situation which goes on and on. My sister is doing what she can, but it is not enough.

Another spiritual friend of mine, still young, has been confined to bed for 15 years. She has a brother, a priest, who is chronically ill, two unmarried sisters, another very pious sister married, who awaits with tears and prayers the conversion of her husband and eight children.

Add to this the terrifying drought on our land; if the harvest fails, the only resource in my town, we shall be faced with real disaster. Finally, peace for this country ravaged by wars and factions, by servility, indifferentism and scepticism.

Pray, Father, pray. Speak to our good Jesus about us all, speak to Him about me and tell me, good Father, what He has to say in reply. Don't worry if you cannot answer me at once, for I don't want you to tire yourself on my account. Write to me at your own convenience, whenever you can, but please don't delay so very long as to change my expectation into anxiety and then to agitation.

What can you expect? Your words do me a great deal of good and they calm me. For me to receive your letters means a feast for my soul. My own letters, on the contrary,

---

[1] Rosina or Rosinella, who will often be mentioned in these pages.

must be a source of nausea, vexation and bother to you! Forgive me. This is a stubborn and unruly sheep that you must bring back to the fold of the Good Shepherd.

What do you think of these poor writings of mine, dashed off in a free-and-easy manner, without head or tail? Do you destroy them when you have read them? If they are harmful to my soul, burn them all. Have the patience to tell me. I want to know if it is necessary to repeat my address at the end of each letter.

How pretentious I am towards you, as if I had known you for a great many years. Attribute this to the great, unlimited, holy confidence with which you inspire me. If I could only speak to you, I should have so many things to tell you: all the evil I have done and continue to do, all the doubts and darkness of my soul, and if some ray of light comes through, I always consider it illusion, all illusion due to my subtle self-love.

Such pride! How can I eradicate and destroy this evil and poisonous plant which has taken root so deeply in my heart? I have no idea. Please tell me. Sins and distress form such a labyrinth that I do not know how to escape from it. When I look at Jesus I want to feel He is smiling, I want to hear and understand Him and to know how to act.

I realize that I have wearied you enough. Tell me if these poor pages of mine tire you and if you destroy them afterwards. Tell me everything. Pray and speak a whole lot to Jesus about me and about my poor sister. She is by no means well either in body or soul and this is a source of consternation and torment for me, Father. May Jesus' Cross and Mary's Sorrows always stand between God's justice and my sins. Don't forget my brother and his wife. May light, love and peace be theirs in mind and heart.

I return a hundredfold your kind greetings for the holy

Easter feasts. Taking refuge with my sister in the adorable Heart of Jesus, I beg His holy blessing and yours.

A poor tertiary.

Address to: Raffaella Cerase, Palazzo Notari.

P.S. Herewith the usual closed envelope[2]. In obedience to you I am not sending this letter by registered post. Pray, write to me and forgive me.

---

[2] Containing the letter from the same priest as before (see p. 61), dated 19 April 1914.

6

Pietrelcina, 25 April 1914.

Storms and temptations are signs of divine predilection. God does not permit the enemy to win. Love and fear make us run in the path of virtue. She is not to worry too much about the impossibility of receiving Holy Communion. Her sister should receive Holy Communion. Signs which show whether the light comes from God or from Satan. He takes to heart all her suggestions. The attitude to be adopted towards those who are obstinate. Their correspondence.

Beloved daughter of Jesus,

May the peace of Jesus be always in your heart. Amen.

I am consoled to hear that the storms are increasing, for this is a sign that God's kingdom is being established within you. Keep cheerful and don't be discouraged. The temptations and storms that are circling around you are sure signs of divine predilection. Your fear of offending God is the surest proof that you are not offending Him.

Place your unlimited trust in the divine goodness and the more violent the enemy becomes, the more you should abandon yourself trustfully on the breast of the most tender heavenly Spouse who will never allow you to be overcome. God Himself has solemnly announced through Sacred Scripture: *God is faithful and He will not let you be tempted beyond your strength, but with temptation will also provide the way of escape, that you may be able to endure it*[1].

To convince yourself of the opposite is infidelity and may God guard us from falling into similar absurdities. Even St. Paul was restless and besought the Lord to free him from the trial of the flesh: he too was very much afraid that he would yield, but did he not receive the assurance that grace would always be sufficient for him[2]?

Our enemy who plots against us wants to persuade you that the very opposite is the case, but despise him in the name of Jesus and laugh heartily at him. This is the best way to make him beat a retreat. He plucks up courage when dealing with the weak, but when anyone takes up a weapon and faces him he becomes a coward. You may fear, if you like, but it must be that holy fear, I mean to say the fear that is never separated from love. When fear and love are united, they help each other, like sisters, to remain on their feet and to walk securely in the Lord's paths.

Love makes us hasten with rapid strides while fear, on the other hand, makes us watch prudently where we place our feet and guides us so that we may never stumble on the road leading to heaven. I know, my beloved sister, that the cross is painful and that for those who love, a thing is almost unbearable when it exposes them to the danger of offending the One they love and adore. But Jesus tempted in the desert and hanging on the Cross is a most clear, obvious and very consoling proof of what I tell you in the name of the most tender Spouse of souls. That is to say, for a soul that is seeking God in all things and longs above all to possess Him alone, that yearns to have Him reign as King in the depths of her spirit and ardently desires to be entirely and totally possessed by Him alone and in all this is much more jealous than

---

[1] 1 Cor 10:13.
[2] Cf. 2 Cor 12:9.

any two people who have passionately vowed to love each other, for such a soul the storms of this life are a most evident sign of the special charity and exceptional mercy of God's loving providence, which He does not bestow on all souls, not even on those who are particularly privileged.

Courage, then, and go ahead. God is with you and hell, the world and the flesh will one day, to their confusion, have to relinquish their weapons and admit once more that they are powerless against the soul that possesses and is possessed by God.

You are tormented by the fact that you are unable to leave the house because of your delicate health and are therefore deprived of the immaculate Flesh of the divine Lamb. Moreover, you believe, or rather the enemy tries to make you believe, that this is a punishment from God. No, no, don't listen to him. I tell you in all sincerity that this is a particular predilection of the heavenly Father towards you. He wants to make you similar to His beloved Son who fasted from earthly food in the desert for 40 days[3]. By depriving you of this beneficial food, He wants to inspire you more and more with great reverence towards his Son in this sacrament, to enkindle within you an ever greater love for the sacred table, for it is at the moment of privation, when God Himself brings this about, that the soul has a deeper appreciation of the greatness of this gift.

From these assurances you will understand that when you are convinced that deprived of Communion you will go from bad to worse, it is then that the shadows which have fallen on your soul do not come from the Father of light but from the tempter who wants to torment you. The unclean beast understands only too well that he is powerless to make you deviate from your duty, so he intends to vent his hatred on you by terrorizing you.

---

[3] Cf. Mat 4:2.

War has been declared upon you, my dear, and you need to be watchful at every moment, to put up a strong defence, with the eye of faith always fixed on the God of hosts who is fighting along with you and for you. You must have boundless faith in the divine goodness, for the victory is absolutely certain. How could you think otherwise? Isn't our God more concerned about our salvation than we are ourselves? Isn't He stronger than hell itself? Who can ever resist and overcome the King of the heavens? What are the world, the devil, the flesh and all our enemies before the Lord?

I agree that you would go from bad to worse in the paths of the Lord if failure to approach the sacred table depended on your own choice, but since everything has been regulated by the heavenly Spouse, your soul will suffer no loss but will benefit all the more. You do well to desire to be united with Him every day and the best proof of this is that, whenever you can, you never neglect to go to Jesus in the Blessed Sacrament to give and receive the kiss of peace.

Calm yourself, then, and rejoice, because in all this it is the Lord who is acting within you. You desire nothing else than to walk before Him all the time, so let Him guide you on the difficult journey of this life. Give Him your total assent so that He may act in the manner most pleasing to Him.

I am confused and I don't hide from you the fact that I feel continually a pang of grief with regard to your sister who approaches the altar so seldom to receive Jesus. This conduct really seems to denote indifference even if we don't want to call it—allow me to use a rather harsh expression—contempt rather than love for Jesus. Oh, if men could only appreciate this gift we should certainly not see such small numbers of communicants! These are very sad times, but what can be done? O unfortunate times on which we have fallen!

Let us pray to our most merciful Jesus to come to the aid of His Church, for her needs have become extreme.

You say that you are unable to distinguish whether the rays of light which appear at times in the depths of your soul come from God or from others and that you fear to be deceived in everything because of your subtle self-love.

Here, then, are the signs by which to know if these rays of light come from the Father of all light. These signs may be reduced to three. The first is that these lights produce an ever more admirable knowledge of God, who, while revealing Himself to us, gives us a deeper and deeper knowledge of His incomprehensible greatness. In a word, this light leads us to love God our Father more and more and to increase the sacrifices we make for His honour and glory. The second sign is an ever greater knowledge of ourselves, a deeper and deeper sense of humility at the thought that such a wretched creature should have had the effrontery to offend Him and still dares to look at Him and tend towards Him. The third sign is that these heavenly rays produce in the soul an increasing contempt for all that belongs to this earth, with the exception of those things which may prove useful for the service of God.

Now, if such rays of light produce these three effects in your soul, consider them as coming from God. Neither the enemy much less our own imagination can produce these effects in the soul.

I have taken very much to heart all those needs which you have explained to me. May our most sweet Jesus bring peace to all these afflicted hearts. I tell you sincerely and without fear of lying, beloved daughter of Jesus, that my soul can say with the apostle St. Paul (although, alas, I haven't even the thousandth part of the charity that burned in the heart of this holy Apostle): *I could wish that I myself were accursed and cut off from Christ for the sake of my brethren*[4]. Yes, let our most sweet Lord excommunicate me, separate me from Him, abandon me and allow me to suffer the shame and sufferings earned by my brethren; let Him even cancel my name from the Book of Life as long as He saves my brothers and my companions in exile and does not deprive me of His grace, from which nothing can separate me.

Pray to the Lord that He may gratify these desires which are burning up my internal organs and causing me to die continually.

You are distressed, moreover, by man's ingratitude towards God and you do well to weep over their misfortunes. In reparation to God, offer Him your blessing and all your actions, making sure that all of these are good. But after you have wept privately over the misfortunes of others, it is well to imitate once more Our Lord and the Apostles by dismissing these things from your mind and turning to other matters and other occupations more useful for God's glory and the salvation of souls. *It was necessary that the word of God should be spoken first to you*, said the Apostles in addressing the Jews. *Since you thrust it from you and judge yourselves unworthy of eternal life, behold, we turn to the Gentiles*[5]. *The kingdom of God will be taken away from you*, says the divine Master in the holy Gospel, *and given to a nation producing the fruits of it*[6].

To spend too much time, then, in deploring the state of those who obstinately persist in sinning would be a waste of time which could be appropriately spent and should be spent in promoting the salvation of others and in works for God's glory.

I am obliged to stop at this point, but before ending I

---

[4] Rom 9:3.
[5] Acts 13:46.
[6] Mt 21:43.

make a last effort in order to urge you not to bother thanking me, because I certainly do not deserve it. Address all your thanks, instead, to the heavenly Father. Don't worry and don't be racking your brains about your inability to express your needs clearly, for in this matter I don't expect a lot by any means. Far from reproving you, I admire and am pleased with your simplicity in explaining all your needs with holy confidence. May the merciful Virgin relieve your distress and bless both yourself and your sister.

Your servant,
Padre Pio, Capuchin.

7

Foggia, 13 May 1914.

Letters filled with "complaints and troubles." Her family situation. She wants a reply to all her questions. How she prays. Requests for prayers. Her attitude towards creatures and towards Jesus. Postscript. Further requests for prayers.

Jesus alone! Most Holy Spirit, help me!

Reverend Padre Pio,

I delayed a while before answering your last precious letter, for I wanted to give you good news, since my poor letters are full and overflowing with complaints and troubles. Unfortunately, however, Jesus permits me to tell you invariably of conflicts and tears, failings and discouragement, miseries and deep darkness. At the foot of this mournful picture of my life I wish I could add just two words: love and sacrifice. Instead, I am very far from this. The Crib, Calvary and the Tabernacle show me the way; they urge and attract me to the true life, but I am deaf, blind, wicked, and I resist. When shall I make up my mind?

The storm which I mentioned in my last letter is over, it seems, but traces of it remain: terror and desolation. It would seem that my brother has at last recognized his duty and retired within bounds. Next September we ourselves, after seven years in exile, will come into our own, that is to say, we'll return to our old home.

We don't know what awaits us within those walls which hold so many precious memories and so many objects of affection for us. Almost all my family have passed away, so many loved ones who are now enjoying the Supreme Good and will protect from above the two unhappy survivors who remain all alone, defenceless, a continual target in furious battles, exposed to veiled resentment and malicious insinuations.

My unfortunate sister, invariably misjudged and misunderstood when she acts with a right intention and with great generosity, is worn out mentally and physically. Jesus alone is capable of consoling her, but she succumbs to indifference and apathy. Her entire life is one long series of conflicts, contradictions, sighs and tears. Oh, no! It is not as you say contempt for Jesus which prevents her from approaching the Eucharistic table! Far from it! Oh, no! Never, never, never! Do not judge her harshly, do not be so severe with her, holy Father. My sister is very, very good. She lives like a cloistered nun, dividing her time between work and prayer. She has a heart of gold and great ideals.

Hers is the only holy affection which Jesus has left me on this earth. Bless her for me, Father, and get Jesus to bless her always. Tell Him that I want to see her at His sacred feet, that I want to see her always united with Him, that I want her to be holy. What is more, I consider that if she has not yet become a fervent Christian, it is nobody's fault but mine. I have denied her the necessary help, timely advice, holy counsel and good example. Quite the opposite, so that the fault is entirely mine and I feel that I alone am responsible before God.

How can I make reparation on my own behalf and for her? How can I make reparation, expiate and atone for these things? I don't know, I am completely at a loss. Speak to

Jesus, tell Him everything I have told you and He will certainly answer you.

I implore you, good Father, to write and tell me everything that holy Jesus says to you. Don't be stingy towards me. Why don't you answer me on certain matters? Why don't you throw light on certain desires of mine? I don't know whether you can read my poor letters over again, because I don't know whether you destroy them or not, but if you reread them you will be aware how you keep silence on some points. You are extremely good, you treat me with such very great charity and indulgence that I just don't know how to thank Jesus for it (since you yourself refuse all expressions of thanks).

In your seraphic patience you will have to bear with me, to make allowances, to tolerate and pardon this miserable creature who does not know how to correspond to the immense gifts, the great graces our good Jesus bestows on her. Ungrateful, wretched worm that I am, when shall I begin in earnest?

I don't know why it is that almost invariably in my very brief and imperfect meditations my mind turns on what I must say to Jesus through you. Is this good or bad? Please tell me. You alone, good Father, are my precious and charitable interpreter with Jesus. I know that He speaks to you every day. What does He think of these holy conversations of ours? Is He pleased? You encourage me to write continually to explain to you in holy simplicity and confidence all my needs. Does He, then, approve of this? Tell me something, my dear Father, and don't keep silence with me. I know all about you, so why do you keep silence with me, why conceal anything?

I realize that I am presumptuous and indiscreet. Forgive me, for it is the confidence of a poor unfortunate daughter which leads her to speak to her good Father, the confidence of a stubborn and wicked patient towards her compassionate and charitable physician.

Keep on praying for my sister, for my friend and for all the needs of my relatives and friends of which you are already aware. Pray for my brother, who is furious with us and for his wife who is even more furious. When will all this end between us? When shall we reach the peace for which we long?

In my dealings with others, mere creatures, I am most anxious to see and hear the Creator alone. I should like to prolong for all time the fleeting moment in which Jesus seizes me really and truly. I should like to hold on to it in order to gaze on Jesus alone and feel Him everywhere. Instead, I find a void, an indolence with regard to what is good, violent passions, hypocrisy, egoism, attachments, deep love for myself. This is the kind of life I am living, dragging along with difficulty. Pray and please write to me.

Hidden along with my sister in the Most Sacred Heart of our loving Jesus, I ask your holy blessing.

A poor tertiary.

P.S. I have reopened this letter. I ask your special prayers for my sister. Last night she suffered a great deal from the usual complaint (a sick stomach brought on by continual worry).

I also ask prayers for my poor niece (my favourite, the widow of the unfortunate man who committed suicide, of which you are already well informed)[1]. Complications follow one another without a break and we are threatened with most painful consequences.

May our merciful Jesus ward off the violent storm, the

[1] See letters Nos. 51, 52.

plot that has been hatched by the enemies of peace. Every day brings these thorns. I know that before the thorns encircled Jesus' sacred Head, they pressed upon and were driven into His Most Sacred Heart. As for myself... I am scared and chase them away. Pray.

8

Pietrelcina, 19 May 1914.

Anyone who is intended to reign with Christ must be remodelled by blows of the chisel. Physical and moral trials should be a source of joy to such a person. It is enough to know that one is not offending God. Banish all doubts. He urges her to follow the Spouse wherever He may go. It is necessary to submit. "All is a trick a love." "The more a soul loves God the less it feels this love." "Your love is not indolent." Frequent Communion on the part of her sister. Why he forget some thing. The meaning of a phrase. He asks for a special grace.

J.M.J.D.F.C.

Beloved daughter of Jesus Christ,

May Jesus and Mary be always in your heart and may they make you holy.

By repeated blows of the efficacious chisel and by diligent polishing the divine Artist prepares the blocks of stone which are intended to form part of the divine edifice. Thus sings our most tender mother, the holy Catholic Church, in the hymn of the Office for the Dedication of a Church[1], and this is very true.

Every soul intended for eternal glory can very well be

---

[1] Hymn at Vespers in the old breviary.

considered a stone destined for the erection of the eternal edifice.

The soul that is destined to reign with Jesus Christ in eternal glory, then, must be remodelled by the blows of hammer and chisel. But what are these blows of hammer and chisel by which the divine Artist prepares the stone, that is to say, the chosen soul? Dear sister, these strokes of the chisel are the shadows, fears, temptations, spiritual torments and agitation, with a dash of desolation and even of physical pain.

Thank the infinite mercy of the eternal Father, then, for treating your soul in this way, for it is destined to be saved. What I say is, why not rejoice at this loving treatment by the best of all fathers? Open your heart to this heavenly Physician of souls and abandon yourself with complete confidence in His most holy embrace. He is treating you as one chosen to follow Jesus closely up the Hill of Calvary and I observe with joy and keenest emotion this action of grace in you. Be quite sure that all that is going on within your soul is decreed by the Lord and for this reason you must not be afraid of acting wrongly, in a word, of offending God.

Let it suffice for you to know that in all this you are by no means offending the Lord and that, on the contrary, He is glorified all the more by it. If this most tender Spouse hides from your soul, it is not because He intends to punish your infidelity, as you imagine, but because He wants to test more and more your faith and steadfastness and at the same time to purify you of certain little attachments which to the eyes of the flesh do not appear as such. I am speaking here of those affections and faults from which not even the righteous are exempt, for it is written in the holy pages that *a righteous man falls seven times*[2].

Believe me, if I did not see you so disconsolate, I should

---

[2] Prov 24:16.

be less satisfied, for I should see the Lord bestowing less jewels on you. Hold firm, then, and banish as temptations all doubts on the subject, for they are really temptations. Do this in the name of Jesus on whose behalf I tell you that in all these spiritual combats you are not offending God, you are not committing sin and your soul derives much profit from it all.

Once more, get rid of all those doubts which are clouding the heavens of your soul, such as the idea that you are deaf to the divine call, that you resist his tender invitations, that you yourself are the only obstacle in the way of perfection on the part of your sister, for this does not come from the good spirit but consists in the devil's cunning attempts to turn you aside from your purpose, or at least to make you pause in your progress towards perfection and lose heart.

I hope I have said enough on the subject and that you will heed what I say. I urge you to pray continually to the heavenly Father that He may always keep you close to His divine Heart, that He may make you hear His loving voice more and more clearly and lead you to correspond with increasing gratitude. Ask Jesus with boundless confidence, like the bride in the Song of Solomon, to draw you after Him and let you smell the fragrance of His anointing oils[3], so that you may follow swiftly with all the faculties of your soul and body wherever He goes[4].

I exhort you once more to abide steadfastly by all that I have told you up to the present, to believe that this is how the matter stands, namely, that the raft which conveys us to the haven of salvation, the divine weapon which leads to victory, consists in full and unquestioning submission of our own judgment to the injunctions of the one to whom is en-

---

[3] Cf. Song 1:3-4.
[4] Cf. Rev 14:4.

trusted the task of steering us through the shadows, perplexities and battles of life. Holy Scripture itself confirms this with infallible authority: *The obedient man will speak of victory*[5].

If Jesus manifests Himself, thank Him and if He remains hidden, thank Him just the same: all is a trick of love. I earnestly hope that you will come to breathe your last with Jesus on the Cross and with Him softly exclaim: *It is finished*[6].

Your desire to feel the Creator alone in all things and the tedium you experience in approaching and dealing with creatures is a most singular grace of the divine mercy which is not granted to all poor wayfarers. Make sure, then, that you know how to profit by it and thank God for it. Don't listen to what your imagination tells you, for it is upset and powerfully attacked by our enemy, who wants you to consider your life unproductive of good. This is merely a clever plot contrived by the devil. The grace of Jesus, my dear, makes you only too watchful with regard to what is good. You are trying to measure, understand, feel and touch this love which you have for God, but, my dear sister, you must accept as certain that the more a soul loves God the less it feels this love.

The thing seems too strange and impossible in the case of transient love for creatures in this poor world, but when it is a case of love for the Spouse of the soul, things are very different. I am not able to explain this truth very clearly, but you can take it as certain that the matter is as I have said. God is incomprehensible and inaccessible; hence the more a soul penetrates into the love of this Supreme Good, the more the sentiment of love towards Him, which is beyond the soul's

[5] Prov. 21:28 (Vg.)
[6] Jn 19:30.

knowledge, seems to diminish, until the poor soul considers that it no longer loves Him at all.

In point of fact, in certain instances it seems to the soul that this is really the case, but the events prove the very opposite. That continual fear of losing one's God, that holy circumspection which makes one look carefully where to place one's feet so as not to stumble, that courage in facing the assaults of the enemy, that resignation to God's will in all life's adversities, that ardent desire to see God's kingdom established in one's own heart and in the hearts of others, are the clearest proof of the soul's love for the Supreme Good.

No, your love is not indolent, nor is it sterile. You ought rather to say that you love your heavenly Bridegroom, but that you want that love to grow continually.

The divine Master has left us in writing the injunction to recognize as our brethren those only who do the will of His Father[7]. Well, then, do you not desire and make every effort to conform at all times to the divine will? Would you not give your life a thousand times rather than resolve to go against God's will? You are quite sure of this and you feel it in your heart. Let this, then, be the touchstone by which you recognize and convince yourself that your life is well spent.

Oh, how far you are from that which your feelings would lead you to believe! You love this most tender Spouse, but this seems very little to you because you desire to love with a perfect and consummate love. To us wretched and unfortunate mortals this love, at least in its fullness, is only granted in the next life. O wretched condition of our human nature! May our heavenly Spouse break through this thinnest of thin veils which separates us from Him and grant us at last that

[7] Cf. Mt 12:50.

perfect love; otherwise our life is no longer life, our illness incurable and our sojourn here below a most bitter and prolonged agony.

You have interpreted too rigorously the sentiments I expressed when I wrote to you about your sister. I never once doubted that her soul is pleasing to the Lord. All I said was that I disapproved of her conduct with regard to the Eucharistic table. In these sad times when so many souls are turning away from God, I cannot convince myself that anyone can live the true spiritual life without the food of the strong. In these days in which we are continually surrounded by people who harbour hatred for God in their hearts and who blaspheme continually, the sure means of remaining immune from this pestilential disease is to strengthen ourselves with the Eucharistic food.

Now, to remain immune from sin and make progress on the path to perfection is not possible for those who remain for months on end without partaking abundantly of the immaculate Flesh of the divine Lamb. I do not know what others think about this, but to me it is very clear that in the circumstances in which we live at present, for those who limit themselves to receiving Communion once or twice in the year, it is illusory to want to convince themselves that they can take even one step towards perfection.

I cannot tell you how distressed I am about your sister's health and only the Lord knows how much I pray for her spiritual rather than her corporal well-being. May my feeble but constant prayers be acceptable to the One who rules over and governs all things, for our welfare and his glory. She is lucky, though, to have been made worthy through no merit of her own to share the Cross of the One who for pure love for us immolated Himself to the eternal Father.

I never cease to present to Jesus all those persons and all the needs which you have so much at heart.

You complain that I don't answer all your questions and

you chide me gently on this account. All I can do is ask your pardon and beg you not to be angry with me, for I am not to blame. For some time past I have been suffering from forgetfulness, despite all my good intentions to satisfy every demand made on me. I am told that this is a very special grace of the heavenly Father, but is this a fact[8]?

The Lord only allows me to recall those persons and things He wants me to remember. In point of fact, on several occasions our merciful Lord has suggested to me people whom I have never known or even heard of, for the sole purpose of having me present them to Him and intercede for them, and in this case He never fails to answer my poor feeble prayers[9]. On the other hand, when Jesus doesn't want to answer me, He makes me actually forget to pray for those persons for whom I had firmly decided and intended to pray.

This forgetfulness frequently extends even to the things most necessary to our human nature, such as eating, drinking and the like. I thank divine Providence in the meantime that I have never been led to forget the obligatory duties of my state.

Judge for yourself, now, if I am guilty or worthy of your compassion. I exhort you, however, when you do not receive a reply to some question, to be so good as to remind me the second and third time, without any human respect. If in such cases you do not receive satisfaction, then adore the divine judgment and do not doubt that if He allows you to remain in the dark on these matters it is for your own good. He will not allow any good thought of yours to go unrewarded.

I cannot reply adequately to the question you state as follows: "I don't know why it is that almost invariably in my brief and imperfect meditations my mind turns on what

---

[8] See *Letters, Vol. I*, No. 169.

[9] See Padre Pio's letter to Padre Benedetto, from Pietrelcina on 20 December 1913: *Letters, Vol. I*, No. 169; *ibid.*, No. 250.

I must say to Jesus through you," because I don't quite understand your question. If possible, please explain yourself more fully. For the moment it is enough for you to know that in this I don't see the slightest shadow of anything wrong.

For several days past I feel as if my soul were tightly bound by an iron band. Pray, therefore, to the most bountiful God to give me the strength to conform meritoriously to this burdensome desire of his. I shall be eternally grateful to you if you add to these prayers the three novenas to Our Lady of the Most Holy Rosary of Pompeii with the Communions you receive in the meantime, all according to my intentions, to obtain a grace which I await from the Lord's goodness, a grace which to me seems to be for the glory of Jesus. However, if all this is seriously inconvenient for you, just dispense yourself from it.

I am obliged to end here for reasons which are well known to you.

May God bless you along with your sister and may He calm your sufferings. May He turn His merciful eyes upon you and console you by His compassion.

Fra Pio, Capuchin.

9

Foggia, 27 May 1914.

Kindness and severity of his direction. Grim picture of the state of her soul. He is to make known her needs to Jesus. Their correspondence. Family matters. Living on Calvary. An exchange of prayers. Her sister's Holy Communion. She asks him to write to her.

Jesus alone! Most Holy Spirit, help me!

Reverend Padre Pio,

I am exceedingly thankful to the Heart of Jesus (*you* don't want my thanks) for the beautiful letter that has reached me. It brings great gladness to my poor soul, but as usual my gladness is marred by a great many doubts. You are extremely kind to me, you invariably treat me with indulgence and gentleness and you always forgive me. I don't deserve any of this and I am afraid I take advantage of it. Be severe and strict with me; I deserve the whip which Jesus used to drive out those who profaned his temple.

Doesn't my rebellious, wicked and proud ego continually profane the temple which Jesus has entrusted to me, namely, my own soul? How bad I am! Yet my malice whispers to me that I am good. May Jesus set me free from this sin which is more dreadful than any other, a sin I don't want to commit on any account. It was this that caused the downfall of Lucifer. I am afraid, very much afraid of my weakness and wretchedness. I don't want the ugly passions which rule me to be so active, relentless and incessant and yet, at times, they save me from my monstrous pride.

I read and think and speak of many fine things, but they don't affect me and much less do I put them into practice. On the other hand, the bad things affect me deeply, exuberantly and powerfully. Where and how, then, am I to put down pride, presumption and conceit?

I admire true virtue and delicacy of conscience in many good and simple souls who love Jesus, while I myself am embarassed, blush for shame and am disheartened.

I should like just once, my dear Father, to speak to you in the confessional in order to give you a right idea of my conscience. My writings reveal a great amount of presumption, self-love, pride, illusions and deception, but not sufficiently. I am invariably very much afraid of myself for I am my own deadly enemy. I am very wicked; help me, holy Father, to be converted. Pray hard and constantly for my true conversion; ask Jesus to transform me into Himself.

You who speak to Jesus every day, speak to Him about me, tell Him that I don't know how to repay Him for the good He does me by allowing you to write to me with that angelic charity worthy of a son of the *Poverello* of Assisi. Tell Him that in spite of His help and grace I am still the same victim of my passions. All my resolutions, all my desires get me nowhere. Facts and not idle talk are needed. His true lovers practise virtue and live constantly in solitude, silence and suffering.

Those who live the interior life experience deep peace: this is one of the fine, good things I think but don't appreciate. But to appreciate a virtue yet never put it into practice—what kind of life is this that I am living? Yet you, good Father, speak to me (I am using your very own words) of "great profit for my soul, tricks of love on the part of the heavenly Spouse" and you tell me that my love "is not unproductive or sterile." Is all this possible in me?

Either I explain myself imperfectly or else Jesus never speaks to you about me. Either one or the other is the case, but tell me which and I must believe you blindly. So what? You will consider it impudence on my part if I venture to argue with you; forgive me, Father, and punish me, but I must tell you everything that passes through my mind and all that occurs in my soul. Make allowances for me and treat me with severity, but tell me what you think about this.

Tell me, too, my dear Father, what our dear Jesus thinks of these holy conversations of ours (this is one of the questions that has remained unanswered and that you kindly ask me to repeat "the second and third time without any human respect," to use your own words). How am I to answer another passage which runs as follows: "You complain that I don't answer all your questions and you chide me gently on this account. All I can do is ask your pardon and beg you not to be angry with me, for I am not to blame?"

What sort of language do you use in dealing with a wretched insect? I am mortified, humiliated, crushed. Please don't abase yourself like this with me; I beg you not to do so any more. Forgive me and punish me.

Now let's go on to perceptible things. Troubles, nothing but troubles. My poor sister continues to suffer—what is to become of her at all? Pray. She needs a change of air but we are uncertain where to go, what direction to take. What is Jesus' will in this regard? We are invariably afraid of making a mistake. Tell Jesus about it and let me know, I venture to say, immediately. We should prepare our travelling bags, but where does Jesus want us to go in order to be united with Him, to find peace of mind, to obtain an improvement in my sister's health which is greatly impaired? Tell me, Father, and don't forget it.

Please pray for my brother who is at war with us all the time. What will happen in September when he will have to vacate our house and leave us free to live there? Let Jesus arrange it. The unhappy widow, my niece, is still in great distress; her father cannot have her in the home because the family is a big one. With three young children she is looking for a house. She is very downhearted and unhappy, suffering in silence and hoping for the best. Last evening she came to see me (as she very often does) and she was most distressed. I watch her, I fully understand and am tormented on this account. It is not for nothing that she has been attached to me from early childhood (she has the same name as my own saintly mother on this earth and our most holy and tender heavenly Mother). Among my many nephews and nieces, grand-nephews and grand-nieces, I feel a particular tenderness for this one who has suffered so much adversity: ten years of married life, of suffering and tears and in the end the tragic suicide; in addition, financial disaster.

Ask Jesus to give her strength, resignation, appropriate graces, and let us hope he will reward her for all she has suffered. Continue to remember the needs of all, with which you are now quite familiar. Remember me in a particular way, as I am in need of everything.

I have a worry, a regret deep down in my soul, something that amounts to a sin. May Jesus set me free from it, for I don't by any means want it. Every day from sundown until morning the darkness makes me afraid and oppresses me, while reminding me of Gethsemane and Calvary where true love is to be found. When the light dawns, since I am fond of the sun, all my fears vanish.

Jesus has convinced me, it is true, that if I want to love in earnest I must live on Calvary. But weak, lazy and hypocritical as I am, I run away, for I am still very much attached to the world and to myself. Speak to me, Father. May Jesus enlighten you as to the true state of my poor soul, so that you may be able to guide me and give me light in this darkness. But who am I to expect you to devote yourself to me continually? I steal a great deal of your precious time, poor Father, obliging you to read my silly letters and to write me long ones in reply. What a burden I place upon you! Don't doubt that Jesus will repay you. But does He want it? This is what I am anxious to know. If He doesn't, then I am ready to sacrifice this one relief for my soul. Never mind! All alone with Him, bewildered, no longer able to remember anything, uncertain, crushed, where can I find shelter? I rely on my good angel.

If Jesus sends me help and comfort and I profit by it, well and good. But if, on the other hand, I seek these things myself and make poor use of them, this is bad and I ask His pardon. May He take absolutely everything from me as long as He leaves me Himself. I know, however, that He always brings with Him troubles and the cross, so may He sustain me by His holy grace.

I am surprised, amazed, astounded that you ask me, *you*, to make the three novenas to Most Holy Mary of Pompeii and to offer my poor Communions. In order to obey you I am doing what you ask. Are you satisfied?

On Saturday my sister went to your Capuchin church[1] (one of the Fathers is her confessor) for Confession and her Easter duty. She has continued to receive Holy Communion. Are you pleased? Ask Jesus to hold her close to His Most Sacred Heart and never let her go. Thank Him on my behalf. Praise be to Jesus!

This morning in church, seeing her united with me (and with my spiritual friend) at the feet of Jesus for Holy Communion, I felt very happy, yet I was unable to say anything to Jesus. I am cold, ungrateful and wicked, always and

[1] St. Anne's Church in Foggia. Cf. *Letters, Vol. I*, p. 869, Note 1.

everywhere. May Jesus forgive me. Oh! If only Jesus wished to bestow on her also His Eucharistic embrace every morning, what a paradise on earth this would mean for me! I desire this all the time but I do not hope to see it come to pass. To Jesus nothing is impossible and it is I who place obstacles to prevent the spreading of His kingdom of love.

Pray very hard for my conversion. I am very, very bad; will Jesus forgive me? Will you write to me? May Jesus have the patience to remind you of all that it is necessary to tell me for the good of my soul.

With deep respect I kiss your hand. Bless me continually, together with my sister.

A poor tertiary.

10

Pietrelcina. Feast of Pentecost, 31 May 1914.

Strategy by which to overcome the enemy. He knows her fully before God. Their correspondence is pleasing to Jesus. Time spent in the best way. He regrets her sister's poor health. He asks for prayers. Illness prevents him from continuing.

J.M.J.D.F.C.

Beloved daughter of Jesus Christ,

May the Holy Spirit fill you with His most holy gifts, may He sanctify you, guide you along the path to eternal salvation and comfort you in your innumerable troubles.

Why are you so afraid of your adversary, my good sister? Don't you know that our good Jesus is invariably with you and that the enemy of souls has no power over those who have resolved to belong entirely to God? In reality the more you are afraid, the safer you are and the more tepid you feel, the more secure you are.

You say that you pity yourself because you see yourself full of pride, with no trace of humility, always falling down and never able to stay on your feet, but all this is quite untrue. It is a snare set by Satan to make you lose heart and to hold you up, if that were possible, on the way of love by depicting the path of perfection as too difficult for you.

Banish these false persuasions from your mind and have no fear, because you have no reason to be afraid. Get rid of your conviction that evil passions are too lively in you. Listen to me, my dear sister: let your mind dwell as little as possible on this matter, for thoughts of this kind usually do more harm than good. They dry up our hearts rather than enkindling in them the fire of love for the Supreme Good, just as the north wind dries up our fields.

Pray, of course, and ask the heavenly Spouse never to allow this harsh northerly wind[1] to blow over the little garden of your soul, but to deign in His compassion as Lover to send invariably the south wind which is the only one capable of awakening chaste and holy love. When similar disturbing thoughts come into your mind, drive them away as temptations, for this is what they really are. Say to yourself at once: I am conceited, I am loaded with sins. I am a profaner of the temple (namely, my soul) which Jesus has entrusted to my care, I rebel against the divine inspirations, I am really wicked, yet this soil brings forth these fruits. If I have not lived well in the past I intend to live well in the future, with the divine assistance.

Then take your mind off these disturbing and tormenting thoughts, open your heart with boundless confidence to the only One who is able to console and save us. Have no fear for the future, for God is with you and He is supremely faithful and will not allow you to be overwhelmed by our enemy. This divine Lover will never allow a soul that is consecrated to Him in a most particular way to remain a victim of the most implacable of all its enemies. No, no. The enemy will never obtain this victory.

Remember what I told you in one of my letters, namely, that your soul is in the arms of your divine Spouse, like a baby in its mother's arms. You may sleep in peace,

---

[1] Cf. Song 4:16.

therefore, for this heavenly Spouse will guide you in the way which is to your greatest advantage.

Don't think I told you this as a formality or because I wanted to treat you gently. No, this is not true by any means. If things were not as I told you, I should have acted differently towards you.

You tell me you would like to speak to me just once in the tribunal of Penance, so as to give me an exact picture of your soul and hence you are convinced that I do not know you sufficiently. No, my dear, this is perhaps one of the worst traps set for you by that ugly wretch who wants to bring his noxious influence to bear on everything. This is one of the deepest snares he intends to place in your path, in order to draw you into his net. Cast this temptation far from you, then. Don't let it even take root in you and never dwell on it deliberately.

Believe me, if I did not know you before the Lord I could never use the language I have used with you up to the present. I repeat and assure you once more that your soul is gaining great profit, that your love is not inactive or sterile and that all that is happening within you is a trick of love on the part of the heavenly Spouse. I should be extremely displeased if you were to try to persuade yourself to the contrary, for this would also displease Jesus.

I am consoled to find you always anxious to know whether Jesus is pleased or not with these holy conversations of ours. I admire with great satisfaction this holy solicitude on your part. The soul which really loves Jesus seeks and studies in all things and in all its actions to give Him satisfaction and until it is assured of this it groans and sighs continually, for it fears it may disgust Him.

On this point the loving soul is quite jealous, with a jealousy which I am unable to compare with any which exists in this wretched world. From my manner of dealing with you up to the present, you ought to have realized that

Jesus is highly pleased with these holy colloquies and conversations of ours.

Besides, if I had perceived the divine Spouse's displeasure in this regard I should not have hesitated to make this known to you in due course. What else does my soul desire but to please Jesus in all things?

You must therefore be reassured, for in this we shall meet with Jesus' good pleasure.

Time spent for God's glory and the salvation of souls must never be regretted, for it is never badly spent. Don't worry, therefore, about stealing my time, because the best way of spending one's time, as I have just told you, is to spend it in furthering the salvation and sanctification of others. I don't know how to thank the heavenly Father for His mercy when He introduces souls to me to whom I can be helpful in some way.

Oh, yes! If it had only pleased heaven to let me spend my whole life in this holy ministry, so that I might not behold myself so disfigured in the sight of the Most High! But instead, wretched as I am, I have wasted time in offending and hating God and by my evil life I have snatched from Jesus many souls whom He redeemed by His Blood! In this I have been worse than Lucifer. I know that nobody is clean in the Lord's sight[2], but my own uncleanness, my dear sister, is unlike any other. I see myself so disfigured that it seems to me as if my very clothing is horrified by my filthiness. But praised for ever be the goodness of the God of our fathers who has never withdrawn His mercy from my wretched soul!

Continue invariably to explain all your needs to me with complete trust and simplicity and you may be sure of doing me a favour, while at the same time pleasing Jesus.

I am unable to put into words my deep distress on learn-

---

[2] Cf. Prov. 20:9.

ing how severely your most dear sister is afflicted by physical and moral sufferings, and I can't tell you what I wouldn't do to bring her back to perfect health. If only Jesus would accept the offering of my poor person in place of hers! Pray to Jesus, you also, for this purpose.

The Lord wills that as far as possible, any change of climate should be in accordance with the doctor's suggestions. Follow this course and have no fear of making a mistake. Besides, Sacred Scripture tells us to honour the physician for the love of God[3].

It breaks my heart to see the conditions to which that poor widow, your niece, is reduced. But let the poor girl take courage, for the longer the trial to which God sometimes subjects His chosen ones, the greater His goodness in consoling them during this time and raising them up after the combat. I shall never forget to pray, unworthy though I am, for the needs of this poor soul, just as I shall not forget any of the others whom you made known to me in the past.

I have neither adequate words nor feelings by which to thank you in a fitting manner for the charity you show towards my poor soul by invoking the Lord's mercy on me. Continue to do me this charity, keep up the novenas to the beautiful Virgin of the Rosary of Pompeii and offer your Holy Communions for me still, for God's hand is coming down on me more and more heavily. My poor soul is on the point of drowning in the waters of affliction and tribulation and I see no way of escape except through the prayers of others.

Yes, pray and beseech more insistently the divine compassion of our God that He may have mercy on me and not be mindful of the sins of my youth, that He may not take His revenge for these sins which He had already forgotten. Knock again at the door of the divine goodness so that He may allow

---

[3] Sir 38:1.

me to weep over my misfortunes and leave me free to deplore the fact that I issued forth from my mother's womb. Would it not perhaps have been better for me to have died therein before any eye had seen me[4]? Praise be to Jesus! He alone is my strength, He alone will defend me from the enemies who have planned my destruction; He alone can induce me to overcome the fear of death which invades my soul!

Forgive me, my dear sister, for having exceeded the limits, alas! I had forgotten that I was speaking to a soul confided to my care by God in order that I might console her! Ah! For pity's sake forgive me and do not blame me if by pouring out the affliction of my soul I have overshadowed or indeed increased your own distress, even to the slightest extent.

I am obliged to end here and you may be sure that I am consumed by the desire to write you a really long letter, something I am unable to do at present as I have been really ill for the past few days. It seems as if the Lord intends to make me pay for the health I enjoyed some years ago, as I used it so badly. But may the hand that strikes me in this way be for ever blessed.

May Jesus bless you and comfort you along with your sister and may He introduce you one day into the splendour of his immortal youth.

Your unworthy servant and brother in Jesus Christ,

Fra Pio.

[4] Cf. Job 3:11; 10:18.

11

Foggia. Feast of Corpus Christi, 11 June 1914.

She thanks him for the previous letter. Tension in her family. She asks prayers. Their correspondence. Her desire to go to Confession to Padre Pio. Her sister has a relapse. "I am worn out in soul and body." Postscript. Prayers. Communion on the Feast of Corpus Christi.

Reverend Padre Pio,

Praise be to Jesus! Praise be to Jesus! Praise be to Jesus!

"From my manner of dealing with you up to the present, you ought to have realized that Jesus is highly pleased with these holy colloquies and conversations of ours. Besides, if I had perceived the divine Spouse's displeasure in this regard I should not have hesitated to make this known to you in due course. What else does my soul desire but to please Jesus in all things?" And further on: "Don't worry, therefore, about stealing my time, because the best way of spending one's time, as I have just told you, is to spend it in furthering the salvation and sanctification of others."

What am I to say to you? How am I to answer these two passages of your precious letter which reached me on the first of the month? No words of mine are adequate. I remain perplexed, embarassed, plunged in the depths when I reflect on the mass of graces which our good Jesus has unexpectedly poured down on my undeserving, ungrateful, sterile soul.

Again: "Continue invariably to explain all your needs to me with complete trust and simplicity and you may be sure of doing me a favour while at the same time pleasing Jesus."

How am I to thank you? How can I repay you? May Jesus do this, for I am no use. An adequate response is necessary when we receive great graces. What a responsibility! I am bewildered, frightened and discouraged. I am too wretched, but Jesus is infinitely rich and He covers all with His compassion and love. What He hates is my malice. How can I obtain pardon for it? I just don't know.

My dear Father, come to my assistance. I have committed so many sins in the last few days... afflictions and sins have alternated continually. Instead of corresponding with fresh graces, I become more ungrateful and wicked. How am I to escape? Only through your prayers and your powerful mediation with Jesus. In your constant private colloquies with Him, tell Him not to fall asleep over my family matters, but to rise up and by His omnipotent voice subdue the fierce storm and restore complete calm.

May He calm and subdue the infernal anger which fans and enkindles the fire between brother and sister. It will soon be ten years since my saintly father's death and his three children are not yet at peace, through the influence of one who nevertheless goes to Confession and receives Communion continually. The three heirs[1] are still unable after ten years to avail reasonably of the honest fruit earned by their holy parent who toiled up to the age of 84, to the eve of his death[2]. All this, because injustice and arrogance stifle the voice of conscience, denying and trampling on the most

---

[1] Raffaelina herself, her sister Giovina (who died at the age of 70 on 6 October 1931) and their brother Matteo. Cf. p. , Note 1.

[2] Michele Cerase, aged 85, died in Foggia on 6 October 1904, in Via Manzoni, 57.

sacred obligations. What does our brother want from us, egged on by his wife? He is rich and childless, yet what sacrifices we have made for him, holy Father, Jesus alone knows.

Although I believe by God's just permission that things have come to a head, we are now faced with threats, calumnies, insults, sentence and condemnation. We are drowning and how can we save ourselves? Are injustice, arrogance, monetary interests and egoism to have the upper hand? I want to know from you, Father, who are well informed about the matter.

Endless, unlimited sins, this is the result, especially in my own case, of this long, underhanded and relentless war. I feel quite unbalanced spiritually and physically. My brain is reeling all the time, my heart is agitated by ugly passions contrary to Christian charity, while my will is opposed to what Jesus disposes and allows for his own lawful and holy purposes.

Where shall we end up? What will happen in September? Let Jesus see to it. Please see to it yourself, my dear Father so full of charity, if you want me to be at peace, if you are concerned as I see you are about my poor soul.

Pray, beseech and compel Jesus to hear us (I am asking a lot). He won't refuse anything to you who love Him so much. I must admit that I envy you, Father, who are capable of loving Jesus so much, who know how to speak to Him, very often see Him (how wonderful!) and hear Him speak. Must not all this be a delightful reward for the great desolation you experience in His holy service? Forgive me, good Father, I am just pouring out my thoughts to you.

"My poor soul is on the point of drowning in the waters of affliction and tribulation and I see no way of escape except through the prayers of others" (your own words). Poor Father, how you must be suffering when you speak like that! What would I not do to bring you relief! It is Jesus who must do so, do you not count on Him at all?

I know everything. Will this letter reach you in Pietrelcina or at Morcone friary? I am most anxious to know. Shall we be able to continue our holy correspondence? Your saintly Father[3] has assured me that this will be possible, but I ask you to confirm it. I'll be most anxious until I receive word from you.

I have a holy envy for your calm and resigned attitude, for your sublime assent to God's will in all your trials. As for myself, it would be very necessary to set up that tribunal of Penance between me and yourself just now! Forgive me if I invariably tremble and am fearful in face of what you tell me. Is this also a sin on my part? Tell me frankly, my dear Father, if this is so. Don't stand on ceremony or think you have to treat me gently. Rebuke me, accuse me, punish me severely and I shall be very, very, happy.

The day before yesterday Jesus punished me, but not as much as I deserve. My good sister had such severe stomach pains that she remained in bed. I was able to make the sign of the cross and mumble a few prayers after midday. It was a day of tears, anxiety and worries to which I can't give a name, a day of real torment. Since yesterday my sister is much better, no longer in bed, for which I thank Jesus exceedingly.

Tell Jesus, Father, not to play this trick any more, to do everything to me, to me alone, but to spare my good sister who has already suffered so much and given up everything. Goodness, beauty, education, social standing—nothing of all this has been of any use to her. May the most holy will of God be done at all times!

I am worn out in soul and body and my wretched, wicked soul is grovelling in the dust. What of the holy spiritual energy so necessary for the generation of physical strength which causes the soul to proceed in the midst of trials with

---

[3] Padre Agostino of San Marco in Lamis.

its gaze fixed on heaven and its will resolutely united to the most holy will of Jesus?

I understand this, but I don't put it into practice.

Pray very hard for this poor soul of mine. Bless me, holy Father, now and for ever, together with all my relatives.

A poor tertiary

P.S. Pray a lot for my brother and his wife. May Jesus bless them. May He transform the tears we shed into heavenly consolations for them. Pray for this change of air which is urgently required. May Jesus inspire us, guide and accompany us. May He be our leader and our defence.

Today is the feast of faith, the feast of love, just like Holy Thursday. Am I right? Correct me. Praise be to Jesus in the Blessed Sacrament! Ask Him to bind and chain my heart to His tabernacle for ever. I offered my poor Communion this morning for all priests, especially for the bad ones. Pray for their conversion. How atrociously they pierce the Most Sacred Heart of Jesus! Pray for one of them who is not from Foggia but who has brought ruin and destruction to souls in this city.

I await, if you can, the promised "really long letter." "You may be sure that I am consumed by the desire to write you a really long letter." These are your own words.

I thank you in advance. I could go on writing to you for ever; forgive me if I take advantage of you.

12

Pietrelcina, 15 June 1914.

The painful experience of his stay in Morcone. How to overcome the feeling of one's own malice. "God is with you." "Physically exhausted." Postscript. He asks prayers.

J.M.J.C.F.C.

Beloved daughter of Jesus Christ,

May the grace of the divine Spirit be always in your heart.

With trembling hand I hasten to write these few lines. May the Lord reveal to you, my dear sister, how much I have suffered in the last few days. I returned yesterday from Morcone[1] where, in the course of a very few days, my health was reduced to an extreme point. Now more than ever I am feeling the full effects of the damage caused by this most recent trial willed by Jesus. I have become very thin, am weakened to an extreme degree and can scarcely stand.

Blessed for ever be the mercy of our most sweet Jesus who has been pleased to test His servant by the trial of fire! You too, beloved sister, give thanks to the infinite mercy of the heavenly Father for not having allowed the enemy to

---

[1] Cf. *Letters, Vol. I*, Nos. 193 ff., pp. 535 ff.

touch my soul during this extreme trial, in spite of my great unworthiness.

How delightful it is to live all the time in the shadow of the Lord, there in the sacred cloister! Perhaps I was quite unworthy to rest within that sacred enclosure to which He called me with such great love, and that because of my ingratitude the Lord has been obliged to send me away. May His will be done, for all that He ordains is right! He intends to put the faithfulness of His servant to the supreme test. To my detriment the Lord intends to hear the prayers of all these devout people here who want, it would appear, to keep me against my will in their midst, by sending up prayers and almost doing violence to the Heart of God to obtain their great desire.

This is no personal opinion of mine. No, they have demonstrated this desire in various circumstances, especially on my return this time, for I must tell you that I had hardly entered the town when they all came out to greet me, adding to their thanks to the Lord their cries of "Long life!" and "Welcome back!"

I was moved to the point of tears! But I am horrified and tremble, my dear, at the thought that the Lord intends to reward me in this life for something done for love of Him. Pray to Jesus, pray that He may keep the reward for me in the next life.

You tell me you are frightened by your malice and you want to know what more you can do to rid yourself of it. Humble yourself before the Lord with complete confidence and don't be afraid by any means, for no harm will come to you. Your malice, moreover, is not, as you think, of such a nature as to incur the displeasure of the divine Spouse. Beseech our divine Lover to free you from these excessive fears, which instead of opening the heart to Jesus' love tend to close it.

Let the delightful thought console you that you are always in the presence of Jesus who sees and knows and weighs up all your actions. You ought to rejoice at this thought, for all your actions are directed towards a good end. I assure you of this in God's name and ask you to let this assurance calm you.

I find it hard to believe that you offend the Lord even in small things. Only too well do I see you walking before Him. The storms that are raging around you will turn out to be for God's glory, your own merit and the good of many souls.

Although unworthily, I pray constantly to the Father for all your intentions. Be at peace, for in these harsh trials of love (to which the heavenly Spouse subjects those who love him) the Lord will never allow the enemy to harm your soul or that of your sister. Take courage, then, I repeat, my dear sister; you are quite safe, for God is with you. What, then, have you to fear? Allow yourself to be led by divine grace and be at peace, for He will be glorified in you.

Regretfully, my dear, I am compelled to stop at this point. I feel physically exhausted. Make allowances for me if I cannot satisfy all your holy and quite lawful questions and please understand that this is not due to any bad intention on my part. Meanwhile do not deprive me of your correspondence, which is pleasing to Jesus.

Pray more insistently for the one who desires your sanctification and may the Lord fill both you and your sister with his heavenly blessings.

Your most affectionate
servant and brother in Jesus,
Fra Pio.

P.S. While thanking you most earnestly for the prayers you offer to the Lord for me, may I ask you to keep me informed, if you don't mind, when you have finished the three novenas to Our Lady of the Rosary of Pompeii and if you have been so good as to offer your communions to the Lord for my intentions. Forgive me if I am taking too much advantage of your kindness.

13

Foggia, 17 June 1914.

She is very sorry to hear of his bad health. Offering of prayers. A trip to Liguria. Some Mass stipends. A request for prayers.

Jesus alone! Most Holy Spirit, help me!

Reverend Padre Pio,

I am writing briefly so as not to tire you. I am very sorry to hear the news about your health, which reached me yesterday. I place immense trust in our good Jesus and hope that this will find you much improved. Your native air will certainly revive you. May our holy Jesus grant you good health for His glory and for the benefit of troubled souls.

In your great humility you ask me for an account of the three novenas to Most Holy Mary of Pompeii. In order to satisfy you, and for no other reason, I reply that I finished them this morning, but as usual I am not quite sure on what day I started, so I prefer to add a further three days and finish on Saturday.

But... you have reversed the order of things. *To whom* do you turn for prayers? May our dear Jesus forgive my impertinence. I have obeyed and no more. Good Father, if you only knew what my prayers and Communions are like... they are nauseating. May Jesus continue to have mercy on me, may He guard and protect me in all things.

We are leaving next week. With God's help we'll go to Liguria, to Savona to be exact, where we'll stay in a convent. Let's hope we'll find it all right.

May Jesus restore her former health to my sister, first of all to her soul and then to her body. Pray very hard, good Father.

As regards myself, may He enable me to find everything necessary for my spiritual life, for I am really in great need in this respect. Pray hard that Jesus may keep me from all temptation, danger, emotion, excitement and distraction. I remain in fear and trembling on my own account, for I know myself sufficiently well. I am afraid of all contact with others. I fear my interior and exterior enemies. I am afraid of everyone and everything. I want to enjoy holy freedom, holy indifference, peace of mind, continual union with Jesus and I abandon myself to His fatherly embrace. May He guide us, accompany and protect us and bless every step we take. We have nobody except Him in whom to trust.

I'll write to you from there and give you my new address. I hope to do this at once, but I won't be so free as regards my time when I am there. Never mind! I venture to ask you in the meantime, when you can, to answer all the questions I asked you in my last letter written on Corpus Christi. Please don't forget. (You need great patience with me, but it will earn paradise for you twice over). It will be quite all right to send your letter to the usual address, because I am leaving my spiritual friend here in our house and she'll take care to forward your letter to Savona.

I am enclosing ten lire for two Masses to implore divine grace: one Mass in honour of the Eucharistic Heart of Jesus and the other in honour of my Mother of Sorrows, for the complete cure of my poor sister and for the success of our journey. All for God's glory and the good of souls.

For the sake of greater privacy I am sending this money without registering the letter. I am not afraid that it will go astray, as all my letters reach you safely and the same will apply to this one. At all events, please be so good as to let me know at once when you receive it.

Ask Jesus with all your heart for the graces for my sister. Let us confide to His keeping all our tears and anxieties, our hopes, our life, the present and the future. When you see Jesus, good Father, give Him a glance for me, a smile, a greeting, and kiss His adorable wounds for me. Together with my sister I hide in these wounds.

Give us your blessing.

A poor tertiary.

P.S. May your ardent prayers accompany us and obtain for us peace of soul and body. Our enemies in the family are not sleeping; how are we to overcome them? May the most holy will of God be always blessed! Pray. Please pray also for my good spiritual friend whom I am leaving all alone in the combat, to deal with our domestic enemies. May Jesus help her. She is the third member of my little family. She has lived with us for 25 years[1] yet she is the object, like ourselves, of calumnies and curses. Heavens above! May Jesus enlighten and convert everyone. May He convert me and save me from all upsets and every evil. Amen.

[1] Rosinella. Cf. p. , Note 1.

14

Pietrelcina, 21 June 1914.

Purpose of the prayers offered and requested. Assurances as regards the coming trip. Defence against Satan's snares. Her desire to go to Confession to him is a sign of lack of acceptance of the assurances received. False interpretation of her sister's behaviour. Exhortations.

J.M.J.D.F.C.

Beloved daughter in Jesus Christ,

May the grace of the divine Spirit comfort your heart at all times and make you holy.

I have no adequate words by which to thank you as you deserve for the fervent and constant prayers you are sending up to the Lord for the restoration of my health. May Jesus reward you doubly a hundred times. Let me remind you, however, that I am more concerned about spiritual than corporal health. Would it not be well, perhaps, to beseech the divine mercy to demolish, at this stage, the very thin veil which separates me from Him?

I am already weary of life and my soul longs ardently for death, just as the thirsty hart longs to arrive at the flowing streams[1]. Do not believe, though, that I long for death

[1] Ps 42:1.

in order to be set free from the suffering of this life. There is a much more sublime reason.

Life is intolerable to me and I only endure it in order to please the Spouse of souls who wants things like this. But I do not hide from you the fact that I have to do great violence to myself in order to pronounce this act of resignation. At certain moments I have to force myself to such an extent to do so that all my bones are dislocated. The desire to be dissolved in order to be united with Him is a sword which has pierced and transfixed my heart for several years now. It is a flame that is slowly consuming me. How harsh and atrocious does life become, my dear sister, for the soul to whom God is continually manifesting fresh secrets of His boundless greatness!

Make allowances for me and do not envy my state which is very pitiable. I am continually dying for the sole reason that I do not die. Ask the heavenly Spouse in His immense goodness to set me free very soon from the prison of this life. I can hardly go on any longer.

Don't be prevented from praying for this intention, my beloved sister, by the thought of losing the one who can—if this is true—help you to some extent in the Lord's ways, for I assure you that your soul would stand to gain much more if the Lord were to call me to Himself. I can solemnly promise you that I should not cease to assist you and watch over you and those who are dear to you.

But may the Lord's will be done at all times!

I hope and firmly trust that the change of climate will be very beneficial to your sister's health and also to you. Meanwhile, with this lively hope in my heart, I will not cease to pray in my own small way and to do violence to the merciful Heart of Jesus for this purpose.

Don't worry, then, and don't have any fears about this trip. Your soul will suffer no harm and the journey will be for God's glory and will benefit your own soul. Get rid of all fears to the contrary; the Lord is always with you wherever you go and He will always fight for you and along with you. The victory is certain and the enemy's confusion will be enormous.

I strongly urge you to be very reserved, as far as this is possible, where you are going. *It is good to guard the secret of a king*[2]. You will forgive me if I am too pretentious and even indiscreet on some points.

In your second-last letter you wrote that you were bewildered, frightened and discouraged, because you do not correspond adequately to the great graces that Jesus is bestowing on you. Pay attention and be very watchful on this point. Your sentiment, in itself, is holy from a certain point of view, but you know very well that the devil invariably tries to turn things upside down. I want you to refrain from dwelling on this matter, because the discouragement you feel when you deplore your failure to correspond with grace comes from the enemy. Even if he doesn't want to make you turn back, he wants at least to bring you to a standstill on the way to perfection.

For the moment that ugly wretch would be satisfied with this, but you mustn't give him this satisfaction. Hence, what I want you to do is to keep your soul at rest, as far as possible, in contemplation of the infinite treasures of the heavenly Spouse, which He is pouring with a lavish hand into your soul. Rejoice in His riches and stimulate within you the desire to possess them.

I should like you to imitate in this the brides of this poor world, who admire and take pleasure in nothing else but the fine gifts and qualities of their husbands, without bothering in the least whether or in what manner they correspond to their husbands' demonstrations of affection. If you make an

---

[2] Tob 12:7.

effort, as I hope you will, to follow this suggestion of mine, your soul will derive great profit from it.

"It would be very necessary," you also wrote, "to set up that tribunal of Penance between us." You want to know if any sin is included in this desire. I can assure you that you are not committing any sin by this desire, but I perceive in you a lack of docility since you fail to be convinced by my assurances.

Do you not see that it is the devil who wants to make you lose at all costs that trust and abandonment towards the one who is your spiritual guide? Moreover, when all is said and done, this is a real waste of time and prevents you from advancing rapidly. I cannot spare you this time from a gentle brotherly reproof.

In speaking of your sister you tell me that the poor thing gave up everything, and that her goodness, beauty, education and social standing have been of no use to her. This expression sounds quite worldly and on your lips it is like blasphemy!

I want to ask you a question: did she or did she not make this total sacrifice for love of Jesus? If she made it for love of Jesus, then from Him alone should she expect her reward. Jesus keeps nothing for Himself of what is done for love of Him and He will repay us very lavishly. Don't let us make our happiness depend on enjoying wonderful health, or else we should be just like those foolish worldlings to whom it is not given to know the secrets of heaven.

On your lips, my dear, how wrong that expression sounds: "having given up everything, none of this has been of any use to her!" May God forgive you, for this time you have made a really big blunder. Take care not to fall into similar exaggerations in future.

Calm yourself, then, and abide firmly by the assurances you have received with regard to your soul which is very pleasing to Jesus. Continue to love Jesus and make an effort to love Him more and more, without wanting to know anything else. He alone will steer us to the haven of salvation. I send you His fatherly blessing, which is also for your sister, as a pledge of that blessing which He is to give you at the entrance to the heavenly Jerusalem.

I must end here as I am quite unable to continue. May Jesus and Mary together with Jesus' putative father assist and console you.

Believe me always,
Your humble servant,
Fra Pio.

P.S. I received the ten lire for the two Masses and I thank you most sincerely for putting yourself out so much. Ask that good spiritual friend of yours to pray for me, as I do constantly for her. As soon as you reach your destination, don't fail to write to give me news of your sister's condition.

15

Savona, 8 July 1914.

The convent in Savona. "I was in very bad humour." Her only book is Jesus crucified. Her sister's health. A Capuchin confessor. She asks for prayers and blessings.

God alone! Most Holy Spirit, help me!

Reverend Father,

A fortnight ago this evening I set out on my trip. After stopping in Florence for a day-and-a-half, with God's help we arrived at six o'clock on Saturday in this holy spot in Savona where we are lodged[1].

This is a school run by Sisters who also keep a boarding-house for ladies. It is beautifully situated, with marvellous views of sea and hills and luxurious vegetation. The silence and quiet, the tranquillity of nature, reach the body and speak to the soul. Here one's spirit is delighted and rests serenely, completely removed from all the annoyances of life—it rejoices and continues to rejoice between these holy walls, surrounded by virginal souls dedicated to God by the three solemn vows; pious, beautiful and holy souls.

---

[1] The Cerase sisters reached Savona on 4 July, where they stayed at the Institute of the Purification of Our Blessed Lady, a local foundation which has its Mother House in the same city.

In the dear little church, in the galleries, refectory and gardens, in the vast corridors, I continually see these people who really love Jesus and sacrifice themselves for Him: Sisters, oblates, postulants, pupils, all of these speak to me of Him and silently and severely, unknown to themselves, they reproach me for my indolence and condemn my selfish, easy-going, empty and useless life.

This is an infinite grace which Jesus has granted me through you. If I am not *converted* now, in this holy retreat, I'll never be converted. What must I do? Please tell me. What return can I make to our good Jesus for all this? How am I to respond and repay Him? Please suggest to me what I can do, holy Father. I am no good at anything. I can only hide my face for shame. How wicked and ungrateful I have been and how many sins I have committed!

For several days after my arrival, due to a hundred insignificant things, I was in very bad humour and annoyed my poor sister who is so dearly in need of consolation. Not even Jesus always present in the beautiful chapel, not even Holy Communion succeeded in calming me. I was dissatisfied, listless and sleepy and I felt like crying all the time. I don't know what it was that irritated me continually and made me suffer. This is how I was for a great many days (perhaps you abandoned me during those days and didn't remember to pray for me).

How many sins... that tribunal of Penance. And now? After a fortnight, I am a little calmer, but apathy, indifference, absolute frigidity grip my soul. What am I to do? Tell me, good and holy Father, for I am at a loss.

The chapel is very dark (to my shame, it makes me fall asleep). I can't read, even with my glasses. To me this is really distressing, as my wretched tongue can say nothing of its own accord to Jesus. Oh, my dear Father! Tell Jesus that I cannot and do not want to read other people's books any more. I want my only book to be Himself, Jesus crucified, Jesus in the Blessed Sacrament. May He be my only Teacher. Obtain this for me from Jesus, good Father, otherwise I'll be able to do nothing, absolutely nothing. Whenever I write, moreover, may my pen be one of His nails, my ink His Most Precious Blood, my feelings, affections and all my utterances His wounds, His thorns, His adorable words.

Speak to Jesus about me. Pray to Jesus for me. Thank Him very much for all He is doing for me and for us. We have been guided, accompanied and helped on our way and in every event by Him. In Florence alone my sister had a slight attack of her usual stomach trouble. Here she has had nothing of the kind, or at least so she tells me. I don't know whether she is hiding something for fear of upsetting me.

I myself am continually afraid, continually in doubt and I worry absolutely all the time. There is a very sharp thorn in the depths of my soul which pierces me through and allows me no peace. To you, holy Father, everything is certainly known, all is clear as regards the most holy will of God. Tell Jesus to cure my poor sister completely. I have no one else on earth except her. If He would only call us both to be united in death as in life. I don't want to see her suffer, as she has already suffered a great deal.

She has certainly not chosen her present state of her own free will. Quite the opposite. After 12 years of combat, anguish and tears, Jesus called to Himself her handsome, excellent and pious young fiancé, who died of a brief heart disease. Thus my sister found her future shattered and her life empty, and she was always dissatisfied while longing for peace and affection in the home. Solitude is making her very sad and it frightens her. She is partially sustained and comforted by her holy faith. But to her great misfortune it doesn't mean everything to her and hence she is discontented and is resigned almost against her will.

This, briefly, is the sad story of my unfortunate sister. I spoke to you in my last letter about her complete sacrifice of everything. If she had made this total sacrifice for love of Jesus, who would be happier or more fortunate? Instead, she gave up everything of necessity, due to the course of events. So, with regard to your harsh rebuke in your last letter, dated 21 June, when you wrote: "May God forgive you, for this time you have made a really big mistake. Take care not to fall into similar exaggerations in the future," did I really deserve that rebuke? Tell me quite frankly, good Father. On the other hand, I am thankful to you, for this is how you ought to deal with this bad tertiary (a tertiary only in name). You should treat her with severity, scold her and punish her.

Always as a result of your prayers, Jesus has enabled me to meet an elderly Capuchin[2] who comes here for the nuns' Confessions every Thursday. However, I went to Confession to him for the first time in the church attached to his friary, a short distance from the convent, in a magnificent position, a solitary place filled with divine peace, the antechamber to paradise.

What more do I need now in order to save my soul? The love of Jesus, that is all. You alone can obtain this for me. Implore for me true humility, patience, absolute conformity to the most holy will of God, love of the cross and of suffering. Implore for me His beloved blessing on every step we take, on our holy desires, on everything that belongs to us, on all our affairs, on all our unhappy relatives, on my spiritual friend whom we left down there in charge of our house. I beg, moreover, your own holy blessing for myself and my sister.

A poor tertiary

---

[2] Padre Paolo of Sestri Levante, who lived for about 40 years in Savona, where he died on 8 February 1924, gratefully remembered by the local people. Cf. S. F. MOLFINO, *The Genoese Capuchins: VI, Necrologies*, Genoa, 1939, pp. 444 ff.

My present address: Raffaella Cerase, Sisters of the Purification, Ladie's Hostel, Villetta, Savona. I anxiously await a most precious and really long letter from you. The refectory bell is ringing. Praise be to Jesus!

16

Pietrelcina, 14 July 1914.

He regrets having to live outside his community. Signs by which to distinguish God's action from that of Satan. Seeing ourselves in Jesus as in a mirror. Love of the cross. Aridity does not mean that we are abandoned by the Lord. Substantial devotion. Reading holy books. Her sister's health. A reproof. Making use of prayer.

J.M.J.D.F.C.

Beloved daughter of Jesus Christ,

May the grace of the Holy Spirit transform you entirely and make you ever dearer to the heavenly Spouse.

I thank the divine mercy for having allowed you to experience the delight which is to be enjoyed in the shadow of the sacred cloister. And while I rejoice with you on this account, my dear sister, I cannot, unfortunately, restrain my tears when I see myself driven by main force, as it were, from the holy cloister to which our merciful Lord called me with most tender love. This memory is for me a sword which pierces my heart and causes me constant agony. The thought of being separated more and more from my community is slowly eating away my life. May the will of the heavenly Father be accomplished at all times, for all that He ordains is right.

The things that are happening to you are such as to leave no room for doubt regarding their origin. Be quite at peace, then, for it is the Lord who is acting in you. Cast aside all fear. The action of Satan is now quite distinct from the movements of grace within you and you will now be able to note the difference.

The one who upsets and torments you is Satan; the One who enlightens you is God. The soul that tends more and more to abase and humble itself before its Lord and at the same time is induced to suffer and bear all things with a view to winning the approval of its heavenly Spouse, cannot fail to recognize that all this comes from God. The soul's ardent and loving yearnings for its Lord are not and cannot be hallucinations or illusions. Hence I assure you once again that the grace of Jesus is the source of the beautiful things that are happening to you. You must therefore allow your divine Spouse to act in you and to lead you by the paths He chooses.

All that you feel within you at the sight of so many holy people around you, all of them devoted to loving and serving the Lord, is a sign that your soul is itself ardently seeking its Creator. The fact that you feel ashamed of yourself on seeing so many souls who love God is a good sign. I exhort you to humble yourself before the Lord at the sight, but to be on your guard against the false humility which brings discouragement with it, for this leads infallibly to despair.

What you must do is to thank the Lord and be very glad that in the midst of an unholy nation, generous souls are not lacking, all intent on loving Jesus. You must make an effort to be more and more careful in observance of the divine precepts and of the duties belonging to your own state.

Unite your heart with the Heart of Jesus and be simple-hearted as He desires. Make an effort to reproduce in yourself Jesus' own simplicity and keep your heart far from earthly prudence and the shrewdness of the flesh. Take care at all times to keep your thoughts pure, your ideas straightforward and your intentions holy. Let your will seek nothing other than God, His pleasure, His glory and His honour.

Let us look at ourselves in Jesus, my dear, as our mirror, in Jesus who led a hidden life. All His infinite majesty was hidden in the shadows and silence of that modest little workshop in Nazareth. So let us, too, make every effort to lead a completely interior life, hidden in God.

Don't be daunted by the cross. The surest test of love consists in suffering for the loved one, and if God suffered so much for love, the pain we suffer for Him becomes as lovable as love itself. In the troubles which the Lord bestows on you, be patient and conform yourself gladly to the divine Heart in the knowledge that all is a continual game on the part of your Lover.

Tribulations and trials have always been the heritage and the portion of chosen souls. The more Jesus intends to raise a soul up to perfection, the more He tries it by suffering. Rejoice, I say to you, in seeing yourself so privileged, in spite of your own unworthiness. The more you are afflicted, the more you ought to rejoice, because in the fire of tribulation the soul will become pure gold, worthy to be placed and to shine in the heavenly palace.

I cannot understand how you could ever even suspect that I had stopped praying for you during those days when you were in very bad humour. May your Guardian Angel reveal to you and convince you how far you are from the truth. God alone knows what violence I did to His divine Heart in order that you might come out of the state without injury to your soul! Never have I prayed the divine mercy for you with such insistence as I did during those days of your deep spiritual mourning. I know that I presented you during that period not less than 100 times a day to our most merciful Lord. Moreover, you ought to be glad that your soul suffered no harm whatsoever but gained quite a lot from that trial.

Don't be discouraged if you experience spiritual dryness. This does not mean that the Lord has abandoned you, as that ugly wretch, Satan, would unfortunately have you believe. You are too dear to the Heart of Jesus and all that is happening in your soul is due to the exquisiteness of Jesus' love for you. He wants you entirely for Himself, He wants you to place all your trust and all your affection in Him alone and it is precisely for this reason that He sends you this spiritual aridity, to unite you more closely to Him, to rid you of certain little attachments which do not appear as such to us and which, in many cases, we do not even recognize or detect.

I am aware that the state of the soul placed in such straits is a sad one, when it really seems to us that all is ended and that the Lord has left us for good because He is tired of bearing with us. Instead, things are quite different. The Lord is never so pleased with us as He is at such times as this. He is always there, close to us, or rather within us, invisibly encouraging us to endure the combat. Don't worry, then, because the Lord will fight for you and will never withdraw from you.

What you must do when Jesus, in His goodness, puts your faithfulness to the test, is to show at all times great promptitude in the observance of your duties, without neglecting any of the practices which you perform in times of consolation and prosperity, without paying any attention to your lack of all pleasurable feelings, since such feelings are merely accidental and can often be quite dangerous to the soul. True and substantial devotion consists in serving God without experiencing any sensible consolation. This means serving and loving God for His own sake.

Until the soul has arrived at the acquisition of this substantial devotion, it is in a precarious state and must go forward with great prudence and discretion.

Help yourself mainly during this period by reading holy books. I earnestly desire to see you reading such books at all times, for this reading provides excellent food for the soul and conduces to great progress along the path of perfection, by no means inferior to what we obtain through prayer and holy meditation. In prayer and meditation it is we ourselves who speak to the Lord, while in holy reading it is God who speaks to us. Try to treasure these holy readings as much as you can and you will very soon be aware of a spiritual renewal within you.

Before beginning to read these books, raise your mind to the Lord and implore Him to guide your mind Himself, to speak to your heart and move your will. But this is not sufficient. It is also advisable before you start to read, and from time to time in the course of your reading, to declare before the Lord that you are not reading for the purpose of study or to satisfy your curiosity, but solely to give Him pleasure and enjoyment.

I also want you to let me know what books you would like to read. You may read as many books as you can obtain which deal with the lives of the saints, but even in this regard I would ask you to keep me informed at your convenience.

I recognize only too well that I ask too much of you and therefore merit your deep commiseration, but God knows that I am not doing so without good reason.

I thank the Lord and am very glad that your sister's health continues to improve and I firmly believe that the Lord will endow her with such good health as to give both of you deep satisfaction.

I do not withdraw the reproof contained in my last letter with regard to your beloved sister, much less do I accept your excuses on the subject. It is true, my dear, that actions performed deliberately by one's own choice are very meritorious and therefore deserving of greater merit than those performed, as we say, by virtue of necessity, but this does not mean that the latter are worthless. The Lord generally makes use of secondary causes for the fulfilment of His plans and indeed this is the way He usually acts.

Don't worry about your inability to use the vocal prayers from devotional books, due to the lack of light in the chapel. You should not, indeed, make too frequent use of such prayers, for they can easily weary and impoverish the soul. Train yourself, as far as you can, to make frequent use of mental prayer and holy meditation.

I must stop here. I am really unable to continue as my physical strength is failing me. Before closing, though, I ask you once more to beseech the divine mercy on behalf of my soul. Go on praying all the time according to my intentions.

May God bless you and alleviate your own anxieties, those of your sister and of all the others who are dear to you; may He look upon you and console you by His mercy.

Your poor servant,
Fra Pio.

P.S. As soon as you receive this, send me a picture postcard.

17

Savona, 22 July 1914.

"I mustn't conceal anything from you." Possibility of an apparition. She hides her wretchedness in her director's hands. Need for a peaceful haven so that she may not offend Jesus. She plans a trip to Lourdes. Graces to be asked from Jesus. Their correspondence. She thanks him.

Jesus alone! Most Holy Spirit, help me!

Reverend Padre Pio,

I complied at once with the wish you expressed in your last precious letter, which reached me on the 14th of this month. You will certainly have received not one but three picture postcards, one showing the splendid panorama of this Capuchin friary and another the grassy path leading to the friary church.

In this connection, why should I not tell you about a day-dream, a pious desire of mine? I cannot and must not conceal anything from you, for I seem to have known you a hundred years. It was on the morning of the Feast of Our Lady of Mount Carmel, my good Mother. Oh! I spent my early childhood in a convent dedicated to her, in Lucera, under the vigilant eye of a cousin of my saintly mother, a Carmelite nun who died in the odour of sanctity eleven years ago. She was my second mother and I shed many tears when I was separated from her... but where are my thoughts leading me? Enough of this. Let me go on.

I was on my way to the Capuchins for Confession, all alone, walking along that beautiful path shown on the postcard, immersed in the deep silence of the natural environment and looking towards the door of the church which can be seen through the trees. My mind wandered and suggested to me: supposing, by God's power and a miracle which could easily happen in the case of His true servants, supposing Padre Pio were to appear here or in the church, what should I do? I should certainly consider it to be a hallucination or a trick of the devil. But no, with my knees knocking and my heart in my mouth I would ask him his name. Then, overwhelmed and not yet convinced (what can you expect? I am always afraid of God's wonders, even of the most astounding miracles), I would ask my confessor and once assured of the truth I would speak and say many many things to Padre Pio. I would confess my sins and cry and continue to cry. What would I not say to him?

Occupied with these thoughts I reached the church which I found deserted. I rang the bell and the old Capuchin who was my confessor appeared. I went to Confession and returned to the convent without having seen Padre Pio except in my imagination.

Now, what will you say, holy Father, to all this? Was it useless, stupid, a day-dream? Tell me quite frankly.

I am most grateful to you for the prayers you send up for me in the combats I endure. Even if I said nothing to you (and my pen will never be able to convey to you all that passes in my soul) you would know absolutely all by divine revelation. It does not matter if I am unable to explain myself sufficiently. All is clear to you as the light of day, of this I am quite certain.

I feel strong in my great weakness and extreme wretchedness, because you are praying for me. I lean upon you as my sure defence. Oh, your words and assurances bring me joy and light and peace! But some of the expressions you use: "You are too dear to the Heart of Jesus and all that is happening in your soul is due to the exquisiteness of Jesus's love for you," astonish me, confuse me, overwhelm me and cast me down into the depths.

As I know myself thoroughly, I am tempted not to believe all this, but you speak to me, you assure me it is true and by struggling enormously, by making a greater effort than I have ever made before, I am obliged in spite of everything to believe what you say. The sight of my wretchedness and my malice very often consoles me, since it saves me from pride. I hide this wretchedness and malice in the hands of Padre Pio and by his powerful intercession he obtains for me pardon and peace from Jesus.

What a paradise on earth it would be to live spiritually united with Jesus, with the hope or rather the certainty of never offending Him any more. Father, on my knees I beseech you to obtain this for me. Please hear me. Far from the occasions of sin and from all concern for this life, in an atmosphere charged with faith, love and purity, with eyes fixed on heaven and heart detached from everyone and everything, awaiting ardently and in all freedom the supreme goal, such is the daily life of these holy virgins who surround me.

Why does Jesus not grant me, grant us some safe haven, some peaceful harbour? I ask this continually for myself, my sister and my spiritual friend, but Jesus does not hear me. Wring this grace by main force from His Eucharistic Heart.

Why does He make us live in continual occasions of sin, in the midst of conflicts, afflictions and enemies of all kinds? We are weary, our souls are now weak, exhausted and in need of peace. After so many storms we need some holy oxygen for our souls and this we can breathe and absorb in solitude and silence in an unsullied environment where faith and charity reign. Do you agree? Will you ask Jesus and oblige Him to lead us at last to this necessary haven? Good Father, I feel sure you will.

Although the trip would be too tiring for my sister, I myself would like to go on to Lourdes with a devout lady whom I met here and who is going there on a pilgrimage. This is a dream I have cherished for a long time and it is now before my mind. Will the White Lady, my good Immaculate Mother, grant my desire? What have you to say about it? Tell me frankly. Will Jesus be pleased to bring it to pass for His glory and the good of my soul? If not, then it is no, never, never. May His most holy will be invariably fulfilled in me. Obtain for me, Father, continual unceasing union with His holy plans and desires; repugnance for everything that does not concern Him; a full knowledge of my own wretchedness; total self-denial, zeal for His glory, an apostolic spirit, love for the cross, for sufferings and sacrifice, deep interior life with Jesus, divine Love, in the Blessed Sacrament and... a haven of salvation, I repeat, a peaceful spiritual haven for all three of us.

Wring by main force from the divine Heart, holy Father, all these graces which the urgent needs of my rebellious spirit demand. Force Him also to give me the grace to pray, which is something I am unable to do, the grace of holy meditation which I never want to face because I find it difficult, arduous and abstruse. Occasionally it fills my heart with serenity and light, but almost invariably it is empty and futile. For some time past, to my shame, I haven't meditated at all.

Reading, on the other hand, brings me relief. I am extremely fond of it and spend hours at it without realizing it. (In the past this was the case with profane books, novels, etc.). You ask me what I read and I am ready to tell you at once. I am a subscriber to several Catholic papers, periodicals and bulletins, but among these I enjoy and derive great spiritual nourishment from *L'Aurora del Secolo del Sacramento*, *Il Carmelo* and *L'Emmanuele*[1], which are written very well, with great unction, profound doctrine and in modern style.

What can you expect? I always prefer the modern free-and-easy style. I read a great many old-fashioned books years ago, but I have no use for them now, just as I very often (to my great shame) have no use for the Book of books, the chief of all books, the holy Gospel, merely because I have read and reread commentaries on it for 20 years and perhaps more. It is very old, but to me it appears to belong to the last century.

You consider this to be a fault on my part, don't you, good Father? But I am fickle, indolent, bad, as you know better than I do myself. A short time ago I read the lives of Gemma Galgani[2], Caterina Volpicelli[3] and Sister Thérèse of the Holy Face[4]. Free-and-easy and pleasing... this is the type of book I would like to have on hand at all times. A heavy and abstruse style of writing, even in articles, makes no appeal to me.

I own a library of books, ancient and modern, and I should like to devour them all, but I lack the patience and the will to do so.

I have confessed everything to you and would like to tell you more on the same subject if I could have the good for-

---

[1] Three periodicals published in Northern Italy at the turn of the century.

[2] Probably the classic biography of the Servant of God, Gemma Galgani, written by her spiritual director, GERMANO DI S. STANISLAO, C.P. and published in Rome in 1910.

[3] Cf. M. IETTI, *Caterina Volpicelli* (died 1894) *Foundress of the Handmaids of the Sacred Heart*, in 3 vols., Naples, 1900-1907.

[4] *History of a Soul. Life of the Servant of God, Sister Thérèse of the Child Jesus* (died 1897), Florence, 1910.

tune to speak to you. But this is enough, I am tiring your invincible patience and seraphic charity.

I thank you for the interest you take in my wretched soul. Don't tell me that you are pretentious where I am concerned; you displease me when you speak to me in this way. On the contrary, I have every reason to authorize you to examine, interrogate, investigate as you think fit everything that miraculously entrusted to you. For this I thank you and will continue to thank you with deep feeling for ever more.
continue to thank you with deep feeling for ever more.

When you can do so without tiring yourself, write me a long letter; instruct me, scold me when I deserve it and punish me.

Let me have news of your most precious health.

Bless me and bless all my dear ones.

A poor tertiary.

P.S. Forgive and absolve me for all the blunders of every description in these awful letters of mine. My sister is preparing just now to go to Confession tomorrow at the Capuchin church, to the same priest who is my confessor. I should be very happy to see her receive Jesus for several days along with so many beautiful souls. Bless her, Father. May Jesus induce her at last to decide to take this holy path. May He make her His own for ever. Praise be to Jesus for ever and ever!

18

Pietrelcina, 28 July 1914.

She must beware of the devil, the "great artificer of evil." Desires to free ourselves from our enemies do not come from the devil. God does not allow us to be tempted beyond our strength. The pilgrimage to Lourdes. Spiritual and profane reading. The saints recommend the reading of Sacred Scripture. Authority of St. Augustine. Testimony of St. Ignatius. Efficacious for spiritual progress. St. Jerome.

J.M.J.D.F.C.

Beloved daughter of Jesus,

May the grace of the heavenly Father be ever in your heart and grant you, through His most beloved Son Jesus, to be set free from all evil and to obtain complete victory over the enemy of all.

Your desire to see me in order to tell me many things, all of which concern Jesus, is a holy one. Do not be afraid that in this you are going against God's will. I warn you, however, not to abandon yourself excessively to this desire to see me even miraculously, for this could be dangerous for you. When such a desire stirs in your soul, drive it away at once. In this way you will close the door to any deception by that wretch.

The devil, as you know, is a great artificer of evil in

which he has been engaged only too long. When he sees how keenly you desire it, he could deceive you by some diabolical illusion or apparition disguised as an angel of light. Who would believe it? This unhappy apostate even knows how to disguise himself as a Capuchin and to act the part quite well. I beg you to believe one who has undergone an experience of this nature.

What I have said on this point is sufficient for the moment. To me it seems that I have said even more than prudence demanded.

You long to be set free from the enemies who surround you, because as apostles of Satan they are all intent on making us act dishonestly. I assure you that the distress you still experience in seeing yourself continually exposed to occasions of offending God is entirely the effect of divine grace which the most merciful Lord has poured abundantly into your heart.

All this is a most sure sign that the love which the Holy Spirit has poured into your heart[1] is not dead, but active. Similar desires, combined with the humility which springs from a low opinion of yourself, cannot by any means conceal a diabolical deception, for the will to be freed from enemies who are intent on causing us to act dishonestly and offend God, the desire to see yourself released from the occasions which put your fidelity severely to the test, completely exclude the cunning of the enemy who is unable to produce such sentiments.

You act very well, in the meantime, when you ask the Lord continually to be so good as to set you free from these occasions and from your enemies. But when you have done this it is well to resign yourself humbly to the divine designs. Even the apostle St. Paul, constantly placed among the

[1] Cf. Rom 5:5.

enemies of Jesus and of his own soul, seeing himself faced almost without respite with occasions of offending Jesus, yearned and implored with sighs and groans, with tears and ceaseless prayers to be set free from this harsh trial[2]. He too was afraid of being overcome, but God assured him that the help of His grace would be sufficient for him.

You, however, do not want to be convinced and I hear repeated in my ear, as it were, that phrase in which not a little diffidence can be detected: "Father, but St. Paul was a saint, he was filled with the Holy Spirit and therefore had nothing to fear, while, on the other hand, I see myself weak and exhausted in spirit, which is precisely the reason why I fear to be overcome."

Very well, but has the Lord not told us that He is faithful and promised never to allow us to be vanquished? God is faithful, and He will not let you be tempted beyond your strength, but with the temptation will also provide the way of escape, that you may be able to endure it[3].

How could you persuade yourself of anything else, my dear sister? Isn't our good God far above anything we can conceive? Isn't He more interested than we are in our salvation? How many times has He not given us proof of this? How many victories have you not gained over your very powerful enemies and over yourself, through the divine assistance, without which you would inevitably have been crushed?

Let us consider Jesus' love for us and His concern for our well-being and then let us be at peace. Let us not doubt that He will invariably assist us with more than fatherly care against all our enemies. If it was left to ourselves, my dear, to remain on our feet, we should never be able to do it. At the first breath of air we should fall down and certainly have no hope of rising again. The more numerous your enemies

---

[2] Cf. 2 Cor 12:9.

[3] 1 Cor 10:13.

become, the more you ought to abandon yourself with complete trust in the Lord. He will always sustain you with His powerful arm so that you may not stumble.

Before the Lord abandons us, we should have to abandon Him, in a word, we should first have to close the door of our heart to Him, and even then, how many times does He not stretch out His hand to us to arrest our headlong dash towards the precipice! How many times, when we had abandoned Him, has He not readmitted us to His loving embrace!

How good our God is! Blessed for ever be His hand which many times alleviates our sufferings and marvellously heals our incurable wounds.

I believe it is God's will for you to go to visit the beautiful Virgin of Lourdes and I don't think this long journey would be prejudicial to your sister's health. However, let her act according to her own prudent judgment and if possible on the doctor's advice.

For many years I too have been longing to go there, but I am aware that this will never be anything more than a pious desire. I would ask you not to let slip this wonderful opportunity that heaven offers you, not to fail to put into effect this most holy sentiment and give free play to your devotion. Go there indeed, I beseech you, to visit the White Lady and pray to her for the needs of holy Church. Pray in a special way for my own wretched soul that it may never again be unfaithful to its God and pray for all those who are dearest to me. Lay at the feet of this most holy Mother an aspiration of mine. Oh! If only I could follow you in this visit, how fortunate I should be and what a wonderful favour from heaven would be mine! But may the Lord's will be done.

As regards your reading, there is very little to be admired and hardly anything by which to be edified. It is absolutely necessary for you to add to such reading that of the holy books so highly recommended by all the holy Fathers of the Church. I cannot dispense you from such spiritual reading, for I have your perfection too much at heart. If you want to gain the quite unhoped-for fruit from such reading, it will be well to rid yourself of the prejudice you have with regard to the style and form in which these holy books are set forth.

Get to work, then. Make an effort in this respect, and don't neglect to ask the divine assistance with all humility. There is a deep deception in this matter and I cannot and do not wish to conceal it from you. I want to tell you, to my great embarassment, that I too was similarly deceived and if the merciful God in his goodness had not revealed this deception to me in due course, who knows where a headlong fall might not have landed me!

I really owe this testimony to the truth, namely, that I never felt the least attraction for the type of reading that might sully moral innocence and purity, for I held quite naturally in greatest abhorrence even the slightest obscenity. In my readings, which were not improper but were invariably profane, I sought merely scientific satisfaction and the pastime of honest mental recreation. Yet in spite of my innocent intentions, such readings produced deep wounds in my heart and if they did nothing else they kept me at a standstill and never helped me to acquire even a single virtue. The worst aspect of this was that my love for God grew colder and colder.

The grace of our heavenly Father, ever attentive, saved me from many dangers and seemed somehow to be battling with my will so as to prevent me from being entirely lost. It seemed as if the good God, with fatherly solicitude and loving insistence, was seeking an effective means to call me back to Him, while I myself was foolishly fleeing, always fleeing from Him. But in the end I was vanquished by divine grace. Oh, how happy I was to have been conquered by so dear a Father! Oh, blessed for ever be this most tender Spouse for His exceeding patience and goodness towards such a wretched creature as myself!

I am horrified, my dear sister, at the damage done to souls by their failure to read holy books.

Listen to the way the holy Fathers express themselves when they exhort us to apply ourselves to this type of reading. St. Bernard, in the scale of values he established for his cloistered monks, recognizes four degrees or means by which to reach God and perfection, namely, reading and meditation, prayer and contemplation. As proof of what he says, he quotes the divine Master's own words: *Seek and you will find, knock and it will be opened to you*[4]. He goes on to apply these words to the four means or degrees of perfection and says that by reading Sacred Scripture and other holy and pious books we are seeking God; by meditation we find Him, by prayer we knock at the door of His heart and by contemplation enter the theatre of divine delights which has been opened to our mental gaze by reading, meditation and prayer[5].

Elsewhere the saint tells us that reading is, as it were, spiritual food applied to the palate of the soul; meditation chews it by its reasoning, while prayer savours it. Contemplation is then the very sweetness of this spiritual food which restores the soul entirely and comforts it. Reading stops at the bark or outer covering of what is read; meditation penetrates into its core; prayer goes in search of it by its questions, while contemplation enjoys it as something already possessed[6].

The esteem which St. Jerome had for the reading of holy books is incredible. He exhorts Salvina to have holy books always at hand, for these are a strong shield to ward off all the evil thoughts which attack people in their youth[7]. He

---

[4] Mt. 7:7; Lk 11:9.

[5] St. Bernard, *Scala claustralium, sive Tractatus de modo orandi*, Chap. 2: PL 184, 476, No. 2.

[6] St. Bernard, *ibid.*, cf Col. 475-476, No. 1.

[7] St. Jerome, *Epist. ad Salvinam*, 79: PL, Vol. 22, Col. 730-731.

teaches the same thing to St. Paulinus: "Always keep the holy book in your hands," he tells him, "that it may nourish your soul by devout reading[8]." To the widow Furia he suggests frequent reading of Sacred Scripture and the writing of those Doctors whose doctrine is holy and wholesome, in order to avoid the fatigue involved in searching for the gold of holy and healthful teachings in the quagmire of false documents[9]. To Demetriade he writes: "Love reading Holy Scripture if you want to be loved by divine wisdom, if you want her to guard and possess you. You used to adorn yourself in various ways," adds the holy Doctor at once, "you wore jewels on your bosom, necklaces at your throat, jewelled earrings. For the future let holy readings be your gems and your jewels by which to adorn your soul with holy thoughts and devout sentiments."[10]

St. Gregory expressed himself in the same way, using the allegory of the mirror: "Spiritual books are like a mirror which God places before us in order that we may see ourselves in them and hence correct our faults and adorn ourselves with every virtue. Just as vain women look at themselves frequently in the mirror and there remove every blemish from their face, adjust their hair and adorn themselves in a thousand ways in order to appear charming in the eye of others, so, too, the Christian must frequently place the holy books before his eyes in order to perceive the faults he must correct and the virtues by which he must adorn himself so as to be pleasing in the sight of his God[11]."

I refrain from mentioning other authorities. However, I point out to you the power of holy reading to lead even worldly persons to change their course and enter on the path

---

[8] Cf. St. Jerome, *Letters*: PL, Vol. 22, Col. 579.
[9] *Ibid*: PL, Vol. 22, Col. 550.
[10] *Letters*, *cit*.: PL, 22, Col. 1124.
[11] St. Gregory, *Moralia*, Lib. 2, c. 1.

of perfection. For this purpose it suffices for you to consider the conversion of St. Augustine. Who was it that won this great man over to God? His ultimate conqueror was neither his mother by her tears nor the great St. Ambrose by his divine eloquence, but the reading of a book.

Those who read his *Confessions* cannot keep back their tears. What a desperate battle, what violent conflicts he endured in his poor heart because of his enormous reluctance to give up his lewd sensual pleasures. He says of himself that he was compelled to utter groans and laments while his will was bound as if by a strong chain and that the infernal enemy confined his will in the fetters of a cruel necessity. He goes on to say that he experienced mortal agony in abandoning his loose morals and adds that when his mind was almost made up, his former follies and pleasures pulled him back from his good resolutions and murmured around him: "Are you giving us up, then? From this moment on are we never to be with you any more?"

But while the saint battled with such tumultuous feelings he heard a voice which said to him: take up and read. He at once obeyed this voice and as he read a chapter of St. Paul the thick darkness in his mind was dispelled, all the hardness vanished from his heart and he became perfectly calm and serene. From that moment he made a clean break with the world, the devil and the flesh, devoted himself completely to the service of God and became the great saint who is honoured today on our altars[12].

History also tells us that St. Ignatius of Loyola, as the result of a spiritual reading which he made from no spirit of devotion but with the sole desire to escape from the boredom of a painful infirmity, was transformed from a cap-

---

[12] ST. AUGUSTINE, *Confessions*, Bk. 8, Chap. 12.

tain in the army of an earthly king into a captain at the service of the King of heaven[13].

Again, we read of St. Columban that through reading a holy book[14], to please his wife rather than from devotion, he found himself completely changed and consecrated his life entirely to God.

Now, if the reading of holy books has the power to convert worldly men into spiritual persons, how very powerful must not such reading be in leading spiritual men and women to greater perfection?

I deal with just one example here, namely, that of St. Jerome. He himself relates how he withdrew from the splendour of Rome and retired to Palestine, where he spent his days and nights in fasts and vigils, in prayer and harsh penances. Even in a life of such severity, he still had a fault which was very detrimental to his spiritual progress. This was his immoderate love for profane books and a certain repugnance for reading holy books because of what he considered to be the uncultured literary style in which they were written. As he himself admits, he saw a defect and a fault in the sun instead of recognizing a defect of his own eyesight.

A severe remedy was required to make him come to his senses. The Lord sent him an infirmity which reduced him to the point of death. When he was about to die the Lord carried him in spirit up to the Judgment Seat, where he was asked who he was. The saint replied: "I am a Christian and I profess no other faith than yours, O my Lord." "You are lying," replied the divine Judge, "you are a Ciceronian (the

---

[13] The change brought about in St. Ignatius of Loyola after he had read the *Life of Christ*, by the Carthusian Ludolph of Saxony and a Castilian *Lives of the Saints*. Cf. Christopher Hollis, *St. Ignatius*, Sheed and Ward, London 1931, p. 25.

[14] *Vita S. Columbani abbatis, auctore Jona*: PL, 87, Col. 1016, No. 9.

[15] St. Jerome, *Letters, cit.*: PL, Vol. 22, Col. 416; cf. *Acta Sanctorum*, sept. t., VIII, Antwerp, 1762, p. 440.

saint was very fond of Cicero's writings) for where your treasure is, there is your heart also." Then the divine Judge ordered him to be scourged. The pain of the blows caused the saint to weep and ask for mercy, crying out in a loud voice: "Have mercy on me, O Lord."

The Angels who stood before the Judgment Seat began to implore mercy for him, promising the divine Judge on his behalf that he would make amends for his fault. Then St. Jerome swore and promised with all the ardour of his soul that never again would he read secular and profane writings, but only holy books. At this point he returned to consciousness, to the astonishment of those present who had believed him dead.

The saint goes on to tell us that this was no vision or illusion, for when he came to himself his eyes were full of tears, his shoulders bruised and his flesh wounded from the severe blows he had received. After this event the saint gave himself up with great fervour to the reading of holy books which were of very great benefit to him.

I end here, as I am quite unable to continue, and I exhort you to take up meditation again. Pray for my soul, for I am extremely disconsolate.

May the Lord give you peace and consolation in your troubles, together with your sister.

Your servant,
Fra Pio.

19

Savona, 12 August 1914.

She wants to abide by his teachings. Her confessors are firm and decided. The pilgrimage to Lourdes is cancelled. Anguish at the thought of returning home and on account of her sister's health. A retreat. In search of "health and peace."

Jesus alone! Most Holy Spirit, help me!

Reverend Padre Pio,

In a postscript to my last letter I asked your pardon for the blunders of all descriptions in my writings. I ought to have added "for the scandal I give you," filled as you are with ardent faith and divine love.

Forgive me, holy Father, and take pity on this soul still far, very far from being converted.

My manner of speaking greatly scandalized you and you rebuke me by giving me a lecture full of profound truths and holy examples (while I deserved something very different!).

When am I going to decide to put these holy teachings into practice? I am exceedingly attached to my own will and this is the trouble. Very often I cherish the fond hope that something is God's will, while all the time it is my own will which prevails and wins out. I frequently fail to distinguish between desire for God, my own will and the promptings of the devil. To tell the truth, I never think of the devil, and I don't know whether this is good or bad for me. In this world I see nothing but God and my own soul; nothing else.

I believe the devil keeps his place, but when we want him to. On the other hand, it is my own malice which causes me to act as I do and to commit sin. I am not familiar with the devil's temptations, or rather, I am unable to perceive them (if he amuses himself with me); I always say that it is myself, it is my perverse will, my malice and not the devil, of whom I never think at all and whose very existence I forget. Is this good or bad for me? I don't know. Please have the patience to explain this important point to me.

Jesus has arranged that I should meet with confessors who speak very little and very well. My ordinary confessor speaks as much as is necessary to make me holy (if I wanted to and could be holy). This elderly Capuchin whom I met here and who, they tell me, is worn out by penances and not by his age, speaks very little. Both, however, are firm and decided in obliging me to receive Communion daily.

How good Jesus is with this unfaithful servant of His! Oh, my wretched, miserable Communions! They arouse compassion and perhaps... horror. What am I to do? All I can do is obey. I am scandalizing you and I should scandalize you even more if you could hear me in the tribunal of Penance. On paper what can I ever convey to you? I don't dare to open my conscience in the light of the sun, but there in the dark, on the contrary—for I always confess my sins with closed eyes—there behind the grille of the confessional you would hear so very much that you would be horrified and would punish me.

In the past I refused to heed the heavenly calls. An elderly Capuchin, learned and holy (whom you certainly knew, for he was formerly your Provincial, Padre Maria Francesco of

Apricena, who died suddenly on 18 July 1900)[1], worked hard on my soul. But I was deaf, ungrateful and unfaithful and failed to correspond. My soul remained hard and barren ground, covered with scrub, sharp thorns and loathsome weeds, without any sign of improvement. The silence or the few words of those to whom I entrust my wretched soul is the lawful consequence, the just punishment for my lack of correspondence. (Speak to me about this). Blessed for ever be the most holy will of God!

The beautiful dream of Lourdes has vanished. It was too beautiful. The whole thing has collapsed, as we have been terrified by the rumours of war.

I am passing through a period of dreadful anguish and I spend hours, even days in real agony. Has my good angel come to tell you about it? I want to know if he has, so please tell me. Far from home, about 1000 kilometers away, exposed to endless dangers, alarms and fears, what course should we take?

We have no home until the 8th of next month. Our rented house is all upside-down and almost empty, because my friend packed up everything as soon as we left. Our own home is still occupied by our brother until the 8th of September and even then, is he going to leave calmly and reasonably, without venom or resentment, along with his wife? It remains to be seen if they will let us move peacefully into our own home.

Shall we return home safe and sound? To our father's house? When must we return? How much longer must we

---

[1] He died on the 16th and not the 18th of July 1900. Born on 16 December 1832, he was twice Provincial Superior of the Capuchin Province of Foggia and was recognized by all as a perfect religious and an expert in the ecclesiastical sciences. Cf. CIPRIANO DA SERRACAPRIOLA, *Necrologia dei frati minori cappuccini della provincia religiosa di Foggia*, Foggia, 1969, pp. 449 ff.

stay here? All is quite dark as we wait in anguish and painful anxiety. You know everything already; tell me, have pity on me.

Add to all this the health of my sister, my martyr. Since yesterday she has been anything but well, with an attack of her usual stomach trouble for the first time since we came here. It came on while she was before the Blessed Sacrament, just at the solemn moment of Benediction. She thought she was about to die and it was a genuine miracle that she did not fall down in a faint there in the church. Imagine the state I am in. She remained in bed and this morning rose quite late, but she is still suffering.

Every morning she gets up at five in order to receive Holy Communion. For her this schedule means a big sacrifice, because she is not accustomed to it, but she is glad to do it for Jesus' sake. Willingly and with real enthusiasm she followed the exercises of the six-day retreat for all the ladies staying in this boarding-house for the bathing season, with two sermons preached each day by a fine missionary priest. Several of these sermons applied to me and several of them, by God's grace, did not concern me.

Each year the good Sisters do some fine work among those who come to stay at the sea from Lombardy and Piedmont, married and unmarried ladies and young girls, about a hundred in all. Among them there are always some unfortunate ones who have not made their Easter duty for years and years. This year all of them corresponded with the grace of our good Jesus in a General Communion, a beautiful and touching ceremony crowned and sealed by the Papal Blessing. Praise be to Jesus for ever.

May Jesus be praised not only in joy but also in suffering! It costs me a great effort to say this, for it does not come from my heart and will, which would be impossible. Don't be scandalized. We came up here to obtain a little health and peace, but I see neither one nor the other purpose being fulfilled, for everything is upset by my sister's insidious illness and by the disturbing effects of the war.

We desired very much to stop in Bologna on our way home, so that my sister might be examined by some well-known specialist for her stomach trouble. But what are we to do now? Perhaps we barely have time to dash off home. Here in Savona, so close to France, the rumours are very alarming. But where are we to go, I repeat, if the house is not available? Oh, how I long to be back in my own town!

I have to conceal my terrible anxiety from my sister who must be spared even the least upset which would bring on her stomach pains at once. I don't know which way to turn. I feel I am drowning in a sea of sorrow, of heartfelt agony. I shed bitter tears without obtaining any relief. What is Jesus doing? Is He asleep that He doesn't hear me? It is my own sins that draw down such scourges on the nations, but where is my repentance?

Father, pray and continue to pray for me, for my sister (may Jesus restore her completely in soul and body), pray for universal peace, for the conversion of the enemies of the faith. Father, advise me at once as to a way of escape. Have pity on us. I can't go on any longer. Help! Give us your blessing.

A poor tertiary.

P.S. Thank Jesus immensely for the great grace He has granted me, namely, for leading me to you to whose seraphic heart I can pour out my woes continually.

Give me news of your own health. Write to me. I am waiting anxiously to know what is God's most holy will.

20

Pietrelcina. Feast of the Assumption, 15 August 1914.

"Spiritual rather than bodily illness." For the moment it is better not to return home. Her fears are prompted by the devil. "Foolish are those who fail to fathom the secrets of the cross." "Jesus wants to make you holy." The joys of heaven are proportioned to the humiliations endured on earth. Effects which he expects this letter to produce. She is not to heed the promptings of her imagination and of the devil. Reading holy and pious books.

J.M.J.D.F.C.

Beloved daughter of Jesus,

May Jesus and Mary be always in your heart and in that of your sister and may they make you holy.

This time I shall be brief despite my will to act differently. I am compelled to this by necessity. My entire person is a prey to spiritual rather than bodily illness. I am weary of this life and would like to be set free from it. I am bearing it, but not without a supreme effort for love of the One who gave it to me and who wants to keep me alive still. May His will be done at all times.

I hasten to answer your letter at once in order to inform you of God's plan for you. I don't think it prudent for the moment that you should return home with your sister, chiefly on account of the really suffocating heat here in our region. To return when it is so hot would be to undo what has already been achieved.

However, in this matter act as you please. To me it seems that I have indicated God's will for you. You would like to come back home because it seems to you that war could break out where you are now rather than elsewhere. Don't be at all afraid on this score. Even if this were to happen (and may the most merciful God in His goodness save our dear land from this further disaster), Jesus will not allow your souls to suffer any injury. Get rid of the fears that trouble you on this account. The soul that places its trust in God alone has nothing to fear.

All those fears to which your soul is a prey and of which you have told me in your last letter, are unfounded and are suggested to you by the enemy of all, who desires at any cost, if that were possible, to ruin us. I want you to pay no attention to such fears and to consider them as diabolic suggestions, for this is what they really are.

Don't be worrying your brain needlessly and tormenting your heart with such devilish absurdities. Trust in God and hope that in His fatherly goodness He will let the light come through. Lift up your mind full of faith to your heavenly home and may all our yearnings and aspirations be directed there. Admire the heavenly regions which can be reached by no other road than that of suffering. That is our true home. What matter if we reach it by treading no other paths than the rough ones of tribulation and sacrifice?

What God wants from you is always right and good. May He be blessed for ever. Let us get to work; in heaven we'll have no other duty than the fulfilment of God's will. Let us strive to bless the Lord when we are the object of humiliations and contempt. Let us bless Him in our spiritual trials and our heartbreaks, for all is ordained by God with great wisdom. In a most singular manner and by a special predilection of the heavenly Father this is being accomplished in you. May He be for ever blessed in all our miseries and in all our sufferings.

Bless Him in all that He makes you suffer on this earth and rejoice at it, for each victory gained has a corresponding crown in paradise. Don't be frustrated or cast down by the violence you must do yourself, for the Lord is faithful and will not allow you to be overcome by temptation. The kingdom of heaven suffers violence, says the divine Master, *and men of violence take it by force*[1].

In order to reach our final goal, we must follow our divine Leader, who usually leads chosen souls by the path He Himself has trodden and by no other; by the path, I tell you, of self-denial and suffering: *If any man would come after Me, let him deny himself and take up his cross and follow Me*[2]. Should you not deem yourself fortunate to see yourself treated in this way by Jesus? Foolish are those who fail to fathom the secret of the cross.

In order to reach the haven of salvation, the Holy Spirit tells us, the souls of the elect must pass through and be purified in the fire of painful humiliations, like gold and silver in the melting-pot. In this way they are spared from expiating in the next life: *Accept whatever is brought upon you, and in changes that humble you be patient. For gold is tested in the fire, and acceptable men in the furnace of humiliation*[3].

Jesus wants to make us holy at all costs, but above all He wants to sanctify you. He offers you continual proof of this; it would seem as if He had nothing else to do but sanctify your soul. Oh, how good Jesus is! The continual crosses to which He subjects you, giving you not merely the necessary strength, but superabundant strength to bear them

---

[1] Mt. 1:12.
[2] Mt 16:24.
[3] Sir 2:4-5.

meritoriously, are most certain and singular signs of His deep love for you. Believe me, the strength He gives you does not remain sterile in you; I assure you of this in God's name and you must listen to me in all humility and rid yourself of any sentiment to the contrary.

My dear sister, calm the tormenting anxieties of your heart and banish from your imagination all those distressing thoughts and sentiments which are all suggested by Satan in order to make you act badly. Jesus is always with you even when you don't feel His presence. He is never so close to you as He is during your spiritual battles. He is always there, close to you, encouraging you to fight your battle courageously. He is there to ward off the enemy's blows so that you may not be hurt.

For pity's sake, I beseech you by all that you hold sacred not to wrong Him by entertaining the slightest suspicion that He has abandoned you even for a single moment. This is really one of the most diabolical temptations which you must drive far from you as soon as you are aware of it.

Let it be a consolation to you to know, my dear, that the joys of eternity will be all the more heartfelt and profound, the more numerous the days of humiliation and the years of unhappiness we have known in the present life. This is not just my own opinion, for Holy Scripture offers us infallible testimony to this effect. Here is what the Psalmist has to say on the subject: *Make us glad as many days as Thou hast afflicted us, and as many years as we have seen evil*[4]. St. Paul the apostle, moreover, has told us in the letter to the Corinthians that a moment of our passing trials can win for us unimaginable glory in eternity. Here are his very words: *This slight momentary affliction is preparing us for an eternal weight of glory beyond all comparison*[5].

---

[4] Ps 90:15.
[5] 2 Cor 4:17.

I cannot tell you how much it grieves me to hear of your sister's bad health, but my grief is partially compensated by the holy and delightful thought of the progress her soul is making in the ways of the Lord. I believe most firmly that the Lord will not refuse me the grace which I ask Him ceaselessly. I await this grace through the hands of our heavenly Mother whose Assumption into heaven is being celebrated today by the entire Church. The grace I refer to is that as soon as you receive this letter the *pitch darkness* which envelops your soul and the ailment from which your sister is suffering may disappear almost if not absolutely altogether.

I insist once again that you are not to listen by any means to what your imagination and the devil suggest to you. Your own fancy and the devil would like to have you believe that you are continually offending God and that you always or nearly always resist the divine call. The ever-present grace of the heavenly Father keeps you quite far from falling into similar infidelities. Be quite sure of this. I assure you that such thoughts come from nowhere else than your own imagination and the devil. Be careful not to attach any importance to them; their only purpose is to cool your feelings of affection towards your heavenly Spouse, to make Christian perfection appear irksome by representing it as difficult and impossible for you. Worse still, they aim more directly at drying up and causing to wither every sentiment of devotion in your heart.

Remember what I said to you in my last letter about good reading of holy and pious books and that I want you to keep me informed as to the books you use for this purpose. I hold firmly to what I have told you already. Make up your mind to heed me without delay and may Jesus give you the strength to do so.

Meanwhile you have said hardly anything to me of your impressions on reading my last letter on the subject of spiritual reading. I understand you because you were unable to think very clearly when you wrote to me. I should have a lot more to say to you, but I am quite unable to continue. Please understand me in the meantime and write to me when and as you like.

Pray to the Most Blessed Virgin to free me soon from this body of death, for I find it almost impossible to go on.

May Jesus and Mary deliver you and your sister from all evil and may they console you in your distress.

Your most unworthy servant,
Fra Pio, Capuchin.

P.S. You spoke to me of a certain Padre Francesco of Apricena, formerly Provincial of the Capuchins, but I didn't know him as I was received into the Order in 1903.

21

Pietrelcina, 28 August 1914.

Immediate departure from Savona.

J.M.J.D.F.C.

May the grace of the Holy Spirit make you holy.
Arrange to leave that place as soon as possible.
Be at peace, for the Lord is with you.
Pray for the one who greatly desires your good.
I am writing this in bed, as I am ill.
Regards and affectionate wishes in the Lord.

Your servant,
Fra Pio.

---

[1] This was a picture postcard (a bunch of flowers), posted in a closed envelope.

22

Modena, 1 September 1914.

Departure from Savona. Their stay in Modena: the confessor. Three constant worries, three trials. Postscript.

Jesus alone! Most Holy Spirit, help me!

Reverend Padre Pio,

Before all else I feel the need to ask news of your precious health. Next, I want to thank you very very much for the deep fatherly interest which you showed us by your urgent message on the last card we received just before our departure, while I was already packing our bags. I had already decided to travel next day, the 27th, at 6 a.m., to Modena where we have a very dear friend with a husband and children, a model family from the point of view of religion and upbringing.

Actually, on the afternoon of the 27th, with God's help, accompanied by St. Joseph and by the prayers of many good souls, especially your own prayers, we arrived safely here in Modena after a fairly quiet journey. We made several stops on the way and changed trains without any of the disastrous mishaps on which my dreadful imagination had been busy for a month.

To tell the truth, in the course of our journey, I don't

know exactly where, we forgot a box containing things we need. St. Anthony will help us to find it; pray to him, good Father.

Here we are, then, the guests of this good family (paying guests, of course), for how long we cannot say. Certainly it will be until after our blessed house is left free for us, that is, on 8 September. Do you approve? Are we safe here? Please advise us. Did that urgent message of yours telling us to leave Savona at once mean that danger threatened Savona? What danger? Be so good as to explain and enlighten me about the whole thing.

Always due to your prayers, I found the church quite close to the house, St. Francis Church (our dear Seraphic Father always goes before me). However, there are no friars there, but a parish priest and his assistant. Where am I to go for Confession? I am in a great state of agitation. May Jesus inspire me. Pray, pray. All the good things which happen to me or to us are, I am quite sure, the result of your fervent prayers. When the opposite happens to me or to us, then I think sadly: "Padre Pio has forgotten me altogether."

Inside those holy walls at the convent of the Purification, how many agonizing hours I spent! Jesus knows very well how many agonizing hours I spent! Jesus knows very well how many days of anguish I spent there. Three constant worries, three acute and lasting trials prevented me from finding peace, namely, my sister's stomach trouble, the thought of our return to our old home (the house of sorrow, of tears and sadness) and the war.

As you know, we went away for a while from our own environment to enjoy a little peace, but we didn't find it even inside the four walls of a holy convent, far from the world and its attractions. How is this to be explained? I really have no idea. Is this an effect of my wickedness or is it something permitted by God? I don't know. My weak mind is very confused and things become less clear to me as the days go by. What am I to do? I am in fear and trembling as regards the future and I go on quite blindly. May Jesus leave me at least one bright spot: His most holy will. What supreme happiness it is for a wretched creature to feel sure of pleasing its Creator!

I must stop in time for fear of tiring you. You are ill and you wrote that message on a postcard from your bed. (What charity you have for a soul that has strayed! Who can ever forget it?). I feel a great anxiety on account of this bad news. Write to me without delay to say that you are well. I hope with all my heart that this will find you perfectly all right. Write to me as soon as you can. I await your news most anxiously. Bless me along with my sister.

A poor tertiary.

P.S. I owe you a reply to your letter received on 17 August. I didn't write sooner because I wanted to give you our exact itinerary, and my sister kept changing our plans all the time, according to the news and the course of events. Do you fully approve of our present plan, to remain here in Modena for some time? I am asking you this, holy Father, and please do me the favour of writing to tell me. Will our merciful Lord in His great goodness, His infinite goodness, save our own Italy from the scourge of war? And in other countries, will this war soon end? Will the conflagration in my own family, our fraternal war, soon come to an end? Will all our enemies come back to us? How greatly I desire this and how greatly my poor sister desires it! I should like to avoid upsetting her in any way in view of her stomach trouble.

On our return trip home, passing through Bologna, she wants to have a specialist examine her. I myself am afraid of the diagnosis. What do you say about it? Tell me frankly.

Thank you for everything. Write to me.

I kiss your hand respectfully.

My present address: Palazzo Pagliani, Via Giardini 2, Modena.

23

Pietrelcina, 6 September 1914.

Greetings. Health of body and soul. He rejoices at the trials and suffering which afflict her. Reprimands. Their stay in Savona achieved its purpose. Confidence as regards the future. Their stay in Modena and a visit to Bologna. The war. Death of Pope Pius X. Recommendations.

J.M.J.D.F.C.

Beloved daughter of Jesus Christ,

May our most sweet Jesus come into your heart, bathe it with His heavenly dew and may He so dispose things that the rapid and vigorous development of His gifts in your soul will compel those who witness your spiritual transformation to exclaim in the glorious words of the royal Prophet: *Thou visitest the earth and waterest it*[1].

I am answering you after a delay of two days for the reason of which you are well aware. At present, thank God, I am somewhat better.

I admire your solicitude and concern for my health, but urge you not to be at all distressed on this account; otherwise I shall tell you nothing more about it from now on.

---

[1] Ps 65:9.

I rejoice in my sufferings, for I then see that I am closer to God, the source of all good. Pray, I beseech you to pray, for this is the greatest act of charity you can perform towards me, not so much for my physical health as for my spiritual health which is of great concern to me.

How can I fail to rejoice when I see the increasing weakness of this miserable body, the only obstacle which prevents my entry to the heavenly banquet? Alas! I see that day still far off. What a torment for my wretched soul! May the Lord support me by His arm or else I'll die because I do not die.

You cannot imagine how it distresses me to hear how you are continually molested and tormented by Satan. Yet while I pray the Lord to spare you this torment, a very mysterious and penetrating voice sounds at the apex of my soul, giving me a foretaste of the delights of suffering and the merit your soul is gaining in these combats.

Hence, the fact that you are continually harassed makes me rejoice with the children of God, for I see that God's kingdom is being restored within you. The Lord is always with you, but He is with you in a very special way when the battle is more pressing. God knows if I am lying when I offer you these assurances.

Take heart, then, and don't fear either interior or exterior persecutions, since nothing has power to separate you from the Supreme Good as the ever-present grace of the heavenly Father takes good care of you in this respect. Be grateful to such a good Father for His attitude towards you, as you have done nothing to deserve such a singular privilege.

You need to be a little more docile. You are still a rather capricious daughter and somewhat unmanageable, but will it be possible to make you an entirely faithful servant? Jesus desires this and with His grace all will be achieved.

You are still very much afraid of life and this is what you must set right. Do you know what means to use? Perfect abandonment of your whole self to the divine goodness. Ask

Jesus with holy insistence for this grace, for every perfect gift is from above[2]. I promise you that I will do the same in my own poor feeble prayers.

Now, you complain that you went some distance away from your native town to enjoy a little peace and that you didn't find this even inside the four walls of the convent. I sympathize with you, because you are not fully aware of what you are saying. If you mean peace according to your own imagination as worldlings understand it, then you are right.

You left Foggia in search of an improvement in your beloved sister's health and unfortunately you did not find it according to your own taste and your own very foolish judgment. The Christian soul looks very differently at God's providence for His creatures. Do you consider a small thing the change which has come about in your sister's soul and also in your own? If you looked at the matter sincerely you would realize that the order of things has been reversed. You left your home town in search of better health for your sister, but the divine mercy (see how good God is) willed that you should find chiefly health of soul, to which you paid less attention.

Our God, my dear sister, is admirable in His judgments. You don't understand sufficiently the change which has come about in your sister's soul and in your own, and this is all right. I am glad that this is the case where your own soul is concerned, but with regard to your sister's soul you ought to rejoice and thank the heavenly Father.

My way of speaking on this point seems like Greek to you and you find it hard to believe, but the Lord understands what I say. I am touched to the point of tears when I compare your present with your former state. I don't know how to thank Jesus for the transformation which has taken place in you under the powerful influence of his grace.

---

[2] Cf. Jas 1:17.

I ask you to abide by this statement of mine which is the truth. It is about time you rid yourself, once and for all, of so many foolish and unfounded fears which pass through your mind, weigh upon your heart and keep it bound with harsh chains. Do you entertain doubts about the future? But have I not assured you that the Lord is always with you? Is not the future the same as the present in the sight of the Lord? What, then, do you doubt? I know and understand that your fear is based on a principle that is holy three times over. Yes, you are afraid of acting badly and of offending God. But rest assured, most dear daughter of Jesus, and be quite at peace, for the ever-present grace of Jesus will take good care to save you from being unfaithful.

Calm your immoderate fear, I repeat, for I assure you in Jesus' name that as long as you live you will always do His will. Grace will not be lacking, so make an effort to correspond to its impulses.

I am deeply grateful to the heavenly Father now that I see you quite safe in the house where you are staying. I offer you a feeble word of advice, namely, not to be in any hurry to return home. Try to prolong your stay in Modena, possibly until about the middle of this month.

Before returning to Foggia it will be well to go to Bologna to consult some reliable physician. Jesus appears to desire this. If you need to go to Confession during your stay in Modena, it seems to me more advisable that you go to the parish priest rather than to the curate, always supposing that this is possible.

While war and deadly, brutal hatred reign among the nations and keep them in a state of extreme agitation, let us not cease to beseech and implore peace from the eternal Judge who is justly angry with the nations for their evil conduct and their failure to pay any heed whatsoever to the law of love.

First of all let us seek to propitiate the eternal Judge with regard to our own dear country, Italy. She, too, has accounts to settle with the Lord and she doesn't want to cry out for mercy. Let us earnestly hope that the misfortunes of France, her sister, may serve to bring her to her senses in time, to make her return to her God with a truly contrite and humble heart.

Let us also thank the Lord for having come to the aid of His Church and consoled her widowhood by sending her a Pastor. Let us ask the Lord to make the new Pope a worthy successor of Pius X, a really holy soul, a supremely peaceful monarch, the "sweet Christ on earth," who died to this world by the ardent love which burned in his breast. I believe that his holy soul has no need of our intercessory prayers, but let us pray for his eternal rest just the same, since our prayers will never go to waste[3].

I end here. My strength does not allow me to go on and you who are so good will understand me if I am unable to answer all your questions. I hope to be deserving of your understanding if you find anything discouraging in this letter. In the meantime, may I remind you that you have many accounts to settle with me, for which I await your return home. I understand you, poor thing. You are like a bird outside its cage.

Write to me frequently and open your heart to me without reticence or reserve. I'll answer you whenever I am able. You want to pay back with interest the postal expenses; very well, then, I don't intend to cause you distress.

Convey my affectionate regards to your sister and believe me always.

Your most humble servant,
Fra Pio.

---

[3] Writing to Padre Agostino on 7 September 1914, Padre Pio expressed warm praise for the deceased Pope Pius X (1903-1914) and the earnest hope that the new Pontiff, Benedict XV, who succeeded him on 4 September, might be "a truly worthy successor of that great Pope, Pius X." Cf. *Letters*, Vol. I, Nos. 206 and 207.

24

Modena, 15 September 1914.

Padre Pio's health. The confessor in Modena. She doesn't believe in her spiritual transformation. Difficulty of explaining herself in writing. Their correspondence. She replies to his reprimands. The desired peace. Problems concerning her return to Foggia. She fears she is the cause of the conflicts in her family.

Jesus alone! Holy Spirit, help me!

Reverend Padre Pio,

On receipt of your most welcome letter on the morning of the Nativity of Most Holy Mary, I recited the *Te Deum* to the Lord and the *Magnificat* to our most holy Mother in thanksgiving for the good news concerning your precious health. In spite of your ardent desire to leave this valley of tears without delay, to fly away at once to heaven to be with Jesus in bliss, I don't hide from you my very great satisfaction on hearing that you are now fairly well. I am selfish; I want you on this earth, here among us for a long time to come, for God's glory, for the good of souls and... for my own benefit in particular. Don't scold me; on the contrary, you should consider me quite right. May Jesus, then, be infinitely thanked and for ever!

I awaited your letter in order to know what to do about Confession, but as the days passed and I felt the need, while I was undecided as to the choice, Jesus inspired me through a priest I had seen for several mornings there in the confessional (he is always there from 6 to 8 a.m., as is the curate also, both of them ready to receive anyone who desires forgiveness). Seeing the priest there before me, it seemed to me that Jesus intended me to go to him. I don't know who he is (I was told he is the second curate); all I know is that on the morning of the Nativity of Our Lady I went to him and found peace and comfort for my soul. However, before I approached the confessional, I recited the *Glory be to the Father* three times to your own saint and three times to your good Guardian Angel, so all that I found easy and good is due to you.

When I returned to the house I found your precious letter containing so many beautiful things. You speak to me of nothing less than a "transformation of my soul." Here are your own words: "I am touched to the point of tears when I compare your present with your former state. I don't know how to thank Jesus for the transformation which has taken place in you under the powerful influence of his grace."

Is all this possible? You assure me of it and I believe it with my eyes closed. But if I were to judge myself with open eyes I should tell you to my exceeding shame that I feel I am just the same as ever: passions, faults, wretchedness, sins, always at the same point. If at times some of these things are lacking, it is only because the occasions are lacking. Prayer, Masses, Confessions and Communions always in the same manner. It's disastrous! It's really... I lack a suitable adjective to give you an adequate idea of this miserable performance.

In church in the mornings I am unable to remain more than an hour-and-a-half, often less, because of my sleepy, distracted, restless and most wretched state of soul. Add to this, many, many times, a physical complaint which invariably torments me in church, so that I have resolved to appeal to you to ask our good Jesus to set me free from it, as I want to spend that short period in church in absolute peace, with nothing to disturb me, oblivious of everything.

My spiritual troubles are already more than enough to make the church a real purgatory for me more often than not; I should be quite satisfied if my bodily troubles were to torment me when I am at home, as long as they did not cause annoyance or suffering to those around me. Do you approve? Will you use your powerful intercession to obtain this grace which to me seems very necessary? I expect you to do so most certainly. Don't consider me arrogant, pretentious and shameless. To whom should I turn for help? To my good Father.

I entrust and confide to you all my miseries and infirmities (even the physical ones), my doubts, perturbations, struggles, fears, tears, torments and worries. And you say to me (your own words): "Write to me frequently and open your heart to me without reticence or reserve." I repeat once more that in order to tell you everything, I should have to speak to you, for the pen does not lend itself for this purpose. Indeed, you look after me too well and what is more, this is the fault of your immense goodness. Your charity is a constant incentive and encouragement to me.

You tire yourself out, therefore, in answering me. Do it a little at a time, half a page each day. This is a big penance among the many others you perform and that Jesus asks of you. And if you want to do another harder penance it will be to read my letters over again whenever you are inspired to write to me, to answer all my anxious questions, all my dark doubts which you no longer remember, while I am awaiting light and serenity from you alone!

I am too daring, I expect too much, I take advantage of you to a great extent. Forgive me, my good, good, holy

Father. Have you some secrets that you don't want to reveal to me? Don't be afraid, I certainly won't compromise you. You understand me. Please speak openly to me, explain to me all that Jesus tells you. Don't keep it all for yourself alone, I beg you on my knees.

You say to me, moreover (your own words): "You have many accounts to settle with me, for which I await your return home." Explain, my dear Father. Tell me frankly what these accounts are. Have the patience to explain yourself, for I am very stupid and I ask you to pardon me.

You also say: "You need to be a little more docile. You are still a rather capricious daughter and somewhat unmanageable." (Please explain also what you mean by this).

How thankful I am to you, good Father. But scold me more, much more and punish me severely, for I deserve much more. You also tell me that I didn't understand the most wise action of divine Providence, who bestowed peace of soul on my sister while I was looking merely for her bodily well-being with the peace it would bring. My dear Father, if you only knew how much I yearn for virtue and holiness in my Giovina! Jesus knows it and this is what I invariably ask of Him: first of all health of soul and then of body; spiritual peace in the first place and then temporal peace.

But undoubtedly in the case of such miserable creatures as we are, I must admit to you that if one does not enjoy peace, relative peace, in material things, in daily life, the soul can never enjoy the peace it needs. Driven like two leaves before the violent winds of arrogance, injustice, spitefulness, abuses and discord, how can we find peace in our own home? But what is more astonishing than anything else, I repeat, is that we did not find it even inside the four walls of a convent.

I am immensely glad and thank Jesus with all my heart for the change which has come about in my sister's spiritual state, as you tell me. However, she is worried all the time, sad and sometimes irritable, while at other moments she is more relaxed and taken up with her prayers. Daily Mass would be a great help to her, but either because the Masses were very early in Savona or because the church is not very near the house here in Modena, she has decided to attend only on Sundays.

I am ready to do anything in order to make it easy for her to go to church. She remains there very willingly, but either her health, or indolence, or some other circumstances keep her away continually. How is this to be explained? I am quite at a loss.

May the peace enjoyed by the worldly be far from us. Rather may the peace of Jesus which He has promised to men of goodwill never be lacking in our hearts, in our families, in the whole of society. I hope I have explained myself on the points on which you misunderstood me.

My sister has been quite well. (How can I thank Jesus sufficiently? Please do it for me). Here she has had no trouble with her stomach and we are quite tranquil in this blessed house. Jesus suggested to my sister this haven where we are safe from the clamour of the European war and from the no less dreadful and disastrous war waged by our brother and his wife. They have now moved to their own house, leaving our home stripped of everything. We shall hear a lot of things on our return home, which Giovina wants to fix for the 20th of this month.

Up here we are in ignorance of the unpleasant things and everything else that is going on, so as to avoid upsetting this poor martyr who is so greatly misunderstood. Still, on account of some news which has necessarily reached us my sister has suffered a shock which has made her weep and worry and torment herself, which has had an immediate effect on her stomach. For several days past she has been suffering physically and morally. I don't know what to do. I am disheartened and am suffering torment. These are agonizing struggles and dilemmas involving the solution of vital and decisive questions.

Prayer, light and good advice have not served to ward off conflicts, resounding clashes both moral and material, which I should have wished to avoid at present for the glory of God and to ensure peace and concord and affection among the last three survivors of a big family that has endured trials and torments of every description. I ought to say: "May God's will be done," but it costs me a dreadful lot to say it!

Will the "Way of the Cross" end here? I doubt it. Painful and belligerent consequences have followed. How long are they to go on? This is a mystery! I am weary by now and unable to bear this disruption of my home and of my unfortunate family. But supposing I myself have been, from the very beginning, the cause of all this? Should I suffer remorse for my whole life? Tell me frankly if this is so. You will be aware of everything, holy Father, and if it is true that I have been and still am the cause of this family conflict, it is only right that I myself and not other innocent people should suffer, expiate and make reparation.

Do you agree with me? Speak to Jesus about it on my behalf and let me know what is His most holy will and His answer.

Overwhelmed by it all, I implore along with my Giovina your holy blessing.

A poor tertiary.

P.S. You still have to explain to me why you told us to fly from Savona, which I beg you to do.

Here, again, is my present address: Palazzo Pagliani, Via Giardini 2. My new address in Foggia is: Via Manzoni, Foggia.

25

Pietrelcina, 19 September 1914.

Afflictions are a proof of love. The present state of her soul is good. The Christian's motto is the cross. Indisposition during prayer. The effects of our sufferings on those around us. Relationship with the rest of her family. Why he does not answer all her questions. His desire to die.

J.M.J.D.F.C.

Beloved daughter of Jesus Christ,

May Jesus and Mary always be with you. May they set you free from the cunning snares of the Evil One and console you in all your afflictions.

It breaks my heart to see you continually tossed about by new and furious storms, but I rejoice within me in the certainty that the fury of the waves in your case is permitted by a special providence of the heavenly Father, in order to make you similar to His beloved Son who was persecuted and tormented to the point of death, and death on the Cross!

The greater your sufferings the greater God's love for you. May they be, my dear, as the touchstone of His love for you. You will recognize God's love by this sign, by the sufferings He sends you. This sign is in your hands and your mind is capable of grasping it. Rejoice, then, at the very raging of the storm. Exult, I tell you, with the children of God, because all this is due to the most singular love of the divine Spouse for you. Humble yourself once more before the majesty of God and consider how many there are in the world who are more worthy than you, endowed with greater intellectual gifts and greater virtues, on whom God does not, unfortunately, lavish this most singular love which He shows in dealing with you.

Yes, this merciful Lord wants to be glorified in you, so take care not to become unfaithful to Him by denying Him the possibility to act freely and fully in you. Seeing you weighed down by so many anxieties and sufferings, I do not hide from you the fact that my lower nature, which is still very strong, would like to see you delivered from these torments. However, in the end the sight of the great benefit you receive from your enemies' attacks fills me with loving resignation to the divine will and, let me say so quite frankly, it makes me glad, for I consider your combat as a piling up of trophies.

Let Satan wage war either directly by his evil promptings, or indirectly by means of the world and our own corrupt nature. Let this unhappy apostate create an uproar, let him even threaten to swallow you up, it doesn't matter, for he can achieve nothing against your soul, which Jesus has now clasped to Himself and sustains in a mysterious manner by His ever-present grace. Cheer up, beloved daughter of Jesus, for I am telling you the truth: never before have you been so well spiritually as you are now.

Don't imagine that your sufferings have been inflicted on you in reparation for sins you committed, but consider that the Lord himself is afflicting you in order to adorn the diadem with the jewels He has decreed for you. Moreover, what must be the Christian's motto? Let us leave it to the Apostle of the Nations to tell us: *Do you not know*, says the holy Apostle, writing to the Romans, *that all of us who have been baptized into Christ Jesus were baptized into the death*[1]?

According to St. Paul, then, baptism by which we become children of God and heirs to His throne is a sign and a reproduction of the death of Christ and a sharing in His death. Baptism is a sign of the death of Jesus Christ because, just as Christ suffered by means of the Cross, baptism is conferred on us by the Sign of the Cross. Just as Jesus was placed in the sepulchre, we are immersed in the waters of holy baptism.

Baptism is, moreover, a sharing in the death of Jesus, for it applies the mysteries it represents and thus produces the effects of our Redeemer's death. The death of Christ is applied to us in baptism as if it were our own and as if we were crucified with Him. It is in virtue of this death that all our sins are wiped out, both sin itself and the punishment due to it.

Finally, baptism is said to be a reproduction of the death of Jesus. According to St. Paul we have been baptized *into His death*, that is, to imitate the death of our Redeemer. Hence, what the Cross was for Jesus Christ, baptism is for us. Jesus Christ was nailed to the Cross that He might die in the flesh. We are baptized that we may die to sin, that we may die to ourselves. Jesus Christ on the Cross was mortified in all His senses; similarly by baptism we must bring the mortification of Jesus to bear on all our senses. This, in point of fact, is what St. Paul writes in the second letter he sent to the faithful of Corinth: *Always carrying in the body the death of Jesus, so that the life of Jesus may also be manifested in our Bodies*[2].

Yes, my dear, let us be consoled when we find ourselves continually oppressed by suffering. Let us thank the divine

---

[1] Rom 6:3.
[2] 2 Cor 4:10.

mercy which makes us sharers in the Passion and Death of our divine Master. Until we are able to say: "This Christian is another Christ," do not let us pause in our ascent of the Hill of Calvary. Let us remember, when we are suffering torment, when we are attacked by Satan, that after Calvary comes Tabor, so that we may not yield to his promptings.

You tell me that on account of your sleepy, distracted, fickle and most wretched soul, frequently with the addition of physical complaints, you cannot bear to remain in church for more than an hour-and-a-half. Don't worry on this account, just try not to give in to this. Make an effort to overcome vexation and boredom and don't weary your mind excessively with very long and continued prayers when your heart and mind are not so inclined.

Try, meanwhile, to withdraw during the day, when possible, and in the silence of your heart and in solitude offer your praises, your blessings, your contrite and humble heart and your entire self to the heavenly Father. Thus, while the goodness of the divine Spouse is forgotten by the majority of His creatures made to His own image, let us remain always close to Him by these periods of withdrawal and these exercises.

You do well when you also desire to suffer physically and you do still better when you ask the Lord not to let those around you be troubled by your physical and moral sufferings. Continue to pray to Jesus for this intention, but if the Lord sometimes allows your troubles to cause annoyance to others, don't be distressed. Don't attempt to complain on this account, because the Lord is offering those others the means to acquire merit and you must not deprive them of this opportunity.

I am very pleased with your exquisite concern and desire to see an improvement in your dear sister, both spiritually and physically. Don't torment yourself, though, if you fail to see any rapid change in her. Let us silently adore the divine dispositions. You would like to see her become holy all at once, but this is not in our power, no matter how holy our desire for it may be.

For your own part, don't fail to use that holy diligence with which Providence has endowed you, to draw her closer to Jesus by the fragrance and the practice of the holy virtues.

It makes my heart ache to hear that the conflicts with your brother show no sign of coming to an end. Let us adore in silence God's designs when He allows this situation to continue as a further test of faithfulness on the part of both of you. Pray to the Lord that all may work out for His glory and for the good of souls. I don't need to tell you how much I am praying for all your intentions and especially for this matter of your brother. I call on God to witness the truth of what I am telling you.

After all, the Lord is so good that He never fails to tone things down. The storm will not be as furious as you imagine. Don't worry about it, and make sure to sustain in mind and body that poor "misunderstood martyr," your sister.

You ask me if in this business of your brother, which torments you so grievously, it is possible that you yourself are the cause of such painful consequences. I don't see any fault of yours in this. What do you say yourself? Are you aware before God of your guilt in this respect? It's about time for you to calm yourself and put an end to these fantastic doubts.

My dear, we don't commit a sin without first being aware of it. Undoubtedly, even after all these assurances you still have doubts, and thus you begin all over again. There is need for a little more docility in your attitude. For the second time I tell you, and very much to the point, that you are still a rather capricious daughter and somewhat unmanageable. I hope you now thoroughly understand this expression of mine. If not, don't hesitate to let me know.

A great misfortune was about to occur, especially

beneath the beautiful sky of Savona. Victims and prayers succeeded, at least for the moment, in restraining God's anger. Your departure from that city was imposed on me from above and I could not ignore that injunction. I should have liked very much to spare you such emotion, but one doesn't go against God.

My desire would be to satisfy all your questions but you know very well, as I told you in a previous letter, how liable I am to forget. So when I fail to answer your questions, please keep on reminding me until you get an answer. You who are so compassionate must understand me if I am asking too much of you. I am not at fault in this forgetfulness and I cannot find words to tell you how much it distresses me.

As regards the accounts to be settled when you return home, there will be something to say later. Don't be worried on this score, as they are accounts which can easily be settled.

I end here as I am really unable to go on. Don't forget me before the Lord; I am unfortunate from every point of view. I am greatly in need of the divine assistance in order to bear the trial to which God has been pleased to subject me.

Don't be selfish; ask our most sweet Jesus to undo without delay the harsh fetters of this body. I am continually dying a thousand deaths for the sole reason that I myself am still alive and far from my heavenly home. Don't deny me this charity; from up above I'll be able to do more for you, because I'll be closer to the source of life.

May Jesus protect and console you together with your sister, while your humble servant never ceases to pray to Him for this intention.

Fra Pio.

26

Foggia, 8 October 1914.

She returns home after seven years in exile. Without sacramental Communion. The chapel in her home. Her sister's illness. The walled-up door. "I rely on these words of yours."

Jesus alone! Holy Spirit, help me!

Reverend Padre Pio,

With the help of God, in the company of Jesus, Mary and Joseph and of the Guardian Angels (especially your own) we arrived home safe and sound on the 23rd of last month after an absence of a full three months.

We are back at last in our old home, in our father's house in which we were born, after seven years spent in exile. It seems to us that we have come from another world. Our still and silent house with the big terrace and the arbour creates for me the illusion of a convent. Towards sundown the immense solitude fills me in spite of myself with melancholy, with a deep sadness. For me this is a sin, I know, and I want to get the better of myself, to appear happy, to smile at all times, at all hours of the day. How am I to do it? I just don't know.

In addition, a film is passing continually before my mental gaze: in every corner of the house I behold my dear departed ones, my parents, my four brothers, a sister[1], uncles and grand-uncles, and further back, grandparents and other relatives. I hear all their well-known voices and hope I receive their blessing.

To tell the truth, I should have liked to have the blessing of Jesus, through His minister, come down at once on this unfortunate home of mine, but for the present this is not possible. We found everything in great disorder and it is still in the same state. General repairs are urgently required, but Giovina has postponed them until the spring as we are already into the cold season. We'll get ourselves fixed up as well as we can, but when? Who knows? I am in a state of great agitation and am irritated with my sister who says I scandalize her by my failure to adapt myself, which is quite true. But it is also true that she seems to me, which is unusual, to be systematically perverse, capricious and impossible to satisfy. In her case in theory, in my own case in practice. I just don't know what I am to do.

On arrival here I was unable for three days to go down for Mass to my dear little church, St. Joseph's, a few yards away from my home. Last Sunday I took up my normal habits again, but always hastily, distractedly, until Friday, when I ran a temperature with a severe pain in the chest, on the left side (which I hid completely from Giovina). Later

---

[1] It is not possible to give full particulars of the Cerase family, as there is no record of them in the municipal files in Foggia. On a tombstone in Foggia cemetery we find an inscription stating that the head of the family, Michele Cerase, son of Matteo (Michele died on 6 October 1904), "with a husband's love and a father's tenderness, inspired by deep religious sentiments, brought together in the same tomb the bones of his wife, Maria Barisani, and of his sons Raffaele Giuseppe and Salvatore Luigi Pasquale in 1892. His son Matteo died 10 October 1924; his daughter Anna, married to Antonio Zicari, died in Naples at 53 years of age, 20 March 1909 and was buried in Foggia. Luigia Raffaella (Raffaelina), aged 47, died at 5 a.m. on 25 March 1916; Giovina, aged 70, died 6 October 1931.

the pain disappeared miraculously, just as I was miraculously saved last winter from pleurisy on the right side (which has left me very fearful and cautious, certainly not for my own sake, but for the sake of this blessed sister). Hence, a further three days privation, without leaving the house.

On the feast of our dear Mother of Pompeii and of our holy Patriarch this privation made me very downcast. I am an unworthy child of Mary and a false tertiary, which is why they did not want to accept anything from me on that day. (Is this really a fact? Tell me; have the kindness to answer me).

I am in dreadful distress. Mind and tongue and heart fail to render to Jesus that which they ought and need to offer Him and which would satisfy them. I am greatly tormented and don't know what to do.

Here in this holy solitude I ought to begin the work of my conversion. I sense this and am aware that Jesus desires it, but indolence, forgetfulness, distraction and confusion get the better of me and I remain frightened, disheartened and weary.

Help me, holy Father, instruct me (answer me on this point). In this respect, moreover, I have a great deal to tell you! I'll do this later on in another letter when I'll try to have greater calm and order in my poor weak mind.

Did I not suffer the same privation in Modena on the feast of my dear Mother of Sorrows, when I was confined to bed the previous day with a severe headache?

Since then Giovina has been afraid to let me go to church early in the morning and she is in a continual state of agitation. I have to listen to her all the time, to her fears and her alarms. I have decided from now on to have Mass celebrated here in the house on a temporary altar during the winter months. The necessary steps have yet to be taken.

For the moment it isn't possible to have a chapel, because we have no room sufficiently isolated for the purpose. Later on, when the contract expires, we'll be able to use a part of the house which has been rented as an office for several years. Tell all this to Jesus on my behalf and let me know His answer. Please don't forget it.

By your worthy prayers, then, hasten all the necessary steps for the installation of this temporary altar, otherwise I'll be deprived of who knows how many Communions and these privations will amount to a series of Lents extended for months and months.

Apart from myself, Giovina will find it very convenient to hear Mass every morning without being exposed to the cold air which does her so much harm. She is fairly free from her stomach trouble at present, thank God. Thank Him yourself also. Through a series of unforeseen circumstances which it would take too long to relate, she was unable to have a medical examination in Bologna. However, she was advised by some experienced people to go to a stomach specialist in Modena for an examination, which she did. He made a thorough examination which was quite satisfactory. The diagnosis is that her liver is affected and she has stones which are still small. The doctor prescribed a suitable treatment and warned her that if she neglected it her illness would become really serious.

I confess that I consider the diagnosis to be mistaken, for I fear she has something worse. You can remove this doubt of mine which is killing me. Tell Jesus about it and ask Him if the diagnosis is correct and exact, then let me know the answer. Don't forget it.

With God's help we survived the horrid and bitter surprise prepared for us by our brother, that is, the walled-up door. Similarly, with His help, we overcame the serious matter of separation: the quite unexpected solution of the knotty problem which had tormented us for ten years, ten years of conflicts and tears.

Communication between us is therefore cut off. The Lord will have arranged things in this way for His own glory and the greater peace of our souls. What have you to say about it? Speak to me and do not forget it. On Sundays we are there in the same church and they look at us like strangers, or rather like enemies. What will they say when they see me approaching the altar to receive the God of love and peace? Moreover, what scandal is given to others! I am suffering and offering it up to God.

On the other hand, all are aware of the facts and of the reasons involved. Pray for holy peace and for some sort of agreement. Another matter remains to be cleared up between us. Pray hard to Jesus to settle this matter without delay so as to prevent further sins. I'll tell you about this some other time. I take too great advantage of your charity and in the name of this same charity I beg you to answer me fully, without forgetting anything.

My good Father, I have given you a little respite by delaying my answer to your last letter which reached me on the 20th of last month. Here are your own words: "He can achieve nothing against your soul which Jesus has now clasped to Himself and sustains in a mysterious manner by His ever-present grace. Cheer up, beloved daugther of Jesus, for I am telling you the truth: never before have you been so well spiritually as you are now."

I rely on these solemn words of yours. I am a little too confident and take too much advantage. I am going calmly on without anxiety or fear, yet a horrible doubt perturbs me, the thought that I am under a great illusion. But what I write to you is true, I feel sure of this. And even if I were to harbour illusions as to my spiritual state, you, to whom all is clear and all is known, could never, never deceive me, for you receive light directly from the One who is essentially light, who can neither deceive nor be deceived.

The thick darkness has been dispelled in my guilty conscience, enlightened by the One who speaks to you heart to heart, whom you see with open eyes close beside you, in loving ecstasy. Hence, there is no illusion, no deception, no guile, of this I can be sure. Speak to me, my good good, holy holy Father. Forgive me, have pity on me and bless me along with Giovina and my friend.

A poor tertiary.

P.S. I enclose ten lire on behalf of my sister for five Masses, that is, four Masses for the repose of our dear father's soul and the fifth in thanksgiving to St. Joseph.

27

Pietrelcina, 10 October 1914.

A visit in spirit. Reading spiritual books. In what true peace consists. Contempt for "things that afflict" her. "Let us aim at invisible things." Fighting against melancholy. Avoiding immoderate anxiety. He thanks her and asks for prayers.

J.M.J.D.F.C.

Beloved daughter of Jesus,

May the grace of Our Lord Jesus Christ be always with you. My love for you in Jesus Christ. Blessed be God the Father of Our Lord Jesus Christ, the Father of mercies and God of all comfort[1], who, in His goodness, has allowed me during these days to visit you in spirit. Did you have no inkling of that visit? May it please Jesus who consoles me in every affliction to console you also, through me, in every tribulation.

My dear sister, I don't want you to be unaware of my distress on your account, which is so great that it makes me regret that I am alive. I have tried up to the present to bottle it up in my heart, but now the charity of Christ which *urges us*[2] impels and stimulates me and gives me no peace until I make it known to you.

---

[1] Cf. 2 Cor 1:3.
[2] 2 Cor 5:14.

Don't think that I wanted to exaggerate and make the matter appear more than it is, or that I meant to reprove you harshly about it, although I don't intend to praise you. May exaggeration and reproof be a thousand miles away. I merely want to warn you as a beloved sister.

I pointed out to you elsewhere the great spiritual benefit to be gained by reading holy books. I also showed you the need for such reading in the case of those who are seeking Christian perfection. Finally, I added my heartfelt prayer to induce you also to take up this holy exercise. Up to the present you have disregarded all this.

I understand that from a certain point of view you can be excused, as it has been almost impossible for you to do anything about it up to the present. However, you are not completely justified in this, for with a little goodwill you could have done something. This is what I was referring to when I told you that you would have an account to settle with me on your return home. I did not want to show you my rightful disapproval at the time, as I knew you were already suffering sufficiently. Since I didn't want to add suffering to suffering I decided to keep my displeasure to myself.

Now, however, you are in your own home and I cannot tolerate that your soul remain deprived of such healthful food. It is time for you to come out of that state of indifference, for if you continue as before, it could be fatal for you, since the lack of that reading is depriving you of a great many spiritual benefits.

I repeat that I am most anxious to see you take up such reading as soon as possible, freeing yourself from all undue prejudice in this regard. I also want to remind you that I desire to be kept informed as to the books you use, or rather the books you want to use. In this matter I cannot treat you in any other way.

Oh, how desirable it would be for your very dear sister to do likewise! I am perfectly well aware that in this respect she is much more in need than you are, but I should be careful not to make this need known to her. I have no sort of right to do so as nobody has authorized me to counsel her. I leave all this to you and rely on the holy diligence with which the Lord has endowed you so abundantly. Now, however, you must begin to take care of yourself.

I take the liberty of suggesting some books to you which make suitable reading in your present state of soul. The *Life of St. Teresa*, written by herself, the *Way of Perfection* and the *Interior Castle*[3]; the *Confessions of St. Augustine*[4]; Monsabré's exposition of Catholic dogma in 18 small volumes[5], the reading of which is a real spiritual feast. These are the books I suggest at present. God will provide later on.

In one of your letters you complained that you and your sister had left your own town in search of a little peace and had failed to find it even inside the cloister of those good nuns in Savona[6].

I pointed out to you that you were wrong in this respect and, if I am not mistaken, I used an expression which you misunderstood. I said that if you meant peace as worldlings understand it, then you were right in saying you didn't find it even in that holy enclosure. But since I know you and was well aware that you detested the peace sought by worldlings, just as you detest the author of that peace, the devil, I made an effort to explain briefly to you that without realizing it you have reached the true peace of which Jesus is the author,

---

[3] It is not possible to discover what edition of St. Teresa's works he was referring to here. In the list of the books used by Padre Pio no works of this saint are mentioned. Cf. GERARDO DI FLUMERI, "I libri di studio di Padre Pio," in *La Voce di Padre Pio*, July-August, 1973, p. 24.

[4] The same applies to the *Confessions of St. Augustine*.

[5] Cf. *Introduzione al dogma cattolico. Conferenze*, by Rev. G.M.L. Monsabré, O.P. Version with notes by Mgr. Geremia Bonomelli, Turin and Cremona, 1889 and following years.

[6] See p. 169.

even though you believe the very opposite to be the case[7].

You answered me by saying that I had misunderstood you when you spoke of peace, just because I had written: "if you mean peace as worldlings understand it, then you are right in saying you didn't find it even in the cloister."[8]

It is well to explain the matter clearly to you now. By that expression of mine I didn't mean that this was the kind of peace you were seeking, much less did I intend to rebuke you for it. If I had found you at fault in this respect you may be quite sure that I should never have stopped there and confined myself to such a plain, unvarnished statement.

I blame myself for having involuntarily caused you spiritual suffering. Please be indulgent towards me: before God I am aware that I acted with a right intention.

What I want you to do now is to turn your back on these matters which torment you, as they are harmful to your soul, and to set your mind at rest, for you have no reason whatever to worry. I have your eternal salvation very much at heart, no less than my own salvation. God alone knows how distressed and heartbroken I am to see you at grips with our common enemy. God alone knows what tears I shed in the presence of Jesus so that He may grant you complete victory over the enemy. And even when I see you free from the enemy's attacks, don't think I am not praying for you. I am not lying when I assure you that I present you to Jesus no less than 50 times a day.

Now, if your salvation is of such concern to me, judge for yourself if by a deplorable silence on my part I can allow you to follow any other path than the one willed by Jesus. Don't doubt that whenever I perceive this to be the case, I'll be inexorable and unyielding towards you, for if I were to act otherwise I myself should know no peace.

---

[7] See Letter 23, p. 171.

[8] See Letter 24, p. 176.

Remember, moreover, that spiritual peace can be maintained even in the midst of all the storms of this life. As you know very well, it consists essentially in peaceful relations with those around us, wishing them well in all things. It also consists in being on good terms with God through sanctifying grace. The proof that we are united to God is our moral certainty of not having any mortal sin on our conscience. To sum up, peace consists in having achieved victory over the world, the devil and our own passions.

Tell me, now, if it is not true that this peace which Jesus has brought us can continue quite well to be ours not merely when we enjoy abundant spiritual consolations but when the howling and shrieking of the enemy fills our hearts with pain and grief?

I don't deny that when I see you so ill-treated I become very upset and would like our merciful Jesus to pour these sufferings into my own heart. Jesus does not always hear me in this respect. May His will be done. In order that we may willingly accept the tribulations lavished on us by the divine mercy, let us keep our gaze fixed on the heavenly home reserved for us; let us constantly contemplate it and aim at it with the greatest care. Let us withdraw our gaze, moreover, from those good things which are visible to our eyes, by which I mean worldly goods, the sight of which fascinates and distracts the soul and contaminates the heart. Worldly goods prevent us from keeping our eyes fixed on our heavenly home.

Let us listen to what the Lord tells us on this subject by the mouth of His holy apostle Paul: *We look not to the things that are seen, but to the things that are unseen*[9]. It is quite right that we should contemplate heavenly things while attaching no importance to those of this world, since the former are eternal while the latter are merely transient.

What should we say if we were to behold a poor pea-

---

[9] 2 Cor 4:18.

sant almost stupefied as he continued to gaze at a swiftly-flowing river? Perhaps we should just begin to laugh at him and with good reason. Is it not folly to fix our gaze on something that is rapidly passing? This, then, is the state of a person who fixes his eyes on visible things. For what are these things in reality? Are they perhaps different from a swiftly-flowing river on whose waters we have no sooner laid eyes than they disappear from our sight, never to be seen again?

Let the consideration of all those good things to be possessed in that realm provide us with delightful food for our thoughts. Enchanted by these eternal delights our minds to distinguish what is valuable from what is worthless. As for ourselves who have been called, through the goodness of the Most High God, to reign with the divine Bridegroom, whose minds are enlightened by God's true light, let us fix our gaze constantly on the splendour of the heavenly Jerusalem.

Let the consideration of all those good things to be possessed in that realm provide us with delightful food for our thoughts. Enchanted by these eternal delights our minds will then inflame our hearts with love for them. Only then, despite the fact that we are pilgrims in a foreign land, in a valley of tears, surrounded by apparent beauty, by enticements and illusions, only then shall we be able to repeat with full conviction along with the indomitable martyr St. Ignatius: *Oh, how worthless is the earth, when I look at heaven*[10]*!*

I bless the Lord for having brought you at last to the home of your forefathers. I earnestly hope your stay there will be a long and holy one, under the powerful protection of the good angel of the house. I hope the melancholy which is brought on by solitude in the evenings will not trouble you much longer. Fortify yourself against it beforehand and don't

---

[10] Cf. St. Ignatius, *Letters*.

give in, much less place your trust in yourself. Let us expect every good thing from above. Whenever you are seized by melancholy, let your thoughts dwell on that fateful night on which the Son of God began the work of Redemption in the solitude of Gethsemane and offer your own sufferings to the divine Father along with the sufferings of Jesus.

You must also have recourse to some good reading and avoid those distressing readings which are not suitable for you. If, after all this, you still feel depressed, then apply yourself to some manual work or something which distracts you. You might even start singing some cheerful song and if possible invite others to sing with you.

I also want you to talk about this to your sister and to Rosina[11] who is so good. Don't worry, for all will work out for the triumph of God's glory.

If the memory of your dear deceased ones comes before your mind, recommend them all to the Lord and go ahead without dwelling further on the matter. See to it that you submit your own judgment to that of your sister, also in everything concerning your daily food. I want you to extend this submission to everything in which you do not perceive any slightest offence against God.

Don't be excessively anxious about the repairs to be carried out on the house. I beseech you to let Giovina deal with all this. By this I don't mean that you are not to make your views known, much less do I intend to forbid you to do so. Speak out when you think your point of view is better, but I beg you not to pester poor Giovina with your views.

The Blessed Virgin of Pompeii and our Seraphic Father St. Francis will be more pleased, on their respective feasts, if you willingly accept your physical and moral sufferings rather than undertaking bodily fasts. This is what they wanted

[11] A servant in the Cerase home, who will often be mentioned in these pages. See p. 253.

from you on those holy days and let us unite in blessing their most singular love for you.

Try to have Mass in your home in whatever way is best during the severely cold days of the coming winter. Jesus will be very happy about this. Apart from the good you would do to all in the house by this, you would also relieve poor Giovina of her fatal anxiety, as she has reason to be worried about your weak health.

It will be well for your sister to follow exactly the prescriptions of the Modena specialist for the present. Later on, with the divine assistance, something can be done. Please don't be alarmed about her illness. You are making a great mistake by being so pessimistic.

Recommend your brother and his wife to the Lord continually, that He may bring them to a more reasonable frame of mind with regard to you and your sister. Bear this cross which Jesus has offered you and have no fear, for even in this matter Jesus must be glorified.

It is the cunning of the Evil One which leads you to believe yourself the victim of illusion. Despise this diabolical suggestion and don't attempt to let your mind dwell upon it. Are you satisfied? I hope so. I don't intend to waste time on this point, so that my silence may give you to understand how far you are from the truth when you suspect that you are under an illusion.

I had every intention of continuing but for reasons well known to you I am unable to go any further. May Jesus thank and reward Giovina on my behalf for the Mass offerings she has been so kind as to send me. Dear God, what trouble people go to on behalf of my wretched person! What consideration is shown for one who rebels all the time against God's grace! Praise be to the divine mercy!

I should like to ask you, if it is not inconvenient, to do me the kindness of making three consecutive novenas to the Virgin of Pompeii for a grace to be obtained for me from her Son, a grace which will mean a great deal for a certain soul.

During the last few days one of my brother's little boys has died[12]. Pray to Jesus to comfort them all, especially the child's inconsolable parents and above all my poor afflicted sister-in-law.

I send greetings to all in the Lord's holy embrace, while I beseech all of you to pray to the heavenly Father, as I myself do for you, that He may free me from the clutches of our common enemy.

Your servant,
Fra Pio.

P.S. Write to me often and as soon as this reaches you send me a picture postcard. I should like to know if you find it difficult to read my handwriting. Your last letter reached me just as I was about to close this.

---

[12] A little son of Michele (1882-1967), Padre Pio's brother.

28

Foggia, 21 October 1914.

Her illness. When and how did he visit her in spirit? Her reason for not replying sooner. Again without Communion. "Speak to me at great length." Postscript.

Jesus alone! Most Holy Spirit, help me!

Reverend Padre Pio,

I am writing you just a few words from my bed. For several days past I have had a very high fever due to influenza, with pains so acute as to make me weep like a child. (What will Jesus think of me?) In the midst of my sufferings I very often invoke you and call out to you! And you, good Father, do you hear me? Do you answer me? Please tell me.

As regards the visit you were so good as to pay me in spirit (how kind you are to this ungrateful daughter undeserving of anything) what day was it and at what time did it occur? Have the patience to tell me and don't forget it. Wretched creature that I am, I was not aware of anything.

I feel deep remorse of conscience. You ought to have had a card on the 10th of this month, but I did not send it as I always want to write very long letters to my holy Father, which try his invincible patience and charity. But I never found the time to write, extremely busy as I was all the time with household matters and visits each day.

When Jesus will allow me to leave my bed and when I am free to do as I choose, I'll reply to your letter in detail. For the moment all I can do is to dash off these few hasty lines to let you know the reason for my long silence.

The gift[1] I received from Our Lady of Pompeii and from St. Francis was repeated on the feast of my own patron, St. Raphael, namely, privation of Holy Communion. This convinces me more and more that my Communions are not good or acceptable.

Speak to Jesus about these most unworthy Communions of mine, of the Masses I hear (this is my own very special way of helping you), of all the prayers, in general, that I say. Speak to Jesus about it and let me know his answer.

When shall I be able to go to church? I see this day very far off. This year I have fallen ill too soon. Imagine how perplexed Giovina is and how inexorable she will be about my going out. (My poor sister! How she suffers on my account! May Jesus do something, just for her sake, as I have no right to torture her in this way). My fasting from Communion will continue. Pray to Jesus, bring pressure to bear on him for this chapel, always if it pleases him.

I am unable to continue. This position makes my pains worse. May Jesus be blessed! Here I am, in idleness, a nuisance to others. Blessed be Jesus for ever! Write to me, speak to me at great length, my good good, holy holy Father. Pray for me, bless me.

Your poor tertiary.

---

[1] She alludes ironically to privation of Holy Communion as a "gift," with reference to what she wrote to Padre Pio in her previous letter, p. 190.

P.S. I am not obedient, I haven't the patience to suffer and I am giving great scandal to others. Ask Jesus to forgive me.

Just now one of your friars[2] has come to pay me a farewell visit. He is Giovina's confessor and is leaving here. A further blow for my sister. Pray.

---

[2] Probably Padre Bernardino of Guardialfiera, "a religious deserving of admiration and imitation" who was transferred from Foggia to Tora between 15 and 22 October 1914. He was born 26 March 1867 and died 19 April 1920. Cf. CIPRIANO DA SERRACAPRIOLA, *Necrologia*, p. 269.

29

Pietrelcina, 23 October 1914.

Feastday greetings and prayers. The spirit of wisdom: three principal considerations. Christian perfection: internal and external elements. How we must act: mortification and self-denial. Postscript.

J.M.J.D.F.C.

Beloved daughter of Jesus,

May the grace of the Lord Jesus Christ and the love of God and the fellowship of the Holy Spirit[1] be always with you and with your family.

Jesus wants me to write to you for your feastday and I therefore willingly do so. Imagine what my feelings are as I send you my greetings for this day. You are no stranger to my sentiments with regard to your spiritual and corporal well-being and thus we understand each other.

May our most sweet Jesus redouble His heavenly blessings upon you and invariably give you the strength to overcome all the snares of our common enemy. I don't wish you worldly happiness and prosperity, both because such things are by no means suited to a soul espoused to the Crucified and because you have no desire for them.

[1] Cf. 2 Cor 13:14.

Take care not to heed the Evil One if he suggests anything to you with regard to my concern for you. Don't listen to him, for you know he is a liar. Listen to Jesus alone who comes to you in His own name, and that is enough.

Unworthy as I am, although I pray continually for your growth in the spiritual life, I promise you that on your feast-day I will send up my feeble pleas to God's throne with greater confidence and filial abandonment, imploring Him and doing gentle violence to His divine Heart so that He may grant me the grace of increasing heavenly wisdom in your soul, so that you may have a clearer knowledge of the divine mysteries and of God's immensity.

Yes, ask for this grace yourself and ask the heavenly Father to grant it also to me. Do this through the intercession of the saint whose name you bear and through your good Guardian Angel as well. This is the finest grace that can be asked by and on behalf of those who aspire to the spiritual life, namely, an increase of heavenly light. This is a light which cannot be acquired either by prolonged study or through human teaching, but which is directly infused by God. When the righteous soul obtains this light, it comes to know and love its God and eternal things in its meditations with extreme clarity and relish. Although it is nothing but a light of faith, it is still sufficient to produce such spiritual consolation that the earth, in the first place, disappears from view, while all that this world can offer is seen to be worthless.

We must ask the Spirit, the Comforter, to enlighten us with regard to three great truths in particular. Firstly, to make us increasingly aware of the excellence of our Christian vocation. The fact of having been chosen, having been elected among innumerable others and knowing that without any merit on our part, this choice, this election was decided by God from all eternity, *before the foundation of the world*[2],

---

[2] Jn 17:24; Eph 1:4.

for the sole reason that we might be His in time and in eternity, is such a great and at the same time such an enchanting mystery that the soul, even though it understands so little of all this, cannot but melt away with love.

Secondly, let us pray that He may enlighten us more and more as to the immensity of the eternal inheritance which has been reserved for us by the goodness of the heavenly Father. May our discernment of this mystery turn our hearts away from earthly goods and make us eager to arrive at our heavenly home.

Finally, let us pray to the Father of all light to enable us to penetrate more and more deeply into the mystery of our justification, how wretched sinners like ourselves have been led to salvation. Our justification is such an enormous miracle that Sacred Scripture compares it to the Resurrection of our divine Master[3]. Yes, my dear, our conversion from ungodliness is such that it can well be said that God revealed His power more fully in our justification than in drawing heaven and earth from nothing, since there is a greater contrast between the sinner and grace than there is between non-existence and being. Non-existence is less far from God than is the sinner. In point of fact, since non-existence is the lack of being, it has no power to resist God's will, while the sinner as a being, and a free being, is capable of resisting all God's wishes. Besides, in creation there is question of the natural order, while the justification of the ungodly belongs to the supernatural and divine order.

Oh! If all men could only understand the extreme wretchedness and dishonour from which God's omnipotent hand has rescued us. Oh! If we could only perceive for a single instant that which still amazes the heavenly spirits themselves, namely, the state to which God's grace has raised us, to be

---

[3] Rom 4:25.

nothing less than His own children, destined to reign with His Son for all eternity!

When it is granted to a human being to fathom this, that person cannot live anything but a heavenly life. O wretched condition of human nature! How often would the heavenly Father not be willing to reveal His secrets to us were He not compelled to do otherwise, since by our own malice we have rendered ourselves incapable of receiving these secrets. May the Lord be pleased to put an end to such squalor and wretchedness. May Satan's kingdom come to an end once and for all and may justice triumph everywhere.

In our meditations let us frequently dwell on the truths which I have set forth so far, for in this way we shall be strengthened in virtue and our thinking will be rendered more sublime.

Certain that it will give you pleasure, I want to speak to you about something very useful, namely, Christian perfection. I already feel my strength failing me and it would be well to end this letter here, but since Jesus wants me to speak to you a little on the subject I have mentioned, I am making every possible effort to satisfy Him.

(a) The person who desires to be perfect needs to undertake a twofold action: internal action and external action. Let us speak a little, in the first place, about the former, while we can deal with the latter afterwards.

The first virtue required by the person who is striving for perfection is charity. In all natural things, the first movement, the first inclination or impulse is to tend towards the centre, in obedience to a physical law. The same thing happens in the supernatural sphere: the first movement of our hearts is a movement towards God, which is nothing more than loving our own true good. With good reason Sacred Scripture speaks of charity as the bond of perfect harmony[4].

---

[4] Cf. Col 3:14.

Charity has as its close relatives joy and peace. Joy is born of happiness at possessing what we love. Now, from the moment at which the soul knows God, it is naturally led to love Him. If the soul follows this natural impulse which is caused by the Holy Spirit, it is already loving the Supreme Good. This fortunate soul already possesses the beautiful virtue of love. By loving God the soul is certain of possessing Him. When a person loves money, honours and good health, unfortunately, he does not always possess what he loves, whereas he who loves God possesses Him at once.

This idea is not the product of my own mind but is to be found in Holy Scripture where we read: *He who abides in love abides in God, and God abides in him*[5]. What does this scriptural passage mean to tell us? Does it not, perhaps, mean that the soul devoted to God out of love belongs entirely to God, while God gives Himself entirely to that soul?

Joy, then, is an offspring of love, but if this joy is to be true and perfect it must be accompanied inseparably by the peace which pervades us when the good we possess is supreme and certain. Now, is not God the Supreme Good which the soul loves and which it possesses as the result of loving Him?

This Good, as well as being supreme, must also be certain. Our divine Master assures us that *no one will take your joy from you*[6]. What testimony could be more certain than this? Pondering on all this one cannot fail to experience great gladness. This is what leads people to face the most painful trials with a cheerful heart.

It must be noted, however, that as long as we are wayfarers on this earth we can never be perfect, and hence we can never enjoy perfect peace. Trials and contradictions are so many and the conflicts by which the soul is harassed

[5] 1 Jn 4:16.
[6] Jn 16:22.

so numerous as to cause it agony at times, to the point at which life itself becomes unbearable. All this arises because the soul sees itself in danger of utter ruin.

Now, to stand up to such harsh trials the soul needs patience, a virtue which enables us to bear all adversity without giving in. Those who are striving for perfection must attribute great importance to this virtue unless they want their efforts to be completely wasted, for it is this virtue which maintains order in one's interior life.

From what has been said up to this point it is clear that love, joy and peace are virtues which perfect the soul with regard to what it possesses, while patience perfects it with regard to what it endures.

(b) This is what is required for interior perfection. As regards exterior perfection, certain virtues are required, some of which concern the manner in which the one seeking perfection must behave towards those around him, while others concern the control of his own senses.

As regards the virtues to be practised in dealing with others, the first is kindliness. By this virtue the pious soul, by showing agreeable, courteous and polite manners with no trace of uncouthness, draws others to imitate him in the devout life.

But all this is still very little. We must come down to actual practice and here at once we have kindliness, a virtue which leads us to be helpful to others. Here it is well to point out two very important things to those who are striving for perfection. First of all, they must be aware of it if the other person is not responding to the help that is being offered him. Secondly, they must realize it when the other person not only fails to derive benefit from their help but, what is worse, responds at times with offences and insults. The undiscerning are often deceived here. May God forbid that we should fall into such snares prepared for us by the enemy in order to ruin us and deprive us of the reward due to our efforts.

We must therefore arm ourselves against the first snare by the noble virtue of forbearance. This is a virtue which leads one never to desist from one's efforts to help others, even when they are deriving no benefit from this help. We must protect ourselves against the second snare by cultivating meekness, which makes us stifle our anger even when we see our efforts repaid with ingratitude, insults and offences.

But all these fine virtues are not yet sufficient if we do not add to them the virtue of faithfulness, by which the devout soul gains the confidence of others and all become aware that his behaviour is straightforward and free from duplicity.

There are, moreover, three virtues which perfect the devout person with regard to control of his own senses. These are: modesty, continence and chastity. By the virtue of modesty the devout person governs all his exterior acts. With good reason, then, does St. Paul recommend this virtue to all and declare how necessary it is[7]; and as if this were not enough he considers that this virtue should be obvious to all. By continence the soul exercises restraint over all the senses: sight, touch, taste, smell and hearing. By chastity, a virtue which ennobles our nature and makes it similar to that of the Angels, we suppress our sensuality and detach it from forbidden pleasures.

This is the magnificent picture of Christian perfection. Happy the one who possesses all these fine virtues, all of them fruits of the Holy Spirit who dwells within him. Such a soul has nothing to fear and will shine in the world as the sun in the heavens.

Let us now consider what we must do to ensure that the Holy Spirit may dwell in our souls. It can all be summed up in mortification of the flesh with its vices and concupiscences, and in guarding against a selfish spirit.

---

[7] Cf. Phil 4:5.

As regards mortification of the flesh St. Paul warns us that those who belong to *Christ Jesus have crucified the flesh with its passions and desires*[8]. From this holy apostle's teaching it is apparent that anyone who wants to be a true Christian, that is to say, who lives according to the true spirit of Jesus Christ must mortify his flesh for no other reason than devotion to Jesus, who for love of us mortified his entire body on the cross. The mortification must be constant and steady, not intermittent, and it must last for one's whole life. Moreover, the perfect Christian must not be satisfied with a kind of mortification which merely appears to be severe. He must make sure that it hurts.

This is how mortification of the body is to be practised, for not without reason does the apostle call it crucifixion. However, someone may take a stand against this and ask why the flesh is to be treated so severely. Foolish one, for if you considered your words attentively, you would realize that all the evils which hurt your soul can be traced to failure to practise due mortification of the flesh, either through ignorance or lack of the will to do so. If you want to be cured, if you want to remedy your trouble at the very roots, you must master your flesh and crucify it, for it is the source of all evil.

The apostle adds that crucifixion of the flesh is to be combined with crucifixion of the vices and concupiscences. Now our vices are all our sinful habits, while the concupiscences are our passions. We must mortify and crucify them continually if they are not to lead to sins of the flesh. A man who limits himself to bodily mortification is like the fool who builds without laying any foundation.

I also said that if we are to allow the Holy Spirit freedom to act in our souls, we must mount guard over the spirit of self which, if we are not careful, seeps in even when we have mortified the flesh.

---

[8] Gal 5:24.

I began with the apostle and I intend to continue with him to the end. Whenever I read his Letters, which I prefer to all other holy writings, words cannot express how much I relish them. Well, then, he tells us in this respect: *If we live by the Spirit, let us also walk by the Spirit*[9], as if he wished to say for our edification: Do we want to live a spiritual life, moved and guided by the Spirit of the Lord? Let us take care, then, to mortify our selfish spirit which puffs us up, makes us impulsive and leads to aridity of soul. In a word, we must be careful to subdue vainglory, irascibility and envy, three evil spirits to which most men are slaves. These three spirits are extremely opposed to the Spirit of the Lord.

I hope with God's help to show you in a further letter the vileness of these three spirits: vainglory, irascibility and envy. For the moment this will suffice, for I have no more strength. For the past few days I have been more ill than usual. May God's will be done. Meanwhile, let us end with the words of the holy apostle: *Let us have no self-conceit, no provoking of one another, no envy of one another*[10].

I send greetings to all in the Lord's embrace, wishing you His choicest blessings.

Believe me, as ever,

Your poor servant,
Fra Pio, Capuchin.

P.S. Whenever you find anything in my letters which you do not sufficiently understand, please ask me for an explanation. I am saying this once and for all. I don't want to work in vain and fail to obtain the result intended by Jesus.

Why did you not answer the letter I sent you on the 10th of this month? I believe Padre Agostino gave you to under-

---

[9] Gal 5:25.
[10] *Ibid*. 5:26.

stand my intentions in asking you to reply on a picture postcard. I hope you won't refuse me the charity for which I begged in my last letter.

I have now been assured, and you can guess by whom, that a letter addressed to me has just left your hands. I have been told that this letter will cause me great pain. Dear God! What can have happened? It seems to me that I have been waiting a thousand years for this letter[11].

Be consoled in the meantime and consider that although I am in ignorance of the misfortune that has befallen you, I want to tell you that it is Jesus who has been pleased to bestow this gift on you.

---

[11] He is undoubtedly referring to Raffaelina's letter dated 21 October which has not yet reached him.

30

Pietrelcina, 25 October 1914.

Her illness and its progress. The spiritual visit. Sacramental and spiritual Communion. He has given her as a bride to the Son of God. The qualities of a bride.

J.M.J.D.F.C.

Beloved daughter of Jesus,

May the grace of Jesus always be with you and with all those who love Him with a pure heart. May God the Father and Our Lord Jesus Christ give you peace and love with lively faith.

The announcement has been confirmed by the facts, thank God. Your letter of the 21st has arrived. As I read it I cannot restrain my tears at the sad news it brings me. I am resigned, however, and I give thanks to the Lord, knowing that this illness is willed by Jesus, not as a punishment but for the sanctification of your soul.

I pray for you every time I am at prayer, that the Lord may multiply His mercies upon you and make you more and more dear to Him. I am confident that the One who has begun your sanctification will be pleased to give you the strength required to overcome all the cunning and secret snares of the enemy. I also sincerely trust and indeed have the certainty based on my hope that this letter will find you already out of bed. Don't worry, at all events, and keep cheerful, for you are already doing God's will in everything.

You tell me that in the midst of the sufferings which weigh upon you, your thoughts often turn to me and you call out to me. Well, the good Guardian Angel sometimes informs me of these needs of yours and then, unworthy though I am, I always do my duty with Jesus and recommend you to His fatherly goodness.

No thanks are due to me for the visit which the Lord allowed me to pay you in spirit, so let your thanks and praise be directed to God alone. You ask me to tell you the day and the hour of this visit. I am very reluctant to reveal this to you, but as I don't want to distress you I'll stifle the repugnance I feel.

If I am not mistaken a visit of this kind took place on 4 October, the feast of our Seraphic Father, St. Francis, and in the early hours of the following day. I cannot tell you any more about that visit. I can only tell you that it was quite a long one. I beseech you not to say a word about it to a living soul on this earth. In fact, I don't deny that I should very much like you to burn this letter as well as mine of the 10th. What do you say to that? Will my desire be satisfied? However, do as you please in this, for I wouldn't wish to trouble you in the slightest way. Whatever you decide to do in this matter, will you please be so good as to let me know.

You are distressed that your illness obliges you to fast from the most holy Eucharist. This I understand and I do not blame you for it. It is well to be resigned and not to cease imploring Jesus to come to visit you spiritually. When sacramental Communion becomes impossible, spiritual Communion makes up for it to some extent.

I don't hide from you the fact that you are quite wrong to believe that your Communions are neither good nor acceptable to the Lord and that as a punishment for this He deprives you of the Eucharistic food on many mornings. Am I to praise you for this? By no means, and I am sorry that in this matter rather than accept my assertions and assurances, you readily listen to the devil's promptings, for it is really the devil who suggests this to you.

I ask you, please, to listen to the assurances of the one who speaks to you in God's name and to drive away those shadows that are gathering in your soul. They come from nobody but the enemy. Since he cannot deter you from receiving Communion he would like to deprive your soul of the serenity and childlike trust required in those who approach the most holy Sacrament to receive Jesus' embrace.

Take good care not to fall once more into such a diabolical trap, the consequences of which could be quite disastrous for you. Have I made myself clear? Are you convinced that this is true? For pity's sake, don't afford me occasion to speak again on this subject.

You are still a very wayward daughter and it is very difficult to persuade you of anything that differs from what your own crazy imagination suggests. Am I perhaps saying this to mortify you? Heaven forbid! It is the love of Jesus Christ which presses me and the keenest desire for your sanctification. This desire springs from an interior flame which is burning up my entrails and makes me jealous of God's glory where you are concerned, for I have consecrated and espoused you many times to the Son of the heavenly Father, while through me you have received the gifts of this unique Spouse, Jesus Christ.

Hence, as friend and minister of the divine Bridegroom it is my duty to watch over you according to His command. I identify myself, moreover, with His jealous love, so that you may remain a spotless virgin and be able one day to appear before this divine Bridegroom exactly as promised, a chaste and unsullied spouse.

I therefore beseech you, for love of Our Lord Jesus

Christ always to keep in mind what I have told you already, namely, that I have united and espoused you to Jesus and have accepted the task of watching over you, that I may then offer you, bind you, in a word, present you to Him in the next life as a chaste virgin.

Be fully aware of your dignity, that you have been raised up, through me, to such close union with the divine Lamb, similar to the union which exists between husband and wife. Consider for a moment the possessions which a wife naturally acquires by the marriage bond. She certainly acquires all the greatness and honours which her husband enjoys.

No evidence is needed to prove this as we see it happening every day before our eyes. Is it not true that when a peasant girl is taken up to be the wife of some monarch of this world, she becomes by that very act the queen and lady of the nation? Jesus, the King of kings, has been pleased to do this and more in your case when I presented and united you to Him and He accepted you. Take care, then, to remain a chaste virgin as befits a bride of Christ. In a word, I exhort you to keep yourself unsullied in body and mind, to proceed in simple faith, not to allow your soul to be corrupted by any error and to flee from even the shadow of what might mar your bodily integrity.

I would like to continue, but I lack the strength to do so, and in any case you would be unable to read my writing without becoming fatigued in view of your present infirmity.

Write to me whenever you can and when Jesus wants you to write.

Now that I am in extreme need, recommend me to the heavenly Father's mercy. In his name I bless yourself and Giovina and all those dear to you. I beseech His divine Majesty to preserve you, to enable you as a beloved and holy one of His own to grow more and more in His love.

Your servant,
Fra Pio.

31

Foggia, 31 October 1914.

She replies to his three previous letters. Dissension in the family. Submission to her sister. She thanks him for his greetings. She enquires about his "spiritual" visit. Some requests. Keeping his letters. Biographical notes. Her desire to meet him.

Jesus alone! Most Holy Spirit, help me!

My Father,

A few days ago I was cured in a marvellous manner (from one moment to the next)—always through you—so here I come to satisfy my heavy debt to you by replying to all three of your recent most precious letters.

With regard to the first, prostrate face downwards I ask your pardon for all the worry and disappointment which my ungrateful soul causes you. You have run up against too bad, too self-willed and too wretched a daughter, my poor, dear Father.

As regards spiritual reading, holy Father, allow me to submit to you my poor opinion. The books you have suggested, such as the *Way of Perfection*, the *Interior Castle*, etc., seem to me, and this is really a fact, to be too refined for my coarse taste which is of this earth and far too material. What do you say to this? Speak to me.

I am reading the *Letters and Ecstasies of Gemma Galgani*[1]. Have no fear. I'll keep you informed of everything. With God's help I'll obey you and you'll be satisfied. I want to be converted and begin with a retreat, at home and in church when the weather and my health permit.

Have you nothing to tell me about the chapel? Speak to me. The illusion of a convent will be complete when Rome allows me to have Mass in the house (the procedure is taking a very long time!)

The silence of my home does not correspond with the tumult caused by my many worries. The house in which my cousins live is situated to the right of my terrace. They are a family of six old people about whose financial position I have already told you with reference to the only brother's employment. Giovina is doing a lot. She always attends to repairs, especially on the farm, but this is not sufficient. Argue with Jesus and obtain for me this necessary grace. To the left are my brother and his wife, whose attitude towards us remains unchanged. May Jesus bless them. At the centre, adjoining our own home, I can see a window of a house in which I feel God is not present (I would like to be mistaken in this).

How many pitiful cases there are, of soul and body! A cousin of mine in Lucera is threatened with a very nasty disease. May Jesus cure her and provide for her. (Giovina is helping her, but this is not enough). A good and pious woman always asks me in church (and I am asking you) to pray for a nephew of hers who has been suffering for 14 years from acute arthritis and has no income. The poor woman is almost crazy and they have no respite day or night. May

---

[1] Cf. GERMANO DI S. STANISLAO, C.P., *Letters and Ecstasies of the Servant of God Gemma Galgani, a Virgin of Lucca*, Rome, 1909.

Jesus have pity on them! Another very devout woman (she receives Holy Communion every morning) weeps bitterly because her only daughter, a widow with several children, all of them working on the land, is far from God.

I recommend very much to you a silent and recollected woman who is unmarried. We have known her for a great many years and she was formerly a tenant of ours. Giovina has a great regard for her. She receives Holy Communion every morning and is a penitent of your Capuchin confrères. She has a pious sister who is also unmarried and a bachelor brother who is not practising his religion and for whose conversion she is therefore praying continually. She is deeply versed in the ways of God and her life consists in work and prayer. She teaches some school children their catechism and prepares them by degrees for First Communion. Among these is one who when very small was set on the path of virtue by such an excellent guide that at present this plant (at 24) seems to yield fine fruits of piety.

The girl's mother is dead[2], and she has been recommended to us. She is our seamstress at present and I am interested in her situation. I should like to know now from you, good Father, if this soul is travelling along the right road and if Jesus approves of a project which is being discussed with regard to her future. Speak to me, good Father, and you will save me much worry. Don't overlook this.

How many sad stories there are around me, how many tears to be dried, how many evils to be remedied. I am explaining them all to you. You can do everything while I myself am unable to do anything.

Apropos of this, I confess that I don't always practise the complete submission to my sister of which you spoke in

---

[2] Anita of Foggia, who will be mentioned again in these letters. Cf. *Letters I*, p. 601, Note 1.

the first letter, especially on certain occasions. What hurts and humiliates me and causes quite a sense of rebellion in me is the financial slavery. Giovina sees to it that I lack nothing and, in point of fact, she does too much for me and studies even my tiniest needs, but I am deprived of the freedom to give.

She invariably tells me that the good she does (and, holy sister that she is, she does a great deal of it) is mine also, as nothing is divided and we hold everything in common. I look on this as just fine talk which by no means satisfies me. Very often I rebel against the yoke and am in a state of agitation. Then I commit sin.

May the most holy will be done! (Speak to me about this). Similarly may the most holy will of Jesus be done with regard to my sister's health. She often has attacks of stomach trouble which although slight are very frequent. Our own general practitioner thoroughly disapproved of the treatment prescribed by the specialist in Modena. This treatment if followed would lead to other trouble. I am more and more convinced that the illness is very serious and therefore does not respond to any remedy. I consider that the Modena diagnosis is wrong.

I do not hide from you that this causes me hours of great torment. However, I leave it to Jesus who is the true physician and the most effective medicine. I consecrate my sister over and over again to his Most Sacred Heart. She is the only being who binds me to this life, this poor unfortunate who has always been misunderstood and taken up wrong. She awaits, through your mediation, a complete cure of soul and body and the triumph of her pure intentions. May all our enemies come back to us with open hearts. This I greatly desire. May Jesus lavish all good things upon them.

Thank you very much for your good wishes that our stay in our own home may be a long and blessed one, also for the greetings for my name-day conveyed in your second letter. You are so kind and charitable, while my own miserable soul is finding things so difficult! I understand all your most beautiful teachings and holy lectures. You explain yourself wonderfully well. But as to the result, wretched as I am, I am frightened and I tremble in face of my responsibility. Dust and mud and ashes that I am, how can I ever correspond to such treatment? I am discouraged and bewildered. Jesus will ask me for a strict account of all these graces one day and how can I answer Him? Holy Father, help and rescue me. I can read your handwriting quite well, so don't worry. I should like to be able to interpret equally well your intimate loving colloquies with Jesus, your delightful conversations, his daily visits to you and those of our good heavenly Mother and your Guardian Angel.

I return to the subject of your spiritual visit. You tell me in your last letter that is was quite a long visit. What did you say to me and what had I to say during those hours? Did you find me awake or was I sleeping? Tell me everything my holy Father. Do not be afraid, for I will not say anything about it to anyone (not even to your own dear Father[3] who knows all about you? Let me know). I beg you to tell me all and not to be an egoist, if you will excuse the word. Enlighten the pitch darkness of my soul.

I am giving you a great deal to do, a great deal of work not merely for myself but also for the unfortunate ones who have recourse to me. You tell me in your last letter that the love of Jesus is burning up your entrails. Pray, then, for me and for the misfortunes and needs of my relatives, friends and enemies. Pray for all those for whom I have asked your prayers.

Answer me about these, especially as regards the future of that girl. Pray for Giovina. Her confessor has left for Tora and to whom is she to turn now? May Jesus enlighten her and enable her to decide quickly for his glory.

---

[3] Padre Agostino of San Marco in Lamis.

Help her, Father. Make haste to attend to the good of her soul. Answer me on this point.

Why did you tell me to tear up your last letter? Oh, never, never, my dear Father, for I should be committing a real crime. This letter is much more valuable than the others. How many wonderful things you tell me! But I am astonished and amazed and what you tell me appears like a dream, yes, a most beautiful dream. Is it possible? A scrap of dust like myself, a handful of mud, a dunghill piled up with wretchedness. Do you not think, Father, that Jesus is driving me away? This is my powerful conviction all the time and it is perfectly confirmed by events. I have now been 13 days without Holy Communion. Jesus is driving me far from Him and from His house, and in this He is right.

Tomorrow, with His help, I'll begin again. But the rainy days are coming and I cannot go downstairs, so that I am always at the same point. Tomorrow, the great feast of All Saints, is my second name-day and my birthday: 46 years of useless, empty, sinful life. What have I done up to the present, my Jesus? Nothing but sins.

I was in a convent until I was seven. From 7 to 21, an altogether worldly life. (Father, you will be horrified... not even the holy precept). From 21 until this day, sins and sins. I was blind and deaf and wicked. To obtain a temporal favour for my sister, when I was 21 I made for the first time the 15 Saturdays to our dear beautiful Mother of Pompeii. That was the first link in the holy chain which binds me to Jesus and it was all the work of my good Mother.

But I am getting lost. My wickedness and ingratitude are immense. I have a great desire to speak with you, my holy Father! My poor pen does not satisfy or appease my hunger. May I hope for this grace from Jesus? Will the day come when I can speak to you? Wretched as I am, I need to ask from you some very important counsel for my poor soul, but

I cannot set it down on paper. Tell me, Father, that I may be able to speak to you at least once. Do not deny me this, you who are so very kind. Your charity sometimes makes you afraid of distressing me. Now is the moment, now is your real chance to avoid distressing me.

Good Father, pray and pray for my true, real and sincere conversion. Forgive me, scold me and punish me as much as you please.

Bless me with a strong blessing at every moment, along with Giovina and all the others.

A poor tertiary.

P.S. I enclose ten lire for five Masses in thanksgiving on my own behalf. The first Mass in honour of the Most Sacred Heart of Jesus, the second in honour of my beautiful Mother of Sorrows, the third in honour of our dear Blessed Mother of Pompeii, the fourth in honour of St. Gemignano, patron of Modena and the fifth for the poor souls in Purgatory.

Remember all my dear deceased ones the day after tomorrow. I anxiously await your reply to this. Write me a long letter and don't forget anything. Forgive me for all.

32

Pietrelcina, 4 November 1914.

He thanks her. A glance at the past. The Communions she didn't receive. Reading spiritual books. Of one mind with him and with all. Three things she must avoid: disputes, vainglory and preference for her own judgment. Submission to her sister. Jesus' self-abasement. The name of Jesus. He answer her questions. Desire for death.

J.M.J.D.F.C.

Beloved daughter of Jesus,

Grace to you and peace from God our Father and from Our Lord Jesus Christ[1]. I give infinite thanks to my God for all the favours He has already granted to you, especially for having cured you so marvellously of your last illness which made me shed many tears before God's Majesty until I obtained the desired grace for you. I am praying insistently with loving concern and joyful expectation that God may be pleased to multiply continually His infinite mercies in your regard.

I am already aware of the kind of life you lived in the past and I am overwhelmed with admiration at the goodness of Our Lord who has come so promptly to your aid to remove you from the path you were treading so heedlessly and which

[1] Cf. Rev 1:4.

ended in a precipice. If Jesus had not enlightened you with His grace and drawn you to Himself, you would have been like that foolish man who walked unwittingly all through the night along the river-bank, surrounded by deep darkness. When daylight revealed to him the risk he had run, he continued recklessly on his way. Poor unfortunate! At a certain point the ground gave way beneath his feet, he fell in and was drowned.

You, too, followed the road towards the precipice for a great part of the night, but Jesus' grace was so powerful that it was not confined to enlightening you and warning you of the real danger you had run up to that moment. He was pleased to do more for you. He drew you to Himself by the power of love without encroaching in the slightest on your own free will.

You felt this loving power and you could only yield to it. Jesus could have acted towards you as did the light of dawn to the unfortunate man already mentioned. But this did not happen, for in His compassion He wanted you for Himself. Observe the loving manner of this good Father. From that time onward with really admirable tenderness He never left you for a moment. He is always close to you, He rules and protects and sustains you, so that your will may not be overcome by your enemies who are attacking you on all sides.

I have reminded you of this dark patch in your life for no other reason than to invite you to open your heart to trust in God, to recognize the divine benefits bestowed on you by the grace of Jesus and, finally, to lead you, along with myself, to thank the heavenly Father for His mercy.

In your last letter you promised me you would not diverge even to the slightest extent from what the Lord would suggest to you through me. I am very glad to see you so willing to do God's will. Pray, I beseech you, that I may never fall short of my duty. Meanwhile, let us get back to work. I implore you, by the meekness of Our Lord Jesus Christ, not to continue in your obstinate belief that Jesus is depriving you frequently of the Eucharistic food because He is disgusted with you. You are very stubborn about this and you don't want to accept the assurances I have given you on this subject on many previous occasions. I assure you that I deeply regret your attitude. I don't intend to dwell further on the matter and I earnestly hope the Lord will give you the strength to accept with docility all the assurances you receive in this regard.

I am more than a little displeased to find that you make some objection to everything I suggest and almost invariably want to act as the teacher. I should like to know who told you that those spiritual books I suggested to you elsewhere are not suited to your mind. Tell me, have you ever read them? I don't believe you have. You give one to understand, therefore, that you intend to have more than one counsellor. Or am I, perhaps, jealous on this score? Never, and may heaven forbid that I should be. However, as regards the present matter, I should be very sorry if someone had suggested to you that those books would not make suitable reading for you. This would go to show that the person concerned does not know your inner life at all, much less its needs. You will realize already from what I have said that I have no intention of yielding in this matter. Get those books, then, because it seems to me that you haven't got them already.

Listen, now, to what I keenly desire from you. Out of devotion and love for Jesus Christ you make great efforts always to console me in my sufferings. In your charity you find many means to relieve my anxieties. By your sentiments and feelings you are firmly united to me in spirit. You pity the wretched state of many unhappy and needy people and have always endeavoured to get your sister to help them, to dry their tears and relieve their poverty by all those material means with which the Lord has abundantly provided you and of which He has given you charge as the treasurer of the poor.

You, I say, by your highly compassionate heart have been pleased also to bring them spiritual relief and for this purpose you have not spared me either, that I might present them to the Lord. I am pleased by all this.

It is now up to you to make my joy complete and perfect. Up to the present, by your steadfast faith, your generosity in coming to the rescue of poor needy people and by your kindness towards my own poor person, you have brought me great joy. You will see now that I am not going to ask you to do anything new. I am going to entreat you to make my happiness perfect, full and complete. I want you to be of one mind with your sister and with me, to be of the same mind and show the same fondness towards all. Only in this way will my joy be made full and my happiness complete. If you act in this way I'll be certain of your constant progress in the path of holiness to which God, by His goodness alone, has called you.

In order to obtain all this, you must get rid of three things. In the first place, you must take care never to quarrel with any one, never to contend with any one whomsoever. If you act otherwise, it means goodbye to peace and charity. To be inordinately attached to your own opinion is invariably a source and beginning of discord. St. Paul exhorts us to be united in the same mind and the same judgment against this wretched vice[2].

Be on your guard also against vainglory, a vice to be found in devout persons. It leads us without our being aware of the fact to appear invariably somewhat above others, to gain the esteem of all. St. Paul also warns his dear Philippians against this when he says: Do nothing from selfishness or conceit[3].

This great saint, filled with the Spirit of the Lord, saw

---

[2] Cf. 1 Cor 1:10; Phil 2:2.
[3] Phil 2:3.

clearly and fully the evil that would result for those holy Christians if this wretched vice were to succeed in penetrating into their souls, which is why he warned them: *Do nothing from selfishness or conceit*[4].

Against this miserable vice which acts exactly like a moth or a woodworm in the devout soul, oppose contempt for this vainglory. Don't dwell much on yourself; a low opinion of ourselves and the belief that everyone else is better than us is the only way to save ourselves from this vice.

Lastly, we must guard against something else which is no less dangerous than this vice, for it contains the unhealthy germ of division. In this connection we must beware of giving priority to what is advantageous to ourselves rather than what benefits others, because this preference for what is profitable to us rather than to others always tends necessarily to the violation of the beautiful bond of love, a bond which must always unite Christian souls, for love, as St. Paul says, *binds everything together in perfect harmony*[5].

From what I have already said you will perhaps be aware that I look very unfavourably on your indocility towards your sister who is so good, on your failure to submit to her judgment. I want you to submit entirely to her in all that concerns "financial slavery", as you call it. Your temporal goods certainly belong jointly to the two of you. Hence what Giovina does to help others in their misfortunes and the good resulting from these holy works is also held in common by your sister and yourself. Here there is an added advantage for you, for you are saved in this way from the wretched vice of vainglory. Submit to her and when there is question of helping those in need let everything pass through her hands.

I do not intend to forbid you to intervene when you see a chance of coming to the assistance of people in need. In

---

[4] Phil 2:3.
[5] Col 3:14.

such cases you should step in, always in a nice agreeable way, to induce Giovina to help them. This action on your part will be very praiseworthy.

I repeat and insist that you must be submissive towards Giovina. In order to achieve this, consider how the Son of God abased himself in His Incarnation and in His mortal life, especially in His painful death, so that He could say with the Prophet: *I am reduced to nothing*[6]. Let us always bear in mind, moreover, that it was precisely this humiliation which led to His honour and glory, that by His example He confirmed His own words: *He who humbles himself will be exalted*[7].

I want you to meditate every day on the humiliations of the Son of God and the glory to which they led. Let us consider how the divine Word abased Himself. As St. Paul says: *Though He was in the form of God*[8], *for in Him the whole fulness of deity dwells bodily*[9], He did not disdain to lower Himself to our level in order to raise us up to fullness of life in God.

Of His own free will and to the fullest extent this divine Word was pleased to abase Himself to our level, by hiding His divine nature beneath the veil of human flesh. In this way, says St. Paul, the Word of God humbled Himself to the point of emptying Himself, as it were: *He emptied Himself, taking the form of a servant*[10]. Yes, my dear sister, He was pleased to hide His divine nature so fully as to take on the likeness of man in everything, even exposing Himself to hunger, thirst and weariness and, to use the very words of the apostle of the nations: *in every respect tempted as we are, yet without sinning*[11].

---

[6] Ps 72:22; 77:59 (Vg.)
[7] Lk 14:11; 18:14.
[8] Phil 2:6.
[9] Col 2:9.
[10] Phil 2:7.
[11] Heb 4:15.

The climax of His humiliation, however, is found in His Passion and Death, when He submitted His human will to the will of His Father, endured great torments and suffered the most infamous death, the death of the cross. *He humbled Himself*, says St. Paul, *and became obedient unto death, even death on a cross*[12]. As He was the Only Begotten Son of the Father He was not induced to obey by any fear of punishment. Neither did He obey for the sake of reward, as He Himself was God and equal in all things to the Father. His obedience, then, in view of His exalted position, of the arduousness of what was commanded and His alacrity in complying with the heavenly Father's will, was highly pleasing to the eternal Father, who exalted Him and *bestowed on Him the name*—says the apostle—*which is above every name*[13].

It is by virtue of that name alone that we may hope to be saved, exactly as the apostle declared before the Jews: *There is no other name under heaven given among men by which we must be saved*[14].

The eternal Father decreed that all creatures should be subject to Him: *that at the name of Jesus every knee should bow, in heaven and on earth and under the earth*[15]. This is what the apostle tells us and this is true. Jesus is adored in heaven. At this divine name, moved by gratitude and love, the blessed in heaven never cease to repeat what St. John the Evangelist beheld in a vision: *They sang a new song*, he says, *saying "worthy are Thou, O Lord, to take the scroll and to open its seals, for Thou wast slain and by the blood didst ransom men for God"*[16].

---

[12] Phil 2:8.
[13] Phil 2:9.
[14] Acts 4:12.
[15] Phil 2:10.
[16] Rev 5:9.

This most holy name is venerated on earth, for all the graces which we ask in Jesus' name are fully granted by the eternal Father: *Whatever you ask in My name*, the divine Master tells us, *I will do it*[17]. Who would ever believe that this divine name is venerated even in hell? But so it is, for this name is terror to the demons who are broken and vanquished by it: *In My name they will cast out demons*[18].

Through Jesus' obedience the heavenly Father willed that all creatures should confess and believe in this most holy name: *Every tongue (should) confess that Jesus Christ is Lord, to the glory of God the Father*[19]. Is not this verified, moreover, and happening at present when the cross is everywhere adored? On the Judgment Day the damned and the devils will be obliged to participate in this homage when they behold the immense glory of Jesus and experience his infinite power.

If we are imitators of Jesus Christ and face up to all life's battles, we too will share in His victories. In conclusion, with St. John Chrysostom, I say, let us firmly believe that our divine Redeemer is adorned with great glory, but let us continue to live for His glory imitating His example and following out His will. On the other hand, our faith will avail us nothing if our actions do not bear it out.

To me it seems that the state of that soul is good. However, I have not asked nor do I intend to ask Jesus if He approves of that project of which there is talk with regard to her future. I regret very much that I cannot set down on paper my reason for acting in this way. May God's will be done!

Giovina's loss of her confessor is not as you imagine it to be. The Father who has gone away has been replaced by

---

[17] Jn 14:13-14.
[18] Mk 16:17.
[19] Phil 2:11.

another learned and very worthy priest. So don't worry on any account, especially in this connection, for the Lord arranges all for his greater glory.

I have to reprimand you on one account. I have implored you many times to ask the Lord to shorten my exile, yet you have always refused to do me this charitable service. You are really unkind in this and quite selfish. Pray, but pray fervently. My life is becoming such a burden that I can no longer bear it. I feel I am burning up but never see the end of it when I shall be completely consumed.

I assure you that if you will obtain this grace for me from the mercy of the Lord, you will stand to gain a great deal. I promise you that if this happens I'll always remain close to you. Then my visits will really be very frequent.

When I requested you in my last letter not to let any one know about the visit I paid you in spirit, I did not intend to extend that secrecy to my beloved Padre Agostino, from whom I wish nothing to be concealed. I assure you, moreover, that when the visit took place you were awake.

Have you nothing to tell me about the novenas to the Virgin of Pompeii? If you see Padre Agostino in the next few days, do not forget to give him my respectful regards.

I should like to continue but my strength does not permit it. For the last few days I have been threatened with influenza and I foresee that it will be my inseparable companion for the whole of this winter. This morning I had to drag myself to the church to say Mass. Blessed be God! In the meantime, write often, as this gives me very great pleasure.

Greetings to all in the Lord's holy embrace, while I wish you most affectionately and always implore for you the blessing of heaven.

Pray for me all the time.

Your poor servant,
Fra Pio, Capuchin.

33

Pietrelcina, 16 November 1914.

Greetings and thanks. Spiritual reading. How to adorn the soul. St. Paul: his guide and master in doctrinal matters. The twofold life: nature and grace. Fruits and effects of baptism. Christians in name and in practice. The worldly man and his vices. Vices that offend others internally and externally. The twofold image of God. The new man. Charity the bond of perfect harmony. Means to reach perfection: divine law and doctrine of Jesus; to act always for his glory. Conclusion. He desires to die. A note for Padre Agostino.

J.M.J.D.F.C.

Beloved daughter of Jesus,

May the grace and mercy and peace of Our Lord Jesus Christ be always with you all and make you ever more acceptable to God our Father. Amen.

I give thanks continually to God for you, as is my duty, for your continual increase in holiness and for the love of Jesus which is becoming more and more abundant in your heart.

This poor letter of mine will deal with what ought to be the life of one who is living in the spirit of Jesus Christ. It is my intention to place before you an example, a model, so that when you look at this example or model you may be able to conform to it in all things, reproducing all its features, even the less important ones, in your own life. I am aware that my manner of speaking is not, unfortunately, what it ought to be. It is quite harsh and tiresome and precisely on this account I am afraid that I may not make my meaning clear. However, I fix my gaze on the One who moves me to speak and who is the source of wisdom and I earnestly hope that all will redound to His glory.

By a most wise order and a most singular love, our heavenly Father in His goodness makes it impossible for us to remove those bodily deformities which we inherit from nature our mother. If we give much thought and waste much time and effort in trying to correct our superficial bodily defects, even in arranging our hair so that not even a single hair remains out of place, tell me, then, what would we not do to rectify and drive far from us the physical deformities we bear in our bodies?

Unfortunately, we are never done trying to improve our appearence. Indeed, all our efforts are directed towards improving the body and making it more and more beautiful. Less attention is perhaps devoted to the soul, which we may have treated as a negligible quantity.

Well, then, if Providence has deprived us of our motive for neglecting spiritual things while we were busy improving our bodily life, God in his infinite wisdom has placed in our hands all the necessary means for the embellishment of our souls, even after we have disfigured them by sin. The soul's cooperation with divine grace is all that is required to enable it to develop, to reach such a degree of splendour and beauty as to attract, not so much the loving and astonished gaze of the angels, but the gaze of God Himself, according to the testimony of Holy Scripture: *The king*, that is, God, *will desire your beauty*[1].

---

[1] Ps 45:11.

In introducing you here to the model of the true Christian, my guide will be my beloved apostle St. Paul. His sayings, all filled with heavenly wisdom, entrance me. They fill my heart with heavenly dew and take my soul out of itself. I cannot read his letters without experiencing a fragrance which spreads all through my soul, a fragrance that reaches the very apex of my spirit.

May God be blessed for ever, for He alone knows how to bring about these marvels in a soul that always resisted Him, a soul that was the receptacle of an infinite amount of filth. He willed to make me an example of grace and He is pleased to hold me up to sinners as a model, so that none may despair. Let sinners, then, fix their gaze on me, the greatest sinner of all, and let them hope in God.

Fix your attention, then, you sinners, on me, the most wretched of all and be encouraged not to despair of being saved, for the Lord has not only pardoned my sins but has been pleased to enrich me with most precious graces.

But, dear God, where is my mind taking me? Forgive me, most faithful servant of the Lord, for this long digression. I have gone astray, I have wandered from the subject. I wanted to glorify the Lord within me and tell you something about the awful life I led up to the present. Who knows how far I might have gone if a great sob welling up from my heart had not almost suffocated me[2] and brought me to myself.

Pardon me. It is a man madly in love with his God who is speaking to you and deserves your pity.

But let us return to the subject I mentioned. In order to understand each other it should be observed that we have a twofold life. We have a natural life received from Adam through procreation and which is therefore an earthly and corruptible life filled with base passions and love of self. The other life is a supernatural one received from Jesus at bap-

---

[2] Cf. *Letters*, Vol. I, Nos. 192 ff.

tism and therefore a spiritual, heavenly life by which we practise virtue. Baptism brings about a real transformation in us. We die to sin and are grafted onto Jesus Christ in such a way as to live by His very life. At our baptism we receive sanctifying grace which gives us life, a completely heavenly life, making us children of God, brothers of Christ and heirs to heaven.

Now if baptism causes every Christian to die to the first life and rise up to the second, it is the duty of each Christian to seek the things of heaven and not to care about the things of this earth. The apostle St. Paul suggests this to the Colossians: *If then*, says this great saint, *you have been raised with Christ, seek the things that are above, where Christ is, seated at the right hand of God*[3].

Yes, the Christian is raised up in Jesus at baptism. He is lifted up to a supernatural life and acquires the splendid hope of occupying a heavenly throne in glory. What an honour! His vocation demands that he aspire continually to the home of the blessed and consider himself as a pilgrim in this land of exile. The Christian vocation, I say, requires that we do not attach our hearts to this miserable world. The good Christian who really follows his vocation directs all his attention, all his study to securing eternal possession. He must look on the things of this world below in such a way as to esteem and appreciate only those which help him to obtain eternal things and must despise all things which do not help him to obtain what is eternal.

The Christian who has forgotten his true vocation and is merely a Christian in name, a worldly Christian, judges things quite differently. His judgment is the exact opposite to that of the Christian worthy of the name who lives according to the spirit of Jesus Christ. The former judges things from the point of view of their capacity to satisfy his vanity

---

[3] Col 3:1.

and his passions. The latter, on the other hand, invariably judges them in relation to eternal things.

Hence the one that is a Christian merely in name, the Christian in high society, sets a great value on honours, wealth, fleeting things, comforts and all that this wretched world has to offer. O foolish man, enter into yourself and remember that by your baptism you renounced the world and are dead to it. The Holy Spirit tells you so by the mouth of St. Paul: *You have died, and your life is hid with Christ in God*[4].

Remember, foolish one, that the life of those who live according to the spirit of Jesus will not always remain hidden and unknown. Remember what it will be in future in the Lord's day: *"When Christ who is our life appears, then you also will appear with him in glory*[5]. *Beloved*, wrote St. John, the favourite apostle, for the comfort of the faithful, *we are God's children now; it does not yet appear what we shall be, but we know that when He appears we shall be like Him, for we shall see Him as He is*[6].

Is the certainty of such boundless glory, O foolish one, not sufficient to make you enter into yourself and come to your senses, to live the rest of your life according to your vocation?

The life mapped out for the Christian by the apostle consists in stripping oneself of the vices of the old man, that is to say, the man of this world, and in clothing oneself in the virtues which Jesus Christ taught. As regards stripping oneself of the vices he tells us: *Put to death therefore what is earthly in you*[7]. The Christian sanctified by baptism is not exempt from the rebellion of the senses and passions; hence the impelling need to mortify our passions as long as we live.

---

[4] Col. 3:3.
[5] Col. 3:4.
[6] 1 Jn 3:2.
[7] Col 3:5.

The holy apostle himself suffered considerable interior distress from the rebellion of his senses and passions, which led him to utter the following complaint: *I of myself serve the law of God with my mind, but with my flesh I serve the law of sin*[8], (that is, the law of concupiscence). It is as though he intended to say: "I am mentally subject to God's law, but my flesh is subject to the law of sin." This is to be said for the spiritual consolation of many unfortunate people who experience the sharp conflict within themselves to which a hot temper or lustful desires give rise. They do not want to feel or to harbour those impulses, that ill-feeling towards others, those vivid pictures presented by their imagination, those sensual promptings. Poor things! Quite involuntarily these feelings surge up and produce a conflict within them, so that in the act of wanting to do something right they feel violently impelled towards something wrong.

Among them are some who think they are offending God when they feel this violent interior inclination to evil. Take heart, you chosen souls, for in this there is no sin, since the holy apostle himself, a chosen instrument[9], experienced this dreadful conflict within him: *When I intend to do good*, he says, *I find within me a power which inclines me to evil*[10]. Even when carnal impulses are violently felt, there can be no sin when the will does not consent to them.

The sensual passions are the most enticing and they find an outlet in a great many different acts, which the apostle enumerates: fornication, impurity, licentiousness, lust and avarice[11]. The last-named gains such mastery over the soul infected by it that it becomes the idol of that soul to which it sacrifices everything else. St. Paul refers to those in the grip

---

[8] Rom 7:25.
[9] Acts 9:15.
[10] Cf. Rom 7:16 ff.
[11] Cf. Gal 5:19.

of these vices as *sons of unbelief*[12], because these things more than anything else blind a man and make him more readily lose sight of eternal possessions. Only those who have had this sad experience themselves can confirm the truth of what we are saying.

Over and above the vices of the senses, the good Christian must beware of those vices which offend others either by interior acts or by his speech.

(a) The vices which lead us to offend our neighbour by interior acts, according to the same apostle, are: anger, wrath and malice[13].

Anger is a moral passion which also exists in good people and in itself it is not sinful. But if we do not know how to control it, it becomes sinful, as happens when we are angry with someone who does not deserve it, or before we have reason to be angry, or in matters which do not justify our anger. The apostle warns us to refrain from this type of anger. On the same subject St. James tells us: *Let every man be slow to anger, for the anger of man does not work the righteousness of God*[14].

Resentment is an offshoot of anger. It is present when a person considers others unworthy to possess what they have and would like to see them humiliated and disgraced by punishment.

Malice, which proceeds from one and the other, endeavours in every way and makes use of every means to harm others.

These are the vices which when present in the heart offend those around us. Anyone who wants to show himself worthy of his vocation should guard against them.

(b) I also said that we can offend others externally by

---

[12] Col 3:6.
[13] Cf. Rom 2:8; Col 3:8.
[14] Jas 1:19-20.

our speech and this can happen especially in three ways: firstly, by blasphemy, either by rebelling against God in offensive terms, or against our neighbour by harsh and unpleasant words, curses and the like; secondly, by impure language which reveals the nasty fire that burns in the heart and is inclined to spread and affect everyone else; thirdly, by lying. This gives birth to deceit, perjury and a thousand other kinds of roguery which are damaging to others.

The Christian must beware of all these vices if he intends to live according to the spirit of Jesus Christ. Now all these vices and all these sins make up the old man, the earthly man, the carnal man. The apostle wants the Christian to strip himself precisely of this man: *seeing that you have put off the old nature with its practices*[15]. The Christian, then, who has died and risen again with Christ by baptism, must invariably strive to renew and improve himself by contemplating the eternal truths and the will of God. In a word, he must endeavour all the time to reproduce in himself the image of the Lord who created him.

Christian perfection obliges us to all this and the apostle exhorts us to act in this way, telling us with great wisdom that we *have put on the new nature which is being renewed in knowledge after the image of its Creator*[16]. But what is this new nature to which the apostle is referring here? It is our nature made holy by baptism which, according to the principles of sanctification, must live *in righteousness and in true holiness*[17].

We Christians are therefore images of God twice over, by nature and by grace. By nature we are endowed with intelligence, memory and will; by grace we are made holy through our baptism which imprints on our souls the

---

[15] Col 3:9.
[16] *Ibid*. 3:10.
[17] Cf. Lk 1:75.

beautiful image of God. Yes, my dear, sanctifying grace impresses the image of God upon us in such a way that we ourselves become divine by participation, and as St. Peter puts it so beautifully: *We become partakers of the divine nature*[18].

See then, my dear sister, how great a dignity is ours. However, we are great on condition that we preserve sanctifying grace and, alas, how wretched we become when we lose that grace. I was about to say that our wretchedness places us on a lower level even than the beasts who roam the countryside. All is cancelled when sin enters in.

Get to work, then, O Christian. Remember that by baptism you cast off the old nature and put on the new. You have already followed me in considering all that goes to make up the old nature, the carnal, earthly nature. Have patience a little longer and follow me now in considering what goes to make up the new nature, the spiritual, supernatural nature.

Man can consider himself from two points of view: in the state of prosperity and in that of adversity. The apostle wants him, when in a prosperous state, to be filled with mercy as opposed to hardheartedness, with kindness as opposed to a harsh external manner and as regards his own personal life he wants him to be full of humility as opposed to interior pride, to be unassuming rather than given to external show.

Turning to the state of the Christian in times of adversity, the same holy apostle[19] wants him to show patience and to stifle all resentment either internal or external. He expects him to bear with all the vexatious behaviour of others and to forgive them sincerely.

This great saint, however, sets greater store by love than by all the rest of the virtues and hence he recommends it most earnestly and expects it to be present in all we do, for Chris-

---

[18] 2 Pet. 1:4.
[19] Cf. Col 3:12.

tian perfection consists in this alone: *Above all these*, he says, *put on love, which binds everything together in perfect harmony*[20].

Observe, then, that he is not satisfied with exhorting us to be patient, to bear with one another, which are in themselves fine virtues. No, he wants us to love, and with good reason, for it might well be that we bear patiently with the defects of those around us and even forgive them when they offend us, but all this may be of no value if it is done without love which is the queen of virtues and includes all the others.

Therefore, my dear sister, let us greatly esteem this virtue if we want the heavenly Father to show us mercy. Let us be very fond of charity and let us practise it. This is the virtue that makes us all children of the one Father who is in heaven. Let us love and practise charity, as this is our divine Master's precept. By this we shall be distinguished from the unbelievers by our loving and charitable behaviour. In our love for charity, we must flee from even the shadow of anything that might dim its splendour. Yes, in loving this virtue, let us always bear in mind the great teaching of the apostle: *We are all members of Jesus Christ*[21] *who is the head of us all, the members of the body*[22]. We should show great love for one another, remembering that we have all been called to form a single body and that if we keep our love for one another, the beautiful peace of Jesus will invariably triumph joyfully in our hearts.

I must add a further word to what has already been said, namely, to suggest the suitable means for the attainment of Christian perfection. The apostle suggests two most powerful means, which are the constant study of God's law and the performance of all our actions for his glory.

---

[20] Col 3:14.
[21] Cf. Eph 5:30.
[22] Eph 4:15.

As regards the first means, he writes to the Colossians: *Let the word of Christ dwell in you richly, as you teach and admonish one another in all wisdom, and as you sing psalms and hymns and spiritual songs with thankfulness in your hearts to God*[23].

This apostle's doctrine is clear and does not need any comment. If the Christian is full of God's law which warns and teaches him to despise the world and its allurements, wealth and honours and all that prevents him from loving God, he will never fail no matter what adversities may befall him; he will endure everything steadfastly and perseveringly; he will readily forgive offences and give thanks to God for all things.

The apostle, moreover, wants God's law and Jesus' doctrine to be and to dwell abundantly in us. Now all this cannot come about unless we apply ourselves to reading Holy Scripture and books dealing with divine things, or else listening to God's word as expounded by holy preachers, confessors, etc.

Finally, the apostle wishes the Christian not to confine himself merely to knowing the divine law; he wants him to penetrate deeply into the meaning of it in order to be able to regulate his own life. None of this can take place without diligent application to meditation on God's law, which makes the Christian exult with joy and chant sweet psalms and hymns to God. The Christian who is striving for perfection will understand, then, how very necessary meditation is.

As regards the other means of doing everything for God's glory, let us listen to the apostle's teaching: *Whatever you do*, he says, *in word or deed, do everything in the name of the Lord Jesus, giving thanks to God the Father through Him*[24].

---

[23] Col 3:16.
[24] Col 3:17.

By the faithful use of this simple means we do not merely keep far from any sin, but feel the continual urge to aim constantly at perfection.

I exhort you to impress this letter deeply on your mind and endeavour to apply its teaching in a practical way to your own conduct. The Lord is calling you to all this, so try not to let all my care of you be ineffective, letting Jesus' grace remain fruitless in your soul.

I want you, moreover, to rejoice at all times, for the Lord's yoke is an agreeable one. You are glorifying the Lord by your life and he is pleased with you. Never leave any room for sadness in your heart, for this would be in conflict with the Holy Spirit poured out into your soul.

When Jesus wills, I want you to give me an exact and detailed description of the manner in which you ordinarily spend your day. Do not consider me a nuisance on this account. God knows and reads my intentions in this respect. Besides, what use is there in concealing things from someone who already knows them through other channels?

I am in really bad health, so pray the divine Majesty without ceasing, as I myself pray continually for you. Pray, I say, not that he withhold his fatherly hand which strikes me, but that he may give me at last the final blow. I cannot bear life any longer, my dear sister. I see myself in continual danger of offending the divine Bridegroom. It appears to me that I am invariably surrounded and pervaded by a divine flame which causes me to die a thousand deaths at every moment.

Ah! Don't be envious of my state, for I am more to be pitied than envied. Death is the only remedy, the only thing that can reduce this flame which burns but does not consume me. For pity's sake, don't be so cruel and ungrateful. Ask Jesus with filial confidence to break these chains without delay, to open the doors of this dark prison. He alone holds the keys and He alone knows how to open it.

The sheet of paper enclosed herewith[25] is for Padre Agostino. Be so good as to put it in an envelope and give it to him when he returns to you. I haven't put it in an envelope myself as I feared it might weigh too much. I am not afraid to pay double postage, but merely want to avoid arousing suspicion.

May the Lord bless you.

Fra Pio.

---

[25] He is certainly referring to the letter he wrote on the same day, 16 November, to his director, Padre Agostino, and which appears in the first volume of his letters.

34

Pietrelcina, from bed, 17 November 1914.

He shares her grief over a distressing attack suffered by Giovina.

J.M.J.D.F.C.

Beloved daughter of Jesus,

May Our Lord Jesus Christ visit your soul and console you as he always does. Amen.

Your unexpected telegram[1] was a complete shock to me. I suffered more than you yourself on account of poor Giovina's distressing attack. I brought great pressure to bear on the Sacred Hearts of Jesus and Mary and I intend to do so again so that they may take this urgent matter into their hands.

I believe most firmly that the hurricane which has struck poor Giovina so violently will soon pass. Please keep me informed as quickly as possible about the happy ending to this trouble.

Don't give way to sadness, for the Lord is with you all, always. Aren't you all in the hands of Providence, a fonder mother than we can say or imagine? Take heart, then, for Jesus won't leave you for a single instant.

---

[1] The text of the telegram is not in our possession. See next letter.

Kindest regards to Giovina in our Supreme Good, and may He be always within her soul and deliver her from all harm.

May His divine Majesty sustain you in your trouble and make you grow in His love.

Pray to Jesus all the time for me.

Your poor servant,
Fra Pio, Capuchin.

35

Foggia, 19 November 1914.

Giovina's recovery from her illness. "Confined to bed and fasting." She will reply to the letters received. Overcome with grief. Requests and prayers.

Jesus alone! Most Holy Spirit, help me!

Father,

I am writing you a few lines from my bed, with my head in a whirl and with very little strength.

Thanks be to our good Jesus (thank him yourself exceedingly on my behalf) my holy sister got up this morning. If you only saw the state to which she is reduced; she looks as if she had been ill for a year. From five in the morning until ten she suffered atrocious and indescribable pain. Her stomach didn't allow her a moment's respite. She seemed to have gone crazy and she called on all the saints in paradise especially her dear St. Joseph, but all in vain.

When my agitation was at its height and I was nearly going mad, I called on you and sent you the telegram. Shortly afterwards I received your own long letter, while four doctors were at Giovina's bedside to bring her some relief.

After an injection of morphine the pain was less acute, but it persisted along with the liver pain for the whole day and the following night. The only food she took on the first day was half a cup of coffee and yesterday, which was the second day, she took two cups of soup and nothing else.

Where are we to turn? I consider and insist that the trouble is very serious, but all the others, doctors and relatives, make a great fuss and assure me to the contrary. However, unknown to Giovina I told the doctor who is attending her and all the others that they are just fooling me and I don't believe any of them.

In the midst of this great tempest I am all alone with the four doctors, alone with Jesus and Our Lady of Sorrows. My sister-in-law and my nephews are vexed with me and feel offended by my neglect of them. I just let them talk.

Since Thursday, eight days ago, a Eucharistic fast. I went to confession but was unable to receive Communion even once. On Friday the weather was bad and I didn't go to church because Giovina didn't want me to. On Friday evening I had a fever and I didn't get up again until late on Monday. On Tuesday morning we had a storm, as you know. I was in agony all day and cried continually. By the evening I had such a dreadful fever and violent headache that I could no longer understand anything. I am still in bed, powerless and of no use to myself or anybody else.

My poor tormented sister was in great need of assistance and I could do nothing for her. Instead, weak and suffering as she is, poor thing, she has to take care of me. For several days now, by God's grace, Rosinella[1] who is also quite ill has been on her feet. The maid who has been with us now for six years is old and unsuitable (an impoverished lady) and we tolerate her for fear of something worse. Giovina would like to find a good strong robust woman, religious and

---

[1] Rosinella lived with the Cerase sisters for over twenty-five years and had become one of the family. She kept house for them and also helped with the management of their affairs.

honest. But where is she to be found? Jesus alone is capable of sending us such a person. He sends us ailments and we have no strength, but domestic help is not to be found even at a very high price. Please see to this yourself.

Your most precious letter of yesterday's date gave me momentary relief (I have still to reply to your two previous letters which I will do when I am calmer). Give me a little time, let me have a little quiet and I'll do everything you wish, always with Jesus' help.

I am very bad, very weak, very wretched. I have scandalized everyone by my tears (just as I gave scandal up there in Savona by my fear of the war). There you have my life: sins and scandal. I look at the cross as it approaches and would like to flee before it. I try to grasp it with both hands but I feel the weight of it. I drag it along and am rebellious. I don't know how to pray and I weep bitterly. It is a real agony.

My poor martyr is suffering very much in soul and body. She cannot eat, even sparingly, like all other human beings. She is the light, the strength, the defence and protection of our home. When she is ill I am horribly upset, confused and muddled, for I myself am no good at anything. What do you think of me, almost fifty years of age and accustomed by my sister to be guided like a child of five? Will you scold me too? Will you tell me I am wrong? I have nobody else in the world except this good sister who is so unfortunate.

We have a brother who has all the good will to approach us, his two solitary and unfortunate sisters, but others sow the seed of discord and keep him away, as will always be the case.

You are my only hope. A complete cure would be a miracle. You can obtain it from that Heart so good and merciful. I deserve nothing, that is, I deserve only one thing: hell. I desire nothing for myself, but for this holy and neglected martyr, dead to the world, buried in this old house, my holy sister who has no desires or aspirations, I ask a little peace, a little health, for her, who has suffered so much bad health. Pray, obtain for us this grace. Otherwise I'll quarrel with you and call you cruel, selfish and uncharitable.

Poor Father, how can you bear with this intolerant and crazy soul? Your spiritual illness alarms me. Knowing that you are in bed, I would like to afford you some relief and satisfaction, but you receive nothing but trial and torment from me. Forgive me. I am bad, bad, bad. I cannot go on any longer.

Bless me always, at every instant, together with my poor martyr.

A wretched tertiary.

P.S. Pray for Rosinella. I sincerely hope that this letter finds you fairly well. Just as soon as I see your holy father I'll give him your note. Pray. I enclose five lire for two Masses in thanksgiving, one to my dear Mother of the Seven Veils, the great protectress of Foggia, and the other to St. Joseph. Did you receive the other ten lire which I enclosed in my letter? I ask you this because you have made no mention of it and I fear some nasty trick of the devil. Please set my mind at rest.

36

Pietrelcina, 26 November 1914.

Giovina's recovery. Confidence and trust in God. Giovina will not be completely cured. A grace through Our Lady of Pompeii. "Be always firm in your faith." Love for tribulation. His illness.

J.M.J.D.F.C.

Beloved daughter of Jesus,

May Jesus console you at all times and keep you for ever in His holy love. Amen.

I bless and pray to the Lord at every moment of my life on your behalf. I give thanks to Him incessantly for the many gifts and favours granted to yourself and your sister. May the Father of orphans be blessed for ever for having in His infinite goodness brought poor Giovina back to life. I don't hide from you the fact that she was in extreme danger, more serious than you imagined. She has been snatched from the jaws of death. It had been intended conditionally that she should join her parents up above and it was only the many prayers that suspended the fulfilment of this intention.

I am revealing this to you, not because I want to cause you unnecessary fear and terror, but to arouse in you a sense of liveliest gratitude towards the giver of all good things and exhort you to confide more and more and abandon yourself to divine Providence. Oh, how good our God is, my dear! He has been pleased to spare you such a great misfortune.

Once again, then, I urge you to have ever greater confidence in God, for it is written that those who trust in Him will never be forsaken[1]. Don't turn in on yourself as so often happens, unfortunately. In the midst of the trials which may afflict you, just place all your confidence in our Supreme Good in the knowledge that He takes more care of us than a mother takes of her child[2].

Don't allow any sadness to dwell in your soul, for sadness prevents the Holy Spirit from acting freely. If we insist on being sad, then let it be a holy sadness at the sight of the evil that is spreading more and more in society nowadays. How many poor souls are every day deserting God, our Supreme Good!

To refuse to submit one's own judgment to that of others, especially to those who are quite expert in the field in question, is a sign that we possess very little docility and an all too obvious sign of secret pride. You know this yourself and you agree with me. Well, then, take heart and avoid falling into this fault again. Keep your eyes wide open for this wretched vice, knowing how much it displeased Jesus, for it is written that *God opposes the proud, but gives grace to the humble*[3].

Take courage, then, I repeat, and have courage at all times. The Lord is with you, always ready to welcome what you confide to Him in secret. What a great consolation it is to know that we always have access to such a dear friend, to such a loving Spouse! The apostle of the nations raised his voice to cry out: *If God is for us, who is against us*[4]?

---

1 Cf. Sir 2:10.
2 Cf. Sir 4:10.
3 Jas 4:6; 1 Pet 5:5.
4 Rom 8:31.

While I have really brought and always bring pressure to bear on the heart of the heavenly Father for Giovina's health and also for your own, He alone knows what tears I shed and what severe penances I am doing for this purpose. However, I must tell you for your own comfort that a complete cure of the disease from which poor Giovina is suffering would not be for God's glory, for the salvation of her soul and the edification of those who live according to the spirit of Jesus Christ. Hence I cannot insist, I cannot demand from the divine Heart to grant her this favour. I will certainly pray and never forget it, since this is the Lord's will wherever I am and no matter in what state I may be, that the Lord may be pleased to grant her constantly at least the degree of holiness necessary for the fulfilment of her duties. Does this satisfy you?

I am confident that the Lord God who is so good to His creatures will not refuse the poor prayer of His servant. In fact, I hope He will grant more grace to the poor martyr than I dare to ask.

The other reason why I refrain from asking a complete cure for Giovina is because this illness is for her a most powerful means of practising many virtues. I cannot deprive this generous soul, who is so dear to Jesus, of such great treasures through a mistaken sense of pity and affection for you.

You must remember, moreover, that if you are on the right road now it is due to that grace which Our Lady of Pompeii obtained for your sister[5]. Remember this grace, I repeat, and consider, too, that this was the first link which bound you to Jesus from that time. Think of all this, give thanks for it to the divine mercy and take care not to want what God does not want. Do not ask for a miracle, not because the Lord is not disposed to grant it, but take care not to ask it because your own faith is far from perfect.

---

[5] Cf. Letter 31, p. 225.

Ponder on what I have told you and may the Lord enlighten your mind about the whole matter.

Be steadfast and firm in your faith and be on the alert, for in this way you will avoid all the evil snares of the enemy. This is precisely the warning given us by the prince of the apostles, St. Peter: *Be sober, be watchful. Your adversary the devil prowls around like a roaring lion, seeking someone to devour. Resist him, firm in your faith*. Then for our greater encouragement he adds: *knowing that the same experience of suffering is required of your brotherhood throughout the world*[6].

Yes, beloved daughter of Jesus, renew your faith in the truths of Christian doctrine, especially at times of conflict. And renew in a most particular way your faith in the promises of eternal life which our most sweet Jesus makes to those who fight energetically and courageously. You should be encouraged and comforted by the knowledge that we are not alone in our sufferings, for all the followers of the Nazarene scattered throughout the world suffer in the same manner and are all exposed like ourselves to the trials and tribulations of life.

O Raffaelina, let us remember that the lot of chosen souls is to suffer. God, the author of all grace and of every gift leading to salvation, has decreed that glory will be ours on condition that we endure suffering with a Christian spirit. So let us lift up our hearts full of confidence in God alone. Let us humble ourselves beneath His powerful hand[7], let us cheerfully accept the trials to which the mercy of the heavenly Father subjects us, so that He may raise us up at the time of his visitation. Let all our concern be "to love God and be pleasing to Him," paying no attention to all the rest, in the

---

[6] 1 Pet 5:8.
[7] 1 Pet 5:6.

knowledge that God will always take more care of us than we can say or imagine.

Oh, how sublime and sweet is the divine Master's delightful invitation: *If any one would come after Me, let him deny himself and take up his cross and follow Me*[8]! It was this invitation which caused St. Teresa to come out with that prayer to the divine Bridegroom: *Either to suffer or to die*[9]. It was this same invitation which made St. Mary Magdalen Pazzi utter the words: *Always to suffer and never to die*[10]. It was this invitation also which caused our Seraphic Father St. Francis, caught up in ecstasy, to exclaim: *So much good awaits me that every suffering is a joy to me*[11].

Let us not complain by any means of all the affliction and infirmities that it pleases Jesus to send us. Let us follow the divine Master up the steep slope of Calvary loaded with our cross, and when it pleases Him to place us on the cross by confining us to a bed of sickness, let us thank Him and consider ourselves lucky to be honoured in this way, aware that to be on the cross with Jesus is infinitely more perfect than merely contemplating Jesus Himself on the cross.

I am aware that both Giovina and yourself, with God's help, are improving in health and I cannot express to you the immense joy this brings me. It is my earnest wish to see you reach a more stable state of health.

Please be indulgent with me for the many days' delay in answering your letter and understand that this is not due to negligence but to my malady which is growing steadily worse. I spend more hours in bed than out of it. May the

---

[8] Mt 16:24.

[9] St. Teresa, "Libro de la vida" in *Obras completas*, Madrid, 1972, p. 188.

[10] Cf. Gesualdo Dello Spirito Santo, *Santa Maria Maddalena de' Pazzi, la santa di Firenze*, 3rd ed., Rome, 1941.

[11] Cf. *I fioretti di San Francesco. Le considerazioni sulle stimmate.* Ed. B. Bughetti and R. Pratesi, Florence, 1960, p. 211.

Lord at last deal me the final blow! Pray all the time for this purpose, if you don't want to be cruel and ungrateful.

Write to me when Jesus wills.

May Jesus grant your soul and that of Giovina and all the others who love Him every charism that you desire for others.

Fra Pio[12].

P.S. Thank you for the Mass intentions, all of which I received.

---

[12] Due to lack of space his signature is written at the top righthand corner of the first sheet.

37

Foggia, Eve of the Feast of the Immaculate Conception,
7 December 1914.

She is comparatively calm in spirit. True conversion. Concerning "total submission." Spiritual reading. Why she does not pray for his death. "I can tell you nothing of my distress." Requests. Postscript.

Father,

Here I am and how many things I have to tell you! Where do I start? I feel comparatively calm in spirit, though peace is lacking on the physical plane as we still have the workmen in the house, both carpenters and painters. This is why I have delayed so long before replying to your four precious letters.

To tell the truth, there was a hurricane in the meantime, which our good, so good Jesus drove away through the prayers of His worthy minister and friend, leaving only some fairly slight traces. Prostrate face downwards I must thank Him and you.

Giovina is fairly well, but suffering all the time from her wretched stomach trouble. She is always cold and tired, worried, depressed and irritable. I watch her, scrutinize her, understand... and suffer torment. This awful cross weighs upon my heart.

Your last letter dated 26 November leaves me trembling and fearful. Ask Jesus to give me strength, patience, resignation and perfect conformity to His most holy will. Argue with Jesus to obtain for me the grace I desire, the grace of my complete conversion. I am blind and deaf to His invitations, I am ungrateful for His very many benefits. I don't know how to thank Him and I don't know how to love Him, yet He bears with me, tolerates me and awaits me. How very good He is with this mass of sin.

You are aware of all my faults, because you say to me in your letter of 4 November: "I am already aware of the kind of life you lived in the past;" and in another letter dated 16 November you say to me: "Besides, what use is there in concealing things from someone who already knows them through other channels?" Hence, you are aware of everything. It makes me blush and I humble myself before God and before you, as I go back over the three periods of my life until now, in the convent, in college and at home; childhood, youth and old age.

But I am not yet converted. When is it to be? I await this gift from you absolutely, since you are so interested and are working so hard for my poor soul. My conversion, my holy sister's spiritual and bodily health, peaceful relations with everybody, provision for the spiritual and temporal needs of poor unfortunates—these are the graces you must obtain for me from our good Jesus.

Apropos of this, I must answer you also on the subject of my total submission. I cannot bring all the pitiful cases to my sister's notice. Very often I have to refuse people I ought not to refuse and then I have to admit to my confusion and mortification that I am just a poor tertiary (how rebellious I am and how full of sin!) Add to this that I have no gentle words, no loving suggestions for those who are poor and afflicted. In a word, I lack the fragrance which proceeds from true charity. I can do nothing, I am no use at anything.

Please make these entreaties yourself, holy Father. Pray for all those whom I know and don't ever, ever forget them.

We come now to another bitter reproof contained in your letter of 4 November. I deserve this. Forgive me, punish me severely, for it will never be too much. You say: "I am more than a little displeased to see how you always have some objection to make to everything I suggest and almost invariably want to act as the teacher," etc. What a humiliation, what embarassment for me! Poor Father, I make you suffer so much, you who treat me so very, very kindly! How horribly ungrateful I am? Who can ever forgive me?

Nobody, absolutely nobody prompted me to object to the spiritual books you suggested for my use. The only counsellor I have is yourself, holy Father full of charity. My confessor tells me in a general way to "do some spiritual reading" and no more. It is therefore only my own empty brain, my own dark and wavering spirit that suggests to me to make known to you the doubts and difficulties which torment me.

Should I not tell you anything further, then? Ought I not tell you any more of all the doubts, all the darkness, the mysteries and secrets that pass through my mind with regard to everything you continue to say to me with immense charity and infinite condescension? Am I to banish to the depths of my conscience all the doubts, difficulties, fears and anxieties, and present myself to you as certain of myself, imperturbable and untroubled? Oh, good Father, I don't know how to do this. I simply must tell you what I feel, I must tell you everything. I cannot do otherwise. It is impossible.

But, for pity's sake, apart from my objection to the spiritual books, in what else have I displeased you? I examine myself and remember nothing. My heedless wretchedness betrays me. That phrase "you always have some objection to make" is stuck like a nail in my heart. Poor Father, I am suffering a lot because of the way I hurt you. In order to repay your continual favours I don't know what I would not do, but I am a nonentity, and what can be expected from nothing? I have, it is true, a soul that is immortal like its God and to this God I always pray for you, that He may grant you what is for His glory and for the good of souls.

I just cannot concede the favour which you ask of me in almost all your letters, namely, to beg Jesus to break the fragile thread of your life. I tell you so with all frankness. It is something beyond my strength. I cannot feel one way and act in another. This is impossible, so I cannot satisfy you. Rebuke me, even punish me as much as you like, for I accept everything from you.

You will fly to Jesus whenever this is His will. Resign yourself to it. You will have to go on working to gain your crown. Some further flowers and jewels and some more rays of light and glory are still needed. Resign yourself. You already possess Jesus very completely, you enjoy Him here below and you will possess Him most perfectly in heaven. You hear and see and speak to Him on this earth. You are continually united to Him in an ecstasy of love and you are transformed into Him. What more do you desire?

I understand that as you come to know Him, the desires and flames of love are kindled more and more. But have a little patience, remain with us a little longer, for we are ignorant and unfamiliar with the noble science of love.

How are you at present? I want to have your news without delay. I am always afraid of fatiguing you by my correspondence. I have no adequate words in which to thank you for what you are doing for me. May Jesus and Mary reward you.

I have begun the third novena to the most holy Virgin of Pompeii; I was already doing the second one when I fell ill and had to interrupt it. I began again when I was able to receive holy Communion once more. Since my return trip on 24 September I have been laid low with a fever four times. The last time it meant fasting for 19 days from the Eucharist.

Do not throw your pearls before swine, says the holy

Gospel[1], but to you I can say nothing of my anxieties as you will be angry with me. Ask Jesus to purify me. I want to lose all taste even for lawful things: the taste for food, the taste for moral satisfaction, for everything. What I desire, what I want is mystical death.

Pride and all the passions have control over me. I am unable to overcome them and indeed I easily yield to them. This is my life. Stop me, good Father, on this fatal descent. I must take another road. I must climb the steep slope of Calvary and this is what frightens me. I am convinced that there is no true love without real suffering and I endeavour to avoid suffering. My weak and cowardly spirit loaded with earth and mud flees in horror from suffering.

Tomorrow, on the great feast of our beautiful Immaculate Mother, I ask you to place my poor lily in her immaculate hands. How extremely rash I am! I am afraid to present it to her myself, wretched as it is, faded, shrivelled up and withered. I blush deeply with shame and I hide. I am leaning on you for support. Defend me (reply to me on this point).

I want to know the exact time at which you say Mass every day and the time of your Mass on Sundays. Don't forget this.

In one of your letters you wanted to know how I spend my time[2]. I'll tell you in detail in another letter. I am afraid of abusing your charity. I always write you fairly long letters and I am afraid of tiring you.

Pray hard for my Giovina. Apart from her union with Jesus she is in great need of holy companionship on the material plane to boost her morale, the kind of company suited to her cultured mind and to her refined, affectionate, sensitive and demonstrative nature. Do you agree with me?

---

[1] Cf. Mt 7:6.

[2] Cf. Letters 33 and 40.

Pray for Rosinella, for her old father who is very ill and for her engaged sister. Jesus has not yet been pleased to settle things for the latter. Her fiancé has now been in the army for two years and there is no mention of his obtaining leave in these difficult times. You may imagine the constant worry and responsibility this brings poor Rosinella. She is older than her sister but timid, uncertain and very ingenuous.

Pray for peace in Europe and that Italy may remain untouched by the terrible scourge of war. Pray and pray and give your blessing continually to,

Your poor tertiary.

P.S. Yesterday, the 6th, was the first anniversary of the death of our holy aunt who was quite unparalleled, a cloistered nun in the convent of the Most Holy Redeemer in Foggia[3]. She had been inside the convent walls since she was nine and loved Jesus very much. Is she now close to Him or is she still in a state of purgation? I am asking this of you who are in a position to know the answer. Please reply to me on this point.

You have forgotten to tell me whether I'll be able to speak to you one day. My very poor pen is never satisfied. It would never stop and yet this is nothing in comparison to what my tongue would have to tell you. The pen cannot and does not know how to explain itself as the tongue would. This is impossible. Allow me to hope. You who show me such great kindness, do you refuse me this? I cannot allow it. Our Seraphic Father would condemn you. Do you agree? Speak to me.

A great many ideas slip my mind and I cannot recall

---

[3] This was Sister Marianna Cerase, daughter of Matteo and Raffaella Albanese, the Cerase sister's grandparents. She died on 7 December 1913 in Vico del Salvatore, n. 4, Foggia, at the age of 88.

them. My mind is confused by a dense fog. Desires and remorse are suffocating and tormenting my spirit. The world fascinates and attracts me and keeps me in fetters. When will everything be extinguished in me, when will it all die?

I am quite right in saying that my poor pen cannot stop. It runs on and on to tell everything to good Padre Pio, but it is never, never satisfied.

Give me some news at once of your precious health. Have you left your bed? Please reply to all my questions. What patience you must have with me, crazy and ungrateful as I am!

I kiss your hand respectfully.

38

Pietrelcina, 10 December 1914.

He awaits news. He wants to be sure he is not deceived. Why he fears the enemy's deceit. She must never slacken on the path of virtue. Sowing abundantly. Regards and good wishes.

J.M.J.D.F.C.

Beloved daughter of Jesus,

May peace, mercy and grace be with you always and with all those who sincerely love our Lord Jesus Christ. Amen.

I wrote to you quite a while ago and have received no letter of yours up to the present. How are you? In the midst of all my troubles and ailments which the heavenly Father in His goodness has been pleased to send me, it is really distressing to have no news from one who means so much to me.

Since I am aware of your exceeding diligence and your singular courtesy, I cannot fail to be extremely worried by this long silence on your part. I sincerely trust that the infinite mercy will grant me the grace to learn that you have been prevented from sending me your news merely because you are so very busy. I hope this is the only reason for your neglect of the one who sends up prayers for you uninterruptedly to God and with tears, while thanking the heavenly Father continually for the many favours granted to you.

With unflagging patience I await the sight of your handwriting in order to have accurate news of you and your whole family, especially as regards Giovina, who is so precious. I ask her prayers for my spiritual health, with your own prayers and those of Rosina.

I have been assured that your own health has improved and I can tell you frankly that my heart rejoices at the news for which I thank the Lord. But as no letter of yours has reached me I am extremely worried, for I suspect that I may have been deceived this time. Moreover, a few days ago the Lord allowed me to pay a visit to Giovina and on that occasion He lavished many graces upon her. It seemed to me at that time that her health was much better than it had been in the past. Am I perhaps mistaken? I don't think so. At all events, relieve my mind of this anxiety.

I earnestly ask you not to allow anything to leak out to Giovina about the visit I paid her. Otherwise you would greatly displease me and at the same time cause me deep embarassment. *It is good to guard the secret of a king*[1].

I am very much afraid that this long silence of yours may be a snare of the enemy from whose wiles you must always defend yourself by paying no heed to his wicked insinuations.

Don't consider me weak in spirit and over severe if I perceive dangers on all sides. Souls cost too much to God and one can never do too much to save them. You who have come to share my secrets, according to what Jesus has disposed, do not consider my concern for your salvation to be mere foolishness. You must also remember that I have espoused you, as I told you elsewhere[2], not to a prince of this world, but to Jesus. You will understand, then, how jealously I desire that your body and your heart be kept pure as when you came forth from baptism.

---

[1] Tob 12:7.
[2] See Letter 30.

For pity's sake remember and never lose sight at any moment in your life of the very strict responsibility I assumed for you before Jesus, to take watchful care of you at all times. Bear in mind that this obligation binds me to keep every breath of pestilential air far from you. Finally, remember that I took it upon myself to present you to the divine Bridegroom when He comes for you, as a virgin chaste in mind and body.

Woe betide me if I were to fail to fulfil this office! I beseech you, then, by the meekness of Jesus and by the bowels of mercy of the heavenly Father, never to slacken on the path of virtue. Keep on running and don't ever make up your mind to stop, for you know that to stand still on this path is equivalent to retracing one's steps[3]. Don't ever disregard my suggestion and, for pity's sake, don't render fruitless and don't neglect the grace which was bestowed on you at baptism and has been increased in great measure by means of the other sacraments.

Be watchful, I tell you, and never place too much trust in yourself or count excessively on your own strength. Try to advance more and more on the way to perfection and practise charity more and more, for charity is the bond of Christian perfection[4]. Throw yourself confidently into the arms of the heavenly Father with childlike trust and open wide your heart to the charism of the Holy Spirit who is only waiting for a sign from you in order to enrich you.

Yes, let us do good. Now is the time for sowing and if we want to reap an abundant harvest it is not so necessary to sow a lot of seed as to scatter it in good ground. We have already sown a lot of seed, but it counts for very little if we want to be gladdened at harvest time. Let us sow now and continue to sow, my dear, and let nothing grieve us on this account. Let us make sure that this seed falls in good soil

---

[3] Cf. St. Bernard, *Epist.* XCI, No, 3; PL Vol. 184, c. 222-24, No. 3.
[4] Cf. Col 3:14.

and when the heat arrives to burst it open and bring forth a plant, we must still be on the watch and take good care that the weeds do not smother the young plants.

I would continue further, but my head is spinning and I feel my strength growing less. Write to me when Jesus permits it and don't hide anything from me.

May Jesus bless you always, together with Giovina, Rosina and all those who live with you and in doing so may He grant my desire to see you all become holy.

Fra Pio, Capuchin[5].

---

[5] For lack of space, his signature is written at the top right-hand corner of the first sheet.

39

Pietrelcina,
Fifth day after the feast of the Immaculate Conception
(12 December) 1914[1].

He acknowledges receipt of her letter and thanks her. Desire for death. The reason for this desire. Explanation of a rebuke. The beautiful flower of purity. The prayers requested.

J.M.J.D.F.C.

Beloved daughter of Jesus,

May the Father of Our Lord Jesus Christ fill you continually with his choicest blessings and make you an ever more worthy bride of His divine Son. Amen.

Our letters crossed in the post. I am surprised how long it took your own greatly-desired letter to reach me. Satan has had a hand in this, for he would have liked to send your letter astray. But praise be at all times to the Immaculate Virgin Mary who did not permit this and will never permit such a thing, I feel sure. This is one more great victory over that nasty wretch.

I cannot tell you how much I rejoice in the midst of my troubles on receiving by your letter a further confirmation of what had previously been affirmed through other chan-

[1] Date of the postmark.

nels, just as I told you in my last letter on the subject of Giovina's health and your own. Blessed be God the Father of Our Lord Jesus Christ, the Father of mercies and God of all consolation[2]. May this good Father continue to show mercy and console us in all the events of life. I really cannot tell you how grateful I am to so tender a Father for the many benefits He continues to lavish on us, in spite of our unworthiness and ingratitude, especially my own which has reached the limit. May He be praised and blessed for ever by all creatures.

I won't go to any pains to find suitable words and expressions to thank you properly for the prayers you are offering for me to the beautiful Virgin of Pompeii. I am well aware that if I tried to do so I should meet with very little success. However, I earnestly trust that Jesus will reward you to the full. It goes without saying that all these delicate attentions of yours are for me so many more reasons for pleading your cause more and more with our most sweet Jesus, although I myself, in the first place, am in great need of His help.

I am amazed and at the same time I commend your sincerity when you tell me you just cannot beseech the Bridegroom of souls to sever without delay the bonds that keep me united to this fragile body. However, I cannot deny that this news is to me like a double-edged sword which goes right through my heart. This admission of yours has greatly increased my agony.

I make allowances for you and may the Lord pardon you, for you do not understand the sad state of a soul that is sick with love for its God. How often is this soul not driven by an irresistible force to shout loudly in the ear of its lover: "Show Yourself and may the sight of You and of Your beauty kill me! Know that love's sweet longing cannot be appeas-

---

[2] Cf. 2 Cor 1:3.

ed except by the presence and the sight of the loved one[3]."

Oh, how often, at the mercy of the flames which burn its innermost recesses, does the poor soul not raise its voice and say: "Extinguish my pains, You alone have power to calm them, my eyes behold You, for You are their light which I want to keep for You alone[4]."

Ah, why am I denied this charity? I no longer dare to call you cruel towards the one who suffers so much and this is only because you have been sincere. But by the bowels of mercy of the incarnate God I still dare to entreat you to act differently in the future. Otherwise, may God forgive me, you will become a murderess.

What have you to say to this? Answer me. Shall I be alone in praying for this purpose? I shall never be heard, for I am well aware that my heart and all the parts of my body are rotten with sin. Ah, don't continue to turn a deaf ear, otherwise who knows how long my soul will have to go on rotting in this putrified body.

I would willingly accept your exhortation to wait patiently for my death if your uncalled for remark were true, that is to say, that I must still labour to complete my crown which needs some more flowers and jewels to finish it. But, dear God, not even the framework of this crown has been made. There can be no talk of flowers or gems, for I have done nothing at all. And if I have not been burnt up it is a pure act of the divine mercy.

Should I begin now to weave the crown, to stud it with gems and make the flowers bloom? Alas! Spring is already gone and the time is not suitable. My soul was deaf to the voice of the Bridegroom when He invited me lovingly to follow Him when the bad weather was over, when the winter was

---

[3] Second strophe of the *Canticle of the soul and the Bridegroom*, by St. John of the Cross.

[4] *Ibid.*, strophe 10.

gone[5]. My soul slept all through the spring. It was the sleep of the ungrateful and too late did I awaken. My soul sought its lover in everything and by God's mercy it found Him seated in the midst of many loved ones whose hands were full of flowers of which they offered Him the perfume.

My soul recognized the mistake it had made and endeavoured to follow Him, occupying the last place. Up to the present moment it does not know what to offer Him, since it has nothing of its own. But observe the goodness of this divine lover who does not rebuff the soul, but draws it towards Him by loving gestures. But, dear God, how do I respond to so many delicate advances of Your love? By ingratitude, that is all. Meanwhile my soul grieves about all this and would like to put an end to its infidelity. But it is invariably surrounded by infinite dangers which cause it to be unfaithful once more.

This is one of the reasons which powerfully stimulate my desire lo leave this life. But let us be done with these laments and come to yourself. Are you still so indifferent that you will not yield to my pleas? For pity's sake, do not be so cruel and barbarous towards this poor unhappy one. I appeal to the nobility and generosity of your great heart, that is all.

I do not cease to marvel at your very rigorous interpretation of my words: "I am more than a little displeased to see how you have some objection to make to everything I suggest and almost invariably want to act as the teacher," etc. I really intended to reprove and rebuke you by these words. But I never intended and it never occurred to me nor could it ever occur to me to forbid you to tell me about all the anxieties and doubts that revolve in your mind. This is quite the opposite to my intention and to do so would be contrary to my will. By that rebuke I meant to reprove a certain obstinacy

[5] Cf. Song 2:11.

on your part in not wanting to calm yourself with regard to matters in which you have been assured you have nothing to fear.

If you understand my reprimand in this sense, then it certainly served its purpose. Meanwhile, just continue to inform me of all that goes on in your soul in the certainty that you will meet with my approval and also please Jesus. Moreover, when you receive an assurance of the true state of something, then I want you to calm down and not act like a teacher who has some fresh objection to make. Do I make myself clear?

Please clear up one point for me. You are to be quite at peace, my dear sister, and you must not take such an admonition in bad part. What I said did not come from any ill-will towards you but from my really deep love for you in Jesus Christ.

Don't be distressed about the suffering you caused me, for all is now forgotten. May Jesus repay my sufferings by bestowing on you just as many consolations and even more. I beseech you, my dear, not to imagine that I am by any means angry with you on this score, for you haven't offended me at all. If I was and still am saddened by this behaviour of yours, I shall be immensely happy when our good Jesus will give me the consolation of seeing you rid yourself of this hideous imperfection.

I am perfectly sure that my good Raffaelina will not deprive me of this great satisfaction. I am so certain of this that I am already thanking the Lord in advance and sending my Raffaelina warm congratulations.

The Immaculate Virgin has already accepted your little bouquet presented by my hands. This good Mother, it is true, found it a little faded by reason of the somewhat cold dew that fell on it, but this is only a slight defect and you will be able to restore it to full bloom by the warmth of love.

Yes, my dear, it must never seem to us that we have too

much of this virtue. Although I find you far advanced in this respect, I never cease to exhort you to an increase in charity, as this is the virtue greatly preferred and recommended to us by our divine Master. He was pleased to give all His followers a commandment with regard to this virtue, a commandment of His very own and altogether new[6], something quite unknown to the majority of our Old Testament ancestors.

I am sorry to be unable to give you an answer here with reference to your aunt's holy soul, as the Lord does not allow it. I hope to do so later on.

At present I am out of bed, thank heaven, but I am in very bad shape. But please do not be anxious about me and take good care not to ask the Lord to free me from my physical ailments. Let all your prayers be concerned with my spiritual state alone which I have very much at heart. I venture to ask the same charity from our very precious Giovina, from the gentle Rosina and from all those who love Jesus.

Assure our good Rosina that I remember her constantly in Jesus' presence and ask her not to disdain to keep a little place in her prayers for my own wretched soul also.

I should like to continue, but... you know all.

In blessing you at all times, may Jesus grant my desires to see you holy. To all those who love Jesus, remember the one who always remains,

Your most humble servant,
Fra Pio, Capuchin.

[6] Cf. Jn 13:34.

40

Foggia, 15 December 1914.

She replies to the previous two letters. She asks that her own letters be burned. Will they meet before they die? The hours of his Masses. Jesus' soul. Preoccupations. Her daily timetable. Preparations for Christmas. Requests.

Jesus alone! Most Holy Spirit, help me!

Father,

I hasten to answer your last two letters, for I see that our good Jesus inspires you to take a deep interest in my poor soul.

The suffering you endured while awaiting my last letter is a very clear proof for me and the sentiments you pour out to me in your second-last letter leave me no further room for doubt. May Jesus be infinitely blessed. What beautiful things you tell me! I am pervaded with deep joy and among your many most valuable reassurances these precious words of yours: "Finally, remember that I took it upon myself to present you to the divine Bridegroom when He will come for you, as a virgin chaste in mind and body. Woe betide me if I should fail to fulfil this office!" leave me quite beside myself, for they reveal to me quite clearly that when I die I shall be presented by you, still on earth, to the heavenly Father.

I shall die, therefore, recommending soul and body to the hands of my good Padre Pio! As minister and friend of the Bridegroom, he will ask peace for my soul in expiation. What good fortune for me! But what have I done to deserve such protection? And when, when will I leave this world? You certainly know this. Will it be soon, as I hope? Father, tell me. Father, hasten it. Ask Jesus to make it soon, soon. If I don't know how to love Him, what is the use of living? What more can be expected of me? He knows me through and through. I would like to know Him, to love Him. Instead, I am sinning all the time, offending and disgusting Him.

When you hear of my death, I want you to do something which is very important for me. My poor letters are written for you alone, they contain all that concerns my conscience and also family matters. To you alone I confide all, so I ask you to burn them. In this regard, set my mind at rest, reassure me, reply to me. Who knows what you will say to these poor, silly, incoherent letters of mine. You who are so good, please make allowances and forgive me for them.

For the third time you have forgotten and omitted to tell me if before I die, which I hope will be soon, you will do me the kindness among the many favours you do me continually, of allowing me to speak to you at least once. I beg you on my knees to grant me this grace. Answer me on this point.

You have also omitted to tell me the exact time at which you say Mass each day and on Sundays. Remember to do this.

By this time you ought to have no secrets from me. Do you not demand that I hide absolutely nothing from you, although you already know all through other channels? All that you know about me is misery, earth and mud. Whereas what I want to know from you is light, virtue, love, holiness, perfection; tears, throbbings, colloquies, ecstasy, union, transformation in immense love. May my poor cold soul, in your image, be converted and corrected. (In your last letter you expressed your "warm congratulations in advance," to use your very words).

By your ardent and continual supplications and according to your own image, may this cold soul be shaken up, renewed and revived. May it be warmed, strengthened and adorned. Tell Jesus that I want to see the ugliness of my soul (even in a dream) so that I may detest my sins. I would like to keep a holy and continual watch in order never to commit any sins again. (Answer me on all these points).

Jesus' life is the highest and most intense expression of love and suffering. And what about my own life? In the little room of His love in which Jesus remains a prisoner and where He continues to think of me, to love and favour me, two eternal deep and powerful words are imprinted: "suffering and love." And my own life, how disheartening it is! Help me, Holy Father. Your holy words stimulate me for a while and then I fall back. I am too weak, too bad.

I am very worried at present about Rosina. As I told you, her father has a very bad heart condition and the end is feared from one moment to the next. As she has at home just one young sister, a beautiful girl engaged to be married, poor Rosa must now leave my home after 25 years with us, to look after this sister.

You can imagine how worried I am. We first met in the church, during the month of May at the feet of our beautiful Immaculate Mother. We met in the spirit and we understood one another. Jesus willed this at the time, but now? My whole household is in the hands of this good spiritual sister of mine and I myself don't attend to any household duties. Imagine how upset I am! If she leaves, this whole responsibility will fall on me. There will be no more spiritual peace for me, for the quiet and calm I need will be lacking. I experienced this several times, on the various occasions when Rosina was away and it was a very sad experience for me.

Our maid (a lady who has come down in the world) is no use at these things. She has neither the will nor the strength for them. Giovina detests having new faces around the house, so she tolerates her. Always nervy and difficult, impossible to please, invariably diffident towards everything and everybody, Giovina is not willing to accept anybody but Rosa, whose affection alone leads her to bear this responsibility, for she has no need to work. (I myself am all the time between Scylla and Charybdis).

I shrink from this responsibility and I am really frightened and worried. May Jesus provide for everything. He knows all and you too are aware of my critical situation. Pray and pray hard. May all be for His glory and for the well-being and peace of all concerned. (Answer me on this point).

I am now ready to satisfy you with an account of how I spend my time. I rise in the morning at 6.30 in winter, because Giovina doesn't want me to get up any earlier. At about 7.30 I go down to the church for Mass (when the weather is good). Rosa comes along later, in view of her duties.

I invariably find Jesus all alone. Gemma Galgani says that before Jesus crucified she used to suffer and before Jesus in the Blessed Sacrament she used to pour out her love[1]. What of myself? What a difference, like the difference between heaven and earth! Two or three women and a man or two assist at the great sacrifice. What desolation and how it must pain the Most Sacred Heart of Jesus! I am the last to leave Jesus all by Himself. The church is then closed and

---

[1] "One day while she (Gemma) was in ecstasy she was heard to say confidentially to the Lord: 'Listen, Jesus, to the question my confessor asks: 'What do you do, Gemma, when you are before Jesus?' 'What do I do? If I am with Jesus crucified I suffer, and if I am with Jesus in the Blessed Sacrament I pour out my love.'" GERMANO DI S. STANISLAO, C.P., *Biografia della serva di Dio, Gemma Galgani, vergine lucchese*, 4th ed., Rome, 1910, pp. 310ff.

I return home at about 8.30. Shortly afterwards I go to waken Giovina. (Now that the weather is cold and she is always ailing to some extent, she wakes very late). We take coffee together and chat for a while (sometimes quite a lot). Giovina then gets up and I return to my own corner. I take up my prayers again and end at about 10 if I am not interrupted. On the other hand, when I am called frequently I don't end until half-an-hour later, or even more. I then see to various things and do some needlework. At about 1.30 p.m. I have lunch. An hour later I devote half-an-hour to prayer once more, then I work or read. When the Angelus rings I say the Rosary etc., then, if we have no visitors, I read and work.

This is my normal programme, but it varies according to the circumstances. This holds good when things are going smoothly, but when there is a storm or even when the course of events varies, my poor brain is all upset and I can't make head or tail of things.

What more should I tell you? Question me, ask me to give you an account of whatever you please and I'll always be quite sincere and happy to satisfy you.

During these holy days I should like to dwell in the blessed grotto. I should like to move around continually in those poor and holy precincts, thinking, working and loving the Infant God. The fine ideas which occupy my mind do not affect my heart, which remains deaf and cold and hard all the time, more insensitive than marble or bronze. What am I to do to soften it? You who are a master in the art of love could teach me and help me to practise it. You who are aflame, who burn and are consumed by love of Jesus, have you no pity for hardened frozen souls? You are selfish and cruel, for you take everything for yourself! Answer me on this point.

I wish you a holy time during the feastdays, blessed and happy with the Infant Jesus. I wish you greater holiness and just one degree of beatitude, just one degree less than the complete and entire and perfect beatitude you will enjoy in heaven (after my death, though, let it be understood; satisfy me in this). Satisfy me also by making the Infant Jesus give holy peace to all my relatives, to all men of good will and even to those of ill will, by turning them towards good, towards virtue and brotherly harmony.

Can you give me any hope that my brother will cease to be so bad-tempered during this feast of peace in which the beautiful values of the family emerge so clearly? This is a gift I expect from your charity during these Christmas feasts. If you are willing, all this will come about; our good Jesus invariably listens to His minister and friend. (Please reply to me about this).

Never forget my unhappy ones and pray hard for them all. Pray a great deal for my Giovina, for her health in soul and body, peace and serenity in mind and spirit. Pray for me during that blessed night close to the cradle of the Infant Jesus and keep this unworthy disciple of yours in mind. During your daily Mass, never forget the last of your daughters, the worst and most wretched of them all. Pray that I may be detached, dead to the world, to creatures and to myself. May novels, balls, theatrical performances and all worldly amusement (I am afraid I am scandalizing you) which belong to the past be far from me.

My dear Father, keep my imagination and my heart far away from such ugly things of this earth. May I forget all this completely, may it all die within me. Do not be horrified, holy Father, and do not draw away from this dunghill. I am in need of help and forgiveness, so do not deny me anything. Yes, help me, forgive me and bless me always, always, always.

A poor tertiary.

41

Pietrelcina, 17 December 1914.

He offers prayers. He asks prayers. Approval of her daily schedule. A few points to be set right. How to behave with regard to imperfect actions. Never forget the divine Presence. Prayer before and after meals. Examination of conscience. The Guardian Angel. Explanation of a phrase about death. Their correspondence. The time of his Mass.

J.M.J.D.F.C.

Beloved daughter of the heavenly Father and betrothed of His Son,

May the divine Spirit come down into your heart and fill it entirely with heavenly charisms. How good our God is who lavished so many graces upon us and loves us so dearly although we do not deserve it. May He be for ever blessed by all creatures.

At the opening of the sacred novena in honour of the holy Child Jesus I felt my soul being born, as it were, to a new life. My heart felt too small to contain the heavenly favours and my soul seemed to disintegrate in the presence of this God who took human flesh for our sake. How can we help loving Him more and more ardently? Oh, let us draw near to the Child Jesus with hearts free from sin, that we may discover how sweet and delightful it is to love Him.

I will never fail to pray to this divine Child for all men, and much more will I pray during these holy days. I will pray especially for you and for all those whom you have so much at heart. I will ask Him to give you a share of those charisms He has poured out and continues to pour all the time into my own soul.

Do not fail to pray particularly during these days for my own soul, that all may go well with it. My soul is greatly in need of the divine assistance. I see how great my need is of gratitude towards the supreme Benefactor. I am aware that I pay Him absolutely no debt of gratitude and that this is a dreadful thing for my soul. Wretched as I am, I wish I were not in such extreme spiritual poverty, but I do not know how to avoid it.

This would be a most singular grace for me if the divine mercy were pleased to grant it through your own prayers. I expect everything from the Lord's most generous hand and I also expect this grace, solely through the merits of the Incarnate Word. Do not fail to send up your supplications for this purpose, especially during these days when heaven is open more than ever to send down divine graces upon us.

Pray, then, and do sweet violence to the little heart of this tender Infant who is filled with deep affection for us. Thank you for the beautiful greetings you sent me for the imminent feasts of the Child Jesus. In return I ask Jesus to repay you a hundredfold twice over. May He grant to your own soul all the charisms you desire for mine.

I am consoled by your way of life. I assure you that this is very pleasing to me and I give infinite thanks to Jesus for it. You say nothing about how you pass the night hours, something no less important. You do not tell me at all whether you make an examination of conscience and how many times you usually do this during the day. Why do you tell me nothing about these things? I make allowances for you, as I realize you have given no thought to the matter.

Now I am going to entreat you to set some aspects of your life in order. I ask you to fix two more periods for holy meditation and in view of your present state of health these should be preferably in the morning, before you go down to church, and in the evening after you have said the Rosary. As the weather is very rigid at this season you may even make your morning meditation in bed before you rise. The Lord will be satisfied with this. Will you also satisfy me in this? I am sure that you will do so in a spirit of deep submission. At all events, please give me your assurance of it.

I also want to hear from yourself the manner in which you have been taught to meditate and how you actually do it. I want you to tell me this very accurately and clearly. Take care, moreover, not to lose the presence of God by any action whatsoever. Never undertake any work or any action without first raising your mind to God and directing to Him with a pure intention the action you are about to perform. You should do likewise at the end of every action. Examine yourself as to whether you have done everything with the right intention you had at the beginning and if you find you have been at fault, then ask pardon of the Lord with humility while making a firm resolution to correct your faulty conduct.

You must not be discouraged or let yourself become dejected if your actions have not succeeded as perfectly as you intended. What do you expect? We are made of clay and not every soil yields the fruits expected by the one who tills it. But let us always humble ourselves and acknowledge that we are nothing if we lack the divine assistance.

To be worried because something we have done has not turned out in accordance with our pure intention shows a lack of humility. This is a clear sign that the person concerned has not entrusted the success of his action to the divine assistance but has depended too much on his own strength.

My Raffaelina is to guard against this secret reasoning

which comes from Satan and to reject his promptings just as soon as she becomes aware of them.

May the ever-present grace of the Lord invariably prevent you from being a prey to this evil spirit even to the slightest extent. It is never a small matter when a soul espoused to the Son of God succumbs to the wiles of this dreadful monster even in little things.

Never let your mind become so absorbed in your work or in other matters as to make you lose the presence of God. For this purpose I ask you to renew very often the right intention you had at the outset. Now and then you should say some short prayers which are like so many darts which wound the heart of God and constrain Him, if I may use such an expression which is no exaggeration in your case, to grant you His graces and His help in everything you do.

Do not sit down to a meal without having prayed first and asked the divine assistance, so that the food you are about to eat reluctantly for the sustenance of the body may not be harmful to your soul. Hence, as you sit down to table, call to mind some pious thought. Picture to yourself the divine Master in your midst with his holy apostles just as he was during the Last Supper before he instituted the Sacrament of the Altar.

To put it briefly, let us make an effort to ensure that the supper by which we satisfy the body may be a preparation for the altogether divine supper of the most holy Eucharist. Let all this be done without excessive spiritual fatigue. Have I explained what I mean?

Never rise from the table, moreover, without having given due thanks to the Lord. If we act in this way we need have no fear of the wretched sin of gluttony. As you eat, take care not to be too difficult to please in the matter of food, bearing in mind that it is very easy to give in to gluttony. Never eat more than you really need and endeavour to practise moderation all the time. You should be very ready to refuse what you need rather than what is in excess of your needs. However, I don't mean to say that you should rise from table without eating. No, this is not my intention. Let everything be regulated by prudence which should be the rule in all our actions.

Never lie down to sleep without having first examined your conscience on the way you have spent the day and without first turning your thoughts to God. Then offer and consecrate your whole person and that of every Christian, especially my wretched self, to God, just as I do for you.

Offer, moreover, to the glory of His divine Majesty the rest you are about to take and never forget your Guardian Angel who is always close to you, who never leaves you no matter how badly you treat him. O unspeakable excellence of this good angel of ours! How many times, alas, have I made him weep when I refused to comply with his wishes which were also God's wishes! May this most faithful friend of ours save us from further unfaithfulness.

Try to have in mind some thought concerning the painful Passion of Jesus before you fall asleep. I advise you, as you go to sleep, to have before your mental gaze the picture of Jesus as He prayed in the Garden. But all this must be done, I repeat, without overtaxing your mind.

As regards those words which I used in my last letter: "Finally, remember that I took it upon myself to present you to the divine Bridegroom when he comes for you, as a virgin chaste in mind and body," you have taken them to apply to the too near future. In saying that I would present you to the divine Bridegroom when he called you, I did not mean that you would go to the heavenly homeland before me. You are in too great a hurry, my dear, to leave this land of exile before I do. You still have to fight further battles in God's name and further crowns have been prepared for you by the divine mercy. Do not be frightened by this statement. There will be a terrible conflict, but there is no fear of your losing the battle, for the Holy Spirit will give you such great strength that you will be able to endure and overcome all opposition.

You will leave this extremely dark prison when you will have run the entire course mapped out for you by the Most High, and as I see it you still have a long way to go. Make haste, then, so that you may finish the course in a shorter time. Keep looking ahead and never call a halt.

If I precede you into eternity, the strict duty I have assumed of presenting you to the divine Bridegroom as a virgin chaste in mind and body when He comes for you, will be fulfilled from up above. Have no doubts, for all will be carried out as I have told you.

As regards your letters, you mustn't worry about what is to happen to them. You have no further rights in this respect. All will be done as God wills. Be at peace, then, on this score and let vain fears about your letters be far from your mind.

You ask me for the second time to tell you the hour at which I usually say Mass. I regret very much that I forgot to tell you this in my last letter, but you who are aware of everything as I mentioned to you on another occasion will not, I hope, hold me to blame. You are very kind and precisely on this account I feel you will be indulgent. I beg of you to remind me continually until you receive a reply whenever I fail to answer you on some matter. In the meantime, forgive me and make allowances for me.

On weekdays, during the winter season, I usually go down to say Mass at about 8.30 or 9 a.m. On Sundays and holydays of obligation, ordinarily after 11 a.m. As you see, I am rather a lazybones, but it is not entirely my fault. My wretched illness compels me to behave in this way.

I leave it to you to imagine my feelings with regard to the misfortune which has befallen poor Rosina's father, but let us trust in divine Providence. All will be for the best both for yourself and for her[1]. May the Child Jesus inspire your brother to have better feelings towards you. In this connection we must wait for something else to happen. Do not torment yourself on this account, but take courage when you consider how long the Lord has shown patience towards him.

Do not get tired of praying for me and for my family, knowing that I do the same for you and for all. I should be very grateful and obliged to you if you would offer up for my intentions your Holy Communions until the eve of Christ's Nativity. I require an urgent favour from this tender little Child, so pray and get others to pray for this purpose.

I don't know whether I have satisfied all your requests and I should be very sorry if I had neglected any of them. At all events, you know how to act towards me. I end here, as I am unable to continue.

I wish you once more, not only yourself but all those in your household, a most happy celebration of the feastdays in our most sweet Lord Jesus Christ, and while I implore the heavenly Father to bless you, I remain,

Your servant,
Fra Pio, Capuchin.

---

[1] See below, Letter 43.

42

Pietrelcina, 22 December 1914.

Renewed Christmas greetings. The beautiful virtue of charity. Requests.

J.M.J.D.F.C.

Little bride of Jesus,

May the grace and peace of the heavenly Father be with you always and make you more holy.

Here I am once more with greetings for the feasts of the holy Child along with your entire most precious family. May the Lord and the most holy Virgin make you ever more worthy of eternal glory. With this faith and this desire I want you all to be very happy during the feastdays of the most holy Nativity of the Child Jesus and I earnestly hope you may repeat this celebration during the longest possible life, growing all the time in charity, which is the queen and mother of all the virtues.

Oh, how sublime is the beautiful virtue of charity which the Son of God has brought us! All must have it at heart, but more so still those who aim at holiness. Without any merit on your part, the Lord has called you; and even though I see you far advanced on the way of charity, I never cease to insist that you continue to advance along this path.

The Child Jesus is offering you a new chance to practise this virtue. Do you know who it is that I mean to mention to you? It is that poor child, the seamstress who has lost her mother and to whom you will be so kind as to forward the enclosed envelope[1]. I am well aware of the affection you have shown her already and I want to tell you how very pleased I am on this account. May Jesus reward you abundantly. Continue to show her charity so that she may feel as little as possible the loss of her mother. I want you to take on the noble task of counsellor and mother to her, a twofold office that I trust you will fulfil well and very scrupulously. Let me tell you that you have to deal with a simple soul, a good soul who is very dear to the divine Master. You must be, in a word, her protecting angel.

This is sufficient about the matter for the present. More about it at a more suitable time.

All my love to every one of you in Christ Jesus.

Fra Pio[2].

---

[1] He is referring to Annita, of Foggia.

[2] For lack of space his signature has been written at the top righ-hand corner of the first sheet.

43

Foggia, 26 December 1914.

The title "bride of Jesus." Remembering a dead man. Household duties and pious exercises. The bitter chalice prophesied. She'll reply later when things are calmer. Counselling the little seamstress. Beside the Holy Child's cradle. Faults of the past. Requests.

Jesus alone! Most Holy Spirit, help me!

Father,

In this letter I don't know whether to burst out into a hymn of joy or a cry of pain. A hymn of joy for the holy and dear title by which you addressed me in your last two letters duly received: "Betrothed of the Son of God. Little bride of Jesus" (your exact words). Is this possible? I'll never succeed in understanding it. It is true that I call Him Father, Brother, Friend, because the ungrateful daughter knows she is understood by her good Father, the sister is sure that she is constantly loved by her fond Brother, the unfortunate and guilty friend knows she will find a response and forgiveness in the heart of her true Friend. But the bride, oh, the bride must be one body and one heart with her spouse: thoughts, feelings, anxieties, palpitations, ardour, flames, her entire life must be for her spouse. This is why I consider that these forms of address are not for me but for some other soul directed by you, someone who is truly a bride of Jesus.

I am very much afraid, my dear Father, of being deceived and of deceiving you. I am incapable of anything but chatter and daydreaming. Tell me frankly if this is the case. Clear up this doubt for me; speak to me.

The cry of pain is due to a storm which is throwing my whole existence into confusion. That which I feared has now come to pass. Poor Rosina's father got a stroke at 10 a.m. on the 21st and at 11 p.m. he blessed his daughters with the crucifix, kissed it three times, then, fortified by the comforts of religion, died the death of the just and passed to eternal happiness.

Our poor friend received a brusque call that morning at my home and she has not returned here. It is useless to mention again the cause of this as you are already aware of everything. I am all alone, Father, both spiritually and materially, and I have no company in church or at home. If one were in good health it would not be so bad. But Giovina in particular has her ailments and her dreadful attacks. Left alone with only the maid, I am lost. I am afraid to remain alone in the midst of sickness or when there are thunderstorms. Giovina is looking for a reliable maid to take Rosa's place, some good, trustworthy and devout woman. But will Jesus send her to us? What do you say about it?

At the moment I am faced with great responsibility and many duties. I am doing all for Jesus in great haste. I can barely steal the time to write to you. Giovina is perturbed all the time. The day before yesterday, eve of the great day, she wept at table because, as she says, we are left too much to ourselves. She suffers a lot especially on feastdays from the lack of family affection. I don't know where to turn or what to do to satisfy her. I should need great physical and moral strength to continue doing what I have to do at present.

For two days I was unable to go to Mass due to an attack of migraine. Two evenings later while saying the Rosary I was seized by a physical ailment which I have had for a long time and had to go to bed at once. Next day I did not go to church and I spent the eve of the great feast without receiving the Eucharist. There you have, in brief, the fine life I am leading. What should I do? How am I to act? I don't know and I feel really lost. I have a sword stuck in my heart as I see myself deprived of my shadow, of my poor friend. I have to pretend and hide everything from my sister who is unreasonably irritated by my quite justified complaints. She behaves very unjustly towards Rosa and is ungrateful, because, it seems to me, she is more than a little jealous. And I myself? I just suffer, suffer, suffer.

What does Jesus want from me? I feel I haven't the strength to go on like this. I am very much afraid of the bitter chalice which you foretold in your second-last letter. I am convinced that the cross is the thermometer of love and I am very far from putting this theory into practice. The fire in me is clearly just a flash in the pan. I cannot bear to suffer. I am not willing to bow down and submit with resignation to the most holy will of the One who does all things well.

I spend hours in deep anguish. I cry bitterly as I ponder on many many things. My heart is breaking. The joy I expected to experience at the holy grotto has turned into bitter grief. I no longer think of anything, for Giovina's physical troubles and the household duties fill my time and my mind. I am anxious and breathless all the time. The days go by in a whirl. During the day in an occasional brief interval I curl up in my little corner and pray badly, listlessly, distractedly and in a state of irritation.

I ought to speak to you and to reply in detail to the questions you asked in your second-last letter, that is, as regards the night hours, examination of conscience, meditation, vocal prayer, the presence of God, nourishment, confession, Communion, my Guardian Angel, the prophesied Calvary, all of them matters of which it would take some time to give you an account. I'll do this in another letter when I can. Give me a respite, give me time, holy Father. Plead my cause, you, my powerful advocate, for I find I am lost.

You who know all about my life, tell me clearly what Jesus says to you. Tell me frankly what sins I commit day by day. Speak to me without reserve or constraint. May Jesus inspire you with regard to the true needs of my poor soul. Oh, if I could only rid myself of the secret and subtle pride which infects and ruins the holiest works! I hope for everything from you, I expect all from your boundless charity. Speak to me on this point.

Does Jesus approve of my language? Please give me an answer. Oh, my poor letters! May Jesus permit them to be seen by no other eyes but yours for you alone are my counsellor. Pray continually and plead my cause as my powerful advocate before my judge (and you call me a bride! I am something very different; I am very, very bad).

To me, bad as I am, you entrust a "good simple soul very dear to the divine Master." What would I not do to obey you and to satisfy you! But note well that I have no freedom and can do absolutely nothing. This person has no need spiritually. Giovina, moreover, has taken a great interest in her material needs by writing again and again to obtain particulars about adoption (she has received very exact information in this respect) and also about a possible place in a convent. We are awaiting her decision, or rather, news from the one who will induce her to decide.

As regards the note you enclosed for her, I am most willing to oblige you, but allow me to point out a difficulty. I have never spoken of you to this person, much less of my spiritual correspondence and I am unwilling to reveal it in the present circumstances—I am very, very jealous—so I am awaiting your holy Father[1] in order to send it to her through

[1] Padre Agostino of San Marco in Lamis.

him. Do you approve? Am I right? Tell me frankly, give me your advice.

Some time ago your holy Father wrote to inform me of this enclosure of yours[2]. I should have answered him and put forward the same difficulties that I have mentioned to you, but I prefer to do this orally and am waiting until he comes. I heard indirectly that he is to pass through Foggia after the holidays. At all events, I think I am right to guard my spiritual secret carefully. No one except Rosa and another holy and discreet person (this orphan's teacher whom I mentioned to you in another letter) shares it with me.

In the absence of Rosa I went to the three Masses on Christmas morning with this person. I listened to her sighs and weeping and loving palpitations there beside me, but my own heart, on the contrary, felt frozen and harder than flint. Oh, my wretched Communion!

This morning there was no Mass at St. Joseph's. After quite a long interval I went to your own friars' church[3].

---

[2] Cf. *Letters* I, Nos. 217, 218, 221, 222.

[3] St. Anne's Church. The little church of St. Joseph is only a few steps away from the Cerase home. The Confraternity of St. Joseph, erected and founded with the authorization of Monsignore de Sangro, on 19 September 1684, was first located in the Theatine's church where the members had a chapel in which to meet for their devotional exercises. In 1762 the confraternity was transferred to the present little church which the members built at their own expense and dedicated to the holy Patriarch. The interior was damaged the day after the titular feast in 1950 and was then completely restored, including the statue of the saint which was modelled exactly on the one which had been ruined. According to the author of a history of the city, the celebrated Foggian painter Giuseppe Fania who had painted some pictures depicting biblical scenes for use at the altar of repose in several Neapolitan churches in Holy Week, donated these to the little church in honour of his own holy patron, St. Joseph, even though he was far from his native city at the time. It is not known where these paintings are at present. The painting on the ceiling depicting St. Joseph's death, was done in 1903 by the well-known Foggia artist Ottavio Mucelli. The pious confraternity arranges for the celebration each year of the holy patron's feast, preceded by the devotions of the Seven Wednesday and a procession, with no external display. Cf. M. DI GIOIA, *La diocesi di Foggia*, Foggia, 1955, pp. 240ff.

What memories, what regrets, what emotion! There is a beautiful crib there. At the foot of the Eucharistic cradle I wept and prayed. I prayed that all my thoughts might remain there, my tender feelings, my anxieties, doubts, tears, dejection and suffering.

I feel the same all the time, always in the grip of my former sins, always ruled by my passions. However, I told the Lord that even if I were to find myself in the devil's arms I would always and ever hope and trust in Him. I hope, at least, that instead of arousing His contempt, I inspire Him with compassion and mercy. He is so good and generous. Answer me about this.

Obtain calm for my troubled soul, my powerful advocate. How patient you are with me. You will have a further degree of glory in paradise on my account, if you are able to bear with this unworthy creature and Jesus will love you more. For the fourth time I now ask you (I am insisting because you told me to keep on reminding you whenever you forget) if I can speak to you one day? Please give me an answer.

Share with me, pass on to me, even in writing, just a single spark of the great fire that consumes you. Don't be an egoist. Satisfy me for the love of Jesus.

Pray for Giovina, for my distressed friend and for my widowed niece. She comes to see me continually and she always cries. This is one of the many sorrowful mysteries which surround us and it is one of the many wounds in my soul. I'll tell you about it some other time.

I kiss your hand and ask you to continue all the time to bless

Your poor tertiary.

44

Pietrelcina, 29 December 1914.

News in brief. The title "little bride of Jesus." The signs of true love of God. "I see you well advanced in love." He hopes to make her acquaintance. Counselling the seamstress.

J.M.J.D.F.C.

Little bride of Jesus,

May the Infant Jesus load you with His charisms and fill your heart with His heavenly consolations.

Rejoice in the Lord, my dearest Raffaelina, even though you feel oppressed by many sufferings. Rejoice, for Jesus is with you and He wants you to suffer with Him.

Do not expect a long letter from me this time. I'll write you a long one as soon as Jesus allows me to do so. Just now it is not possible. Meanwhile, make allowances for me and do not on this account say that I am cruel and selfish. I take all your troubles to heart as if they were my own and I hope the divine Bridegroom will be pleased in His goodness to remove their weight from your soul.

Elsewhere I also called you "little bride of Jesus, betrothed of the heavenly Father's Son" and you really deserve this title. You should calm yourself and yield more and more to the love of our divine Spouse. I urge you not to let yourself be persuaded that I have perhaps been deceived about the true state of your soul. This is a real temptation which you should drive far from you, as you are accustomed to do.

I cannot refrain from blaming you when I see how very attached you are to your own judgment as regards your love for your heavenly Bridegroom. You are mistaken, greatly mistaken, when you want to measure the soul's love for its Creator by the delightful feelings it experiences in loving God. This kind of love belongs to those who are still spiritually immature and it could prove fatal to a soul that abandons itself too fully to it. On the other hand, the love of those who have left this spiritual infancy behind them is a love which experiences neither taste nor delight in what is called the sensitive part of the soul.

We have a sure sign that these people really love God when we observe their readiness to keep God's holy law; their constant watchfulness so that they may not fall into sin; their habitual desire to see the heavenly Father glorified, while losing no chance to spread the kingdom of God as far as lies in their power; when we see them praying continually to God the Father in the same words of our divine Master: *Our Father... thy kingdom come*[1].

I see you far advanced in this love of God and I merely urge you to grow more and more in it. I ask you not to worry about this matter and not to be troubled if you do not experience any sweetness in your love. With the divine assistance I hope to speak to you at greater length on this subject in another letter. For the moment let it suffice for you to know that you love God and that God has a very deep love for you. Make an effort to bear with steadfast patience this new trial which the Lord already made known well beforehand through me. The mercy of the eternal Father has reserved many crowns for you because of this present trial.

---

[1] Mt 6:10.

Do not doubt, my dear, that the beautiful noonday sun will soon shine. Without your being aware of it, Jesus is detaching you little by little, imperceptibly, from all that places an obstacle in the way of this heavenly union. Oh, how good Jesus is, my dear Raffaelina, with all, but how good He is showing himself to us in particular! Let us open our hearts trustfully to him and allow him to work on us.

You ask me if the Lord will grant us the grace to meet one day face to face, to tell each other many things concerning Jesus, things that the pen cannot put on paper. I don't know what I would not do to satisfy you in this respect but my condition prevents me from doing so at present. I am confident, however, that our joint desire will be fulfilled one day which I hope is not far away.

You cannot imagine how sorry I am to know that my letter has not yet been passed on to that poor little soul. May Jesus forgive you. You never do anything for me as it should be done! There is no need to mention my name to her, as the thing goes without saying. Please give her the letter immediately as it contains the Lord's wishes.

While I regret my inability to continue writing, I wish you and Rosina every good thing from Jesus.

Your servant,
Fra Pio.

P.S. I wish you a fine ending to this year and an excellent beginning of the New Year.

45

Pietrelcina, 9 January 1915[1].

Her love of God is increasing all the time. Light will appear in the darkness. Substantial and accidental love of God. The image of the mother nursing her child. Application. The soul's reaction. This painful state is a purification. The soul does not understand it. Why is this? This is the case of the soul receiving direction. Spiritual cleansing is necessary; a) aridity; b) very bright light. An exhortation to humility. The reason for these explanations. Her illness. Their correspondence. "We feel that Padre Pio gives us, in this letter, a personal insight of his mystical experience, which leads to union with God."

J.M.J.D.F.C.

Beloved daughter of the heavenly Father,

May divine grace abound more and more in you. May Jesus and Mary always reign in your heart and give you a foretaste of the delights reserved for you in the abode of the blessed. Amen.

Further to my last letter[2] in which I urged you to be at peace with regard to your love for God, I do not cease now

---

[1] Date of the postmark.—We feel that Padre Pio gives us, in this letter, a personal insight of his mystical experience, which leads to union with God.

[2] Cf. Letter of 29-12-1914.

to address the same exhortation to you. In my last letter I told you that I intended to repeat in this letter the same reassurances, namely, that your love for God is growing and being consolidated continually.

Your fears on this score are groundless. I tell you that you are greatly mistaken when you think this love is lacking in you, just because you do not feel in your will or in your heart any sweetness due to this love. This is very painful and I fully understand your state of mind, but it is necessary in a soul that is called to a high degree of holiness.

I said with good reason that this is a most painful state of soul, for although the poor thing makes ingenious efforts to serve and please God in every action, as far as it can see it has no proof of its love for God. In fact, in every devotional act it finds that the will usually remains dry and the heart quite hard, devoid of all feeling for supernatural things. What is worse, the poor soul very often feels itself involved in a horrible conflict, for when the higher part feels the urge to love God, its supreme Good, the lower part, that is to say, the sensitive appetite is torn and tormented by ennui, tediousness and many other vague feelings of a painful nature.

But do not be frightened at the state in which your soul is placed by the goodness of our most merciful heavenly Father. Rejoice, because when you least expect it, the Lord will make light shine in the darkness: *Then shall your light rise in the darkness*[1]. Even in the midst of all this darkness you can be consoled and receive within you as much light as suffices to prevent you from yielding to despair.

Let us dwell for a moment, then, on the virtue of love of God. What is this love? Before answering this question we must remember that substantial love of God is one thing and accidental love another, and that in the latter we must

---

[1] Is 58:10.

distinguish between accidental love which is perceptible and that which is purely spiritual. Having made this distinction we can now reply to the above question.

Substantial love of God is that simple and straightforward choice by which the will places God before everything else because of His infinite goodness. One who loves God in this way loves Him by an act of substantial love. But if this substantial love of God is accompanied by a sweetness that is entirely confined to the will, then we also have accidental love of a spiritual nature. If, moreover, this sweetness reaches the heart and produces ardour and delight, then we have perceptible accidental love.

When God in His infinite goodness wants to raise a soul up to great perfection He usually treats it as a mother treats her baby. Note all the ingenious attentions which a mother devotes to her child. She is all tenderness for her dear little idol. Immediately after she has given birth to her child she does not take it to her breast to feed it, for two reasons. The poor mother is very much afraid that the milk which is not yet completely purified of caloric content in her breast might seriously harm the fruit of her own womb.

But a further reason also induces this good mother to act so prudently: the milk that is not fully purified does not appeal to the palate of the newborn child and the loving mother has good reason to fear very much that if the little child is sickened at such an early stage by the disagreable taste of her unpurified milk, he may later on refuse to suck at all. So the poor woman is content to feed him initially with very sweet nourishment such as sugar.

Later on when this most affectionate mother has treated her baby in this way and her milk has acquired the property of healthy nourishment, we soon see her drawing her baby to her breast with holy motherly eagerness to give him her milk.

When the child has reached the age of weaning, this

tender mother begins little by little to give him some other foods as well as her milk. Meanwhile she is almost imperceptibly withdrawing her milk from him by giving him less and less and not so often, until the day comes on which she stops it altogether.

Does all the mother's care for her child end here? I leave it to anyone at all to judge. But do not let us lose sight of the baby. The weaning causes him to suffer and certainly to suffer a lot at first. We often see the child languish for awhile, but later on he will revive in health, his limbs will grow stronger and he will become a fine man, which could never be the case if his mother had been content to give him her milk all the time.

God deals with our souls in this manner and in an even better way. He wants to win us over to Himself by having us experience abundant sweetness and consolations in all our devotions, both in will and heart. But who does not see the great danger which surrounds this kind of love of God? It is easy for the poor soul to become attached to the accidentality of devotion and love of God, while paying very little attention to substantial devotion and love which alone make it dear and pleasing to God.

When we are placed in such grave danger, our most sweet Lord hastens to the rescue with extremely delicate concern for us. When He sees that a person is strongly consolidated in love for Him, attached and united to Him, when He observes how that person has drawn away from the things of this world and the occasions of sin and has acquired sufficient virtue to perservere in His holy service without the attractions and sweetness which arrive through the senses, He then intends to promote that person to greater holiness of life. He therefore removes the delightful feelings we have experienced in all our meditations, prayers and other devotions. What is more painful still for the soul in this state, it can no longer pray and meditate easily but is left in the dark, in complete and painful aridity.

In addition to all this, other external torments and innumerable vexations are not lacking. In a word it seems to this unfortunate person that everything contributes to his destruction and eternal condemnation. In these circumstances he is terrified at first. Believing all this to be due to his own culpable negligence, he makes an effort even by indiscreet means to awaken his dormant feelings of love. But when all his ingenious efforts to recapture his previous state of soul prove useless, the wretched creature is assailed by extreme and deadly fear and begins to suspect very strongly that the cause of all the trouble is some serious sin into which he has unfortunately fallen, something he had previously failed to take into account.

Then, without any delay, that person begins to examine his conscience, to scrutinize all his actions and when he fails to discover anything for which to reproach himself or which seems to him to account for his great misfortune, he concludes that everything is finished for him, that he has been abandoned by God, that God's justice has caught up with him at last, that the whole thing is a penalty for the sins of his past life or else a punishment for his daily failings.

Dear God, how easily he has been deceived! What the unfortunate soul calls abandonment by God is nothing else than a most singular and special attention on the part of the heavenly Father. This transition which is taking place is no more than incipient contemplation, dry at first, but if that person is faithful he will be trasferred from the meditative to the contemplative state and all will become palatable and delightful.

All that has been said so far is useful for the acquisition of contemplative prayer, which can never be reached unless the soul has first been purified of what is called accidental perceptible love of God. The new and most painful state of which I am speaking is intended to purify this love, but unfortunately the person concerned is unable to find peace. For him there is no comfort and he feels that nobody has grasped his real state. Even though the reassurances which are offered him bring some small relief, this does not last and in fact it vanishes almost immediately. His entire torment can be summed up in the words: "I have no love for God."

Oh, if the poor creature could only understand that he does not lack divine love, then he would consider himself happy even in the midst of all his sufferings! If he could only realize that this suffering is not due to his own fault! If he could understand that this impossibility to fix his imagination on any truth whatsoever in order to meditate on it is due to the fact that God has withdrawn from his imagination all the light which shone on the images of supernatural things and made discursive prayer easy and effective! If he could realize, I say, that God withdraws this light in order to infuse into his mind at the same time a more perfect light, a much more spiritual and a much purer light by which he can fix his eyes on God and on divine things and without any words just contemplate Him with a simple gaze, a pure, delightful, delicate and divine gaze! Then would this most fortunate soul be heard to confess that he is happy and would not exchange his present state for all the good things of this world.

But at this point, and with good reason, I seem to hear the objection: if this is much more perfect light, then the soul ought to experience this new and better light of contemplation in the spiritual faculties of intellect and will. But, if you please, do not let us be so hasty in this matter. What usually happens at this stage is what happens unfortunately to those whose palate is unaccustomed to anything but coarse material foods. If you were to offer such a man very delicate foods, he would find himself initially at a great disadvantage and would not appreciate them. Indeed, he would willingly put aside such foods and help himself to coarse material nourishment.

The same thing usually happens to the soul, although we don't realize it. The one who is unaccustomed to such spiritual food and is still used to the coarse material nourishment of perceptible consolations will not perceive and will not be capable of appreciating this higher favour from God, this more refined light of contemplation. It will only be perceived and appreciated when, in the course of this aridity, or rather as the process of purification evolves, that soul gives up all attachment to feelings and to perceptible light.

This is how things stand with you, my dear Raffaelina, and you must be convinced that your soul is not lacking in love for its God. The aridity and darkness which envelop you do not make you fall back even very slightly in God's service, as you yourself can see. You are now more concerned about serving the Lord and you are very much on the alert so as not to fail God. You experience within you a certain vigour and a certain holy desire to practise virtue constantly and perseveringly. Am I perhaps deceived? No, be sincere at least with yourself.

Now I ask you, where does your soul get this great strength to act so virtuously in your present state of aridity and darkness? It certainly cannot come from the feelings, for this area of your soul is entirely plunged in desolation. I am therefore quite right when I conclude that this strength must have a spiritual origin.

Dear God! But if the spirit is also enveloped in darkness, you must agree with me this time that within this fog there is a clear, pure, delightful divine and delicate light, as I have already told you. You cannot discern this light, but it is none the less true that precisely this light strengthens and invigorates you in the service and persevering love of the Lord.

It is this light, moreover, which is for you and for your soul the beginning of contemplation. You cannot fully achieve this contemplation until you have submitted humbly to the purification of the senses already described. Contemplation, Raffaelina, is something completely spiritual, and until the soul has been completely spiritualized it can neither possess nor know it.

But we are still at the weaning stage. Please keep in mind and never lose sight of the mother's concern for her little child. In order to make this child a strong and sturdy adult the mother must begin to provide him with more substantial and flavoursome food than her own milk.

If it is to pass on to adolescence the soul must submit to another and much harder trial than the one already described. Our merciful Jesus calls us to this. Let us see for a moment what this new trial is to which the Lord wants to subject us. As I have already mentioned, after the purgation of the senses which you are undergoing at present, our heavenly Father has decided to raise your soul to a higher degree of perfection and it is therefore necessary for you to be subjected to a much more severe purification which is known as purgation of the spirit. Consider yourself most fortunate, then, O Raffaelina, and let this be, as it were, a shield which will enable you to face this fresh trial humbly and steadfastly.

This trial will most certainly be a very severe one, but do not be frightened. The Lord, as always, will be with you and will console you. This new purification will consist entirely in detaching you from what is called accidental spiritual devotion and love of God. Now, the first and principal means towards this end is spiritual aridity which consists precisely in absolute privation of all comfort of a purely spiritual nature. Your present state is very painful, but there is question here of cleansing your love and your devotion to God from every trace of sweetness and enjoyment that can be relished by the sensitive appetite. Hence, in itself, it does not exclude during your devotions and various loving transports towards God that while the senses are utterly arid you experience a certain refreshment and consolation at the apex of your spirit. This is precisely what we here call accidental spiritual devotion and love.

I repeat that the aridity experienced during the purgation of the senses does not in itself prevent one from enjoying a certain spiritual refreshment at the apex of the spirit. In itself aridity does not place an obstacle here, but it ordinarily happens that when the aridity at the level of the senses is not too pronounced, it makes itself felt also at the apex or fine point of the spirit and hence we often find souls deprived even of this comfort. This happens, as I have said, not of itself but indirectly by a sort of redundancy, as is the case when one's body is a prey to really acute pain which torments the sufferer also on the spiritual plane.

Of itself, we said, sense aridity does not prevent us from experiencing a certain refreshment at the very centre or apex of the spirit. Now the further purgation consists in being deprived of this refreshment. When the Lord shall be pleased to place you in this state you will suffer a pain so severe as to exceed any idea it has been possible to form about it before. When that happens, however, remember that the love of God is growing all the time in your soul. The sign by which you can recognize this is that you will feel more and more willing to face everything that offers service and honour to God. This readiness on your part, however, will not depend on even the smallest enticement and there will be no feeling at the spiritual level. Rather will you feel yourself enveloped in deep darkness and all activity at the spiritual level will be difficult and repugnant to you.

You will then be serving and loving God with a purer love, even though you will not be aware of it. You will not even perceive that you are acting well. This lack of perception on your part is due to the fact that God has withdrawn from you His reflected light through which we come to know and love Him and to act virtuously. When all this happens, rejoice, for then you will already possess that substantial love and devotion by which we love God disinterestedly.

I do not know if such purgation will stop at this point. An interior voice tells me that the Lord is inviting you to a higher degree of contemplation and that consequently the purification will not stop here. If, then, the divine Physician intends to raise you up to sublime heights, as I sincerely hope, I have nothing to add except to implore you to be faithful and humble and always to keep the great Mother of God before your mental gaze, she who humbled herself more profoundly the more she was exalted.

It is therefore with the certainty in my mind that God intends to raise you up to perfect mystical union in love that I forewarn you that aridity and privation of the reflected light are not sufficient for spiritual purification. Another painful interior process is also required, which penetrates into the most secret recesses of the soul, pierces it to the depths and renews it completely. This is nothing but a very bright light which gives the soul a clearer view of its faults than we can possibly conceive and consequently plunges it into an abyss of darkness and most painful anxiety. In a word, this very bright light penetrates and envelops the soul so thoroughly as to cause it extreme torment and interior agony. And if that person does not die it is because the Lord keeps him alive by a continued miracle. Oh, if such people were only allowed to die how happy they would consider themselves! Death is for them a relief from their great sufferings. They are not deceived in their judgment when they reckon that death itself does not bring with it as much suffering as they endure in their present state.

Yet, O Raffaelina, who would believe that this light which in the beginning invades the soul with such desolation and pain is later to raise it up to mystical and transforming union? But to tell you the truth, I don't understand exactly how this comes about. I can only say, without fear of being mistaken, much less of saying what is untrue, that this and nothing else is what happens. If I were to give my poor opinion on the matter, I would say that it seems to me that this is how things should be. When this same very bright light which is to join the soul to the divine Bridegroom in perfect loving union finds that soul at first unprepared for such a high degree of union, it subjects it to pain and desolation. Instead of being enlightened, then, the poor soul is plunged into darkness and instead of being strengthened it is pierced through and through. The sensitive appetite undergoes extreme torment, while the spiritual faculties suffer a deep-seated mortal agony. The atrocious pain experienced by the soul at this stage is so deep and searching that we can only find a faint and feeble resemblance to it in the sufferings endured by the souls in Purgatory or even the damned in hell. And when the soul has been purified by this light which causes such atrocious suffering and has been made fit to receive the kiss of perfect loving union, then the same light will become more illuminative.

This is how I see the matter. Perhaps those who have had quite a long experience of it in their own lives will be better able to understand and explain it than I am.

Before bringing this letter to an end, even though I am aware of your humble attitude before the Lord, I entreat you to be always on your guard against thinking yourself to be of some importance, since these poor writings of mine have shown you the dignity to which our most sweet Jesus has been pleased and is still pleased by His goodness alone to raise you. The knowledge of God's plan for you must serve, on the one hand, to arouse gratitude in the depths of your soul towards so good a Father, so that you may give continual and heartfelt thanks to your heavenly benefactor. You should unite your praise to that of Mary Most Holy and Immaculate, of the angels and all the blessed inhabitants of the heavenly Jerusalem. On the other hand, this knowledge must serve as an incentive to lay aside all fear and not come to a halt halfway on your journey, because of the sufferings and trials which must be endured if you are to reach the end of this extremely long road.

The Lord has allowed me to show you all these things chiefly to prevent you from any uncertainty as you travel this road. Run, then, without growing weary, and may the Lord direct and guide your steps so that you may not fall. Make haste, I tell you, for the road is long and time is very short. Run, let us all run so that at the end of our journey we may say with the holy apostle: *I am already on the point of being sacrificed, the time of my departure has come. I have fought the good fight, I have finished the race, I have kept the faith*[1].

At this very moment I have been handed Giovina's very precious little letter and I thank the divine Majesty for having made me acquainted with the writing of this excellent sister of yours[2]. I learn from your sister that you have been in bed for several days with a heavy attack of influenza. You can imagine how this news distresses me. I know that this illness is expressly willed by Jesus for you and I am resigned to His will which is right and holy.

It is also true that I ought to have written this letter quite some time ago, but I must tell you that the Child Jesus has given me a little present for his feastdays also. How good Jesus is to all, but especially to this unworthy and rebellious son of His! I know I do not deserve his crosses, yet He never fails to hear me and to satisfy me also in this.

I feel it is unnecessary to tell you to keep quiet during your present indisposition, for I know you will do so in the knowledge that you are acting exactly as Jesus desires.

---

[1] 2 Tim 4:6-7.

[2] This "little letter" from Giovina Cerase, dated 8 January 1915 from Foggia, will be published in the next volume of Padre Pio's correspondence.

I want you to keep this letter carefully so that you may show it in due course to Padre Agostino. In this way, when I myself am gone, he will know the road which the Lord has called you to follow. This is the only reason for which I want him to read this letter. Have you any difficulty in doing as I say? When you will no longer have me, it is my intention to place you under the guidance of this dear father.

I end here as I cannot continue to write for reasons well known to you.

I ought to address this to good Giovina, but knowing how you share everything I dispense myself from doing so. However, I feel it is my duty to send her through you my deepest and most sincere thanks for the affectionate concern she shows for me.

I take leave of you in the Lord's holy embrace along with Giovina and all those who are seeking Jesus.

Padre Pio, Capuchin[3].

P.S. I patiently await news of your health.

---

[3] For lack of space his signature is written at the top right-hand corner of the first sheet.

46

Pietrelcina, 23 January 1915,
Marriage of the B.V.M.

Greetings. Fortitude under trial with Jesus' help. Reassurances. She is not to doubt that he knows her well. Her present state is an enviable one. His own sufferings. He is by no means indifferent to her spiritual trials; he asks the Lord to end them. A holy fear. The chapel. Their new maid. His desire for their meeting.

J.M.J.D.F.C.

Beloved daughter of the heavenly Father,

May the grace of the Holy Spirit be ever more abundant in your soul. May it give you strength to endure the fight and the trial to which Jesus our Spouse is subjecting you for your own sanctification and the edification of many others. May you and all those who are united with you in the same spirit enjoy grace and peace from God our Father and from Jesus Christ our Spouse.

In the first place, I give infinite thanks to my God with many tears on your account. This I do through Jesus Christ, mediator and priest close to God the Father, through whom alone we have access to the Father[1], for the strength and steadfastness you have shown in the very great trial to which

[1] Cf. Eph 2:18.

our most sweet Lord has willed to subject you. This has been and continues to be pleasing in His sight. Courage, then, courage all the time, for the Lord has never been so close to you as He has been and still is in this trial.

May this knowledge fill you and hearten you continually with fresh courage to face up to all the trials the Lord has predicted through me. The cross will not be as heavy as the one carried by the Only Begotten Son of the heavenly Father. Jesus, who is infinitely merciful, will not fail to give you now and then a respite from the trial He has sent you. He is so good that He will never allow you to give in.

You have every reason to be frightened when you measure the trial by your own strength, but the knowledge that Jesus never leaves you even for an instant should bring you the greatest consolation. God himself tells us that He is with those who are afflicted and in distress: *I will be with him in trouble*[2], that He even comes down to dry their tears. Be comforted, then, by the delightful thought that after such pitch darkness the beautiful noonday sun will shine. In this light you will contemplate our heavenly Spouse with a clear and limpid gaze. Do not be inclined to believe, my beloved sister, that you are more or less forsaken by the Lord and that for you there is no salvation. Cast this thought far from you, for it comes from our common enemy. Arm yourself with the beautiful virtue of trust in the Lord and take heed of the assurances which God gives you through me. Your soul is in perfect agreement with God. Do not let the mass of your infidelities frighten you, for the Lord who in sheer goodness has chosen you to be His beloved spouse has pardoned and forgotten all.

The trial to which God the Father has subjected you is not a punishment for your unfaithfulness. This is not so, I repeat, for He has forgotten everything. The trial has been

---

[2] Ps 91:15.

sent to you in order to make you a more and more worthy bride of His beloved Son. This very harsh trial is offered to you to enable you to collect more and more prizes and crowns to be presented to your Spouse when you are united with Him in heaven.

Believe me, Raffaelina, and do not heed your imagination in which the devil is powerfully at work. Believe me, I beg you by the bowels of God's mercy and by the meekness of Jesus, for I am telling you the truth and I have no reason to lie or to deceive you. Remember the strict obligation I have to present you to Jesus as a chaste virgin when He comes and that if I were to see you in danger I could not hesitate for a moment to raise my voice to warn you. Ponder well on the significance of this obligation I have assumed towards Jesus, for it means that if I fail to ensure your salvation, the penalty will be the exclusion of my own soul from eternal glory.

Be reasured, therefore, my dear Raffaelina. Be docile and obedient and do not give way to sadness, for in view of the obligation I have assumed before Jesus in your regard, if you were to be lost, which God will never permit, this would mean my own eternal reprobation. Allow me to tell you that the time has come to give you a brotherly reproof, for it seems to me that I am quite right in this. It is time, I repeat, for you to put out of your mind once and for all the alarming and devious doubt you have as to my own full awareness of your state of soul. What does this matter to you? Just obey and you will never be mistaken. *The obedient man will cry victory*[3], the Holy Spirit tells us. Just obey and you will not have to give an account to the Lord of what you do for the sake of obedience.

Will it ever be true that I am mistaken with regard to your spiritual state, that I do not know the life you lead? Can you ever say this without temerity? Has Jesus not given you

---

[3] Prov 21:28 (Vg.)

very many proofs of it? I am aware of everything, of your life and your interior spirit, and all this is due to the divine mercy. Jesus is yours and you belong entirely to Him, you love Him ardently, He is well pleased with you and provided you remain faithful to Him you are destined to go to enjoy Him as a bride in the heavenly homeland.

Despise, therefore, all fears to the contrary. Treat them as diabolical suggestions, for this is what they really are. Believe me, for I am speaking to you in all sincerity, without ambiguity or duplicity. I told you that the Lord had given you proof of this, which you believe and cannot deny. It is true that you have never opened your heart to me, and that we have never met. Yet our most merciful Lord reveals your interior life to me with a view to your sanctification and for your consolation in your troubles, especially your present ones and those which may come to pass in the future.

According to God's designs I have already notified you in my last letter of all the sufferings to which your soul is a prey at present and will be in the future. It is now up to yourself to judge whether I hit the mark by what I told you. Just tell me to my embarassment if what I have said is not true. Come on, then, Raffaelina, and reduce me to silence, for which I'll be grateful to you provided you know that my description of you does not correspond to the facts.

When I meet you, I'll humble myself in deep confusion under the right hand of the Lord[4]. I'll weep for my fault, I'll declare that I was foolish and deluded. But you will never be able to do this. In you, all is sufficiently clear and eloquent and I was very sure of the truth I disclosed to you in that letter of mine. If things stand exactly as I told you, I ask you who could ever have revealed to me what was going on in your soul, even in its most secret recesses hidden from all creatures and only fully known to God and partially to yourself?

---

[4] Cf. 1 Pet 5:6.

Did you, perhaps, disclose to me what was going on within you? You may be quite sure that I did not hear these things, for you did not reveal them either to me or to any one else. Hence you must convince yourself that if I learned of them it could only have been through the channel of which you are well aware.

Well, then, if the most high God deigned so much for our joint edification and sanctification, you ought to be at peace and believe all the other assurances I gave you. Do you believe this? Yours is an enviable state, my dear Raffaelina. The trial is a very hard one, but the Lord who is so very, very good will not fail to lighten the cross from time to time. Be quite sure that all will turn out for God's glory, for your own sanctification and for the edification of a great many people.

Thank the divine Master for the deep love He has for you and that in spite of your unworthiness He is pleased to treat you in this way and to hold you up to others as an example of His favours. Thank this most tender Spouse for this grace. In the case of those who pass through the state in which He is pleased to place you, He does not always reveal and foretell what He has revealed and foretold to you through me.

According to the divine plan you have been informed of what the Lord has done and is still doing in my own soul, which invariably rebels against everything connected with God. It is no longer necessary for me to conceal from you something that should afford you comfort even in the midst of all the sufferings you are enduring and must still endure.

I don't deny the great repugnance I feel in being obliged to make known what the Lord has done within me, but I perceive and feel a very strong impulse which urges me to say what I am now about to tell you. I am doing this so that I may not go against the divine will and also because Jesus has willed that you be informed of something He has done in my own soul.

I am very well aware, my dear Raffaelina, that *it is good to guard the secret of a king*[5], but I also realize that we should *gloriously reveal the works of God*[6]. Our most sweet Jesus has deigned to favour me also with the trial through which you are passing and with the new trial you will still have to endure whenever God wills. Well, then, when I was subjected to such extreme trial, what would I not have given to know that someone was speaking to me in God's name, that all this was just a trial imposed on me and willed by God, not as a punishment for my sins which are, unfortunately, very many, but for the purification and sanctification of my soul?

Oh, if I could only have known at that time that I was not an outcast from the land of the living! If I had only been able to recognize, as you yourself have been assured, that even in this state I loved God more than I did in times of prosperity, I would have chosen to remain in this state for all eternity if this were pleasing to His divine Majesty!

Your own pain will enable you to imagine mine, so very much sharper than yours, since I was deprived of all consolation and assurance. To all this you must add the fact that nobody understood me, so that I was obliged to keep silence. Dear God! What unheard of cruelty it was to oblige a martyr in extreme torment to remain silent, and all this because of the ignorance of our times.

Alas! What has escaped my lips? Pardon me, my Raffaelina, if I have accused of ignorance those whom I should not have accused. All this was arranged in such a way by God because my moral disorder, my bad habits and evil inclinations called for nothing less than a most severe purgation. Don't worry, then, because you have never loved God as much as you do in this trial He has sent you and you are

---

[5] Tob 12:7.
[6] *Ibid*.

loved in turn by Him in His fatherly mercy. Take courage, then, and go straight on, for it won't be long before the sun shines through the darkness.

But do you perhaps think that while aware of your torment I remain indifferent? No, you are very familiar with the brotherly concern I have had for you up to the present and you know that divine Providence has entrusted you to my care. I share everything with you, in times of prosperity and times of trial. Hence my heart cannot fail to be stricken with the most acute pain when I see you, so very dear to me, placed in such harsh conditions by a trial willed by God for your sanctification.

Meanwhile I never cease to pray to our merciful God to make haste and bring to a speedy end this period of trial. At the same time I neglect no effort with our most tender Lord to induce Him to alleviate now and then your torment in this time of trial. I am praying, or rather I am continually pestering the heart of the divine Master, to allow me to feel, if not all at least a part of your torment, on condition that He lessen and lighten your own sufferings.

Moreover, for fear of being unjust to you and depriving you of merit, as might be the case by my acting as I do, I strike a bargain with the Lord and tell Him that I want the merit to be yours. In all this, thanks to our most tender Spouse, my poor weak prayers have been heard in accordance with all the conditions laid down. Are you satisfied with this?

I am well enough aware that a very great fear pervades your mind. Do you want to know what this fear is? You are afraid that you will become proud and vainglorious. Am I perhaps mistaken? Well, then, don't worry on this account, for this is a holy fear and as long as you are afraid of falling into pride and vainglory you will never be a victim to them. Have I made myself clear? Take care that this holy fear never leaves you. When a person no longer feels this holy fear or tries to rid himself of it, let him take care that the

Lord does not leave Him, if He has not done so already.

I learned with immense satisfaction that Jesus has at last granted you the grace of setting up the altar in your home. I feel happier now in the knowledge that you will be less exposed to the bad weather while at the same time being able to fulfil your obligations and your devotions. The installation of this altar will be of spiritual benefit also to Giovina and all those persons who make up your household.

Our very dear Padre Agostino, who came to see me a few days ago, has told me that Jesus has at last sent you the kind of maid you desired. May our most sweet Jesus be infinitely thanked for this further favour. I had prayed and prayed to the divine Master for this intention and in this too I have been heard by this Father who is so good. May He be blessed for ever!

God whom I serve with all my heart is my witness that I have remembered you continually in my prayers. How much I should like to be close to you in the hours of suffering in order to console you! May my good angel do this for me.

Let us also ask the Lord to grant us at last, according to God's will, an opportunity to speak to one another face to face. I too, like yourself, have a keen desire for our meeting, so that we may both be consoled by our mutual faith.

How is Giovina just now? Don't fail to give her my most respectful regards and don't deny me the charity of recommending me to Jesus, for I feel greatly in need of his help.

Tell me something also about poor Rosina.

I have been in bed for several days. I got up this morning for the first time but am feeling fairly bad still. It can be said that the bad weather is conspiring to destroy me.

Although I have a great desire to receive your news especially during this trial you are undergoing, I don't want you to write unless Jesus wants it and only when you can do it.

I leave you in the Lord's holy embrace.

Fra Pio.

47

Foggia, (26 years today since the death of my saintly mother), 26 January 1915.

Darkness and distress. Their correspondence. She thinks he has forgotten her. The maid's behaviour. The letter to the seamstress. She replies to his letter of the 23rd.

Jesus alone! Most Holy Spirit, help me!

Father,

Darkness and distress; an occasional ray of light or a trickle of comfort (your letters) then even deeper darkness and more painful distress. I am overwhelmed by a continual storm and if there is a momentary lull I look around me in fear and trembling and ask myself what more can happen to me. Jesus wants it like this and so be it. But it is difficult for me to accept and my will has no part in it. What am I to do? Advise me, holy Father.

How much you work for my ungrateful soul and do I correspond? Tell me frankly and don't forget it.

I reply to two of your letters, the second of which contained a holy treatise on the love of God. I must admit that I found it hard to get your holy father to read it according to your instructions. As soon as he returned from his visit to you he repeated your orders and I obeyed, certain that I was doing the will of Jesus and not my own. Never, never my own will; it could deceive me, betray me and cause me to fall.

I had two long conversations with Padre Agostino about that letter. What patience with this rebellious and obstinate worm! All the holy and sublime things you say to me bring me light, relief and strength in my great spiritual and bodily trials. But I should prefer to be ignorant on certain matters because this miserable clay, this handful of mud very often—you will be horrified—becomes puffed up with pride. My pride is great and subtle and hidden and I am very much afraid of it.

Don't say anything to me, my Father, leave me in my abjection, treat me invariably with contempt and severity. Humiliate me continually. I am not afraid of the devil but I am afraid of myself. You who are spiritualized by divine love use a language that is altogether divine, communicated to you by divine revelation. You use this language with me, mud and misery that I am. I am continually engaged in this fight and I fear to succumb. Advise me, good Father; help me, speak to me at length on this point.

Who knows what you will say to all these objections, always fresh ones, that I put before you? Scold me, punish me, don't feed me with sugar, I beg of you, for this speck of dust will make big blunders (speak to me about this).

At times, I don't know why, when the hand of Jesus comes down heavily on me (it is never too much for my sins), I begin to think you have forgotten me. Is this possibile? Knowing your immense charity, I cannot suppose that you are not interceding with Jesus to obtain some relief for me in my tribulations.

Your holy father will have told you of my spiritual and bodily state: complete prostration, yet this was nothing compared to what was happening within me. But you know all about me through other channels and do you not pray for me? Do you not plead my cause? Have you really forgotten me? We are two atoms continually overwhelmed by misfortune. I am weary. I can't bear any more, not because of myself but for the sake of my unhappy sister. I am afraid the bow that is bent too far will break. Pray.

I see with regret that the light and heat of faith is partly lacking in her. I understand my duty, that I ought to be an example, a spur and a help to her in virtue. Instead, the very opposite happens and her failings are nothing but the consequences of my own bad example. Isn't this how things are? Speak to me on this point.

Sick as she is in soul and body, she arouses such pity, she causes me such pain that at times—don't be scandalized—my faith wavers. May Jesus keep His most holy hands on my head, otherwise... Without Mass or sacraments, I have never opened a pious book or paper since the day Rosa left our house on the death of her father. Thirteen days absence and you know quite well how I spent those days. On the evening of Rosa's return to my home, it was the most holy will of God that I should take to my bed with a temperature of 40 degrees, hoarse, coughing and choking, etc. A week later Giovina went down also with influenza, with a high temperature, etc., etc. Both of us in bed, desolate in soul and body.

For the past few days, thanks be to Jesus, Giovina has been getting up late, but she is reduced to a thread. Her stomach continues to cause her trouble and suffering and she has a sharp pain especially at night in her right hand and arm, which makes her cry like a child. She has been examined by a number of doctors (one of them even came here from Naples) and had treatment of various kinds, but there is no improvement. And you, do you not say anything to the great and true Physician on behalf of this poor creature who is so sorely tormented in soul and body? May He be moved, in the end, to compassion, He who is so very good and merciful. Speak to me about this.

Due to incompatibility of character between Rosa and

Giovina and between Rosa and the maid, I wanted to settle the matter at all costs in order to avoid trouble. I believed that your prayers had sent me a good woman and, in point of fact (I had known her quite a long time) she was pious, humble and prudent, middle-aged, in good health, a widow with plenty of experience of household duties. I thought I had touched heaven, but she had only been a fortnight in my home when her former mistress with whom she had worked for eight years moved heaven and earth to have her back. She even enlisted the aid of a priest, whose voice the woman was obliged to obey. Against my will I had to call back our former maid (humbling myself, may Jesus' most holy will be done!) who is able to do very little. We have to be satisfied now with the old regime because I am afraid to have anyone new and immoral in the house where we two women live alone. If these different characters could agree, at least for the moment, it would be possible to get along, but to me this seems a riddle. Is it Jesus' will? You alone can explain it to me. Add to all the rest that in her state of health Giovina requires reliable assistance. May Jesus attend to it and arrange things. I say no more. Pray.

Thank you for the books you sent me to read[1]. I hope to return them to you quite soon. Due to a number of unusual circumstances I myself was obliged to deliver your letter to the orphan, who thought I had received it from your spiritual father. She asked me to open and read it and was touched by your words. She told me she would have to reply to you, but she is very embarrassed.

You who are now committed to the care of young, pure, simple souls dear to the heart of Jesus, do not neglect, I beg of you, those wretched ones who are in greater need. I am very jealous—I confess my fault—but do not forget me in Jesus' presence. I have great confidence in your prayers. You

---

[1] See the next letter, Note 4.

are always my powerful advocate, my good father. Always call me daughter, an ungrateful daughter who does not know how to respond to the efforts of her good father, a rebellious daughter, but always and ever a daughter.

My invariably disjointed writings, always full of complaints and tears, bring you nothing but trouble and pain. Of this I am well aware—forgive me. Is this how things are? Tell me. I would like, at least sometimes, to bring you smiles, joys and fragrance. Instead, my dear Father, I am always so sad and I cannot overcome it. I feel quite unbalanced spiritually. I haven't been to Confession for 24 days now and you can imagine how many sins I have committed. Have I Jesus' grace in my soul? Tell me.

I still have so very much to tell you. Before long, then, I'll have a chat with you. May Jesus be praised and blessed for ever! The last word I addressed to your spiritual father[2] was: I expect you in May with Padre Pio. Amen, amen.

I kiss your hand and ask you always to bless,

Your poor tertiary.

P.S. When the most pure shell put forth the divine pearl, when the powerful Mediatrix of men gave us our Redeemer during the holy Christmas feasts, I meditated on the straw on which the Infant God was laid, the straw from which I saw burst forth the golden ears which matured and were then transubstantiated in the bread of heaven, the heavenly bread of which I have been deprived for so many days. My meditation stopped there. The ears changed into sharp and bitter thorns. Tribulations paralyse my flights of faith and love and drag me down to earth, then the earth swallows up soul and body, ideas and feelings, everything. What wretchedness!

Write me a long letter and do not neglect me. This letter

---

[2] Padre Agostino of San Marco in Lamis.

which I started on the evening of the 21st has been written in bits and scraps. My time is no longer my own—blessed be the most holy will of Jesus. I write to you whenever I can. Pray a great deal for me.

P.P.S. I have reopened this to tell you that the day before yesterday I received another most precious letter of yours. What am I to answer? I feel humiliated, embarrassed, wiped out. I don't know how to thank the divine goodness and yourself, good and holy Father. I blindly believe all you say to me. I obey your every command. Do with me as you wish. By myself I am unable to understand or define the most harsh trial to which Jesus is subjecting me. All I know is that I am suffering and that this is caused by a mass of human, earthly, moral, spiritual and temporal things. I know I spend some very delightful hours and some sleepless and restless nights. I often call you and you, perhaps, do not hear me. I tell my good angel to inform your own angel of my sufferings and plead for some comfort. But nothing happens, all is silence. However, you are informed of everything through other channels. What more can I say to you? My soul, my conscience is before you like an open book. You are aware of all my great unfaithfulness and you assure me that Jesus has forgotten and forgiven me for all.

Ah, Father, Father, help me to thank and bless Him and to love Him very much, to correspond to such great mercy. I am no good at anything, I sink into the dust. My wretched soul is safe in the light of your blessed words: "for in view of the obligation I have assumed before Jesus in your regard, if you were to be lost, which God will never permit, this would mean my own eternal reprobation."

But what did I ever do, good Jesus, which allows me to listen to such words from a worthy and beloved minister of Yours? What have I ever done to hear that you take all my sufferings upon yourself, holy Father, while leaving me the merit? How can I repay you for such very great charity? I am really lost when I think of this. May Jesus repay you for me: may He grant you greater perfection for the conversion and sanctification of souls.

The altar is not yet fully installed, but the Brief from Rome has reached us. May Jesus hasten this beautiful day for His glory. Pray and pray very much. Yesterday, after four full weeks I went to Confession (at home) but I have been without Jesus for a full 24 days. What have you to say to this? Pray.

Three days ago I was honoured by the visit of Very Reverend Father Provincial (accompanied by Father Guardian)[3]. He had already called on me several times, but this was the first time in my present home. He told me how very glad he was to see us back in our own home. How good he is! I am more and more edified by his profound doctrine and great virtue. Giovina was deprived of this comfort as she was in bed with a fresh attack of fever. I was very sorry about this as I was certain she would have derived great spiritual profit from his visit. She is always saying: "God deprives me of everything, for me it is a continual sacrifice." This is true, unfortunately. Poor martyr! What have you to say about it? Speak to me.

I want this holy sister of mine to have spiritual comfort, bodily health, steadfast faith, peace in the midst of misfortunes and to be well-balanced in soul. You are able to do all, so continue to plead her cause, for you will succeed. This has been a fixed idea with me.

She returns a hundredfold your greetings, with her deep and devoted respects, kissing your hand. Rosina asks your prayers. For the moment she is here in my home as her sister has gone to stay for some time with her brother in Molfetta. Jesus will arrange things for the good of souls.

---

[3] The Provincial was Padre Benedetto of San Marco in Lamis. The Guardian of St. Anne Friary in Foggia was Padre Tommaso of Monte Sant'Angelo (1872-1932) who had been Padre Pio's novice master.

Francesca[4], the orphan's teacher asks you to remember her in Jesus' presence, with her sister and her brother who goes to church but has been absent from the sacraments for a full 12 years. He is very obstinate even with regard to material matters which would relieve the family situation. He has quite an amount of capital, that is to say, a large quantity of iron to be sold, but he refuses to sell it even though he recognizes the financial advantage this would mean for his family. Poor Francesca, she would like to know from you if this is the express wish of Jesus. Please satisfy her.

This is a person who is misunderstood even by confessors, as far as I have gathered. She needs some spiritual comfort. She speaks very little, meditates a lot and is a woman of great depth. She is always alone and recollected and is the only one to whom I reveal in part my secrets and my sufferings.

Together with this good soul I bow down and ask your blessing.

P.P.P.S. An idea has occured to me: what is the further trial you predicted? I want to know this from you because you are aware of everything. Don't tell me I am imprudent. Yet I would greatly like to be spiritually prepared, to be docile and even glad and gay while awaiting the fulfilment of God's will. Instead, I feel a great repugnance for it and would like to drive all trials far from me. Don't be scandalized. Ask pardon for me all the time from God's infinite mercy. Write to me.

---

[4] She was a spiritual friend of Raffaelina (cf. Letters 57 and 97). The "orphan" is Annita of Foggia (see Letter 31).

48

Pietrelcina, 30 January 1915.

The illness of those who love the Lord. One can never take too much trouble for the sanctification of a soul. Acceptance of God's will in time of trial. Her fear of falling into pride because of the gifts she has received. He always remembers her in prayer. Her sister's defects. He makes her a present of St. Francis de Sales' treatise on the love of God. She is in God's grace.

J.M.J.F.D.C.

Beloved daughter of the heavenly Father,

May your soul always be the temple of the Holy Spirit. May Jesus and Mary always be with you and console you continually in your afflictions. Amen.

You will make allowances this time for my brevity. The pen is shaking in my hand, for I am sick at heart. My illness is purely spiritual, but do not imagine that my body does not share it and to a great extent. This is the sickness of those who love the Lord. You can never imagine the sad state of a soul whom Jesus has made love-sick.

If you have any heart at all, pray for my speedy dissolution, for there is no other remedy for my soul. My dear Raffaelina, I see myself more and more weighed down with debts towards our most sweet Jesus and I cannot see how I can pay them. May the flames of divine love consume me without delay! You too must pray for this intention.

Don't be upset if you cause me some trouble. One can never take too much trouble for the sanctification of a soul. For my own part I want to tell you that up to the present you have not caused me any inconvenience. So do not let yourself be persuaded by the devil on this score.

You are distressed, moreover, that your will has no part in your resignation to the divine plan. Are you really sure of this statement? For pity's sake, don't torment me by telling me things about which you yourself are not certain. Unfortunately when you utter your act of acceptance of God's will you want to feel this in your heart also with a kind of perceptible sweetness. But have I not told you that the state of purgation in which the Lord has placed you consists precisely in stripping your soul of that delightful feeling it experiences in the service of God?

Consider Jesus' act of acceptance in the Garden and how much it cost him, making him sweat a sweat of blood! Make this act yourself when things are going well and also when they go against you. Don't be upset and don't worry about the way in which you make your act. We know that nature shrinks from the cross when things are hard, but we cannot say the soul is not submissive to God's will when we see it carrying out that will in spite of the strong pull it feels in the opposite direction.

Do you want a practical proof of how the will expresses its acceptance? Virtue is recognized by its opposite. When the Lord subjects you to a trial, whether great or small, tell me, have you any intention of rebelling against God? Or, better still, let us suppose the impossible, that is, try to rebel against Him. Tell me, are you not horrified at the mere sound of such blasphemous phrases? Well, then, between assent and refusal there is and there can be no middle course.

If your will flees from rebellion you may be certain that

it has tacitly or expressly submitted to God's will and consequently that the will, in its own way, has uttered its act of acceptance. See to it, at the same time, that you combine external with internal submission to the best of your ability.

You tell me you want to remain unnoticed because you are afraid of falling into pride. I myself cannot see how a person can become proud on account of the gifts he recognizes in himself. It seems to me that the richer he sees himself to be, the more reason he has to humble himself before the Lord, for the Lord's gifts increase and he can never fully repay the giver of all good things. As for you, what have you in particular to be proud of? What have you that you did not receive? If then you received all, why do you boast as if it were your own[1]?

Oh, whenever the tempter wants you to be puffed up with pride, say to yourself: all that is good in me I have received from God on loan and I should be a fool to boast of what is not mine. Act in this way and have no fear. As regards your fear of becoming proud, I refer you to my last letter in which I feel I explained myself sufficiently.

For pity's sake cast aside the suspicion you have that there are times when I don't pray for the two of you. I'd like you to know that I offer to the Lord even my most indifferent actions for your spiritual health in the first place and then for your bodily health. God, whom I serve with all my heart, knows how true this statement is.

I don't by any means agree with you that Giovina's feelings are the consequence of your bad example. I'll bet you anything that not even Giovina herself would agree with you on this point. Test this for yourself and I'll be very happy to admit it if I was wrong. The only mistake I attribute to you in this respect is that, involuntarily, you have made the health of this poor martyr much worse by showing her so

---

[1] Cf. 1 Cor 4:7.

clearly that you suffer because of her own sufferings. Am I perhaps mistaken? Have I hit the mark or not? Be more watchful about this unless in your opinion you have as usual some objection to make and consider me to be wrong.

There is no need to thank me for St. Francis de Sales' treatise on the love of God[2] which I sent you by means of my spiritual father[3]. It is I who ought rather to ask your pardon for an act that did not altogether conform to the rules of politeness.

Cast far from you the temptation as to whether the grace of Jesus is in you or not. It seems to me that I have spoken clearly enough on the subject and a great many times. Don't worry, then, serve the Lord cheerfully, trust and abandon yourself to Him at all times. To convince you still further I refer you this time to Sacred Scripture: *Because you were acceptable to God* (said the angel Raphael to Tobit and through him to all of us) *it was necessary for you to be tested by temptation*[4]. I add no more. You know only too well yourself how many temptations and trials you have been subjected to up to the present.

Fra Pio.

(On a little card)

Warm regards to your most worthy sister and may she take courage. Send me some good news continually about her condition.

My love, in Jesus, is with you all.

Your servant,
Fra Pio.

---

[2] The two masterpieces of the holy bishop Francis de Sales (21 August 1567-28 December 1622), doctor of the Church and patron of Catholic journalists and writers: *Introduction to the Devout Life* (which originated in the spiritual direction of M.me De Charmoisy, first published in French in Lyons, 1600) and *Treatise on the Love of God* (conceived as a genuine theological treatise and later urgently requested by M.me de Chantal, also published in Lyons, 1616).

[3] Padre Agostino of San Marco in Lamis.

[4] Tob 12:13 (Vg.)

49

Foggia, 31 January 1915.

Painful effects of a letter which is not in our possession. Epistolary relations with another person. Correspondence with her director. Her sister's health. A thought which she noted in writing.

Jesus alone! Most Holy Spirit, help me!

Father,

I intended to wait before writing to you in order to avoid troubling you, but your last very brief letter[1], received yesterday, induced me to ignore the proprieties.

Your letter of yesterday made me suffer very much. You are angry with me, and why? The last part of that letter, stiff and dry, with stern commands, really astonished me. What have I done to displease you. What wrong have I done you unawares? In what way have I offended you? Explain yourself, speak, for pity's sake. Tell me everything frankly and you will relieve my acute perturbation.

Your second-last sentence convinces me that you have misunderstood me: "I dispense you this time from the task

[1] Letter not in our possession.

of passing on some reassuring words to Francesca, as I am well aware by experience how badly you would serve me. Moreover, you don't want to be disturbed on any account, so let things remain like that. Perhaps I do not deserve it. In the meantime I have entrusted someone else with the job."

What a harsh reproof! You are indeed severe and cruel in judging me so literally! If I did not carry out your instructions regarding the orphan's letter, I repeat that it was merely because I don't want my private affairs to be made known to other persons with whom I am barely acquainted. I am slow to speak and cautious in acting and I get on well like this for the glory of God.

On the other hand, as I have told you over and over again, Francesca for me is an exception. I have known her for a great many years. She is elderly, reliable, tried in virtue, silent as the grave. I tell you once again that I trust her and confide to her all my spiritual and corporal troubles, family matters, everything. Moreover, although she is a plain and simple woman I take her advice and always obtain comfort and relief.

In addition, your last sentence drives me out of my mind: "Please keep all my correspondence carefully, because at the first chance I'll send for it[2]." What kind of language is this? It's a riddle, a mystery. Do you not want to write to me any more? Do I bore you and disgust you? Am I wicked, proud, wayward and pigheaded? Then it is up to you to convert me, to put me on the right road, to correct me. Do I not respond? Is Jesus weary of me and does He tell you to withdraw from me? Tell me, explain all to me, absolutely all and for pity's sake don't hide anything from me. I want to know all the unpleasant things of whatever kind they may be. May the most holy will of my Lord be done at all times!

---

[2] A passage from the letter which we do not possess, evidently written on 30 January as will appear from later letters.

Giovina, my poor martyr, took to her bed again the day before yesterday, with another stomach attack, although less severe than the one she had on 17 November last. Seeing her fast completely for days at a time, racked by bodily pain and torn by moral sufferings, I cannot restrain my tears. Are they displeasing to Jesus? If you think fit, answer me on this matter. Ask Jesus these two favours for me: my own conversion and my death before my holy sister dies. Will you do me this kindness? Do you undertake to obtain these favours for me?

Some days before I received your letter, I had put down in writing the following thought (I sometimes commit to paper some idea that I fear may escape me when I am writing to you, which is certain to happen by reason of my very poor memory): If all these rays of light which come down on my soul by means of you had been received by some other docile and pure soul, oh, how much progress that soul would have made by now on the road to perfection! I myself, instead, wretched and conceited as I am, remain prostrate on the ground and in spite of all the help I receive I am still unable to rise.

I am afraid, and with good reason, that Jesus is offended and weary of receiving no response and that He will deprive me very soon of all this help. Then what shall I do? I would like to be reduced to nothingness so that Jesus might be glorified by it. Mere theory, this, but what of the practical aspect? O Jesus, make me more and more aware of my wretchedness and my malice, so that you may save me from my great pride.

Does this idea of mine tally with the reason for your tacit command to have your letters returned to you? How many doubts are running around in my poor mind! Explain yourself and set my mind at rest.

I intended to write very briefly in order not to bore you, but when I write to my good father my pen runs on and on and will not be stopped, even though I know my good father to be angry, annoyed, offended and no longer willing to have anything to do with this daughter who causes him nothing but trouble and suffering.

I anxiously await an explanation. Bless me all the time.

The least of your tertiaries.

50

Pietrelcina, 4 February 1915.

A letter which we do not possess. The consequences of writing before taking counsel with Jesus. He asks her pardon for having made her sad. He is not offended. Jesus is not withdrawing from her. Another trial in store. Submitting one's own judgment. His illness.

J.M.J.D.F.C.

Little bride of Jesus,

May the heavenly Father not lead you into temptation but always deliver you from evil[1]. May the Holy Spirit fill your soul with heavenly charisms and may Jesus, most pure Spouse of souls, always console you in your afflictions. Amen.

As soon as you receive this I want you to tear up the half-page which was added to my last letter[2]. As regards the letter itself, if you want to tear it up you may do so; if not, don't worry. You will already have realized in view of this command that I didn't intend to distress you by that letter. There is no truth whatsoever in all that was suggested by your

---

[1] Cf. Mt 6:3; Lk 11:4.

[2] We do not possess the half-page which was added to his letter. Raffaelina tore it up as Padre Pio desired.

own mind, powerfully influenced by our joint enemy. For pity's sake, don't listen to him. Treat with contempt his wiles and all the disturbing things he suggests to you.

I am aware, my dear Raffaelina, that I myself have contributed indirectly and involuntarily to your great unhappiness. This is the result I can produce when I fail to take counsel with our most sweet Jesus before putting things down on paper. Blessed for ever be the Lord who has been pleased to humble me in this way and by means of this humiliation open the eyes of my soul to the truth! May this good Father always keep His hand on me so that I may not fall short of what I have promised.

When I promise things, I hope for just as much from the liberality of the divine Master.

You cannot imagine how mortified I was to hear of the unhappiness I caused you. My heart is breaking with pain and God knows how many tears I have shed already and am still shedding on account of your own distress! May our most sweet Jesus forgive my mistake. By the meekness of Jesus and his great obedience to his eternal Father, I ask you, Raffaelina, not to be cross with me and not to deny me your forgiveness. Unhappily I don't deserve your pardon, but I appeal to that charity which is not controlled by laws or restricted by boundaries. I appeal to the charity which unites us all with Jesus. Pray, then, that the Lord may be pleased to pardon my fault. I'll be uneasy until you have assured me of your full forgiveness.

I ask you to dismiss from your mind the idea that I am offended and weary of working for your sanctification. You have been and will always be the object of my interest with Jesus. Stop worrying, then, on this score. Don't listen to anything to the contrary that your imagination suggests after the devil has whispered loudly in your ear.

I have not been offended by you in any way, much less am I tired of working for your salvation. And even if my guidance of you were to create some inconvenience for me, it would never be too much to work for the sanctification of a soul redeemed at such a high price by the Son of God.

From the fact that I told you to keep my correspondence carefully so that I may take it back just as soon as I get a chance, you are not going to believe that Jesus is disgusted with you and for this reason wants to deprive you of my poor services for your timely consolation. My dear Raffaelina, there is no truth in what you have been thinking in this respect. Jesus loves you and wants to make you more and more holy. He never intends me to neglect the obligation I undertook towards you in His name. It's strange how you never stop blundering where I am concerned. I can't understand how you should misunderstand certain things I say to you. From the mere fact that I told you to return my correspondence you go on to draw certain conclusions of which I never even dreamed. You are being fairly hard on me.

Even supposing the impossible, that Jesus had obliged me to give up my direction of you, would it not have been my strict duty to inform you of this? For pity's sake! You want to annihilate me. God alone knows how interested I am in your sanctification and in your continual progress in the ways of the Lord! Rest assured that Jesus doesn't easily withdraw, as you imagine, what he has given out of sheer goodness. This tender Master is always more inclined to enrich you with his favours and never intends to take back what He has once given. He only takes back, and almost against His will, what He has bestowed on someone when that person is unfaithful and closes the doors of his heart to Him. And even in this case, oh, what gentle violence He does to that heart in order to gain admittance to it! Only when we arrive up above will we fully understand this mystery of love.

Let us trust, Raffaelina, that Jesus will never allow you to become unfaithful to Him. You must be more and more reassured on this point; you must open your heart more and more to hope and endeavour to grow in charity all the time.

In the other letter you asked me what was the further trial to which God intended to subject your soul out of sheer love for you. If I am not mistaken, I described this further trial to you in that same letter. Have the goodness to read it over again if it interests you. It may be that I did not describe it or that you did not understand me. At all events, don't hesitate to let me know. I told you in that letter that this future trial would be a harder one, precisely because it is to take place in the most secret recesses of your soul.

I ask you, however, not to be frightened by this new trial that your soul will have to face, both because the Lord will always be with you and because at the end of the trial which is yours at present, your soul will already have made great progress in the further trial. Don't be discouraged by any means in view of the new trial which is to be much harder than the present one, for it will result, as in the present case, with the triumph of God's glory and the sanctification of your soul.

I cannot hide from you the displeasure I felt when I saw how obstinate you were in not delivering at once the letter I addressed to that very good girl, even when I had requested this for the second time. This was the exact reason why I dispensed you from the task with regard to good Francesca. According to your way of thinking, it appears that your interior life is of greater interest to you than to me. You are mistaken and greatly mistaken. When you failed to deliver that letter to the person concerned, after my first request to you, I made allowances for you, but I could not help being disgusted by your failure to comply when I asked you the second time.

I don't like this attachment to your own will. You should obey the one who has undertaken to have full care of you and you should not find fault with what you are told to do.

I am ready to forget all that has happened in the past, but let us take care for the future if you don't want to displease me.

I would like to go on, but the exceptional state of my health won't allow me to write more. The attack which I mentioned to you in my last letter is becoming more and more serious. Do you still refuse to ask Jesus for my speedy departure? You are still cruel! May Jesus forgive you. Speak to me about this. I ask you to be at peace about everything, as you have good reason to be. How is Giovina's health? Give her my kindest regards and assure her that I am attending to her sanctification when I am before the Lord.

I leave you in Jesus' holy embrace.

Your servant,
Fra Pio, Capuchin

51

Foggia, 7 February 1915.

The Pope asks all the faithful for prayers. She relies on Jesus' inexhaustible charity. Peace between them! His desire to die. The "second trial." Her family. Postscript: the desire to die. Her widowed niece.

Jesus alone! Most Holy Spirit, help me!

Father,

A solemn day, a day of general audience, which the King of kings on His throne grants in all the churches of Europe, a day on which Christ's Vicar calls upon all the faithful to assemble and pray for peace. (Shall we have this holy peace? You may know this)[1]. As the last among the last I unite with the intentions and prayers of the Church's head, of the priests and especially with your own prayers, holy Father. I join with all Catholics to implore mercy.

This morning (fast from the Eucharist since 2 January)

---

[1] Benedict XV had ordered for 7 February 1915 "that throughout the Catholic world humble prayers be addressed to the Lord to obtain from His mercy the greatly-desired peace." Among other things a prayer was to be recited which began with the words *Appalled by the horrors* and had been specially composed by the Holy Father himself. Cf *Acta Apost. Sedis* 7 (1915), 8-9.

I succeeded in going down to the church to receive Holy Communion. It was only this morning (an exceptional day) that my superior (my sister) permitted this after she had put forward lots of objections, difficulties, fears and dangers, especially for my wretched health. Blessed for ever be the most holy will of my Lord! But He is right not to want to come into my poor dwelling, for I am very bad and wretched. This morning, however, I told him that by the flames of His holy love He must consume all my sins and by the fire of His infinite mercy He must burn up all my troubles. Answer me on this point.

By now I trust and rely without the slightest fear on His inexhaustible charity which is fathomless and immeasurable. You, good Father, by all your assurances in Jesus' name, have removed from my weak uncertain and restless spirit all fear, all doubt and all anxiety.

Will my whole life be sufficiently long to thank Jesus in the first place and then yourself, holy Father? But much more so must I humbly ask your pardon for disgusting you by my disobedience, as you told me in your last precious letter. This letter, moreover, restored peace to my soul. Your true words, which gently persuaded me of my false and indiscriminating judgment, gave me back the calm I need so much. Pardon me fully, pardon me always.

But what humiliates and mortifies me and makes me sink into the dust are certain expressions you use. You, in your insuperable virtue, ask me to pardon you and make allowances for you. You must abolish absolutely these words in dealing with me, Father. This I ask of you on my knees. Promise to satisfy me. Speak to me about it.

You want me to speak to you about your continual selfish desire to fly away to heaven without delay. But what am I to say to you? In one of my letters I told you what I thought of this. What must I add? I continue to repeat that your love-sickness is such that it makes you deaf to the groans, to the needs of those confided to your care. It's all very well for you to say that up there you will assist and comfort us just the same. Oh, you don't convince me by any means! You would be too far away. I should not hear your words on this earth, your living, warm, persuasive, charitable words close at hand, which bring comfort in sorrow, encouragement in the struggle and spur me on to strong and genuine virtue.

Are you not satisfied, for the present, with blessed flames which absorb and burn up your being? I imagine that the love of Jesus must be delight and pain. Do you love Jesus very much? Love Him a little for me also. How I envy you! Speak to me on this point.

I obeyed you by tearing up the last part of your second-last letter. You tell me I am to read that letter over again to have the explanation of the second trial to which Jesus wants to subject me. Oh, how many times I have read and re-read that letter! I understand perfectly that this hard and bitter trial will come in the deepest recesses of my soul, but what will be the cause of it? On what causes and circumstances will this trial hinge and develop? This is what I want to find out from you. Oh, good Father, tell me, tell me everything, since you are aware of everything by other means! Satisfy me and for this I thank you in advance.

Giovina continues all the time to have ups and downs. May Jesus lessen some of her sufferings. Pray very much for her spiritual and bodily health. Don't forget the family of six, my relatives, of whom I told you several times. May Jesus be moved to pity once and for all to remedy such financial disaster. I recommend good Francesca to you and in another letter I'll tell you more about her. We expect you in May and let our desires hasten this holy and blessed day full of spiritual joy. Amen.

Among the souls entrusted to you, who are pure, simple and exceedingly dear to Jesus, never, never forget and always, always bless the last of them, the very last, who is,

A poor tertiary.

P.S. I return to your favourite topic. While reading the book you kindly lent me I was struck by the following paragraph which applies to you: "St. Paul felt his soul hard pressed by two different desires (Phil 1:23 etc.), by the desire, on the one hand, to depart from his body in order to be with Jesus Christ in heaven and by the desire, on the other hand, to remain in this world to serve in the conversion of the nations. Undoubtedly, both of these desires were in the higher part of his soul, for both proceeded from charity. Nevertheless, in resolving to follow the latter path St. Paul was not guided by reason, but by a simple view and a simple feeling regarding the Master's will. In spite of all that reason could tell him, this great servant consented to this feeling only with the fine point or apex of his soul."[2]

In your own case, after the Master's will comes your own ardent and justified desire. This is the cry of those souls who, yearning to see their good father, their powerful mediator, the minister and friend of the eternal Judge, remain here on this earth.

I kiss your hand.

P.P.S. I am reopening this to enclose a letter from my unfortunate niece, the very unhappy widow. She is unaware, let it be understood, of my correspondence with you. I merely told her that I intended to send her letter to its destination and no more.

Her moral situation is very sad. As things stand she lacks nothing from the material point of view, for the father can and must do his duty. However, she worries a lot about the

[2] St. Francis de Sales, *Treatise on the Love of God*, Bk. I, Chap. 12.

education and success of her two sons. We ourselves can do nothing for her. So the idea which she now submits to you has come to her and she wants to know how to put it into practice. May Jesus inspire you about the real needs of this soul and the right remedies to be applied in this critical situation. Comfort her, good Father, and advise her. This is one of the sharpest thorns in my heart[3].

When she was five years old (and I was 17) I cradled her in my lap. At that time, full of worldly ideas, I foretold for her a future full of roses and happiness. But even had I been completely spiritual I could never, never have imagined her future as the most unhappy widow of a suicide, with three orphans, totally dependent on her father, this woman who is so very good, beautiful and young at 32!

May Jesus help her. Please pray very hard and tell her whether she can and ought to carry out her rather risky plan. Her own peace and ours depends on the success of this plan. What will her holy mother, our deceased sister, say (she was the apple of her eye) as she looks down from heaven and sees how much her poor daughter is suffering? She comes very often to see us and she weeps continually while confiding all her troubles to us. It is heartbreaking to me and to Giovina, powerless as we are to relieve her moral suffering.

The Marquis can do everything if Jesus so inspires him (he is old and very religious; may God see to it).

Write me a long letter. Don't defraud me in order to write to others.

I implore you not to let anything leak out to my niece about your writing also to me. Bless her, Father, with her three orphans. Give her a big blessing and continue to bless her.

---

[3] Maria Zicari Cairelli (died 1964) daughter of Antonio and of Anna Cerase, Raffaelina's sister, had five children. Two died at birth and three survived, of whom the only one now living is Guido. Maria's husband, Luigi Cairelli, in a moment of depression committed the insane act of suicide on 2 August 1913. See the next letter and also Letters 56 and 69.

52

Pietrelcina, 12 February 1915.

Reassurances. He is ill and cannot write a long letter. He encloses a letter for her widowed niece.

J.M.J.D.F.C.

Beloved daughter of the heavenly Father,

May the grace of the Holy Spirit be with you always and make you more and more worthy of the kingdom of heaven.

I give infinite thanks to the Lord for the continual benefits He bestows on you in ever greater abundance. From you, therefore, humility, resignation, prayer and thanksgiving to the good God!

Don't worry about anything. Let divine grace act freely in you and make use of it invariably for His glory, for the salvation of your own soul and of all souls.

My Raffaelina, make allowances for me if I don't continue. I am very ill and have just left my bed for a short while to reply to your niece[1]. The enclosed is for her, so please see that it reaches her.

---

[1] Two handwritten letters from Maria Zicari to Padre Pio are kept in the Capuchin records in San Giovanni Rotondo. In the first, dated 8 February, she explains to him her reasons for feeling obliged to send her three children to Florence, to the home of the Marquis Filippo De Piccobellis, whose lands had been rented by her father: "My Father, I await a word

Who knows when Jesus will allow me to write you a long letter. Write to me meanwhile whenever you feel the need and be sure you will be doing me a favour.

My love is with you always and with all those souls who love Jesus.

Fra Pio.

---

of counsel from you and have opened my mind completely to you. Tell me if *I should* do as I have told you, if there is any hope there. The future of my children depends on you.'' We do not possess Padre Pio's reply, but its content may be gleaned from the second letter, dated 27 February: ''Your letter did me a lot of good, it relieved me in my great depression. You advise me not to *delay* and this word scares me. Perhaps if some further time elapses it will be too late? I think of carrying out my intention immediately after Easter... Pray for me, Father, pray hard for me and bless me.'' Unfortunately this sad affair did not have a happy ending. Cf. Letters 56 and 69.

53

Pietrelcina, 23 February 1915.

The subject he intends to deal with in this letter. A passage from St. Paul to the Philippians. For me to live is Christ. The Eucharist. To die is gain. Uncertainty whether to live or die. The desire of all righteous souls. His own experience. How Raffaella is to act. Conclusions.

J.M.J.D.F.C.

Beloved daughter of the heavenly Father,

May the grace of the Holy Spirit make you more worthy of the heavenly kingdom. May Jesus and Mary comfort you, sustain you and bless you all the time. Amen.

Here I come to satisfy the request you made to me in your last letter, to give you an explanation of what the apostle St. Paul says in his letter to the Philippians, Chapter 1, verses 23-24 (always subject to a better interpretation and to the judgment of the Church, in which I declare my intention to live and die).

In order to understand this holy apostle more fully we must consider his situation at the time of writing this letter. He was a prisoner in Rome at the time, solely because he had preached the Gospel, during the reign of the Emperor Nero. He was therefore hanging between life and death, because it was possible that the wicked Nero would have him martyred, while it was also possible that he would set him free. In point of fact, he was set free.

While remaining in this state of suspense he declared in the first place to those good Christian people that he was ready for anything for the love of Jesus Christ whom he served. He entertained the most firm hope that everything, including the very chains which bound him at that moment, would help towards his salvation, that all would be advantageous to him for eternal life.

This is a truly sublime sentiment which should be entertained by every Christian. For why do we live at all? As a result of our consecration at baptism, we all belong to Jesus Christ. Hence every Christian soul ought to be familiar with this saying of the holy apostle: *To me to live is Christ*[1], I live for Jesus Christ, I live for His glory, I live to serve Him, I live to love Him. And when God wants to take our life from us, our sentiment and our feeling should be those of a person who at the end of his toil goes to collect his wages, who, at the end of the fight, goes to receive the prize.

Let us relish, my dear Raffaelina, yes, let us appreciate this most noble attitude of soul in one who was very much an apostle! Yes, it is only too true that all those who love God are ready for anything for love of that same God, in the firm hope that all will work out for their good. Let us always be prepared to recognize in every event of life the most wise order of divine Providence. Let us adore it and be ready to conform our will in all things and at all times to the will of God. In this way we shall give glory to the heavenly Father and everything will be to our advantage for eternal life.

God, who has bestowed so many benefits on us, is satisfied with such a very insignificant gift as that of our will. Let us offer it to him along with the divine Master Himself in that most sublime prayer, the *Our Father*: *Thy will be done*

---

[1] Phil 1:21.

on earth as it is in heaven[2]. Let us offer this will of ours with the same sentiment with which our divine Master offered it for us to His Father. Let us hand it over to Him in a total offering and let us do this also in our daily life. Don't let us make our offering like those children who, when they have given away something precious as a gift, immediately or very soon regret what they have done and begin to cry and ask to have it back. Made in this way our offering would be a mockery.

The total offering of our will is unfortunately very difficult. We must remember, though, that when our divine Master addressed to His Father on our behalf those words of the Lord's Prayer "thy will be done", his divine mind showed him very clearly how difficult it would be for us to do what He had promised the Father for us. Our good Jesus, Raffaelina, perceived through His divine eyes and weighed up our immense weakness, which very often prevents us from carrying out God's will so that we invent obstacles or rather we pretend not to know what His will is.

Well, then, His immense love, that same love that induced Him to leave the bosom of His eternal Father in order to come on earth and take upon Himself our fragility and our debts and satisfy the divine justice for us, found an admirable means in which He showed us His exceedingly great love for us. What means was this? Oh, for the love of heaven let us understand what our good Master asked the Father immediately after He had offered our will to Him. In His own name and in ours He asked Him also: *Give us this day, Father, our daily bread*[3].

But what bread is this? In Jesus' request here, failing a better interpretation, I recognize primarily the Eucharist. Oh, the exceeding humility of this Man-God! He is one with

---

[2] Mt 6:10.
[3] *Ibid*.

the Father, He is the love and delight of the eternal Parent. Although He knew that everything He would do on earth would be pleasing and would be ratified by His Father in heaven, He asked leave to remain with us!

O Raffaelina, how exceedingly the Son loves us and at the same time what excessive humility is His in asking the Father to allow Him to remain with us until the end of the world! Again, what exceeding love has the Father for us, when He has seen Him subjected to such dreadful treatment and still permits this beloved Son of His to remain among us, to be the target of fresh insults every day!

How could this good Father ever agree to all this? Was it not sufficient, O eternal Father, to have permitted just once that Your beloved Son should be left a prey to the anger of His Jewish enemies? How could You ever agree to His being left among us still, to see Him every day in the unworthy hands of so many dreadful priests, worse than His Jewish enemies themselves? How can Your most merciful heart, O Father, bear to see Your Only Begotten Son so neglected by many unworthy Christians? How can You consent, O Father, to His being sacrilegiously received by so many unworthy Christians?

O holy Father, how many profanations, how many sacrileges must Your merciful heart still tolerate! Who, then, O God, is to take up the defence of this most meek Lamb who never opens His mouth to defend Himself but speaks on our behalf alone? Ah, Father, I cannot ask you now to remove Jesus from among men, for I am too selfish; and how could I who am so weak and half-hearted live without this Eucharistic food? How could I fulfil that petition made by Your Son in our name: *Thy will be done on earth as it is in heaven*, if I did not receive strength from this immaculate flesh? Even now, with the powerful help which Jesus has left us in this sacrament of love, I often feel I am on the point of wavering and rebelling against Your will, so what would become of me if I asked You and You answered my request to take Jesus away from men so that He would not be treated so badly?

Ah, I lack the strength which I should perhaps have if I loved this most holy Son of Yours a little more. But in the meantime, holy Father, I entreat You either to put an end to all the dreadful acts continually committed by men against the adorable person of Your Only Begotten Son. Do this, O Father, since it is in your power. Do it, because the love this Son has for You calls for such an action on your part. Glorify Him as He has glorified You and meanwhile, holy Father, give us today our daily bread. Give us Jesus always during our brief stay in this land of exile. Give Him to us and grant that we may be increasingly worthy to welcome Him into our hearts. Yes, give Him to us and we shall be sure to fulfil the request that Jesus Himself addressed to You on our behalf: *Thy will be done on earth as it is in heaven*.

Alas, Raffaelina, I realize now that I have strayed from the subject! Pardon me and make allowances for me. It is a poor weak-hearted man who speaks to you! Who knows how much further my head would lead me, but I don't want to abuse and sorely try your patience even more than your indulgence.

Let us return to the apostle. He rejoices to think that he will never be confounded and will never fall short in any way of his duty as an apostle of Jesus Christ. He rejoices, moreover, that Jesus will always be exalted in his body even in the midst of all the chains that bind him. If he is to live, he will exalt Jesus Christ by means of his life and his preaching, even while he is in prison, just as he had done before by preaching Jesus Christ to those in the *praetorium*. If he is to be martyred later, he will glorify Jesus Christ by rendering Him the supreme witness of his love.

He therefore declares openly that for him to live is Christ, who is, as it were, the soul and centre of his whole life, the cause of all his actions, the end of all his aspirations. When he has said that for him to live is Jesus Christ, he goes on to say that to die is gain, because by his martyrdom he will bear solemn witness to Jesus of his love, he will make his union with Jesus indissoluble and increase the glory due to Him.

What do you say, Raffaelina, about such talk? When worldly people, who have no notion of supernatural and heavenly things hear such language, they are inclined to laugh, and with good reason, for, as the Holy Spirit tells us, the unspiritual man does not discern the things that are of God[4]. Poor creatures, they have a taste for nothing but mud and earth. They can form no conception of the beatitude which spiritual men say they experience in suffering and dying for Jesus Christ.

How much better would it be if, instead of expressing astonishment and ridiculing these things, they were to recognize their own guilt and admire with silent respect, at least, the loving enthusiasm of those whose hearts burn intensely with divine love. But to come back to ourselves.

The Philippians could have deduced from this kind of language on the lips of such an apostle that he preferred death to life. For the consolation of those good people who were so fond of him, he adds at once that if to live somewhat longer in a mortal body were more beneficial for God's glory and the salvation of souls, in this case he would not know which to choose.

Now, if he was so uncertain at the time of writing as not to know which of the two things to choose, whether to die or to live, the thought strikes me that St. Paul had received a revelation from God, through which it was left in his power

---

[4] Cf. 1 Cor 2:14.

to choose between life, in order to continue his ministry, and death in order to receive the crown of glory.

It seems to me, my dear Raffaelina, that only in this way can we understand better the reason for his great uncertainty as to whether to choose life or death. But in order to make known his sentiment, undoubtedly in perfect charity he says something more. He tells us he is hard pressed, for his "desire is to depart and be with Christ, for that is far better; but to remain in the flesh is more necessary on our account."

Both of these sentiments in St. Paul sprang from perfect charity. The desire to depart in order to be united with Jesus Christ in perfect union in glory, which would have been better for himself, that is, more desirable than continuing to live on this earth, had its immediate origin in his perfect love of God. The other sentiment or desire also had its origin in a perfect love, the immediate object of which, however, was the salvation of his neighbour. In other words, this desire started out from the principal object, God, but was motivated indirectly by the salvation of souls.

His first desire, that is, to depart from this body, is seen by him as more beneficial to himself and he ardently yearns for this as much as any righteous soul can ever desire to be united with its God. Filled as he was with the Holy Spirit, he viewed the second desire, to go on living in the midst of trials and arduous work in order to obtain the salvation of souls, as more necessary for them. Better still, since he had received a revelation that he was not to die just yet (as seems clear from what he says immediately afterwards, and events seem to confirm my interpretation, since he was not martyred at that time but obtained his freedom), he resigned himself to suffer for love of the salvation of souls. In this he resembled a son who tenderly loved his father and due to this affection submitted to all sorts of humiliations and carried out most exactly some very lowly tasks which his father was pleased to impose on him.

This loving son acts in such a way that he not merely avoids transgressing in any way his father's will, but endeavours to please him in everything. This does not mean that the affectionate son, who willingly submits to all things out of purely filial love, ceases to feel the weight of his sacrifices. Rather does the weight increase and become more painful the more the love for his father grows in his heart.

But why should we get involved in comparisons concerning natural love which cannot always be dissociated from many imperfections? Was not the holy apostle's sentiment, perhaps, the desire which also animates all righteous souls? In point of fact, dear Raffaelina, such souls turn their gaze continually towards the heavenly homeland. They are constantly longing to depart from this exile so as to be united with Jesus Christ in the heavenly nuptials. They hasten the arrival of this hour with groans and sighs, with prayers and ardent longing, but since God does not always receive their aspirations in the manner which they desire and understand (for inscrutable reasons which it is not given to miserable mortals like ourselves to fathom) they bear the weight of this present life for the sole purpose of pleasing Jesus in this matter also.

However, in the midst of the really atrocious sufferings entailed for them in being obliged to struggle on still in their exile, they never cease to make use of God's gifts and to win souls for Jesus, by reason of the love that burns in their hearts. To worldlings it seems incredible that there should be people who suffer because they see their life prolonged by God's providence. Yet this is the story of the saints and it has happened and will continue to happen as a lesson to mankind.

From the atrocious pains suffered by just souls in seeing themselves far from their centre, we may form a feeble idea, Raffaelina, of what these souls experience in being obliged to satisfy the more essential needs of this life such as eating, drinking and sleeping. And if God in his mercy does not hasten, especially at certain moments and on certain days, by a kind of miracle, to prevent them from reflecting while they are performing these daily acts which are so necessary, they suffer extreme torment. Their suffering is so extreme in performing even one of these obligatory acts that I can tell you, without fear of being mistaken, that I can only compare it to the agony endured by those martyrs who were burned alive and thus offered their lives to Jesus in witness to their faith.

This comparison may appear an utter exaggeration to some people, but I know what I am saying, my dear Raffaelina. I tell you that on the day of general judgment we shall undoubtedly see these people crowned like the martyrs with the palm of martyrdom even though they did not shed their blood for the faith.

In the case of those who consider exaggerated the foregoing comparison regarding the suffering such people endure in satisfying their everyday needs, I beseech our most bountiful God to give them a taste of this kind of suffering themselves.

Above all, in confirmation of what I have said of such souls, I want to tell you that I am only too familiar with one who has been tried in this way. During certain periods of this person's life in which the Lord did not prevent him from reflecting on these necessary acts which are indispensable for the preservation of life, he experienced a degree of pain in performing them that could not be surpassed, I should say, by the suffering of the damned at the moment of their death.

Do you still obstinately persist, then, in your indifference towards me and refuse to entreat this God of goodness to grant me at last the grace of departure from this life? For pity's sake, if you do not want to have compassion on a poor unhappy man and pray to the heavenly Father for this intention which I mentioned to you quite recently, due to your egoistical and ignoble concern for yourself, I beseech you to listen to me at least in one respect, that is, to refrain from praying for my continued survival. Am I to be satisfied at least in this? May I have your assurance in this respect? Speak and do not remain silent.

If I were aware of being useful in some way by remaining alive, I would be resigned to bear still longer the burden I already carry. But I am very much afraid, Raffaelina, that my fear is no foolish one but is well founded. To put it briefly, I am afraid of failing to fulfil my priestly ministry and therefore rendering useless the grace given me by the imposition of the bishop's hands at the moment of priestly ordination.

Consider, now, if I can desire to go on living. Oh, how hard it is to be resigned in this matter! This is beyond my strength. In uttering such an act of resignation I feel as if all my bones were being rent asunder. Moreover, I cannot give you even the faintest idea of what happens in my soul as I make that act.

I am also afraid that the souls entrusted to me by divine Providence are not being very well nourished by me. One can never do too much for the perfection of even a single soul.

It is useless to speak to you further on this point. You will always turn a deaf ear to me and perhaps the more I speak the more obstinate and pigheaded you will become. May our good Jesus show you my true state! He alone can succeed in softening your heart in this respect. But I must almost complain about our good Jesus Himself. He, too, turns a deaf ear whenever I pray to Him for this intention and it seems to me that He is even harsher than you are. May this good Jesus forgive me such arrogance! However, this is not the first time that I have ventured to approach Him in such a way.

Blessed Jesus! What a lot He has to bear from this rebel son of his! If He were anyone but Himself, He would have cast me off long ago! How patient this Jesus is! How good

He is to everyone but more especially to me. I am really sorry, you know, that I make such blunders in dealing with Him. I would like to mend my ways, but what can you expect when I always want to have my own way? The more imperturbable I find Him, the more I want to have my way. What great patience is needed in dealing with me! Even Jesus Himself cannot move me!

Is your *superior* still so obdurate as not to let you go to Jesus in the morning[5]? She is too hard on you, isn't she? Listen, then, to what I want you to do in this matter. It seems to me high time for her to banish those vain fears she has with regard to your weak health. Here's what you could do during the bad season and your period of convalescence. Continue to rise rather late in the morning, then go to church, receive Holy Communion as soon as possible, spend a short time in adoration before Jesus in the Blessed Sacrament, then return home at once. Make your thanksgiving for Communion at home.

As regards hearing Mass on weekdays, don't be upset and don't torment yourself about it. Jesus knows all and He will also know how to make allowances for you. This is how I want you to behave and I expect you to do it. But will your good superior be convinced? I, too, like yourself, see great difficulty here. Try to convince her yourself and leave no stone unturned in your efforts to achieve your purpose. Jesus will do the rest. At all events, please don't quarrel with her, and rest assured that I don't intend you to rebel against her. Pray, entreat, in dealing with her use all the ingenious methods with which the good God has endowed you only too abundantly.

You are anxious to have some exact information about the second trial of which I spoke to you elsewhere. Please do not worry on this score. If suffices for you to know that

---

[5] He is referring to Giovina.

this trial will be sent to you by God for your greater sanctification. Let it be enough for you to know, moreover, where this trial will take place. For your comfort let me tell you that since the coming trial is a purely supernatural grace of a most singular nature which the Lord grants to just a few privileged souls, it will come down upon you when you least expect it.

The fact of being subjected to this trial does not depend on the soul itself, as it can do nothing directly to bring it about. It depends exclusively on God's will. What I advise you to do is to remain calm and not worry on any account about what it is to be. All will work out for God's glory and the sanctification of your soul.

In addition, remain invariably in an attitude of humility before the infinite goodness of the Lord. Open your heart all the time and give thanks uninterruptedly to the good God for the favours He is continually showering upon you, for the one who fails to be grateful for favours already received is unworthy to receive further graces. Let the divine grace act quite freely within you and make use of it always for His glory, for your own salvation and that of all other souls. Never forget that heavenly favours are granted not merely for our own sanctification but for the greater holiness of others as well.

In your last letter I expected to find a word of forgiveness for the distress I caused you involuntarily by that famous letter of mine dated 30 January last[6]. I have no doubts about your forgiveness, but I expected you to mention it. However, Jesus has willed the opposite and may He be blessed for ever! Meanwhile pray to the good God continually that He may pardon all my faults, especially the one I committed against you in that letter of mine. I expect you to inform me fully about the decision taken by your excellent niece, Maria.

---

[6] A letter we do not possess. See Letters 50 and 51.

How is good Giovina healthwise? Oh, how much I pray to the good God to grant her better health and greater holiness still!

Console good Francesca all the time. She is a holy girl.

Give my regards to our most meek Rosina and pray for me, all of you, as I remember you continually in my own poor but constant prayers.

My Padre Agostino will be nearby these days. I take advantage of and abuse your goodness by asking you to pass on the enclosed note to him[7].

Pray for me all the time.

Fra Pio.

---

[7] This is the letter he wrote to Padre Agostino on 22 February: "I take the liberty of sending you this by means of Raffaelina as the Lord has arranged. I hope it reaches you in time before you leave. *Letters*, Vol. I, No. 230.

54

Foggia, 21-25 February 1915.

The reason for this letter. The trial has begun. "We are denied everything." She has a relapse. Not a glimmer of light is to be seen. "Sometimes I fear I shall go mad." Two cloistered nuns. "You will cry shame." "Here is the fruit of my kitchen-garden." Abominable apathy. Postscript. The chapel. I want this letter to be destroyed. Reply to his letter of the 23rd. Her widowed niece. A prayer for her director. The fresh trial. It is not the devil's fault.

Jesus alone! Most Holy Spirit, help me!

Father,

Encouraged by the charitable words in your very brief letter[1]: "Write to me meanwhile whenever you feel the need and be sure you will be doing me a great favour" (you may be sure I feel the need!), I come as usual to bother you, in search of help, mercy and intercession. (Your letter, by the way, was far too short; I am waiting all the time for a really long one; you must speak to me and answer me on a number of points; I keep on waiting for this).

---

[1] We must remember that her own letter was begun on the 21st, continued on the 23rd and despatched on the 25th February.

Don't be scandalized: I have fallen down. You prophesied a most harsh trial; is this it, perhaps? For my own part I cannot and do not want to endure it. The cross seems extremely heavy to me and I rebel against it, I run away from it and I find no peace. On the first Friday of Lent, how many sins committed. My conscience is completely upset. I force myself to pray, very little and with neither faith nor hope. A very slender thread of faith held me up, sustained and encouraged me before, but since Friday all is changed within me. I feel my lower and rebellious self putting up vigorous and impudent opposition to God's most holy will.

I long for death for I am tired of living in the midst of continual trials. Don't be scandalized! (I speak and let off steam with good Francesca alone, and she is really scandalized). Down with the mask (which I have worn, perhaps, until now). I am always the same, I feel it, always dreadful, proud and attached to a comfortable life full of distractions.

Giovina, my poor martyr, is carrying on between stomach pains, stabbing pain in the hand, and constant spasms of whooping cough (she is now slightly improved). She spends entire nights in pain (she often has to rise from her bed, crying like a child from the stabbing pains in her right arm and hand). I myself am suffering a hellish interior martyrdom, while poor Rosa, under great strain, keeps watch and takes care of us.

During one of these attacks, Giovina, racked with pain, wept as she said to me: "My sister, leave the path of perfection. Do you see how the others are getting on?" I made no answer. Actually, our enemies are enjoying themselves in soul and body. They have Masses, sermons, Confession and Communion whenever they like; then they have outings, visits, family affection, moral satisfaction, lawful amusements. The Lord blesses them all the time, but we are denied everything.

I wanted to try to go down to Mass every Friday and Sunday in Lent, but it would have been better not to think of such a thing! I had a relapse of influenza due to taking a walk on my terrace on a morning that seemed like spring. Then, all over again, coughing, and fever that I endure in secret for fear of making Giovina worse. Poor Rosa was kept on her feet although coughing and running a temperature herself. The maid had a cough and a very high temperature and now that she is convalescent is being helped by us who are in dire need of care ourselves. This is the fine life we are leading: weariness that persists without a respite or a moment of relief.

We see no glimmer of light on any side. All is desolation. We are abandoned by relatives and friends and even by our faith.

We have needy relatives around us all the time, always complaining (one of these comes in every evening to console us) and although Giovina always does something, it is invariably very little. There is continual oppression no matter where we turn. It is an impossible life, a life filled with agitation, afflictions and fear. I myself, in addition, am afraid of thunderstorms, of earthquakes, of the war and I endure spiritual, moral and physical pain. Moreover, to see the one being I love on all the earth suffering so much in soul and body, to see her suffering ceaselessly and with no way out of it, with no sign of an end to it all, is something which is driving me crazy.

Sometimes I fear I shall go mad. I am in the grip of a great sadness. A strong and invincible melancholy has taken possession of me, from the first moment of entering this house. Yet this is our own home where many of our dear ones died (in our own bedroom alone, three of them died), where we shed so many tears and where Giovina was to find (and this is really the case) greater physical sufferings, deeper melancholy and more painful solitude.

Oh, how the solitude weighs me down, drains my strength and embitters me! My family that was so big, all destroyed, wiped out. Just one brother left so near to our home but so far from us as regards affection. Our brother-in-law, the widow's father, in view of his office has suggested to us to open up that communicating door of which you know already. We vigorously opposed the idea, I myself in particular, certainly not because of our brother but on account of his wife. The past has taught and counselled us, filling us with fear and horror.

We are two cloistered nuns surrounded by deceit, ill-will, disappointments, bitterness and suffering without end. I don't know what I am expecting. I expect some new and unusual event which will change this very sad situation of ours. I am not thinking of a momentary change, but of a lasting change which will bring us peace, good health, serenity and spiritual and social consolations such as others enjoy.

Hasn't my poor sister the same right as so many friends of her own age, position and education? Is she alone to be denied absolutely everything? (Am I unjust and ungrateful to speak in this way?) The key to this dismal mystery, the explanation of this perpetual riddle will be known to yourself alone through other channels. I can no longer understand anything. The slender thread of faith, I repeat, has left me, while blind reason, my lower self and my ruling passions are struggling and tearing each other to pieces without ever arriving at a conclusion.

In reading this you will certainly tear at your hair and cry shame! To what depths can a soul descend when it is not sustained and helped by the One who can do all things! I agree that I am deserving of hell and even more. But my sister is not. It is unfair that she who is innocent should suffer for me a sinner. I alone must suffer for a while, unknown to anyone, but I am always frightened, irritated, prostrated and in a state of rebellion.

Here you have the fruit of my kitchen-garden, Father, or rather the weeds, the nettles produced by my ground. What have you to say? You will certainly weep from grief and disappointment. Judge me and condemn me. Moreover, by your powerful prayers you must force this rebellious will of mine to bend to God's most holy will and make me calm and indifferent to everything that happens.

After this period of rebellion I have fallen into a deplorable apathy, an absolute indifferentism. Nothing rouses me, nothing attracts me, nothing distracts me. I find everything boring and even to write to you is very difficult and burdensome, leaving me indifferent (this is something new and horrible which never happened before; for me to write used to be a spiritual feast).

Pray, help and raise up this wretched sinner from the mud. Bless this

Poor tertiary.

Foggia, 21 February 1915.

P.S. I forgot to tell you about another chastisement from God. After all the money we spent, the chapel has not yet seen the light. The wretched carpenter is to blame, or rather this is permitted by God. Poor Rosina can't even go down to Mass, because we are wakeful all through the night or else, at the hour for Mass, Giovina needs our assistance in her attacks. (I no longer know what it is to sleep). The holy martyr gets very little rest, in fits and starts. She eats practically nothing. She spends the whole day withdrawn, suffering, discouraged, physically and morally exhausted.

Have pity on us, you at least. Pray, intercede for us and write to me.

I want you to tear up this letter as soon as you have read it. It is incoherent, disjointed and blameworthy and it deserves to be destroyed, like the one who has written it. Will you satisfy me in this? Tell me that you will.

I kiss your hand.

23 February 1915.

P.P.S. I am reopening this to tell you that I have just received your own most precious letter for which I thank you very much. Blessed are you, enlightened, sustained and made to suffer by faith and love of Jesus (on whom I no longer dare to call). How I envy you!

I told you in my last letter that you should abolish altogether the words "pardon" and "making allowances" in dealing with me. In this I was alluding and replying precisely to your request for my forgiveness for the distress you involuntarily caused me by your letter of the 30th of last month[2]. I thought I had done my duty when I expressed myself in those terms.

My niece tells me she must write to you again. She is calmer now. Pray hard for her. I'll keep you informed of all that occurs. Good Francesca comes quite often to visit and comfort me. For my own part I cheer her up with Padre Pio's holy words (confining myself to what I can say, while my very private spiritual affairs are known only to myself and you). As I told you in one of my letters, the poor creature is thirsting for light and comfort. She needs guidance and counsel for she is full of doubts. The confessors here don't understand her. The only one who does is your own holy father, but he appears here and disappears again like a bright meteor.

Why don't you write a page or two to Francesca herself, making use of me as you think fit? May Jesus inspire you about the real needs of this soul and enable you to apply the holy and necessary remedies[3]. She wants to tell you through me that she has extreme need of a spiritual favour. Pray very

---

[2] A letter we do not possess.

[3] Among Padre Pio's letters to his spiritual daughters there is one which was probably sent to "good Francesca" in October 1915.

much for her brother during this appropriate season of Lent. She is praying constantly for you in accordance with your intentions of which we are well aware.

Francesca is more generous than I am (I am very bad). All I say to Jesus is: "I recommend to you Padre Pio and all priests, good and bad." Nothing more. Are you satisfied? As you see, I don't speak to Jesus of my own desires which spring from motives that are too selfish and paltry, according to your own severe judgment.

I return to my fixed idea and ask you if this is the first or the second trial you foretold for me. I understand absolutely nothing. All I can see in myself is chaos of mind, heart, will and everything else. I don't know what to do or what to cling to either in spiritual or material matters. As far as the spirit is concerned I lack a sense of direction, I lack light and strength (the Eucharistic food—how well you explain yourself on the subject in your last letter!—you must admit that I am right to some extent). As to material things which have to do with my poor sufferer, I would like to take her to a nursing home and stay there with her. I would like to transfer her to a milder climate such as Naples. I would like to obtain some holy companionship for her. I would like to see her devoting her life to a holy purpose so as to see her removed from sordid things and daily annoyances. I would like all this, but by myself I can do nothing unless I have your prayers and your counsel. What do you advise? Speak to me at length and patiently on this point. I am in a state of great agitation and do not know what to do. Answer me on all these matters.

I began this letter on the 21st, but was interrupted hundreds of time. Undoubtedly the devil had a hand in this. Don't tell me, Father, that the present state of my conscience is due to his action. I never think of *him* and it's better that I don't, for it would be very convenient to blame that *ugly wretch* for every sin I commit.

Forgive the blots on this sheet. How very many stains there are on my poor soul. Will Jesus forgive me for them? How do I stand before God? Tell me quite frankly. Yesterday I did as you told me by delivering your note to good Padre Agostino. Pray a great deal for my conversion.

25 February 1915.

55

Pietrelcina, 28 February 1915.

Reassurances. The mystical state. The essence of mystical desolation. Go forward all the time with fresh courage! Respectful regards.

J.M.J.D.F.C.

Beloved daughter of the heavenly Father,

May Jesus invariably remain the peaceful King of your heart, may He console and bless you as always. Amen.

I have received your letter and from all it contains I see clearly that these are the last outpourings of a heart sick with love for God.

On the one hand this letter distresses me immensely, while on the other hand it brings me a consolation that cannot be expressed in human language, for in all this I recognize the fulfilment of God's will. Hence, Raffaelina, we must really be consoled. Have no doubt, for with the divine assistance all will work out for the glory of God and the sanctification of your own soul and other souls.

Meanwhile you must try to be always ready and prepared to do the divine will, which invariably has in view God's glory and the good of our souls. Oh, how delightful is the thought of doing God's will in all things! May our good Jesus enable you to experience its most wonderful effects.

Don't ever fall back on yourself when the storm is raging. Place all your trust in the heart of our most sweet Jesus who is not only mine but your Jesus also. Renew your faith continually and never give it up, for faith never abandons anyone, much less a soul that is yearning to love God.

Withdraw, then, your blasphemous statement that you "have no faith left." The Lord is acting within you by His infinite goodness and you must continue to humble yourself before Him and pour out blessings and thanks to Him. Cheer up, then, and don't listen to the enemy's insinuations.

The trial is very hard, but I repeat for the umpteenth time that you are not to be afraid, for Jesus is with you even when you see your soul, as it were, on the brink of the precipice. You must invariably lift up your voice to heaven even when desolation invades your soul. Cry aloud along with that most patient man, Job, who when the Lord placed him in the state which you are now experiencing, cried out to him: *Even if You are to slay me, O Lord, I will still hope in You*[1]. I understand only too well that a person placed in this state considers himself almost damned. Little by little, as he becomes more aware of his own infidelities to the one who has been such a great benefactor, he feels the hand of the Almighty coming down more heavily upon him. But be consoled, because this does not mean that the soul is getting worse, as it might seem. In reality, without realizing it, the poor soul stands to gain a great deal.

Take care, Raffaelina, not to make up your mind that you have fallen into disgrace with your divine Spouse. This would be to do a great injury to the Lord who is bestowing such abundant graces upon you. In actual fact, what is sweeping over your whole being at present is a most singular grace and it shows you quite clearly what you would be yourself if it were not for divine grace.

---

[1] Job 13:15.

But you will object that if this is a grace why does it cause you desolation and not consolation? This is a strong objection and it is also true if we are speaking of the graces granted by the Lord to souls whom He does not intend to raise up to mystical union. Now, your own state, merely through the heavenly Father's divine goodness, is really the mystical state.

I feel sure that when you hear mention of the mystical state as applied to yourself you will begin to laugh and possibly think me little less than a fool. Well, you may form this judgment of me if you like. In your present state you are permitted everything. For me it suffices not to be a fool and to be fully aware of this fact.

I have said that what is causing great desolation in your soul is a most singular grace which God only grants to those whom he intends to raise up to mystical union. That is exactly how things are, my dear Raffaelina. Unless I am mistaken, the fright and terror which this grace causes in the poor soul acts in the following way.

This grace is a very pure and incomparably spendid and brilliant light. When it first invades the soul it finds it unwilling and unprepared to receive it, and it then produces what is going on within you at present. In order to give you a proof of this, or rather to use an analogy that has nothing to do with the subject under discussion, I propose for your consideration the idea of a man affected by a disease of the eyes. It is painful for this individual to look at the light and he would be inclined to consider the sun as an enemy to his eyes. Now, listen to me. According to universal good sense everyone prefers the sun to darkness, everyone says the sun is good, that it is excellent. Yet those who suffer a disease of the eyes prefer darkness to light and to the sun and they would almost be tempted to call the sun their worst enemy.

Can you tell me what is the origin of this great diversity of judgment, of the diametrically opposed ways in which these two classes of people judge the situation? I mean the ones with good eyesight and those whose sight is bad. Is it, perhaps, that the sun is not beneficial to everyone? You will certainly not think so. The sun, the light is an excellent thing and has the virtue of being good for all eyes. So if those affected by a disease of the eyes are hurt by it, this does not depend on the sun but on the eye that is unfit to receive its light. In point of fact, when these people's eyes are cured, the light becomes beneficial to them also.

I therefore conclude that the same occurs in the case of the soul that is invaded by such a light. This soul is almost ill and is completely unprepared to receive such a supernatural light. Hence, when this light assails it, the poor thing is frightened and terrified and this terror extends to the faculties of memory, intellect and will. Moreover, this terror and dread are also experienced in the interior senses of the body. But when the soul is gradually being healed of its illness, it soon begins to feel the healthful effects of this new grace.

Take courage, then, Raffaelina. Don't be frightened and don't stop halfway on your road. Go forward all the time with fresh courage. Would you believe it? This grace which is causing you such terror at present is precisely what is needed to unite you to the divine Spouse in a mystical marriage.

For pity's sake, though, don't listen to what your sister suggests. Only the devil himself could have put such a notion into her head. I cannot conceal from you the fact that since receiving your letter yesterday up to the present moment I have been unable to restrain my tears on account of that wretched diabolical suggestion of hers. I am so distressed by it that my heart is breaking. The only thing that relieves me somewhat is the thought that you will never put it into practice, much less receive it into your soul.

I end, Raffaelina, by exhorting you to remain firmly and securely attached to the cross, for you have nothing to fear. Jesus will be the helmsman who will steer your little spiritual ship and Mary will be the anchor.

I would like to write more but I feel I haven't the strength to go on. You will always know how to make allowances for me and to pardon me. Isn't that so?

To your excellent sister Giovina and to all those who love Jesus, please convey my most respectful regards.

I leave you in the Lord's holy embrace.

Fra Pio.

56

Foggia, 1 March 1915.

She thanks him. Confidence in her director's prayers. She returns to some questions already asked. A letter from her niece. Requests for prayers.

Father,

I have your most precious letter and warmest thanks well up from my heart towards the One who in the midst of so much mud and misery and darkness deigns by means of your letter to send me light and comfort.

This is only a feeble momentary light and comfort, but it enables me in some way or other to drag myself along in the wake of the cross.

I frankly admit that if all that you say to me about my spiritual state had not been written and confirmed by you and by you alone, I would never believe it. You yourself inform me in advance, through the full knowledge Jesus gives you of my interior life. I am amazed, embarrassed and humiliated. Such ingratitude, perversity and wretchedness on my side and such love and grace and benefits from God! Help me, stand in for me with this admirable and infinite benefactor to love and thank Him while asking His pardon over and over again.

My spiritual state continues as before: rebellion, apathy,

indifference, hardheartedness, human reasoning, paltry earthly desires, endless demands. The continual and painful difficulties still surround me and I place all my trust in your prayers. I count on the friendship, predilection, extraordinary favours and graces you enjoy in the secret loving conversations which Jesus is pleased to grant you, face to face, at all times.

Do you understand, do you sympathize with, make allowances for and forgive those who lack everything, wretched, guilty and utterly poor as they are? Oh, I do not doubt it.

You say nothing about the advice I asked from you with regard to my poor martyr. Have the patience to re-read my last letter and when you see fit, be so kind as to answer me clearly. But now that I think of it, did you tear up that letter as I asked? Tell me, holy Father.

Have you nothing to say to me about Francesca? I know you send her your instructions by another means. Perhaps you will make use this time also of worthy and privileged souls, while I myself withdraw without demur[1]. Have the patience to remove a doubt that is in my mind: why did you use twice, in two separate letters, the same phrase: "treat good Rosina well for me." Tell me what Jesus said to you on this subject. For me this is another hidden and sharp thorn. Is there some other surprise concealed here? I am in fear and trembling. May Jesus see to our case, for I myself am bewildered.

I enclose my niece's letter[2]. Enlighten, guide and counsel her, Father. The enterprise is a difficult one (she is

---

[1] We only possess one letter from Padre Pio to Francesca.

[2] The widow Zicari's reply is dated 27 February 1915 from Foggia. From this letter we learn that Padre Pio had advised her "to lose no time in carrying out a plan on which the good of her children might depend", that is, to place them in the home of the Marquis Filippo De Piccolellis. See Letters 52 and 69.

young and very beautiful, the most beautiful woman in Foggia). Everything must be done very cautiously and nobody must get an inkling about this plan and this trip. And if it turns out well? This is what is causing us great anxiety and agitation. The successful future of two young plants, the future of an unfortunate family and the peace and security of a most unhappy young widow would be sufficiently serious reasons to justify this step. For you, holy Father, all this would be a matter for continual insistent prayers with the holy satisfaction of their being granted to the full. Pray a great deal for the fulfilment of this good work for the glory of God and the good of a number of souls.

I am afraid of tiring you. I abuse your Franciscan patience too much. Forgive me. Pray very much for Giovina's serenity and health in soul and body and for the total and speedy conversion of my own soul. There must be some great obstacle either in myself or in Giovina which is preventing the Lord from granting the spiritual and temporal favours requested. You alone can know what it is. Point out this wretched obstacle to me, Father, and I shall be most grateful to you.

Obtain for me patience, strength, desire and love for the cross, with an ardent longing for the Eucharistic bread. May Jesus, the wise and loving physician, come quickly, very quickly, to examine and heal this poor creature of His, by helping her to follow the path of Calvary, clinging closely to Him all the time.

Bless at every moment,

A poor tertiary.

57

Pietrelcina, 4 March 1915.

Joy and sorrow caused by the new mystical trial. Encouragement. Her one thought must be to grow in love. Uniting with God's will and fearing to offend Him. Objections. Ever closer and more united in spirit. Family matters.

J.M.J.D.F.C.

Beloved daughter of the heavenly Father,

May the Holy Spirit sanctify you more and more, make you worthy of greater charisms and make you a most chaste spouse of the Son of God. Amen.

Infinite praise and thanks to Jesus, King of souls, for treating you as a chosen daughter of His own. I cannot fail to be deeply moved and filled with indescribable joy at the sight of all these most singular gestures of love with which Jesus favours your soul. Seeing you subjected by Jesus to this fresh trial the higher part of my soul rejoices with all the children of God, for I see very plainly the fulfilment of God's plan for you and the crown that is being fashioned for you up above in the heavenly homeland.

I do not deny that in the lower part of my soul I feel as if my heart were being torn to pieces to see you plunged in such a very harsh trial; but as I said to you some time ago, the higher part of my soul is happy to see you reduced to such straits, for it sees the Lord loading you continually with jewels. Yes, I who in holy charity have your welfare at heart as if it were my own rejoice more and more as I think of you in that state.

Courage, then, Raffaelina, courage all the time, for before long it will be bright noontime in the heavens of your soul. Fight the good fight to the last, for Jesus will give you the strength to do so, or rather He is with you and will also fight for you so that you may overcome all obstacles. On your side there must be humility and gratitude to the good God for such outstanding favours.

May Jesus enable you to appreciate more and more, along with all the souls who love Him with a sincere and pure heart, his most loving invitation: *My yoke is easy and my burden is light*[1]. May this most tender invitation of the divine Master console you in this new trial, or rather in this accumulation of divine favours upon you. It can truly be said very well that your new state is a most singular favour of the Lord, a favour that he usually grants only to those strong souls who, in His mercy, He holds most dear.

Rejoice, then, along with me at this outstanding benevolence of our good God. Oh, Raffaelina, how delightful and consoling it is to know that without any merit of our own, this most tender Father has raised us to such high dignity. Oh, open your heart to this Father, the most loving of all fathers and let Him act freely within you. Let us not be stingy with one who enriches us even too much, whose generosity is endless and knows no limits.

Let your only thought be to love God and to grow more and more in virtue and in holy love which is the bond of Christian perfection[2].

In all life's events recognize the divine will, adore and

---

[1] Mt 11:30.
[2] Cf. Col 3:14.

bless it. Especially in the things that are hardest for you, do not be in a hurry to escape from them. Raise up your heart to the divine Father more than ever on these occasions and say to him: "Lord, God of my heart, You alone know and read all my troubles, You alone are aware that all my distress springs from my fear of losing You, of offending You, from my fear of not loving You as much as I should love and desire to love You. If You, to whom everything is present and who alone can read the future, know that it is for Your greater glory and for my salvation that I should remain in this state, then let it be so. I don't want to escape from it. Give me the strength to fight and to obtain the prize due to strong souls."

Don't be upset, either, my dear Raffaelina, because you experience no refreshment or spiritual delight in making such acts of resignation to the divine will. Let it be sufficient for you to be united to God by your will. But you are afraid that you are not united to God even by your will and this is the cause of your interior torment. But be consoled and cast off your doubts, for I tell you in the Lord that your will is united with the will of God. A person who does not love God does not pay any attention to God, does not feel afraid of not loving Him and never troubles to think of God with the sincere desire to love Him. Moreover, if the thought or idea of God sometimes comes into this person's mind, you will find that person dismissing the idea at once or almost at once.

Console yourself, I repeat, that as long as you are afraid that you do not love God and as long as you fear to offend Him, you already love Him and no longer offend Him. Oh, if it only pleased heaven to have everyone feel the fear you feel, offence against God would already be banished from the face of the earth! No longer would we see so many souls lacking in love of God! If this were the case with everyone, would you believe it, we should lose sight of the idea of souls who do not love God, we should no longer have even the concept of sin in human creatures and should only contemplate it in those unfortunate angelic spirits who fell and were stripped of their dignity.

For pity's sake, don't smile a mocking smile at this statement of mine and accuse me of exaggeration. I tell you once more that things would be just as I say and could not be otherwise.

"But, Father," I hear you shouting in my ear, "I am being punished by God. I see my ingratitude and my wretchedness, so how is it possible that my present state can be combined with divine grace, or rather, how can my present state be divine grace itself? Father, your judgment of me is mistaken."

Get rid of this further doubt, Raffaelina, which for you is the most atrocious one. Tell me, is it the sun or is it darkness that lights up and discloses things? I leave it to yourself to draw the true conclusion. God alone is His grace, God alone is the supreme sun and all others are nothing, or if they are anything, it is due to Him alone. God alone, I say, can enlighten the soul with His grace and show that soul what it is. And the more fully a person knows his own wretchedness and unworthiness in God's sight, the more remarkable is the grace that enlightens him and reveals to him what he is.

I understand that the discovery of one's own wretchedness under the action of this divine sun saddens and distresses at the outset. It is a source of pain and of terror for the poor soul that is enlightened in this manner. But console yourself in our most sweet Lord, for when this divine sun will have warmed the earth of your soul with its burning rays, it will cause new plants to spring up, which in due course will yield most delicious fruits, the like of which have never been seen.

Believe me, Raffaelina, for this is exactly how things stand. Console yourself, then, with this delightful thought, with this beautiful assurance. I would like to be close to you so as to be in a better position to fight the good fight along with you, to explain to you more fully your very enviable state. I would like to be near you, in a word, so that we might comfort each other and share many spiritual consolations. But let Jesus, the Most Blessed Virgin and your own good angel stand in for this holy desire of mine. I'll be satisfied to assist you spiritually and to help you as much as I can by other means. I have done this up to the present and in future, with God's help, I will continue to do the same more wisely and more perfectly.

With regard to your question as to what to do for your excellent sister, Giovina, I do not consider it right and advisable for you to leave Foggia at present to have her taken care of in a nursing home. This is my advice to you, but it is, of course, in accordance with human judgment. If you do not find it suits the case, you may act as you please. I would suggest just one thing. I consider it most advisable and necessary for you to accompany her to Naples to be examined by some good specialist. But the time is not yet ripe and we might speak of it later in the season when the weather is better.

And what about the complaints you make to me concerning our good and most pious Francesca? You ought to remember only too well how you failed the first time. The punishment due to your fault was remitted, but not the fault itself. I can only entrust you with the task of reassuring her all the time about her spiritual state.

There is no foundation for your suspicions concerning good Rosina.

Fra Pio[3].

[3] For lack of space his signature is written at the top right-hand corner of the first sheet.

58

Pietrelcina, Feast of the Annunciation of the B.V.M.,
25 March 1915.

Greetings and good wishes. A more spiritual than corporal illness: its intensity and effects. His desire to die. Encouragement. Good wishes for Easter. Content of the letters. Requests.

J.M.J.D.F.C.

Beloved daughter of the heavenly Father,

May your heart always be the temple of the Holy Spirit and may Jesus come to you in your present distress and trial. May He always be the helmsman of your little spiritual ship. May Mary be the star which shines on your path and may she show you the safe way to reach the heavenly Father. May she be like an anchor to which you must be more closely attached in time of trial. May your good Guardian Angel break down and reduce to silence all the tempter's cunning suggestions.

Don't attempt to think that I have forgotten the very strict obligation I assumed with Jesus in your regard, just because I have not shown any signs of life for some time past. If you have had such a suspicion, you have been greatly mistaken. You ought to know that for some time now Our Lord Jesus Christ has been pleased to let me be extremely ill, with an illness that is more spiritual than corporal. This trial is so great that I am staking everything on it. All hell has been let loose upon me. At times I feel as if I am dying and it is really a miracle of God's mercy that I go on living. I am dying at every instant and feel myself crucified by love. This ought to be a source of delight for me, but what do you expect? My soul is still accustomed to very coarse food. I spend entire nights in extreme anguish in view of the trial by which I stand to lose absolutely everything.

Believe me, Raffaelina, that this period of most acute mortification and trial presses down upon me at times to such an extent that I feel I am being crushed beneath its enormous weight. I sometimes think it is a punishment from God for my innumerable infidelities to the great goodness of his divine Majesty, so that all my prayers seem quite useless. Only too well do I deserve to be punished, but is it really possible that the heavenly Father's mercy should be overcome by my wickedness? No, such a thing can never be. Praise be to Jesus! He is with us and we have nothing to fear.

Beseech Him without ceasing for me in the meantime. May He set me free without delay from my present state. May He call me to celebrate Easter in my heavenly home. Oh, how greatly I long for that day! But, alas, it seems to me to be too far away! *As a hart longs for flowing streams, so longs my soul for Thee, O God*[1]. Oh, how sad is this exile for me! Never has it been so painful to me as it is now. My mouth feels parched and I feel my entrails burning. Will our good Jesus take pity on me?

Pray, pray, my dear Raffaelina, that the Lord may put an end to my most painful state and satisfy at last my most ardent longings. Pray, I repeat, for you will reap great fruit from the fulfilment of my desires. No, I feel sure you will not turn a deaf ear this time to my lawful requests.

Did you receive my last letter, dated 4 March? How is

---

[1] Ps 42:1.

it that there has been no reply? It is very painful, while plunged in great dejection, not to have even a line of reply for such a long time from one whose spiritual rather than corporal health I have so much at heart. Don't yield to the storms stirred up by Satan. Place your trust in God all the time. You are advancing steadily in this respect and you must show this especially in the present trial, which must turn out for the glory of God and be a great triumph for your own soul. Don't torment yourself more than is necessary. Rejoice, for the war will soon be over. Before long negotiations will begin and the expenses of the war will be charged to the enemy of God, the enemy of souls. Oh, how beautiful will be the bright noonday that the good God will send when the purgation is over! May this sweet thought encourage you, then, to fight the good fight like a strong one.

I wish you a most happy celebration in the Lord for the beautiful day of our redemption. May Jesus always live in your soul!

I must end here, Raffaelina, for my strength will not permit me to continue. In the meantime, when you do not find your wishes answered and satisfied, please read my letters over again, as I feel they contain everything.

Will the good God grant me to see soon again your greatly-desired and precious handwriting? Answer me without delay, if Jesus wills, and manifest to me your present state of soul.

Remember me to your excellent sister, to the most pious Rosina and to all those who love Jesus. May they pray for me, especially at the present time, as I always do for all of you.

I bless you in the name and in virtue of Our Lord Jesus Christ.

Your poor servant,
Fra Pio, Capuchin.

59

Foggia, Feast of the Annunciation,
25 March 1915.

First ceremonies in the family chapel. In paradise only as regards the body! Further anxiety. Her director's disease is incurable. "Is my state enviable?" Peace for all. Balance sheet of his direction during the year. Postscript. Reply to his letter of the 25th!

Jesus alone! Most Holy Spirit, help me!

Father,

There is a respite and in this Jesus allows a ray of His infinite generosity to shine forth.

Not all my letters must contain tears and distress. Some of them, at least, although this seldom happens, must bring you joy and smiles.

I left you in peace for awhile and my writings have not disturbed your tranquillity for some time. But now I cannot wait any longer. I want to share some good news with you: the chapel is now finished.

Certain to give you pleasure, I want to tell you briefly about the beautiful inauguration ceremony which took place on the morning of 14 March. In one of the rooms, formerly the study, the altar-cupboard was installed. (We did not want to have an open altar, because we intend to transfer it to another room since the present room is one through which we pass). According to my desire the altar is dedicated to the Most Sacred Heart of Jesus. We have a beautiful and most life-like picture which we obtained from the Sacred Art Centre in Milan, along with the other furnishings for the chapel. In this picture of the divine Heart, the Lord's eyes are most tender and seem to follow us all around the room. All those who came for a visit liked it.

On the previous day, a Saturday, the Canon and theologian from the Cathedral (who is at present my confessor and also Giovina's) blessed all the furnishings. It was he who took charge of everything and dealt with the whole business, from the Roman Brief down to the smallest details. On the following day, Sunday, at 8 a.m., we had the blessing of the picture of the Most Sacred Heart, then Mass, Consecration and Litany to the Sacred Heart, plus a fine impromptu sermon by the Canon[1] and the blessing of the whole house. Eight people received Holy Communion, including Giovina, good Francesca, her disciple Annita[2] and several of those who work for us. These were the only people I wanted to be present at the inauguration. We excluded relatives and friends in order to avoid distractions and confusion. Other private reasons which it would take far too long to explain made it advisable for me to act in this way. Thus we avoided explanations and unkind remarks from relatives who are anything but fond of us. What have you to say to this? Do you approve? Did I do right or wrong? Does Jesus approve?

Fresh flowers from our own terrace were not lacking on the altar, along with some plants. A distinct odour of incense

---

[1] Mr. Guido Cairelli (cfr. Letter 52), great nephew of the Cerase sisters, remembers a canon who was chaplain to the Cerase home, a priest named Bucci whose Christian name may have been Pasquale.

[2] The orphan Annita, the Cerase sisters' seamstress.

completed the idea of a chapel. On the second day, Monday, we invited Father Guardian of your Capuchins to say Mass, but this was impossible as all the Fathers were busy. The Guardian came instead to say Mass on the feast of St. Joseph. Two days earlier we had the honour of a nice visit from Very Reverend Father Provincial, accompanied by his secretary and the Guardian[3]. We invited father Provincial to say Mass also, but he could not accept as he had to leave next day at 6 a.m. However, he promised to say Mass for us after Easter and said, in fact, that we would have a nice little ceremony.

As to myself, I am in paradise, but only as regards the body, for I am always at the same point spiritually. I am dissipated, cold and distracted. But shame! After so many graces and benefits from Jesus I ought to be all aflame, all fire and zeal. I ought to respond to many kindnesses but I find myself incapable of this. I can say or feel nothing. I should like to feel Jesus' presence (I now receive Him almost every day) but I do not feel Him within me. Tell me, what does Jesus think of my present ingratitude? Speak clearly to me, for I am very troubled on this score.

Further worries, in fact real torments are never lacking to me on account of Giovina's health. She is comparatively well but always suffering from her ailments. She is pale and thin, shrinking day by day, while I myself live in a continual state of agitation and fear. Add to this my usual great sadness which I just cannot overcome. Every day it invariably seizes me an hour before sunset and disappears at sunrise. During the hours of sunshine I feel I am a different person. This light, this kindly sun makes me calm, cheerful and happy. I bless it for dispelling my interior melancholy, a melancholy which

---

[3] The Provincial was Padre Benedetto of San Marco in Lamis and his secretary Padre Luigi d'Avellino (1884-1959); the Guardian of Foggia friary was Padre Tommaso of Monte Sant'Angelo (1872-1932).

(to my shame) is always due to human motives, earthly considerations, worldly desires and regrets.

Why do you not ask Jesus to cure me? May He who is the true sun of justice, the kindly and holy sun, He who is the divine and powerful physician, heal the disorders which are displeasing to Him and which I myself am unable to discern, discover and define. May He heal in soul and body my Giovina, who now receives Him frequently in Holy Communion. (Speak to me about this). Oh, if these Communions might only continue permanently!

Your own illness is incurable. It is of a very different nature, species and form. Your malady is love, it is the fire that burns, devours and consumes you without any refreshment or relief. But refreshment and relief for you would be a very bad thing, because it would mean slowing down and coming to a halt. Ah, no! You love and you want to and must always love and burn with love for the divine Lover at all costs.

Good Francesca and also Annita told me about your state and of the attack you have had. I suffer to think that you are suffering, but I rejoice in the knowledge of the cause of your suffering and I envy you. If I were a saint I too would experience these most sweet pains, but even without feeling them I imagine and understand them. (Is this too rash on my part? Tell me). This must be the hell of love. However, there must frequently, quite frequently, be a ray of light, a smile, a heavenly joy. Loving feelings and palpitations, secret colloquies, ecstasies, caresses, looking at Jesus, isn't this paradise on earth? (Speak to me at length on this point).

Various things you said in your last letter, which reached me on 4 March, encourage me: "I would like to fight the good fight along with you, to explain to you more fully your very enviable state."

My enviable state? This greatly astonished me. Is the very harsh trial over? Is Jesus very pained by my present state of indifference, of coldness and neglect? You are aware of all, so tell me all, speak to me at length.

With regard to the matter of Francesca, or rather my own offence (quite justified, in my opinion), you are all the time very severe and unyielding towards me. You speak of this with great severity in your last letter. The day after tomorrow is Palm Sunday. Hold out to me the blessed olive-branch in forgiveness of my fault and remission of the penalty. Forgive my former failure and grant me peace. You implore peace for everybody and may Jesus grant it, through your mediation, to the enemy countries, to Italy, to society, to families, especially my own (will there be an end to the situation with my brother?) May He grant peace to my Giovina, to Rosa and her family, to relatives, to true friends and false ones, to all our enemies. And may He grant it to me, His unfaithful servant.

I wish you everything you desire during these holy feastdays. I would like to spend these holy days in great recollection, I would like to spend them in love and compassion for Jesus' sufferings and Mary's, in true repentance for my sins which have caused them and a firm resolution not to fall again. All beautiful foliage, but, as usual, there is no good fruit.

On 29 March, Passion Sunday of last year, 1914, I received your first letter. A year has gone by! A year of your care, your counsel, your instruction. What result have I yielded? What fruit has this barren and thankless soil given you? Tell me yourself. I hide away, I humble myself, I blush and am ashamed to answer. May Jesus still show me a little of His infinite mercy, through your powerful pleading, my holy advocate. I place my trust in you and fear to take too much advantage of you.

Thank you for everything. May Jesus reward you. Forgive me and continue to bless,

Your poor tertiary.

P.S. While I was writing this your own most precious letter arrived. Touched by it, I repeat that I sometimes delay in answering you for fear of making too great a nuisance of myself.

You ask my prayers for a certain purpose, but what use are the entreaties of this poor nonentity? In the attempt to suggest a comforting remedy, I tell you to write to your own holy father. With the insight, discernment, wisdom and inspiration which only uncreated Wisdom can give him, he will bring you relief in your present state.

Poor Father, how I wish I could lighten your trial! But, shameless as I am, what do I dare to say? I am unwilling to face up to my own little battles, implacable enemy that I am of trials and sacrifice! May Jesus console you. May He inspire you for your coming visit to us. The dear little chapel in my home awaits the holy and blessed visit of holy Padre Pio. What do you say? Does Jesus want this? Answer me fully on this point and don't forget it.

Pray for Francesca, pray that we may have an easy chance very soon to reach an agreement with our brother and his wife. Pray a great deal. I'll keep you informed.

I kiss your hand.

60

Pietrelcina, Tuesday of holy Week, 30 March 1915.

Greetings. He praises God's goodness and mercy. Every Christian must be another Christ. Growing in love. His attack continues: prayers are needed. The desire to die. "Don't think me more than I am." The chapel in her home. Fighting against sadness. In peace await God's plan. A message for Francesca. Their correspondence.

J.M.J.D.F.C.

Beloved daughter of the heavenly Father,

May the grace of the Holy Spirit sustain you and enable you to grow more and more in virtue. May Jesus and Mary provide you with the grace to fight all the time with fresh courage against the wiles of the Evil Spirit. May your angel invariably show you the right path which leads to him and may he continually praise the Most Holy Trinity on your behalf. Amen.

I give infinite thanks for you to the Lord who is so good to all His creatures, especially to those who do their utmost to love Him. He never ceases to visit them in time of trial and to send down a heavenly charism into their souls, which must serve them as armour and shield to ward off the blows of the enemy and further misfortunes. Praise be for ever to Jesus and may the divine mercy and providence be praised for ever!

But if ever there was a human being in whom the divine goodness and providence shines forth more clearly, it is precisely yourself. This is how things are, Raffaelina. Humble yourself continually before the Lord, keep yourself always in the last place and never give in to yourself. Have boundless trust in God even when misfortune and the deceitful prompting of the enemy trouble you. He who abandons himself in God and trusts in Him will never be confounded. May your whole life be spent in giving thanks to the divine Spouse, may all your actions, all your sighs and yearnings be addressed to Him. Remain with Him always in times of misfortune and trial. Remain with Him also in your spiritual consolation. Live for Him, in a word, and let your entire life be spent for him. Hand over to Him your departure and the departure of others from this earth, when, where and as He wills. In all things show yourself ever more worthy of your Christian vocation.

Live in such a way that the heavenly Father may be proud of you as He is proud of so many other chosen souls like your own. Live in such a way that you may be able to repeat at every moment with the apostle St. Paul: *Be imitators of me, as I am of Jesus Christ*[1]. Live in such a way, I repeat, that the world will be forced to say of you: "Here is Christ." Oh, for pity's sake, do not consider this an exaggeration! Every Christian who is a true imitator and follower of the fair Nazarene can and must call himself a second Christ and show forth most clearly in his life the entire image of Christ. Oh, if only all Christians were to live up to their vocation, this very land of exile would be changed into a paradise!

Grow always in Christian love and never tire of advancing in this which is the queen of all the virtues. Consider that you can never grow too much in this most beautiful virtue. Love it very much, let it be more than the apple of your eye, for it is truly most dear to our divine Master. In an altogether

[1] 1 Cor 4:16; 11:1.

divine phrase he calls it "my precept"[2]. Oh, yes, let us greatly esteem this precept of the divine Master and all difficulties will be overcome.

The virtue of love is exceedingly beautiful, Raffaelina, and to enkindle it in our hearts the Son of God was pleased to come down Himself from the bosom of the eternal Father, to become like us in order to teach us and make it easy for us, with the means He left us, to acquire this most eminent virtue.

Let us ask Jesus insistently to give us this virtue and let us make greater and greater efforts to grow in it. Let us ask this, I repeat, at all times and more than ever on the feast of the risen Jesus. Ask it also for me who greatly need it if I am not to fall and to betray the goodness of the heavenly Father.

The attack which I mentioned to you in my last letter, Raffaelina, continues with its ups and downs. Praise be to Jesus! This too will work out for the glory of His divine Majesty. I need fresh courage all the time, though, and this I await from heaven through the intercession of yourself and of other souls that are very dear to the divine Heart. For this purpose I ask you in charity, by the meekness of the Son of God, to begin the holy novenas to the beautiful Virgin of Pompeii in whom I have great confidence and through whom I expect all from the generosity of God. I also want you to receive Holy Communion during this time for the same intention. I am asking too much, but do not doubt that Jesus will know how to reward you.

Do not worry, however, for the good we endeavour to do to others will also result in the sanctification of our own souls. This is exactly how things stand and not otherwise. During these holy days entreat as never before the goodness of the heavenly Father, that His plan for me may be achiev-

[2] Jn 15:12.

ed. I am prepared to receive any blow whatsoever as long as I can please the Lord.

I have never hidden, nor do I hide this time from you that my keenest desire has always been to be released from these bonds in order to be with Jesus Christ. I earnestly entreat the Lord to put an end to these ardent desires which, especially at certain times, make me taste every sort of death simultaneously, even though I do not really die. Nevertheless I do not want to leave this prison even for a single instant before the time the Lord has fixed for me.

Meanwhile what am I doing? Am I inactive? No, indeed, and I could never be inactive. By my desire I am forcing the hours, the days and the years to pass quickly and at the end of each day I always feel more consoled—comparatively, of course—for I see slipping off me and growing less the weight which presses upon me and separates me from the eternal sun.

For pity's sake, my Raffaelina, don't think me more than I am from what I have already said about myself. The desire to be united with Jesus is a holy one, but is it so in my case? I do not know and all the assurances I am given in this respect fail to convince me. I doubt and continue to doubt it, for it seems to me that I have no charity at all. In the many years I have spent at Jesus' school all the desires I have for the good God have not yet been satisfied. I feel within me all the time something I cannot define, something akin to a void. I would like my love to be more perfect and no matter how much I strive to do this I continue to feel ever more intensely this desire to love. I understand only too well that this desire can never be completely satisfied as long as we are wayfarers on this earth and this is where all my sufferings start. May the divine will be done! May it soon be granted to me to have an answer to my prayers.

You cannot imagine what a consolation it was for me to know that our prayers had been heard at last with regard to the installation of the altar in your home. May the heavenly

Father be blessed! Be grateful and thankful to God for the great benefits He continually bestows on you. Show Him your gratitude and appreciation by a life that is more and more worthy of a Christian woman. I too am now satisfied, for I see that Jesus can inebriate and satiate you with His immaculate flesh every day. And I am all the more happy in the knowledge that all will work out to the spiritual advantage of Giovina and others also.

When you are overcome by sadness at sunset, then more than ever must you renew your trust in God, humble yourself before Him and praise and bless the heavenly Father with a full heart. Cast far from you all thought of things that cause you to be sad, refuse to harbour all such thoughts just as you would reject temptations against holy purity. You must not dwell any longer on these tormenting thoughts. I wish you to act in this way, in fact I was about to say (if this does not displease you) that I command and insist that you do all this.

In addition you must endeavour to occupy your mind with happy things. Try to dwell, for example, on the goodness of the heavenly Father in giving you His Only Begotten Son, on the beauty of our holy faith, on the happiness reserved for us in paradise, on the Resurrection and Ascension of Jesus, on the glory He enjoys in paradise and which, if we remain faithful to Him, He has reserved one day for us also. Try to have other people keep you company, moreover, and avoid topics that tend to make you sad. Let your speech be edifying and confine yourself to cheerful topics. Sing some songs, too, but let these be religious songs or something similar.

If you had put into practice the advice I gave you elsewhere, perhaps you would not find yourself in your present state. This may appear to you to be a reproof, but I take good care not to reproach you. I merely wanted to remind you of this with a view to stimulating within you the courage and zeal to practise what you have been told up to the present. In a word, I intended by this statement to draw the attention of your depressed and discouraged soul to a point of the greatest importance.

Don't be curious to know whether the very harsh trial foretold to you has already ended. Leave yourself invariably in the arms of your heavenly Father, where you are at present. Peacefully await the fulfilment of God's plan for you and don't bother about anything else. If it pleases the Lord to reveal some future secret to you, as He did before, thank Him for it. But if He wants to conceal everything, then thank Him just the same.

Here is a message for our most pious Francesca. Assure her in the Lord as always that her soul is very dear to the divine Master. Let her not be uneasy or worried if it seems to her that things are not working out as she desires, for this is better for herself, for other souls and for the glory of God. Give her my best wishes for the feasts of the risen Jesus and do the same in the case of your excellent sister, of Rosina and all those others who love Jesus. Assure them all that unworthy and insignificant as I am I send up ardent prayers to the good God for their growth in holiness. I consider it superfluous to ask them to pray for me as I know they are most certainly doing this already.

Tell Miss Francesca not to deny me the charity she is doing me during these days. Our good Jesus will reward her. I don't take the liberty of thanking her for what she is doing, for I should not know how to thank her. I merely venture to tell her, through you, that I see it all with great pleasure and that on this occasion she will always have one of the first places in my constant prayers.

Here is the palm for which you asked me last Sunday. Are you happy now?

Write to me often; I too am in need of relief in my present state. If you don't receive a reply, write again. During this Holy Week and in Easter week, it will be difficult for me to answer you.

My love to you all in Christ Jesus.

Fra Pio, Capuchin.

61

Foggia, 5 April 1915.

"I am still on Calvary." When she comes down from Calvary she will reply to his last letter. Postscript. Visit of two Capuchins. Her sister's sufferings. "Pray for me." "I am continually crying." Their correspondence.

Jesus alone! Most Holy Spirit, help me!

Father,

Holy Week is not yet over for me. I am still on Calvary. My very dear martyr is in bed with one of the usual severe attacks on this day of joy and festivity for the redeemed. It began yesterday evening at nine o'clock and eased off towards four o'clock this morning.

Last night, in moral torment, I said to Jesus: "Very soon You will rise glorious from the dead amidst universal joy; You, Your most holy Mother and the holy women are all happy and brimming over with joy. Do you not look on us who are weeping instead? This poor creature is suffering very much and my own heart is bleeding."

On Wednesday of Holy Week she had another but less violent attack. Your most precious letter reached me while my wretched soul was undergoing a nameless torment which has lasted for five days and has not ceased even on this great day. Tears are my daily bread all the time. I would like to restrain them, but they are stronger than I am. I reply to the greetings of relatives and friends with a lump in my throat and uncontrollable weeping. I am extremely weak. I am all alone and have no one on this earth to counsel me, to help me, to smooth the way towards getting treatment for my holy sister's most precious health.

Ask Jesus to make me strong, very strong morally and materially, in soul and in body. Discouraged, disheartened, crushed by this horrible storm, I am about to give in. I am staggering, I am falling.

How ingenuous I was to ask you if the very harsh trial was ended. I see now that it has hardly begun. Where is it to end? Will there be a tragic sequel? Pray for me, pray for both of us, very weak leaves buffeted by so many tempests. Implore moral and physical strength for her, for me, for poor Rosa who sacrifices herself along with me to take care of her.

When I come down from Calvary and when I feel more at peace I'll reply to your last letter. Keep before you continually my lasting torment. I ought to unite it to the perpetual agony of Jesus in the Eucharist, but I do nothing of the kind. Pray and plead for me. Bless my Giovina all the time. (She is unrecognizable, all her clothes are falling off her. She is fasting almost all the time, for although she would like to eat, she is afraid, and the tiny amount of food she takes is inadequate for her nourishment. So what is to be done? What is to be done? I am lost in this matter and my head reels).

Continue to bless your,

Poor tertiary.

P.S. I began this letter yesterday, taking advantage of the brief interval when my poor invalid was resting. I was interrupted by a visit from Father Guardian and the Very

Reverend Definitor, Padre Francesco[1], your confrères. I took it up again today with an effort as I was in a state of agitation. Pray to Jesus to keep His most holy hands on my head, for if He doesn't, I'll be in great trouble.

I see my sister's enemies rejoicing in triumph. She has many enemies, merely because she has claimed her absolute rights and because she demands justice all the time for herself and others. Her enemies are triumphant and is she, poor thing, to be treated like this by the good heavenly Father and not to be spared even on the day of His most holy Son's triumph? How are our enemies to judge this? That it is according to justice, supreme justice, for this holy creature to suffer, always to suffer? Oh, her whole life has been made up entirely of sacrifice, renunciation, disappointments and physical ailments, and was this not sufficient? An illness had to be added, a horrible illness in my opinion, of which we can understand neither the beginning nor the end.

My relatives speak of the responsibility that is mine, all mine. They say I should assert my authority, take a decision and act, that I should take her to Bologna to be examined by Murri, then retire with her to a nursing home to get appropriate, effective and decisive treatment for her. These are all fine words, all very true, but I have no idea how to begin or go on to act on them. I feel capable of making any sacrifice for my good sister, but Jesus will have to help me. He can do all things if He so wills, He who is the only powerful physician in whom I trust and hope.

Why do you not do me the favour of reciting for me the three novenas to our beautiful Mother of Pompeii? Good Francesca began these prayers for Giovina this very morn-

---

[1] We cannot say exactly who this Padre Francesco was, because in 1915 there were two Definitors, or Provincial Counsellors, of the same name: Francesco Maria of Savignano (10 December 1838-16 February 1916), fourth Definitor, and Francesco of Fragneto l'Abate (9 December 1873-24 October 1934), third Definitor.

ing. I myself also started them for you this morning. But I am in dire need in this great darkness and boundless solitude. I feel I am suffocating beneath the weight of the cross. The saints suffered because they were not suffering, but I am suffering because I don't want suffering. I fly from the cross, the thorns, the humiliations and solitude. I am deeply grieved. I feel death in my soul and Jesus is very dissatisfied with me. Implore for me a new heart, a new soul. Beg for my holy conversion. I have extreme need of prayers, of help, of special, adequate, superabundant strength for myself, so that I may pass it on then to my dear sufferer.

I am weeping continually. During these days I had no thought of Jesus' Passion. Preoccupied, concentrated and absorbed in Giovina's sufferings as I am and in the great immense misfortune which hangs over me, my tears betray me and reveal my agony of mind to those to whom I do not wish to let it be known. May Jesus set me free from this weakness and free me from all the insinuations, temptations, forecasts and melancholy by day and especially by night.

I am anxiously awaiting the end of this life of mine which is full of sins, of fears and dangers. I am extremely tired. I am waiting for death but don't feel at all prepared for it.

Don't be horrified and don't be scandalized by the content of my letters, please. What a difference from those you receive from good souls! In those you will find paradise, in mine... hell.

Write to me when you wish, when you can. All will be known to you by other channels.

I kiss your hand.

62

Pietrelcina, 10 April 1915.

Greetings and good wishes. The brevity of his reply. Her sister's health. "Have trust all the time." "God is with us in our trials." She is worrying too much. Prayers for one another.

J.M.J.D.F.C.

Beloved daughter of the heavenly Father,

May the Holy Spirit fill your soul with His most holy gifts and make you holy. May the risen Jesus make you, too, feel a spark of His holy love and reveal more and more to you the mysteries of the Cross. May the sorrowful Virgin obtain for you from her most holy Son true and sincere love of the cross and may your soul be inebriated with it. Amen.

I intend to be very brief this time, for a twofold reason. First of all, because I am not able to do much in view of the exceptional state of my health and, secondly, because I don't want to bother you with a long letter in view of your own present troubles. In point of fact, I tell you frankly that the latter motive rather than the former induces me this time to avoid writing at too great length. I will limit myself to what is strictly necessary in this.

Poor Giovina's state really makes me groan before the Lord. May our good Father console the poor martyr and all those souls who are fond of her. I do not hide from you the fact that this poor creature's sufferings have increased and made more irksome my own torment, so that I feel crushed beneath the weight of such grievous tribulation. May the most sweet Jesus accept these continual and habitual mortifications and sufferings of mine for the relief of your excellent sister and yourself.

Meanwhile do not lose faith in God's providence. Put your trust in God, abandon yourself to Him and let Him take care of you both, then rest assured that you will not be confounded. I understand and am deeply aware that the trial is hard and the battle fierce. But I also understand that the fruit you will gather in due course is very abundant. The crown that is being woven for you up above is far greater than can be humanly conceived. You will perhaps laugh at me for saying such things which you will consider quite mistaken, but I know quite well what I am saying.

Judge me as you think fit, but what I want from you is that as the trial increases your abandonment and trust in God may also increase. Immerse yourself ever more deeply in humility and in blessing the Lord who in His goodness deigns to visit you in this way so as to prepare you to share in building up the heavenly Sion!

I therefore exhort you again to be trustful. A soul who trusts in her Lord and places all her hope in Him has nothing to fear. The enemy of our salvation is always around us to snatch from our hearts the anchor that is to lead us to salvation, by which I mean trust in God our Father. Let us keep a very firm hold on this anchor and not relinquish it for a single moment. Otherwise all would be lost. Repeat continually and more especially in the darkest hours those most beautiful words of Job: *Even if you are to slay me, O Lord, I will still hope in you*[1]. Always be on your guard and don't

[1] Job 13:15 (Vg.)

become puffed up, considering yourself to be good in any way, or above others. Don't imagine that you are better than them or at least as good, but consider all to be better than yourself. The enemy, Raffaelina, overcomes the presumptuous and not the humble of heart.

Drive away what the enemy is whispering loudly in your ear when he wants you to believe you are almost on the point of being lost. Despise these evil insinuations and live in peace, for the Lord is with you as never before in your tribulations. Sacred Scripture also assures us that an afflicted soul is united with its God: *I will be with him in trouble*[2], God tells us. Take heart, then, and don't be afraid, for it is quite certain that the one who fears to be lost will not be lost and that the one who fights with his eyes fixed on God will cry victory and intone the triumphal hymn. There is nothing to be afraid of, my Raffaelina, for the heavenly Father has promised us the necessary help to prevent us from being overcome by temptations.

To tell the truth I see in a bad light your feverish anxiety about the poor sufferer. It seems to me that the time has come to put an end to this once and for all. Your attitude towards her illness is a sign that you have little trust in the Lord and this seriously wounds the heart of the one who has taken it upon himself to look after you and direct you. May the good God enlighten you with regard to my rightful dissatisfaction on this score.

You are also worried about your sister's enemies who laugh behind her back because of her sufferings. But tell me, please, what more can we expect from them, if they are enemies? Let us remember that if they are her enemies they are also God's enemies. Well, then, the enemies of God insult the Cross and all those who are crucified upon it with the

---

[2] Ps 91:15.

Son of God. For you this ought to be a source of gladness, as it is for many souls.

I'll satisfy you by reciting the novenas to the beautiful Virgin of Pompeii, to which I add the recital of the entire Rosary. Don't cease to pray yourself, then, for the intention of which you are aware, knowing as you do the straits in which my soul is placed.

May Jesus always be with you all.

Fra Pio.

63

Foggia, 17 April 1915.

Her sister's health. Her feverish anxiety. Confidence in prayer. "In what does my life consist?" Their correspondence. "I need light." Daily Communion. Participation in the Mass. Meditation. She wants long letters. Failure to correspond with her director's kind care of her. Their correspondence. "The cross is a token of love."

Most Holy Spirit, help me!

Father,

You want frequent news of my Giovina and here I come to satisfy you. On Thursday of Easter week (as well as on Easter Sunday[1] and Wednesday of Holy Week—which is three times in eight days!) she had another very bad attack, so bad that she had to have a morphine injection. She was utterly changed by the spasms of pain and I feared to lose her from one moment to the next. She is now picking up to some extent, thanks be to Jesus, but my own life has become an impossible one. I am living in a state of agitation, of fear and anguish and continual spasms. (I'll certainly have a heart attack). From one moment to the next I fear and expect some

---

[1] In 1915 Easter fell on 4 April.

very painful surprise. I look into her eyes, I ask her questions, I insist and I worry night and day, afraid that she is partly hiding her great sufferings from me. She really hides them from me to some extent, poor martyr, to save me from continual torment.

What are we to do? Where are we to go? I really do not know. What have you to say to me? I am in need of light, guidance and moral strength to help and sustain me. To whom am I to turn? The dear invalid places great hope in a change of air, some movement and a different life from the present one, by leaving for a while an environment saturated with disappointment and sadness. How can we help being melancholy and keep our minds off painful thoughts, as you advise in your last letter, when a wretched state of health and the painful mysteries that surround us continue to crush us? This is an oppressive moral torment which prevents us from finding a single hour of peace.

I realize that I always tell you the same things, while you listen to me with holy patience. But what can you expect? The situation is always the same, so how can I speak to you of anything else? In your last letter, which reached me on the 10th of this month, you reproved me gently about my "feverish anxiety." Forgive me, make allowances and pray very hard for me. I am in greater need than Giovina, that I may not give scandal to those around me.

I have great confidence in your three novenas to the beautiful Queen of Pompeii. Do I not owe it to you that we have the freedom of our own old home? Nobody could ever have imagined that my brother would abandon this house which he had taken it into his head to call his own. We have no more business dealings with him, except with regard to some land in Lucera (from my mother's family) which is administered by my sister-in-law's brother. He has given no account of this management for fully seven years, so that the matter is a source of accusations and unpleasantness. Giovina would like at all costs to remove this man, but our brother and his wife are holding out with a view to some profit for themselves. Does it not seem so to you? Would this be a rash judgment?

I have explained this affair to you so that your prayers may hasten the day of reckoning and prevent further sins. There is still ill-feeling between us. When, Father, shall we cease to make such an exhibition of ourselves? You certainly know this, so tell me.

Good Francesca asks me to thank you for the fine reassurances you sent her and she continues to pray hard for your intentions. I myself am doing likewise and will continue to pray for what you so ardently desire. But I'll do this on one condition, that is, that Jesus will call me very soon after He has called you. Do you promise me this? Your promise will be sacred for me.

In what does my life consist? It is empty, wretched and useless to myself and to others. I want to serve a holy purpose, to do good to all who approach me, but instead... In the very first place, I invariably cause deep displeasure to my good Father who for a year now has been pouring out all his zeal and charity to enlighten this gloomy being, to straighten up this wretched plant. Unfortunately you are not meeting with success. This thankless and unfaithful ground yields you nothing but thorns and sorrow. I don't respond to your efforts, poor Father. What will you say in your deep disappointment?

Ah, do not abandon me to my own devices, holy Father! You tell me in your last letter that you refrain from writing to me at length for fear of "bothering me with a long letter" (your very words). For pity's sake, don't even think such a thing and don't abandon me. I have extreme need of light, strength, guidance, moral enlightenment, moral and physical strength, guidance in moral and material matters. I am afraid of the darkness, for my mind, my soul, my whole inner being is in darkness. I am weak and am just dragging myself along. For this reason I am very glad when I get a chance to lay down the cross and stop along the way to Calvary, happy and gay, far from sorrows and tears. Good Father, I don't want to suffer.

Our good Jesus in the Eucharist comes to me every morning (when there isn't a storm), but He is not satisfied with me. He comes joyfully and eagerly, yes, hoping to find the virtues, some virtue in me after so many visits. He brings with him an assortment of gifts, graces and favours, but He stops on the threshold of my heart, astonished and distressed at the sight of such wretchedness and desolation, and He weeps. In his infinite mercy and generosity He has pity on me, He forgives me and then waits. Does He carry off with him all the gifts and graces, the benefits, the light, love and fire? I fear this, because my soul remains all the time in the dark; cold, distracted and miserable. Is this how things are? You know all, so tell me if this is the case and speak to me at great length.

Tell me also if Jesus is pleased with the way I hear Mass. During the first Mass in my chapel, and at Holy Communion, I was so very distracted and dazed. However, before the holy Sacrifice began (I forgot to mention this in a previous letter) it occurred to me to whisper to Francesca and Annita: "Let's think of Padre Pio as if he were here along with us." Giovina prepared for me part of the equipment for Jesus in the Eucharist and may He in His goodness reward her with a little health, so that she may be able to attend daily Mass as I desire. Pray very much for this.

A few days ago (what a nasty reproof I deserve from you!) I took up meditation again and if there are no storms I will continue to practise it. I read a paragraph chosen at random from your book and Jesus said the rest to me. Yesterday, for example, I read about John's loving abandonment on the most holy bosom of the divine Master. I reflected that

John reclined on that Heart because he was a virgin, because he was pure. Mary Magdalen stopped and prostrated herself at the Saviour's most holy feet, because she was a sinner. Although she had been born again, rehabilitated by repentance, sanctified by forgiveness and purified by love, that was her place, prostrate on the earth, because she had tasted the earth's abominable pleasures. Reduced to nothingness at the Redeemer's most holy feet, she had to weep and expiate her sins, always remembering them in order to flee from them.

This morning I read of the Eucharistic presence of Jesus in our own hearts and how the mind, faculties and will are absorbed in this infinite perfection, etc. I would like to dwell on and give you an ample account of my very wretched and very brief meditation, but the ideas escape me and once meditation time is over I no longer remember anything. This happens to me more often than not.

As you will find, it's a whole tangle of thoughts and interior acts without head or tail. Don't be scandalized. These are the fruits of my kitchen-garden. Speak to me about this.

While I am meditating my mind constantly turns to what I must write to you, the things I must tell you about my spiritual state and about how my meditation runs while I am speaking to Jesus and to you. I don't know whether I give you to understand the distractions which come to me while I am meditating and frequently after Holy Communion too. In a word, I speak to you while conversing with Jesus.

I feel sure that this confusion is a result of culpable distraction. Is this so? Enlighten me. I don't know whether I do right in telling you how I speak to Jesus. If I am at fault in this, if I am guilty of pride, presumption, self-love, etc., you will be clearly aware of it all and you must tell me everything, including the more unpleasant things. You must convert me. This will be for your holy satisfaction, your glory and triumph. Write me a long letter. Do not deprive me, for pity's sake, of your light and guidance. Don't tire yourself too much by writing a lot to me.

Poor Father! Nothing but your exceeding charity can tolerate my hardheartedness and obstinacy! How many instructions in a year, what zeal, what hard work! And what of me? I am invariably the same, bad and wretched. I am ashamed to ask you for long letters. What will you say? Waste of breath, useless effort. Oh, how scrupulously and exactly your counsels and your guidance are followed by good people, by pure, docile, obedient ones! What a difference you will find between their souls and mine. The difference between Christ and Belial, is that it? Speak to me at length. Be patient with me. May Jesus reward you. Prostrate in the dust I thank you for all you have done for me.

Now, allow me to ask you a question: why did you ask me some time ago for your letters? What was the reason for it? What was your intention? I venture to ask you to answer me. I venture also to ask you to read my confused letters over again before you reply to me, so that you will not omit any of the answers. I await your reply to the many questions, doubts and difficulties I have put before you little by little. I await them like a light from paradise, like beneficial dew on a parched plant.

This false disciple of the Nazarene feels the cross weighing enormously on her heart and goes in search of the merciful Cyrenean who will relieve and comfort her. The cross is a token of love, the cross is a pledge of forgiveness. Love must be fed and nourished by the cross, otherwise it is just a flash in the pan[2]. (This is a point from another meditation of mine about which I feel urged to tell you. Am I doing right or wrong? Is it necessary? Tell me frankly).

These are all beautiful considerations in theory, but as

---

[2] These words: "This is... a flash in the pan" were repeated by Padre Pio in a letter dated 21-4-1915 to Padre Agostino. *Letters*, Vol. I, No. 251.

regards putting them into practice, a greater responsibility weighs on my soul. While receiving so much light, to find oneself in the dark; in the midst of so much wealth to remain so poor, threadbare, tattered and wretched! What does Jesus say about it? And what have you to say yourself? Do you approve of my way of explaining myself? Do you approve of my language? Speak to me clearly.

May Jesus relieve my Giovina in scul and body.

Pray for this trip to Bologna for an examination by Murri in these difficult times. What do you advise? Enlighten and bless all the time,

Your poor tertiary.

P.S. I enclose ten lire for five Masses for our dear deceased ones.

64

Pietrelcina, 20 April 1915.

Good wishes. The Guardian Angel. How he has grieved his angel. The present state of Raffaelina's soul: she is to trust in God and thank Him. The reality of God's love in the soul. Defence of her own interests. Meditation and spiritual reading.

J.M.J.D.F.C.

Beloved daughter of the heavenly Father,

May the grace of the divine Spirit always possess your heart and those of all who want to belong to Jesus! May Jesus disclose also to you the mystery and power of the cross and may He inebriate your whole being with it. May the Virgin Mother be the very one who obtains for you the strength and courage to fight valiantly. May your good angel be your breastplate to ward off the blows that the enemies of our salvation aim at you.

O Raffaelina, how consoling it is to know one is always under the protection of a heavenly spirit who never abandons us, not even (what an admirable thing!) when we are actually offending God! How delightful is this great truth to the one who believes! Who is to be feared, then, by the devout soul who is trying to love Jesus, when accompanied by such an illustrious warrior? Was he not, perhaps, one of the multitude who joined with St. Michael up there in the heavens to defend God's honour against Satan and all the other rebellious angels, to vanquish them in the end and drive them down to hell[1]?

Well, then, let me tell you that he is still powerful against Satan and his satellites. His love has not lessened and he can never fail to defend us. Make a habit of thinking of him continually. The fact that we have close to us an angelic spirit who never leaves us for an instant from the cradle to the grave, who guides and protects us like a friend or a brother, must really fill us with consolation especially in our more dreary moments.

Let me tell you, Raffaelina, that this good angel is praying for you and offers to God all your good works, your holy and worthy desires. When it seems to you that you are alone and abandoned, don't complain that you are without a friend to whom you can open your heart and confide your woes. For goodness sake, don't forget this invisible companion who is always there to listen to you, always ready to console you.

O delightful intimacy, O blessed companionship! If all men could only understand and appreciate the very great gift which God in His exceeding love has given us by appointing this heavenly spirit to guide us! Call to mind his presence very often. We need to fix our spiritual gaze on him. Thank him and pray to him. He is so considerate and sensitive. Respect him. You must always be afraid to offend the purity of his gaze.

You should frequently invoke this Guardian Angel, this kindhearted angel. Often repeat the beautiful prayer: "Angel of God, my guardian to whom the goodness of the heavenly Father entrusts me, enlighten, protect and guide me now and for ever." What a consolation will be yours, my dear Raffaelina, when at the hour of death you will behold this good

---

[1] Cf. Dan 10:13; 12:1; Rev 12:7.

angel who accompanied you during life and was so generous in his motherly care of you! Oh, may this delightful thought make you increasingly fond of Jesus' cross, as this is also the wish of your good angel! May the desire to see this inseparable companion during your whole life enkindle in you the fire of love that will make you yearn to be separated without delay from your mortal body.

Oh, how holy and wholesome is the thought of seeing this good angel of ours! It should enable us to escape before our time from this dark prison in which we are confined. Raffaelina, where are my thoughts leading me? How often, alas, have I made this good angel weep! How often have I lived without any fear of offending the purity of his gaze! Oh, he is so considerate and so sensitive! Dear God! How often have I responded to the generous and more than motherly care of this angel without the slightest sign of respect or affection or gratitude. At present, moreover, instead of being filled with confusion by this thought (alas, as you listen you will be horrified) I am so very heedless that I feel no pain and what is still worse I treat this dear little angel, I do not say as a friend, but as one of my own family. To tell the truth this angel is by no means offended by such treatment. How dear he is and how good!

Ah, Raffaelina, forgive me for this digression and for dwelling at lenght on a subject by no means edifying for our souls. I try your patience too much, don't I? Make allowances for my weakness. Jesus will reward you for all.

As regards your spiritual state, I exhort you in the Lord not to be afraid and in Him I reassure you. I want you to have greater trust in the divine mercy. Humble yourself continually before the mercy of our God and invariably give thanks to Him for all the favours He has granted you. This attitude will be the most favourable for the reception of new graces which the heavenly Father in His absolute love for you intends to grant you. For according to a principle of sound logic, those who fail to correspond with gratitude and continual untiring expressions of thanks for favours received are undeserving of further favours. Yes, trust in God and thank Him continually for everything, for in this way you will challenge and defeat all the anger of hell.

I repeat, my dear Raffaelina, that you are not to be afraid. The One who has helped you so far will continue His work of salvation. Don't have any doubts about the divine assistance, don't turn in upon yourself because of the many calamities that continually surround you, for everything will turn out for God's glory and the salvation of your soul. Tell me, how can you doubt these assurances? Without divine grace, could you have come through all the crises and battles which your soul has had to face in the past? So have confidence always, for all the rest will be done by this same grace: you will be saved and the enemy will be consumed by rage.

Continue to pray, meanwhile, and to give thanks and suffer according to the divine intentions and the divine will, and may you be encouraged to do this by the thought that your reward is not far off. I understand that the trial is hard, that the fight is unspeakably painful for your soul, but great is the merit of victory, ineffable the consolation, immortal the glory and eternal the reward.

You are afraid that your love for God is not true love, that you do not love God at all. Well, I urge you to be quite at peace on this point. Tell me yourself, do you not feel this love in your own heart? What is that ardent desire you feel in your soul? Who placed in your heart this yearning to love the Lord? Do you think that holy desires can be inspired by anyone but God?

Console yourself, Raffaelina, and be quite sure that God is not found where there is no desire for His love. Now, if the soul longs for nothing else than to love its God, which is your case, then don't worry and be quite sure that this soul possesses everything, that it possesses God himself. And if the longing to love God seems to you not to be satisfied, or let us even say that it really is not satisfied; if it seems to you that you always desire without ever arriving at the possession of perfect love, all this means that your soul must never say it has enough, it means that we cannot and must not stop on the path to divine love and holy perfection. St. Augustine says very aptly: *Our heart is not at rest till it rests in the object of its love*[2].

Now, you know very well that perfect love will be acquired when we shall possess the object of this love. But the object of this love will only be possessed when we shall see Him as He is, not through a veil but face to face, as St. Paul says[3], when we shall know Him as we know ourselves, and all this cannot happen until the doors of our prison are opened.

Hence you may imagine the pain endured by a person to whom Jesus has disclosed some of His heavenly treasures, as he sees himself still a wayfarer in a land of exile. It is useless to dwell on this point. It would be a waste of time, for these are things that can only be felt and never expressed in exact terms.

Be quite at peace in the meantime as regards the existence of divine love in your heart. Cast aside all that futile anxiety and have no fear. How could it be possible that a soul consecrated to heavenly love, a soul that is endeavouring with God's help to please Him, that desires and longs more and more for the limpid waters of this divine love, how is it possible, I say, that this soul should lack love? How could it be possible at the extreme hour of our life to depart from this arid cold world without yearning for God, without divine love? Does it not seem to you, Raffaelina, a real contradiction? And would it not be an offence against the divine

---

[2] ST. AUGUSTINE, *Confessions*, Bk. I, 1.
[3] Cf. 1 Cor 13:12.

goodness to believe all this, when God in His goodness not only does not reject repentant souls but invariably goes out in search of the obstinate ones? Come, now, Raffaelina, I beg you in our most tender Jesus not to yield to this fear of not loving God, for to me it seems that the enemy is trying to deceive you.

I understand very well that nobody can worthily love God, but when a person does all he can himself and trusts in the divine mercy, why should Jesus reject one who is seeking Him like this? Has He not commanded us to love God with all the strength we have? Well, then, if you have given and consecrated everything you have to God, why are you afraid? Isn't it a real waste of time to dwell on it, a plot prepared by the enemy of our salvation?

On the other hand, you are always asking Jesus to do what you are unable to do yourself. Say to Jesus, as St. Augustine invariably said: *Give what you command and command what you will*[4]. "Do you want great love from me, Jesus? I too desire this, just as a hart longs to reach a flowing stream, but as you see I have no more love to give! Give me some more and I'll offer it to you!" Do not doubt that Jesus who is so good will accept your offer, so be at peace.

Enough for the moment on this point. It seems to me that I have explained myself sufficiently, have I not? There is one thing I want to urge you to do. Where money interests are concerned, be very ready to yield as far as possible. In this way you will avoid a lot of trouble which can be very harmful and which always bears the stamp of moral offence, especially when such matters arise among relatives. I advise you to act in this way and not for motives of justice, but of charity. When some such affair can be settled peaceably, even with some slight financial loss, do not appeal to strict justice, or rather take care to avoid doing so. Remember that we are

---

[4] Cf. St. Augustine, in *Ep. Tract 7*: PL, 35, Col. 2029, No. 8.

children of an infinitely merciful Father who is very indulgent towards us.

Let us always bear in mind that if the Lord were to judge us according to strict justice, none of us, perhaps, would be saved. So let us make righteousness and peace exchange a kiss[5], which we shall obtain if we always tend towards mercy rather than justice, in imitation of our heavenly Father.

During the time of meditation and prayer, drive far from you all those thoughts which come into your mind with regard to what you should write to your director. There is a proper time for everything. Have I made myself clear? Put this into practice. I highly approve of your spiritual reading, but what I want you to do is to read such books as much as you can.

I am closing this letter without having satisfied all your desires. You will make allowances for me, for I cannot go on. I feel drained of all my strength. Don't cease to pray to the Lord for me in the meantime, for that intention which is known to you and for my present state of mind. I need the divine assistance if I am to endure the fight.

Ask good Francesca and all those who love Jesus to pray for me. I myself continually remember them in Jesus' presence.

Fra Pio.

P.S. All good wishes to excellent Giovina and make me a frequent present of her news.

---

[5] Ps 85:10.

65

Foggia, 10 May 1915.

Putting in a good word for her widowed niece. This niece's distress. Reply to the letter of 20 April. She goes every day to the Capuchin church. The family chapel and her sister Giovina. The Guardian Angel. Dark night. Requests.

Jesus alone! Most Holy Spirit, help me!

Father,

I am urged to write to you by an extreme need and a holy hope. Just now my Giovina sent off a letter to the pious person already known to you, with regard to the well known matter of our most unhappy widowed niece who, in view of the turmoil of war, did not consider it prudent to set out on a journey, as you are well aware. Instead, she sent an appeal in writing, in Giovina's name, or rather in the name of our dear departed one[1], our holy sister, of whom the person concerned cherishes pious memories. In the letter she begged him to grant the wish of a most unfortunate mother by saving her two little boys.

---

[1] This was Raffaelina's sister Anna (cf. Letter 26, No. 1), mother of her widowed niece.

May the letter be under the protection of the guardian angels to whom it was handed over and entrusted and who must enlighten this pious benefactor to perform the great act of charity which will mean the moral and material future of a needy family. The poor mother is very dejected and disheartened. She is surrounded by indifference and selfishness and her faith does not always sustain her. Her sons, backed up by an opposing current which is false and hostile towards her, are disobedient and disinclined to study. Alone in the combat she struggles on, exposed to blows and with impaired health. You can easily imagine the rest. I appeal to you very earnestly so that Jesus may grant her this very necessary grace, He who is the support of widows and the father of orphans. I will say no more, but ask you to plead this cause.

I didn't reply sooner to your most precious letter of 20 April for fear of making a nuisance of myself. It is true that children are never a bother to their fathers, but these are the good, docile, obedient children, while the bad children are different. These torment their fathers and I myself, bad as I feel myself to be, am always afraid of troubling and distressing you.

Your own letter reached me that day just when my Giovina was having one of her usual very severe stomach attacks. Since that day, that is, during the past 20 days she has had three further attacks, although very slight ones. I hope and trust very much in the mercy of our good dear Mother of Pompeii to obtain that other great grace.

Almost every morning since 1 May I have gone out at six o'clock to the first Mass in the church of your Capuchin confrères (I have resumed my old habits). I go across the fields and in this splendid spring weather I get a breath of fresh air. I nearly always find the church deserted and I hide away in the chapel of the most holy Virgin of Pompeii, where I remain for the second Mass at which there are devotions for the month of May. By eight o'clock all is over.

Very Reverend Father Provincial's secretary[2] came to say Mass in our family chapel the day before yesterday, feast of Our Lady of Pompeii. Father Provincial sent word that in a few days time, while he remains in this city, he himself will come to say mass in our home.

My Giovina, praise be to Jesus for ever, goes out frequently for a little walk in the country and to pay some visits. In the evening she likes to stop in some church or other to attend the May devotions.

In addition to the devotions to our Mother Most Pure, I myself add those to the Guardian Angel, for you have taught me to love him. I used to be really careless and indifferent towards my good angel. It was a devotion which I always desired but which always eluded me. This was revealed to you and you were right to rebuke me for it, while at the same time you introduced me into this precious intimacy, this holy friendship. I thank you very, very much. What darkness there is in my soul without your light! How many doubts which find no solution! How many questions go unanswered! Finally, what silence in your last letter! Why do you keep silence? I beg you to answer me at length, if you can, and always correct me severely. Dark nights, hours of agitation, days of abandonment, domination by my passions and moral torment alternate continually. There is languor, coldness, lack of all feeling in my soul. I ask pardon and strength from the One who can do all things. I want a smile and joy, but I am asking too much. How can you smile when the thorns pierce you and draw blood? How can you rejoice when enemies are grieving you and triumphing over you? Only the saints can do such things.

Good Francesca asks me to convey her thanks to you

---

[2] Padre Luigi d'Avellino.

and to Jesus because her brother has fulfilled his Easter duty. She is not satisfied, however, and wants you to pray that he may persevere.

Pray for Giovina. Pray for Maria[3] that she may soon receive an affirmative answer. Pray for Rosa. Pray for peace among the nations and in families. How greatly I desire holy peace with our brother and our other enemies. This is a desire which torments me continually. Jesus commands it, but when will He give it to all of us?

Bless my Giovina and your poor

Tertiary.

P.S. I received no acknowledgment of the five Mass offerings I sent you. I request this because I am afraid of some trick on the part of that *wretch*. I know he always plays tricks on you and that he relishes this. Ease my mind about it.

[3] Maria was the widowed niece, mother of three orphans (cf. Letters 51 and 52).

66

Pietrelcina, 11 May 1915.

Greetings and good wishes. Their correspondence and spiritual guidance. Sincerity in reprimands. Her sister's health.

J.M.J.D.F.C.

Beloved daughter of the heavenly Father,

Let us bless the Lord for He is good, for His mercy endures for ever[1]. May Jesus lighten your load of sorrow and enable you to walk invariably along the path that leads to Him. May the Mother of Jesus and our Mother always look on your soul with a smile and obtain from her most holy Son every heavenly charism. Amen.

For a great many days now the Lord has deprived me of your correspondence. I cannot explain this and it worries me exceedingly. To tell the truth, for some time past I have noticed a great cooling off in your letters. Yet this cannot be explained by your having less need of guidance from the director of your soul. You must agree with me, in fact, if you intend to be sincere, that as you advance in the ways of the Lord you feel more and more the need of guidance by another.

---

[1] Cf. Ps 106:1; 107:1; 118:1,29; 136:1.

Do you think I want to congratulate you on this new attitude of yours? Am I going to praise you for it, perhaps? Quite the opposite, and to be quite frank I tell you that I don't view it without becoming uneasy. I know and understand that you are acting in this way from what appears to be compassion, but I must tell you that this is an illusion and a snare laid for you by the enemy. This is exactly how things stand, Raffaelina, so let us take care, for heaven's sake, and remain on our guard. The enemy is well aware of what a soul gains by viewing and doing everything in obedience to a spiritual director. For the precise purpose of preventing this profit to the soul, he is attempting to gain a foothold if possible in your soul and to break down that filial confidence that everyone should have in his spiritual guide.

It can be understood that once he has succeeded in this intent the enemy is assured of victory, for when that person is deprived of guidance he will fall into every vice, even the most abominable. He will be so blinded that nothing will then avail to snatch him from the road to perdition on which he is launched. Such a person will reach the stage at which he will believe he has no further need of help, even of God's help, and this will be apparent at least from his actions.

As a proof of what I tell you, there is no need to turn to what the history of past centuries teaches us, because we can see it happening before our very eyes and being repeated thousands of times at every moment.

Do not then consider me to be acting very harshly towards you. No, Raffaelina, the good God knows what an effort I must make when I have to remind someone of his duty. Moreover, you understand and are perfectly well aware of the responsibility I have assumed before Jesus for you. If something evil takes place to your spiritual detriment, Jesus will ask me to account for it directly. For pity's sake, listen to my feeble words, be docile and obedient all the time and then don't be afraid of anything. I earnestly beseech you not to be downhearted in the face of spiritual battles or spiritual sufferings, but to continue to place boundless trust in the divine mercy. God loves you very much, so you must respond to the best of your ability to this love. He desires nothing else, so trust in Him, hope in Him, humble yourself and love Him.

If you want to break off relations with me, please let me know in all sincerity. I want to and must know all.

How is Giovina's health? I venture to ask you to give her my deepest respects. Why don't you take her to Naples to be examined by a good specialist? I consider this very advisable.

Looking forward to your invariably good news, I take my leave of you in the Lord's holy embrace.

Your servant,
Fra Pio, Capuchin.

67

Pietrelcina, 15 May 1915.
Ascension of the Lord.

Greetings. The meaning of his reprimands. Fighting against the world, the flesh and the devil. God is faithful. He exhorts her to be humble. Prayer for his death. 'Your suffering is as God wills.'' God wants the spirit, not the flesh. Clinging to the divine will. Her family. Unanswered questions.

J.M.J.D.F.C.

Beloved daughter of the heavenly Father,

May divine grace be more and more abundant in your soul, may it sanctify you and make you ever more worthy of the heavenly nuptials. Amen.

I am extremely glad, after a long and negligent silence on your part to have had the divine grace to see once more your much-loved and precious handwriting[1]. May the Lord enlighten you about that fully justified reproof I gave you in my last letter. May He give me the happiness of never being obliged again to have recourse to such measures in order to recall you to the path of duty. Such measures go so strongly against my nature that when I am obliged to resort to them God alone knows how bad I feel about it.

---

[1] He is referring to the letter of 10 May.

I know that this letter and my last one do not bring you the relief and comfort for which you hoped in the midst of your troubles. I am sure, in fact, that they will cause you some embarrassment, but cheer up and don't let any sadness creep into your heart. Console yourself by the thought that the one who speaks to you like that had no feeling of resentment towards you. Remember that he is that same father who on other occasions treated you with tenderness and that he has not changed towards you even when love induces him to raise his voice with you. If you think of all this, the very reproofs which of themselves embarrass you will turn into a wholesome potion for your soul.

Have I explained myself? Do you understand me? I hope so with all my heart. Well, then, Raffaelina, be at peace in the Lord and think no more about the past.

We must be watchful not to let the enemy find the way to enter our soul and contaminate the temple of the Holy Spirit. Oh, for pity's sake, don't let us overlook this great truth for a single instant. Let us always bear in mind that at our baptism we became temples of the living God and that every time we turn our minds to worldly things, to the devil and the flesh which we renounced at baptism, we are profaning this sacred temple of God.

May you flee from every shadow of imperfection which can give these three archenemies an entry into your heart. Fight all the time against their assaults, keeping faith alive continually in your heart, watered by deep and generous love.

I understand that our enemies are strong, very strong, but when one fights along with Jesus how can one have any doubt about winning the battle? Oh, isn't our God stronger than all the others? Who can hold out against Him? Who can oppose His decrees or His will? Has He not promised all of us that He will not allow us to be tempted beyond our strength[2]? Is He by any chance unfaithful to His promises?

---

[2] Cf. 1 Cor 10:13.

Does anyone believe this? If anyone does, do you want to know who it is? It is the fool, it is the madman: *The fool says in his heart: "There is no God"* (no true God)[3].

The man who sins through disbelief, through lack of trust, Raffaelina, is a madman. You, now, more than ever, have had not just one proof but an infinite number of proofs of this divine promise. These proofs are as numerous as the victories your soul has won over its enemies. Without divine grace, could you have been victorious in all the crises and all the spiritual battles which you have had to face? Well, then, open your soul more and more to divine hope, have more trust in the divine mercy which is the only refuge of the soul that is exposed to a stormy sea. Humble yourself before the compassion of our God who is always ready to welcome and raise up the one who in the simplicity of his heart acknowledges his nothingness before Him.

Flee, then, flee from even the slightest shadow of anything that makes you think highly of yourself. Reflect upon and keep before your mental gaze the great humility of the Mother of God, our Mother. The more she was filled with heavenly gifts, the more deeply did she humble herself, so that she was able to say when overshadowed by the Holy Spirit who made her the Mother of God's Son: *Behold the handmaid of the Lord*[4]. This dear Mother of ours was to break forth with the same words in the home of St. Elizabeth, although she bore in her chaste womb the Word Incarnate[5].

As gifts increase in you let your humility grow, for you must consider that everything is given to you on loan. The increase in gifts must always be combined with humble recognition of such an outstanding benefactor, which should burst forth from your heart in the form of continual thanksgiving. If

---

[3] Ps 14:1; 53:1.
[4] Lk 1:38.
[5] Cf. Lk 1:46.

you act in this way you will challenge and defeat all the anger of hell. The opposing forces will be broken up, you will be saved and the enemy will be consumed with rage. Place your faith in the divine assistance and be certain that the one who has defended you up to the present will continue His saving work.

In your second-last letter you told me you would pray for that intention of mine[6], on condition that Jesus called you to heaven before long. Well, I promise you to make every effort to obtain this from our most compassionate Lord. Pray very hard in the meantime for the same intention. Note that you are now bound in strict justice to do this.

You asked me to throw some light on your attitude towards suffering and told me that you often go in search of comfort, that nature cries out to be spared and hence it seems to you that your love for God is not sincere and perfect. But be consoled on this score, because your suffering is as God wills. If nature suffers and demands its rights, this is a condition of man's life as a wayfarer. Secretely and tacitly he feels the pain of suffering and naturally wants to escape from it, for man was created to enjoy happiness and his trials are a consequence of sin. As long as we remain in this world we shall always feel a natural aversion for suffering. This is a chain that will accompany us everywhere.

You may be quite sure that if in the higher part, at the apex of our spirit, we desire the cross and therefore embrace and submit to it for love of God, this will not prevent us from feeling in the lower part of the soul the demands of nature which objects to suffering. In point of fact, who more than our divine Master loved the cross? Well, then, His most holy humanity prayed during his voluntary agony that the chalice might pass from Him if possible[7].

You must agree with me that your spirit is always willing to do God's will and makes every effort to do it. It is the flesh, on the other hand, that is weak, but God wants

[6] See Letter 63.
[7] Cf. Mt 26:39,42.

the spirit and not the flesh. Let nature object, then, Raffaelina, for this feeling does not depend on the will and therefore it does not make us guilty before God. Rather does it become a cause of merit for us if we hold it in check and subdue it.

Cling tightly all the time in spirit to the divine will, then be at peace and serve the Lord with a joyful heart, for divine love will never grow less in your soul. I ask you, then, not to be cast down because of your attitude to suffering and because of all the other doubts which assail you at present and may assail you in the future. Continue to have boundless trust in the divine mercy.

I assure you once more by this letter that God loves you very much and that you are corresponding to the best of your ability to His love. He desires no more, so continue to trust, to hope and to love.

I just do not know how to acknowledge the goodness of the heavenly Father for the excellent news you gave me in your last letter as regards Giovina's health and the conversion of good Francesca's brother. These news items have been a great relief to me in the extreme spiritual torment to which I am continually subjected. Praise be to God in the highest heavens!

Let us pray for the happy solution of your niece's problem[8]. I should really never have thought the question would be solved by a request in writing. To me this seems to have been opposed to God's plan.

You tell me in your last letter that I left many of your questions unanswered. For pity's sake, you know all! Why don't you repeat your questions, then?

Best wishes to Giovina, Francesca and Rosina.

Pray for me.

Padre Pio[9].

---

[8] For the answer from the Marquis in Florence as regards placing the three little orphans, see Letter 56 etc.

[9] Due to lack of space, his signature is written at the top right-hand corner of the first sheet.

68

Foggia, 20 May 1915.

Their letters. Her sister's health. Reply received by her niece. Conversation with Padre Benedetto. She replies to his last letter. Her present spiritual state. "Do not abandon me." Anxiety because the war continues. Their correspondence. Postscript.

Jesus alone! Most Holy Spirit, help me!

Father,

Your second-last letter and my last letter crossed in the post. What a rebuke! What delightful reprimands! Certain expressions of yours grieve me very much and make me weep: "If you want to break off relations with me, please tell me so and be sincere on this point also. I want to and must know all." It is the devil who suggests all this to you. Forgive me and allow me to tell you so. (He knows well how to make fun of you). I refer to some words of your own: "To tell the truth, for some time past I have noticed a great cooling off in your letters," etc. I have not cooled off, no, but I am finding it very difficult to write and this convinces me that it may be, as you tell me, a snare laid for me by the enemy.

I was not aware of this fact, but to you everything is known. You have revealed it to me and warned me in time, for which I thank you very much. The great difficulty I experience in writing to you (something which did not happen formerly) is partly due to lack of time. How often, when I have time, I mean to take up my pen, but the *wretch* intervenes, then someone comes to visit me or some other impediment arises, time flies and I keep putting it off.

To prevent Giovina from becoming angry, I get busy about the house to make up to some extent for the inadequate service of the maid (an elderly lady and unsuitable). For this reason I lack the time to write and even to read, which for me is a torment.

In addition, I stay close to Giovina and I don't know what I would not do to make her happy about everything. Prostrate with my face to the ground I thank Jesus that she is fairly well, although always very worn-out and irritable. In your second-last letter you told me to take her to Naples for an examination by some good specialist, but how can we travel now when the danger of war is so imminent? We are in great agitation on this account. Giovina is very worried. What is to become of us? Shall we be killed? Will our houses be burned down, our towns destroyed? What do you say about it? What has Jesus to say to you?

I have great faith in the most holy Virgin. She is more powerful than all our enemies, than all hell, and she must triumph here in our own Italy, the cradle and seat of her most holy Son's Vicar. Let us hope so.

That reply to my niece arrived at once after just one day and it was absolutely negative. She got just nowhere and you may imagine the state of that most unhappy mother. She sees her whole life as desperate. Some of her words frighten me, to the point where she says (horrible blasphemy) that she would have believed if the Lord had granted her this grace. I don't insist sufficiently. What ought I to say? How am I to inspire her with faith and hope if everything is going wrong and she feels disheartened, crushed and humiliated, left with three small children whose future is fraught with danger and uncertainty?

This is another headache, holy Father, added to the many I have already, and this one is atrocious, everlasting and without any way of escape. Moreover, all this is doing real moral and physical harm to my poor Giovina who has great need of quiet and calm. What a struggle! What am I to do? Advise me. Pray very much.

On the 14th of this month, just two months after the inauguration, Very Reverend Father Provincial came to say Mass in our chapel[1]. Mass was at the usual time, 8 o'clock, but he remained until 11.30 when Father Guardian came for him[2].

After Mass and after we had drunk some chocolate, Giovina left us alone. I wanted this because during previous visits he had always been accompanied by other Fathers. I wanted to speak to him but was not prepared that morning, nor did I feel like it (I forgot to mention that Francesca came to the Mass also and left immediately afterwards). We spent a little time in general conversation, then it seemed to me that Jesus offered me a chance to speak, so I spoke to him. I told him of my doubts, my uncertainty and fears. I asked for explanations, for light and norms and with Franciscan patience and charity he answered me as a master. He scrutinized my soul, sensed my spirit, penetrated into my conscience and discerned my spiritual state. He enlightened, convinced and calmed me.

We had a fairly long spiritual colloquy. Oh, good Father, how much better is the spoken word than what is written! For this reason I have a great desire to speak to you face to face and at great length! When? Later on, as usual, I wondered had I done well or not in speaking about myself. Had I

---

[1] Padre Benedetto of San Marco in Lamis.
[2] Padre Tommaso of Monte Sant'Angelo.

spoken well or badly? Had I told the truth? Am I perhaps deceived and do I deceive others? Now it is up to you who know everything by other means to set my mind at rest. Tell me everything, correct me frankly. Speak to me on this point and do not forget it.

If I speak to any one other than yourself about my spiritual state, it is only because they are your superiors, that is, Father Provincial and your own holy father[3], I have spoken to nobody else. I am very, very slow to speak because I am sure to sin.

When Father Provincial had left I found your own most precious letter on my writing-desk. I thank you so much for the zeal and interest and concern you show for my good. I am only sorry that I fail to correspond. As far as I am concerned you will always find unalterable, unchangeable filial trust in revealing to you my interior state, in informing you of the circumstances which have helped to change it, more or less. But what is essential, what is necessary is lacking. Virtue is lacking.

If you were present with me in church in the mornings, you would weep with compassion, or rather you would be horrified and nauseated. Before and after Holy Communion, for about an hour: heaviness, sleepiness, weariness, prostration, spiritual laziness are all accumulated in my most wretched soul. Yet, my dear Father, I confess that I delight in my rags, for they keep me safe from pride and presumption. I prefer them rather than union (perceptible, and do I possess imperceptible union?) with Jesus. Explain this to me and speak to me at great length about it. My Communions, Masses and meditations are truly ruinous.

You recall me to my duty by your letters. You do very well and you always do it. You have every right and authority for this, so do not spare me. I beg of you not to abandon

---

[3] Padre Agostino of San Marco in Lamis.

me. I am always the same. I confide my whole being to you and I tell you all the fine and all the ugly things that take place in succession in my wretched existence. My poor soul has incessant need of you. When the battle is raging, when my soul is weary and dejected and also when I am comparatively calm, at home and outside, here and elsewhere, always and everywhere, your holy words are strength and light and comfort to me.

If you were to remain at the friary in Foggia[4] (only a miracle could bring this to pass), who knows if this unworthy, perverse and great sinner might not become a saint? A saint, yes, to please Jesus, to love Him very much. For myself, I long for and expect nothing on this earth. All for Him, in Him, with Him. What do you say about it? Speak to me at great length about it.

Two days ago we all went to the station to greet a nephew of mine from Bari who was perhaps on his way to the frontier. The soldiers themselves were unware of their destination, as the higher officials kept everything a deep secret. He is a brother of the widow and he spent five years in Bologna with the Barnabite Fathers at St. Louis' College.

You can imagine our anxiety about the course of the war. Pray a lot to Jesus and to His heavenly Mother that they may protect this young man and save him from all misfortune. May the comfort of our holy faith sustain and be propitious to him and to the entire Italian army. Oh, may nobody lack this most precious gift and may it be present especially in those who are unaware how powerful, deep and tender it is. May Jesus set us free from this dreadful scourge. Pray and plead very hard.

Whatever happens, I earnestly ask you to take care of my poor correspondence. I beseech you to entrust it to nobody except your own holy father.

---

[4] St. Anne's friary.

All those holy souls to whom you sent good wishes return them devotedly and a hundredfold. Pray for and continue to bless at every moment Giovina and,

Your poor tertiary.

P.S. I ask you, if you can, to write me a long letter. Please do not forget to reply to the many questions on which I want to be enlightened.

You must arm yourself with superhuman patience in order to read my letters a second time before replying to me. Otherwise my questions will easily escape your attention, while for me it is sometimes impossible to repeat them as you desire, because I lose sight of them just as you do. You must accept this inconvenience of re-reading my letters, or else you will commit many sins of omission.

Poor Father! What charity and what virtue you have to practise with this ungrateful daughter! I am speaking to you with holy confidence. You don't mind, do you? (Tell me frankly if you do). Forgive me and punish me.

Pardon me again if I insist for the third time. You forgot to acknowledge receipt of the five Masses and I am afraid the devil may have robbed you of them. Nothing would surprise me, knowing as I do how he amuses himself with you who make things so hard for him.

Please remember the matter of the agreement with our brother. Another headache. Pray.

I kiss your hand.

69

Pietrelcina, 23 May 1915,
Feast of Pentecost.

Greetings and good wishes. A brief reply. He is more distressed by sin than by the war. Explanation of a few phrases. Her difficulty in writing. Her widowed niece. Her conversation with Padre Benedetto. His presence in Foggia is not necessary. Anxiety about the war. Her spiritual reading. Her letters. He may be called up to the army.

J.M.J.D.F.C.

Beloved daughter of the heavenly Father,

May the Holy Spirit fill you with His most holy gifts and make you worthy of the heavenly banquet. May Jesus and
May the Holy Spirit fill you with His most holy gifts and make you worthy of the heavenly banquet. May Jesus and
love as a consuming fire burn up all that is mean and sordid in you and set you free from all spiritual avarice.

I am obliged to be very brief this time, which is contrary to all your expectations. For several days now I have been suffering from a very severe migraine which makes it impossible for me to apply myself to anything. Add to this all the other spiritual torments, plus the continual emotional distress which seizes me at the horrible sight of a fratricidal war and you have the highest degree of spiritual dejection.

Between ourselves, Raffaelina, let me say that what troubles, torments and pains me, what tortures my mind and perplexes me, what makes my hand and my tongue tremble is not merely the war towards which we are advancing but the sins of which we Italians are guilty before the throne of God. They are more abominable sins and as a lawful consequence they are deserving of greater punishment because we have been for a long time spectators of other people's misfortunes. Instead of singing the *Miserere* psalm before the Lord's throne we have become more obdurate then ever in our sin and we have become unworthy of the divine benevolence.

Up to the present nothing has served to make our country enter into itself and come back to God. Alas! Because of our nation's sin, since it has become abominable and detestable in God's sight, I fear that the Lord in His furious anger will punish us according to strict justice. May it please this God of goodness, who is rightly enraged with our country, to behave as a loving father and not as a rigorous judge as we deserve only too well. In the excess of His love for His creatures, may He change the punishment itself into a wholesome cleansing for all of us.

The supplications of Christians must aim at this. We too must commit our whole lives to this, we whose happy lot it is to have chosen the better part, God our Father. Let us pray incessantly and let us suffer according to the divine intentions and the divine will. Let us pray and suffer in expiation of our own sins and those of others.

You tell me that certain expressions I used were suggested to me by the devil. May the Lord look on you with merciful eyes. He knows who placed those questions on my lips. It is evident, however, that you are always wide of the mark and continue to behave as a quite capricious and unmanageable child. Instead of deserving reproof, for me you are an object of compassion. I asked you such a question, not because you could, through your own fault, have considered interrupting our correspondence, for I hadn't the remotest notion of such a thing, but because I feared the devil might have suggested something of the kind to you. Judge for yourself, now, who was the true author of that question. May Jesus forgive you. You are accustomed to look at things from one side only, and hence you are very often mistaken in your judgment.

Now that I have clarified the question, as it seems to me, have the goodness to give me an exact account of it in due course. It is superfluous to tell you that the difficulty you experience at present in writing to your director is a snare of the enemy, and you yourself are only too convinced of this. Knowing who is the author of it, I urge you in the Lord to despise and overcome this difficulty. The Lord wants to put you to the test on this point also, and He has permitted and will still permit the enemy to lay this ambush for you also.

Watchfulness, prayer and humility are the arms needed to overcome all temptations and they must never be unaccompanied by boundless trust in God, so that we never stop halfway.

I am not at all surprised at the Marquis' negative reply to your niece[1]. She delayed a great deal and, what is worse, she dealt with a very important matter by a mere letter of appeal. If she had gone there personally, the result would have been different. It is no use crying now over the mistake. The consequences must be faced and since you yourselves have also been very much at fault in this matter, you will have to bear this cross along with her.

Would there not be some way, Raffaelina, of bringing this excellent niece of yours into your own home? In this way the children's education would be assured. This proposal may seem rather strange at first sight, but in view of Christian charity which knows no limits and seeing your own need of

[1] Cf. Letters 51, 53, 54, 56.

help because of Giovina's bad health, it seems to me that my very poor suggestion might deserve a little consideration.

The matter is most important. Think it over and pray a lot about it, then do whatever you feel inspired to do.

I am very pleased that you opened your heart to Father Provincial on such a suitable occasion. Don't be worried; I am not jealous by any means when you seek counsel on spiritual matters from learned and enlightened persons. I just warn you on one point, that is, you must know how to distinguish between people. Don't pay any attention to what is going around in your mind as to whether you explained yourself clearly or not, for this is nothing but a waste of time. Do likewise in the case of all the other doubts you have about that colloquy. You acted well and you deceived neither yourself nor him.

One does not do wrong without being aware of it. If you acted badly you should see it quite clearly. How can a person be condemned if he is not conscious of his error? Moreover, light and darkness cannot be present at the same time. Now, if you had done wrong you would know it, but with your eyes open can you maintain that you did wrong? The solution lies with you.

I should just like to know how he found you spiritually and if either of you spoke about me. Be sincere as regards this matter which is so important for you and for me, and the Lord will love you more dearly.

Don't be distressed if you cannot have me close to you to enable you to run more swiftly in the Lord's paths, for He will compensate you very fully for this loss. You are with Jesus and Jesus is closely united with you. Listen to His voice.

Put away the fears you have about the war and the injury it might do you in the future. God is with you and not a hair of your head will be touched.

Don't consider me too demanding if I ask you once again to set great store by holy books and read them as much as you can. This spiritual reading is as necessary to you as the air we breathe. Read, read a great deal and never fail to add a fervent and humble prayer to your good reading.

You tell me to read your letters the second time so as not to deprive you of an answer to some of the things you ask me. I do this many times, but what can you expect? Even if I read them 50 times, when I'm writing I only remember what Jesus wants me to remember. There you are! It's too bad, but may the Lord's will be done!

As to yourself, don't fail to conduct yourself as I have told you so many times.

I send greetings to all the souls that belong to Jesus.

Pray for me, for I am greatly in need of this.

May Jesus always be with you.

Your servant,
Fra Pio, Capuchin.

N.B. Read what is written inside the envelope.

(On the inside of the envelope). I am expecting from one moment to the next to be called up to the army. In the midst of the present confusion who knows if they will recognize me as unfit. Pray and get Annita and Francesca to pray too, as well as the others who love Jesus. If you don't mind, begin the novenas to the Virgin of Pompeii.

70

Foggia, 5 June 1915.

Delay in replying to his letters. Padre Benedetto's opinion on her spiritual state. The war frightens her. Her sister's health. Her widowed niece. Their correspondence. Sufferings. "Holy hero of virtue." Postscript.

Jesus alone! Most Holy Spirit, help me!

Father,

I wanted to reply at once to your most precious letter, which I received on the 23rd of last month, for three reasons: firstly, in order to overcome the difficulty of which you are aware; secondly, to ask news of your precious health at once; thirdly, for fear you had been called up to the army, as you mentioned to me in your last letter. However, in the latter case, you who are so good and precise would let me know beforehand for fear that my letters might fall into the hands of who knows who. I can be sure of this, can't I? Let me have a word on the subject that will set my mind completely at rest.

The last time Very Reverend Father Provincial visited me (a gift which he made me three times), I asked in a general way in the presence of the Definitor, Padre Francesco[1], if

[1] Cf. Letter 61.

other Fathers in his Province had been called up. He told me this was not the case, except for the 14 friars who had gone off some time ago. Thus I was reassured about you and I thank our good Jesus for sparing and freeing you and all priests.

You ask me if we spoke about you during our spiritual colloquy. How could we fail to do so? I was the first to mention your name. We spoke about our spiritual correspondence, about which he was already informed and of which he approved. You ask me how he found me spiritually, but what can I tell you on this score? He said that my story was the same as that of many others, etc., etc. My dear Father, by word of mouth I could tell you all, absolutely all, but this is not possible in writing; the pen is insufficient, inadequate. Come here and I'll have very many things to tell you. I'll tell you everything, all that you want and think that you ought to know.

In this conversation, speaking of meditation, I ventured to say to Father Provincial that I was very often tempted to put down on paper what Jesus, in His infinite charity, deigned to put into my poor mind. Well, then, complete darkness ensued. It's not possible to draw juice from a stone. It's a fitting punishment for my presumption. What have you to say about it? Is this how it is? Explain it to me. Darkness, prostration, drowsiness, oppression, mournful forecasts, horrible forebodings by night and by day, all this is building up in my very weak soul.

I am very frightened by the war. Giovina, poor invalid, even more so. The strokes of the big cathedral bell, which rings almost every evening to warn us that enemy planes are passing over, startle and dishearten us. The deep darkness, the shuttered houses and the general terror make me afraid. I see myself alone with my sick sister, with Rosa a semi-invalid and the elderly maid. I am cowardly and fearful to excess,

I who in all circumstances especially in times of sorrow, need lots of company to give me courage and strength.

I think, then, of the Most Sacred Heart of the One who is there in the chapel. He is the king, the sovereign, the master and defender of my home. Besides, your own holy words: "not a hair of your head will be hurt" reassure me, so I am at peace.

Not so with regard to Giovina's health. I find her so weak all the time and she seems to be failing. She has spasmodic stomach attacks, sometimes serious, then slight, sometimes quite frequent, sometimes lasting a long time. She is always so irritable, bored by everything and everyone. She clashes with everything and everyone and is indifferent, apathetic, or worse still she gets annoyed. She repeats continually: "A sad youth, a sadder old age." Her body is very ill, but I sense that her soul is even more so.

What can I do? I myself am discouraged and listless, with a weight pressing all the time on my eyes and my heart and a frequent feeling of bodily illness. Then I become frightened and I tear my hair. Who could take care of my sick sister who is so exceedingly reserved and difficult to please? Who would take care of me? It's a problem already, impossible to find a capable, reliable and devoted maid even by paying a high salary as we do in the case of those we have already. Jesus alone can supply our needs.

You speak to me of bringing our widowed niece to stay with us. I dislike to say it, but Giovina is terrified of such a thing, precisely because she is ill. But even if she had been well she would never, never have shouldered the responsibility of a young family, of two young boys who tomorrow will be men. It would mean running ourselves into a great many difficulties now that we are old and ailing, while our freedom, our independence, as Giovina always says, is the only privilege left to us in the midst of many tribulations. Do you agree?

You have blamed us for the way the whole thing was

handled, with such bad results. But with the war so close to us, it was absolutely impossible to act in any other way. Do you still agree?

I come now to beg you pardon on my knees. I humble myself, prostrate at your feet. It was painful fright and distressing astonishment that drove me to reveal my innermost thoughts to you. It was a diabolical suggestion which made me ask if you wanted to interrupt our spiritual correspondence. Will you pardon me, you who are full of goodness and Christian charity? The *wretch* sometimes cries victory within me, for he induces me to write things which hurt my holy Father, my generous Father. What is more, I am perfectly right when I repeat that I am always the same, bad, wayward and pigheaded.

Oh, I see my conversion as very difficult! I feel so far from Jesus even though I receive Him every morning. How greatly I long to hear His voice! He is silent with me, there is never anything but silence and darkness and it is I who chatter all the time. Twice only did I receive deep, deep down in my soul something like a breath, a whisper, a single word: "Suffer." Nothing more. I understand that everything is included, everything is summed up in that one word. But that is exactly what disgusts me: suffering and sacrifice.

Implore strength for me, courage, energy, readiness, resignation, renunciation, humility, hope, love, trust, abandonment, total and continual mystical death, patience, docility, self-denial, purity, zeal and charity.

You too, poor Father, are suffering very much and in every way! The jewels of your immortal crown are no longer to be counted. Who could ever tell their number? The holy athlete always fights and always wins. The prize is already prepared by Jesus and is ready. Jesus will crown your martyr's forehead with the palms of victory over the world, the flesh and the devil. Take courage and go forward. O holy hero of virtue, do not forget the wretched soul of your,

Poor tertiary.

P.S. Francesca asks me to tell you that she is praying all the time for your intention. Don't forget her or her family. I am making the three novenas you desire (to whom do you turn!). I want to ask you a favour now on behalf of my confessor[2]. He wants me to ask you to do the three novenas to our beautiful Mother of Pompeii for an intention of his. Poor Father, he too is very sad and dejected, I don't know why. It is my duty of deep gratitude that makes me commend him warmly to your fervent prayers. Implore from Jesus whatever he wants. Set him free without delay from all distress. I beg this of you very earnestly.

Have the patience to write me a long letter at once, if you can. Give me some news of your health. I ask you once again to pardon me for all the times I have disgusted you. Make allowances for this poor lunatic.

If you only knew how many times I broke off writing this letter. The devil always does his job, but with Jesus' help I don't yield to him. Am I doing right? Tell me. Pray very hard for me and for my affairs. Pray for Giovina. A hostile environment is tormenting her in soul and body (I confess that it also torments me). Drive it out and may peace be restored, through you, to reign in our home, among relatives, friends and our many enemies. May there also be peace at once in Italy and in the whole of Europe. May this come about without delay.

This morning in the church of your own Capuchin friars they began the novena to the most holy Virgin of Pompeii for peace. Oh yes, we shall now obtain it from her, the Queen of Victories. This merciful Lady will receive the tears of the innocent and the repentant and will present them to her divine Son who is rightly irritated and she will say: "See how many tears, see how much blood. Enough, enough now. May these

---

[2] This was probably the theologian from Foggia cathedral, Pasquale Bucci, See Letter 59, Note 1.

tears and this blood serve as expiation and as a lesson to present and future generations."

Pray for my two nephews who are at the frontier. One of them, as I told you, is the widow's brother and the other (who accompanied us to Liguria last year) is my deceased cousin's son. Pray too for all the sons of several of my friends and relatives. Pray for all the young men who are the flower of Italy and for all the fathers who have to support families. Pray.

I kiss your hand with respect. I entrust this letter to my good angel. I am very much afraid it may not reach you. Set my mind at rest without delay, please.

71

Pietrelcina, 8 June 1915.

Greetings. Comment on the war. Advice. Consequences of suffering.

J.M.J.D.F.C.

Beloved daughter of the heavenly Father,

May the consolation of the divine Spirit always dwell in your heart and in the hearts of all those who love God. May Jesus always be the idol of your soul and may He fill you with His grace, so that you may really experience, even in this exile, how sweet it is to serve the Lord.

I thank you most sincerely for your latest news. Blessed be Jesus' will for ever! May He give everyone at all times the strength to fulfil it devoutly. I thank you also on Jesus' behalf for the fervent prayers yourself and our excellent Francesca are offering up for me to our good God.

I see that my own age-group (1887) will be called up before long. This thought troubles me quite a bit as I don't know how things will work out for me. According to the doctors I am suffering from an incurable disease, but in such sad times who knows if the army doctors will let me pass as unfit? Pray incessantly, then, not merely for this intention but for the present needs of our dear country and of the whole world. May the merciful God have compassion on our wretchedness and our sins.

All of us have duties, very serious duties to perform at this crucial moment, Raffaelina. Let us carry them out faithfully and perseveringly. Those who represent the established authority and who govern our beloved Italy today are calling us[1]. Let us accept courageously and cheerfully the orders which come from the top and let us do our duty in accordance with our state in life.

Unfortunately, Raffaelina, the voice that calls us obliges us to painful separations, but we must accept it all with the courage of strong souls. We may shed tears from the sorrow that rends our hearts, but let them be tears of resignation. In moments of sadness let us raise our hearts up to God from whom all will receive strength, peace and comfort. We must all cooperate by prayer and within the range of our own activity with those who govern and defend the rights of the nation, to ensure the general good.

It is necessary for us to call down upon us the mercy of the heavenly Father in this very grave hour. It is necessary that our life be influenced by Christian principles, that it be ruled by God and by the Church so that we may submit to the orders of all lawful authority. We must be Christian in our daily life and not just in name.

Let us pray fervently, humbly and perseveringly. The Lord is a father, the most tender and best of fathers. He cannot fail to be moved when His children appeal to Him. Moreover, while our valiant soldiers are fighting on the field of honour and duty we must not confine ourselves to empty and fruitless admiration for them. No, we must be close to them in thought and with grateful affection which must be expressed in consolation, help and prayer for them. We must

---

[1] These same ideas are to be found in a letter Padre Pio wrote to Padre Agostino on 31 May 1915. Cf. *Letters*, Vol. I, No. 260.

help and comfort all those wives and mothers and children whose menfolk are under arms, in order that they may find comfort in their sorrow and relief in their sufferings. We are all called and bound to act in this way and we can do great good in this field. Hence we must feel it to be our duty even at the cost of personal sacrifice.

We must know how to face up to this important moment when we are at war and we must not be cast down by it. May the thought of the splendid noontime that will shine forth after this grave hour encourage us to endure the trial. Let us be consoled by the thought that the present upheaval of the nations, by reason of the sorrow and suffering it necessarily entails, will bring forth great virtues and new and wholesome vigour. The grain of wheat does not bear fruit if it does not suffer[2] by disintegrating. So, too, people and countries need trial and suffering in order to come forth cleansed and renewed.

The solemn moment through which our country is passing, Raffaelina, does not mean that heaven has abandoned us. While heaven speaks we are still loved. Wretched are those countries to whom the Lord doesn't speak any more, not even in quiet indignation, for this is a sign that he has cast them off, that they are abandoned and left alone in their blindness and obduracy. In you, wretched nations, there has been fulfilled what God said through the prophet Ezekiel: *My jealousy shall depart from you; I will be calm and will no more be angry*[3]. Tremble, all nations who no longer hear even the angry voice of our God, for this silence is the greatest punishment which heaven has dealt out to you. As the prophet Isaiah exclaimed: *Wilt thou restrain thyself at these things, O Lord? Wilt thou keep silent and afflict us sorely*[4]*?*

Let us be comforted, then, and trust in the Lord, for

---

[2] Cf. Jn 12:24.
[3] Ezek 16:42.
[4] Is 64:12.

He still loves our own Italy. Let us be docile in face of these events which are apparently harsh but are a sign of true mercy. Let us continue to trust, for the God who humiliates us and makes us suffer at present is the God who is still speaking to us, and the God who still speaks to us, Raffaelina, even if He thunders so unpleasantly and severely, is still the God who loves us. He is waiting for the voice of our repentance to silence His thundering. He is waiting for our tears to extinguish His lightning. Well, then, let our tears of true contrition never fail us. Let us lift up our hands to heaven and implore tears of this kind for all our fellow-travellers.

Let us pray to the Lord that He may never permit us to shut the ears of our heart to His voice that is speaking to us today in this way. Let us implore the heavenly Father never to keep silence with our beloved Italy. May He take up His thunderbolts in His right hand; may He cry out continually and thunder within the hearts of us Italians by His inspirations and externally by all sorts of adversities. Let Him frighten us, sadden us, press us down beneath the weight of His divine right hand. May He humiliate us, mortify us, try us as He thinks fit. No matter how severe these punishments may be, they will always be punishments of a very tender father who raises His voice and brandishes the scourge for the correction and salvation of His children.

In His immense goodness may He spare us the tremendous punishment of this silence which is the dreadful sign of and the disastrous prelude to His abandonment of us. May He spare us this grievous punishment for the love of the one *who knew no sin*, but *whom God made to be sin for our sake*[5].

Praise be to God. May it please Him never to allow us Italians to fall short of the plans He has for us in His wisdom. May He find us all in a state which will permit us to use the

---

[5] 2 Cor 5:21.

grave and solemn moment through which we are passing, the trial to which we are all being subjected at present for the benefit of our souls and for our country!

O Raffaelina, don't let us be frightened! Jesus is with us, Jesus is with our own Italy, so who can be against us or against our country? Ah, let us not view the triumph of divine glory in our own Italy from the sinner's wretched hovel, through the pitch darkness of the deepest night we are to experience, for this triumph would then seem too far off. I invite you, instead, to look at this magnificent triumph of divine glory for Italy through or rather from the Lord's own house. How close at hand this triumph will then appear to us!

I exhort you once more in the Lord not to be afraid of the enemy planes or weapons, for the Lord is with you and is watching over you at every hour. You must therefore dismiss all the fear you have of the enemy's weapons. Offer up your distress and desolation for your own salvation and for that of others and for the hastening of lasting peace for our own country and all the others.

Don't have any fear with regard to your letters. Whatever the Lord may have disposed in my regard, they will be in good hands. Let there be no more talk about them.

May I ask you not to be so reticent with regard to your spiritual colloquy with Father Provincial. I want to know all about it from you also, especially his opinion of your spiritual state. Make an effort to obey and the Lord will help you also in this respect.

Don't complain if you find it impossible to put down on paper what Jesus has communicated to your soul during meditation. This is purely and simply a cross that the Lord sends you and would you want to refuse it? Humble yourself more deeply beneath the divine action and have no fear, for everything is decreed with a view to your salvation.

Respond to the best of your ability to the voice that Jesus has allowed you to hear within you, which said "Suffer," and don't be disheartened if it seems to you that you frequently go in search of the Cyrenean, if nature cries out for comfort and if it then seems to you that your love for God is not sincere or perfect. This is just an illusion. When Jesus endured His voluntary agony, His human nature also asked that the chalice might be taken away[6]. Could you conclude from this, without being branded with unfaithfulness, that Jesus' love for His divine Father was less perfect and sincere? The answer rests with you.

At times the spirit is willing and the flesh weak, but God wants the spirit more than anything else. Cling closer and closer to Him, then, with your will, with the highest point of your soul. Let nature feel it and be roused to demand its rights, for nothing is more natural. If nature is also subjected to suffering at present, this is not due to itself, for nature too was made for happiness. These sufferings are due to it because of sin.

What criminal is there who, when subjected to what he recognizes as deserved torture, does not feel the pain and demand to be freed from it? Always bear in mind as a safe general rule that while God tries us by His crosses and sufferings He always leaves us a glimmer of light by which we continue to have great trust in Him and to recognize His immense goodness.

I urge you, therefore, not to be entirely disheartened in face of the cross which heaven bestows on you, but to continue to have boundless confidence in the divine mercy. God loves you very much, Raffaelina, and you are responding in the best possible way to His love. He desires nothing else, so trust in Him, go on hoping, humble yourself beneath the divine action and love Him.

Assure your confessor that I shall always pray to our good Jesus for him, and I am sure that he too will not forget

---

[6] Cf. Mt 26:39.

in Jesus' presence the spiritual rather than the corporal needs of the undersigned.

I stop here because of the obstinate attack of which I told you elsewhere.

May Jesus be with you always. I leave you in the Lord's holy embrace.

Your servant,
Fra Pio, Capuchin.

P.S. Pray and get others to pray, especially the most devout Francesca, for the matter of which you are aware and which makes me feel quite faint. May Jesus deal with me as best pleases Him.

72

Foggia, 23 June 1915.

Her sister's painful situation. A family from Casamicciola. A health resort for her sister. A visit from Padre Agostino. Her sister's confession. Apostolate of the two sisters. Difficulty in explaining herself. Prayers for one another. Their sufferings. "Write to me at once!"

Jesus alone! Most Holy Spirit, help me!

Father,

In your last precious letter, which reached me on the 8th of this month, you kept complete silence on the subject of my poor martyr, whereas I had told you a whole lot about her. I told you about the physical and moral torment she is undergoing. Why this silence? This should have your continual attention since it is the essence of my own life, my whole worry in the past, at present and for the future. How can you, who are so good, so full of compassion and love for others, assist at this painful scene without being moved? How can you fail to obtain from our generous Master calm and healing for that sorely upset and discouraged soul, for that exhausted and martyred body?

Father, here is a soul you love, a being who is bound by a holy tie to another being, that brings pressure to bear on you and seeks to interest you! When I see my sister suffering (almost every day, either in the evening or at night, we are kept awake and we go through a lot), when I see her so very weak, fasting, racked with pain, I can no longer think clearly and then I consider you cruel, deaf to our laments, blind to our tears. Have mercy, have mercy, Father, on these two isolated stones. Money has no value when one is without a family of one's own.

The poor invalid, disgusted and buffeted by everyone and everything, suffers from hunger. Her legs give way and her head reels from extreme weakness and she is unable to take sufficient nourishment. I myself, discouraged, crawl along, dragging my enormously heavy cross, irritated, mute and full of fear. Where am I to find refuge?

Giovina has decided to go to Casamicciola to get a breath of fresh air. For the past 20 years we have always gone there (Giovina went for the mud-bath treatment almost every year) to a holy family: father, mother and two daughters. One of the girls is married and the elder one, whom we met 20 years ago as a child of seven, is now a true bride of Christ. She wanted to be a Sister of Perpetual Adoration, but Jesus arranged things otherwise and she is now carrying on her good work among the boys and girls. Hers is a continual apostolate, a true example of virtue in that small centre. This young and ardent soul is constantly occupied in the care of the church adjoining her home, in catechism and the Apostleship of Prayer of the Most Sacred Heart of Jesus. We are bound to her by ties of holy friendship and we write to each other from time to time[1]. But I have strayed from the subject.

Giovina, as I was saying, wants to go there. I willingly agree, but then fear seizes me, fear of illness, of the war and of the sea. It takes three hours from Naples to Casamicciola.

---

[1] She is referring to Giuseppina Morgera. Cf. Letters 78 and 96.

We have made this crossing tranquilly over and over again in the course of 20 years, but now... May God help and accompany us! What do you advise us to do? We intend to stop in Naples for several days for an examination by a specialist and would then go on to Casamicciola, but I am very much afraid. What should I do? How does Jesus inspire you on the matter? Let me know. I feel tired, extremely tired and dejected. I feel I haven't the strength even to think, much less take on such a heavy responsibility.

Serious illness should only come to those belonging to big families. Giovina needs assistance and she is very difficult about the choice of people to assist her. I am so weak that I am not up to it physically. Moreover, I would have to give up going to church altogether and neglect the sacraments in order to devote myself to her and even then she wouldn't be satisfied. What ought I to do? May Jesus see to it and make provision in time.

The trial is too hard and the purgation too long. The essence of the matter is that I am gaining nothing spiritually, or rather, I am losing more and more in an alarming way.

Some days ago I had a visit from your own holy father. He found me in bed, due to a high temperature on the previous night. We had a long chat about everything and especially about you. He was tranquil enough and sure on the question of your being called up to the army. He said you are ill and that this can be seen with closed eyes. So don't be upset. Remain calm like your holy father. Have no fear. Jesus it there, watching in a particular way over His chosen ones.

By a happy chance, my widowed niece called on me just then and I introduced her to Padre Agostino with her three small children. Two of these, the boys, had made their First Communion the previous day, which was the feast of St. Anthony. The good father had many beautiful words of faith and comfort for the unhappy widow who wept silently and bitterly there beside my bed.

I had desired very keenly for a long time to have her make her confession sometime to Padre Agostino. I asked her if she wished on the octave day to send good wishes to her poor husband (his name was Luigi) as I do with my deceased relatives, but she opened her eyes wide and did not understand me. I answered that she could do this by a good confession to Padre Pio's confessor and a Communion for the repose of her husband's soul. She agreed at once, so I am waiting for Padre Agostino to return to have all this done. I also made him promise that he would say Mass in our chapel. May Jesus console us for his own glory.

I would also like to have Giovina make her Easter confession. In reality she received Communion many times in our own chapel, but not for the Easter precept which should be fulfilled in the church. Pray to Jesus to draw her close to his Most Sacred Heart and make her rest with abandonment and trust on that Heart of father, brother and spouse. I always consecrate this holy sister of mine to Him but it seems that Jesus turns a deaf ear. He doesn't hear me or look at me or pay any attention to me. He is quite right, for I offend Him very often. I am convinced that I have in you alone a compassionate advocate who will plead my hopeless case, that in you alone I have a prop to prevent me from falling inadvertently.

You reproved me silently and rightly in your last letter, on the good I ought to do to many others who are suffering in mind and body. This is a gentle rebuke and you are perfectly right. I do absolutely nothing. In the Catholic Women's Association, of which we are both members, we are ready to make our financial contribution on every occasion, but we have never been willing to help in teaching catechism or in charitable and cultural activities. In the beginning I myself used to attend the meetings, but later, for various reasons,

I withdrew completely. What have you to say to this being who is useless and harmful to herself and to others? Speak to me on this point.

I would very willingly obey you and tell you all about the spiritual conversation I had with Father Provincial, but I am unable to do so. Forgive my ignorance and make allowances for me. Do you call this reticence? Reticence with you? Allow me to tell you that you do not know me yet.

Good Francesca is praying all the time for you and at present she is making a novena to the Most Sacred Heart of Jesus. She thanks you very, very much, through me, for thinking of her constantly and she says she doesn't deserve it. She says Jesus is inspiring you to do this for her conversion.

Pray and intercede for us always. Pray for my Giovina. Pray a great deal for Rosina. I am very distressed about one matter which is another torment for my soul. May Jesus do with me as He wills, but to accept His will costs me a continual effort and an enormous amount of hard work. Calvary's flowers are fertilized by Jesus' Most Sacred Blood and by Mary's tears. Our flowers must not be mere ideal blossoms born in the imagination, but true flowers which spring from our heart's blood, from continual sacrifice, from hidden acts of self-denial.

Forgive the way I write. My brain is not helping me and I am exhausted. Jesus willed to fall three times beneath the cross. I myself, without wanting to, or rather, weary, utterly weary and under strain, fall a thousand times every second. The cross should be carried in triumph, but I am dragging it along the ground. What will Jesus say to my continual complaints? What will you yourself say? Speak to me about this.

You too are suffering very, very much, but you, holy Father, feel Jesus within you, and everything will be a delight for you. I myself, on the other hand...

Write to me at once. Do me this kindness. Speak to me about our trip and advise me, because I want to make arrangements for our luggage. In the meantime I feel I lack the physical and moral strength so necessary in certain circumstances. I am most unhappy, invaded by deep melancholy, and with a void all around me.

Pray and continue to bless,

Your poor tertiary.

P.S. Pray for a successful confession by my niece (when Padre Agostino returns) and also for Giovina's confession. Forgive me for repeating myself.

73

Pietrelcina, 24 June 1915.

Greetings and good wishes. Turning her thoughts continually to heaven. The weapon of prayer. An offering for Masses.

J.M.J.D.F.C.

Beloved daughter of the heavenly Father,

May the grace of the divine Spirit always triumph in your heart and give you more and more courage to face calmly and cheerfully the war waged by your enemies. This I wish for you from the Lord and as you will understand quite well, my assiduous prayers and fervent wishes for you have no other purpose than to see you holy.

How is your health now? Your illness distresses me more than a little, but since I know what Jesus' express will is, I am resigned and give thanks to Him constantly. If God wills to add corporal fragrance to the spiritual, is this not sufficient to make you as happy as it is possible to be in this valley of exile?

What else can we desire than God's will? What other wish can a soul have when it is consecrated to Him? What else do you desire, then, if not that God's plan may be fulfilled in you? Take courage, therefore, and go forward on the path of divine love, with the firm conviction that the more fully your own will becomes united and conformed to God's will, the more you will advance towards perfection.

Let us always keep before our eyes the fact that here on earth we are on a battlefield and that in paradise we shall receive the crown of victory; that this is a testing-ground and the prize will be awarded up above; that we are now in a land of exile, while our true homeland is heaven to which we must continually aspire. Let us live, then, Raffaelina, with a lively faith, a firm hope and an ardent love, with eyes fixed on heaven and the keenest desire, as long as we are travellers, to dwell one day in heaven whenever this is pleasing to God.

Let us keep our thoughts, I say, continually fixed on heaven, our true homeland of which this earth is merely an image. Let us be cheerful and calm in all circumstances whether happy or sad as is fitting not merely to every Christian but to a soul that has received special training at the school of suffering.

May the motives of faith and the comfort of Christian hope offer you continual support in all this. If you act in this way the heavenly Father will alleviate your trial with the balm of His goodness and mercy. The holy and beneficent angel of faith, moreover, counsels and urges us to have recourse by insistent humble prayer to this goodness and mercy of the heavenly Father in the firm hope that we shall be heard. In this we are basing our trust on the promise made to us by the divine Master: *Ask, and it will be given you; seek, and you will find; knock and it will be opened to you... Everything that you ask the Father in my name will be given you*[1].

Yes, serene in our faith and tranquil in soul let us pray and continue to pray, because intense and fervent prayer pierces the heavens and is backed up by a divine guarantee. Let us pray that peace may be restored to all the countries

---

[1] Mt 7:7; Lk 11:9; cf. Jn 15:16.

that are at war. But let us also pray for the souls engaged in spiritual warfare, that they may fight like strong ones.

I hasten to tell you that in the past few days I said the Masses you requested. I realize that you asked me several times already if the offering for this purpose had reached me, but up till now I had forgotten to satisfy your rightful questions. So don't worry, as I have received all.

May I ask you to deliver the enclosed[2] to my Padre Agostino as soon as possible. He'll be in Foggia in the next few days.

I end here as I am hardly able to continue.

I await your news which I hope will be excellent.

Fra Pio.

---

[2] On 24 June 1915 Padre Pio wrote to Padre Agostino: "I have decided to write you this letter which for reasons that may already be known to you I am taking the liberty of sending through Raffaelina" (*Letters*, Vol. I, No. 265).

74

Pietrelcina, 25 June 1915.

He asks for prayers. Useless to give advice about something already done. He threatens not to write any more.

J.M.J.D.F.C.

Beloved daughter of the heavenly Father,

May the grace of the divine Spirit always fill your soul and console you in times of tribulation and trial. Amen.

I feel crushed beneath the weight of my grievous sufferings. Pray very hard to the divine Heart that He may not withdraw His mercy from me. I deserve this, unfortunately, but is it possible for the heavenly Father's mercy to be overcome by my malice?

I consider it useless for me to express my opinion on Giovina's trip since you have already made all the arrangements, and suggestions would lead nowhere. In our present times I consider it too daring and inopportune for you to wish to go elsewhere.

I want you to know that as long as you refuse to answer fully the questions I put to you in my second-last letter, I'll be obliged to my immense sorrow to make you feel the effects of my silence.

I wish yourself and Giovina and all the others who are most dear to Jesus every choice grace from the Lord.

I remain, as ever.

Your servant,
Fra Pio, Capuchin.

75

Foggia, 12 July 1915.

Why she didn't reply sooner. "Alone with Jesus on Calvary." Her sister's health. The trip to Casamicciola. Postscript. Reconciliation in the family.

Jesus alone! Most Holy Spirit, help me!

Father,

I have decided to write to you. The language I used in my last letter disgusted you more than a little, I imagine. Tell me frankly if it did. Your own holy father dispensed me from replying to your second-last and last letters as he replied for me[1]. How good he is, and what charity he shows me, which I don't deserve!

Meanwhile you continue to make me "feel the effects of your silence" (your own exact words). Very well! The confessor scolds me, you continue to sulk, you keep silence and

---

[1] Foggia, 29 June 1915. Padre Agostino to Padre Pio: "Raffaelina let me read your last three letters to her. She told me how distressed she is by your threat to make her feel your silence if she doesn't tell you all about the conversation she had with the Provincial. The poor thing tells me she has made every possible effort to obey you and that her conscience doesn't prick her about anything. I myself examined the matter and find it very simple and by no means alarming..." (*Letters*, Vol. I, No. 266).

remain indifferent to my suffering, leaving me to struggle and weep all on my own.

Deprived of all human comfort (how often I should need and desire it!) I turn to Jesus. I trust in His kind Heart. He is the resurrection and the life[2]; He must not abandon me to myself when He finds me so very, very bad and ungrateful for His graces. He must burn up all my sins in the flames of His love and enable me to start a new life.

I am alone with Jesus, climbing with Him to the summit of Calvary, but I believe I am only halfway up. Is that how things really are? You may know, so tell me.

Thank Jesus in my name for my niece's confession (you know everything already as your holy father wrote to you about it). My dear martyr also went to confession (at home, to my confessor, as she had been accustomed to do since last winter) and she was able to receive Communion just once, at Padre Agostino's Mass in our own chapel.

On Thursday evening, the eve of the feast of Our Lady of Grace, she had a very severe attack which lasted until three in the morning. This prevented her for days from continuing to receive Holy Communion. I am really lost in all this. May God's will be done!

Relatives and friends who see this scene frequently repeated are talking quite a lot about an examination by specialists in Bologna and Naples. The poor sufferer herself cannot make up her mind. Good Padre Agostino as well as our confessor is urging and encouraging us to seek at once a change of air and appropriate treatment in view of the continual deterioration of the dear invalid.

The house in Casamicciola is fixed for next week. There are endless obstacles with regard to a companion. I am very heavy-hearted and perceive nothing but darkness and silence. I assist, in constant crushing agony, as this poor body of hers

[2] Cf. Jn 11:25.

grows thinner and thinner, she who was a pillar of hardiness and strength. Then I think, ungrateful as I am: O Jesus, I did not want to meditate on your bitter Passion and now I am justly condemned to meditate uninterruptedly on the sufferings of the one being left to me on earth, the one I love best in all the world, the one who is my guide, my defence, my protection, my strength and comfort. What chaos there is in my poor brain!

The brief periods of comparative peace are followed by long periods of storm, abandonment and apathy. I very often neglect meditation. My poor prayers, my poor Communions! Jesus is so good. Ask His forgiveness for me. Remember me all the time and do not abandon me. Don't allow the progress and the virtues of Jesus' true spouses to make you forget the wretched ones. My language is always too human. These are the weeds that my ground yields. I know that Jesus is very dissatisfied with me. I am always complaining and weeping over my troubles. I completely forget His sufferings, I speak about myself all the time and never of Him. I weary Jesus and I weary you exceedingly. Forgive me and make allowances for me. I am a worry and a burden to myself and to those who listen to me.

Pray for me, pray for Giovina. Obtain for her light and vigour, strength, patience and resignation. Is my poor sister perhaps a victim in God's sight? Reply clearly to this doubt of mine. For the last five days she has not had the usual stomach-pain. I hope it is not lying low in order to attack her more violently than ever. I am trembling and shaking all the time. Is it you who are working for this poor martyr? Work, then, and go on working for her, for she is very good. Work also for the speedy and complete conversion of,

Your poor tertiary.

P.S. Some good news: the two powers have made peace.

Is this also the result of your work? To God the glory and to you everlasting gratitude.

On the last day of the month dedicated to the Most Sacred Heart of Jesus I was coming from your own friars' church while my sister-in-law was going in that direction to Mass at the church of Our Lady of Grace, which is quite near our home. Our meeting was very affectionate. I myself was calm but very sad on account of Giovina's health. When my sister-in-law asked me about it my only reply was a flood of bitter tears, the continuation of all those I had shed in church and I could not utter a word. My self-love suffered a lot as I revealed my very sad state of mind. I would have liked very much to give the impression, at least on this first occasion, that I was happy, indifferent and untouched by all the disagreeable events. But Jesus arranged things differently in order to pulverize my pride and intolerance. May His will be done!

A few days later I forced myself to go alone to pay them a visit. My sister-in-law continued to be very affectionate while my brother was sulky and pig-headed. The other evening she came by herself to visit Giovina and there were kisses, embraces and tears. (Genuine or false? You alone can see the other side of the medal). Yesterday evening Giovina returned the visit and our brother was more human.

Now, allow me to ask you a question. Might I myself alone have been the cause of discord in my family? Answer me frankly. You alone can weigh up the whole matter now that it's all over. Speak to me and don't forget it. Everything can be fixed up, my dear Father, except for dreadful complicated internal illnesses. Jesus can do all things, if He wills, He who is the resurrection and the life[3]; I have a very slender hope. I see everything collapsing in and around me and He remains my only support. I cling to Him, the anchor of love,

[3] Cf. Jn 11:25.

in spite of my sins, my infidelities, my refusals, my wickedness and wretchedness. He is so good that He will not be able to cast me off; He will console in soul and body the sister who sheds so many tears.

Good Francesca was also present and received Holy Communion along with us at Padre Agostino's Mass in our chapel. She asks me to tell you to thank Jesus for the many benefits He continually bestows on her. She went to confession to your holy father as she would have done to you. She opened her conscience completely to him and told him everything she had been feeling for a long time. For a very long time she has yearned to have sufficient time like this to explain all about her spiritual state without any need to hurry. In the end Jesus granted her this. May Jesus be infinitely praised for ever. Thank Him very, very much. She is obliged to you all the time for the many fine graces she receives and in return she prays continually for you, holy Father.

I add to this that Jesus grants all sorts of help to those who know how to correspond with it. Those who fail to correspond, or rather those who abuse His grace experience dreadful night, darkness and silence. You understand me sufficiently.

I intended to imitate the painful brevity of a great many of your letters (especially recent ones). I resolve to do this but I don't succeed and it is only when I come to the end that I realize I have been too lengthy and tiresome. You will object: so many long letters and to what purpose? You are quite right, good Father, but I cannot resign myself to your brevity, which is a sure sign of your indifference and neglect, etc., etc., although I am convinced that I deserve nothing else.

Write and tell me how you are. Before leaving (if Jesus so wills) I'll write to you.

76

Pietrelcina, 14 July 1915.

Greetings and good wishes. Extreme physical weakness explains the brevity of his letters. He is passing through a crisis. She is not alone in climbing Calvary. Reconciliation in the family. The long letters.

J.M.J.D.F.C.

Beloved daughter of the heavenly Father,

May the Spouse of our souls increase the ardour of the flames of His love in your heart and may he always smile on you and on all those whom He loves. May Jesus' Mother and ours continue to obtain for you the necessary strength to fight and win all the battles God has decreed for your benefit. May your good angel remain watchful by your side, may he protect you and support you with his hands lest you dash your foot against a stone.

When you open this and see how little I am writing to you this time also, your first thought will certainly be that I am still angry with you. Am I perhaps wrong? At all events, you are accustomed to judge me severely and in this you are greatly mistaken. From the tone of my last letter you thought and continue to think that I am annoyed with you and I want to tell you before the Lord that I was never annoyed with you and much less am I annoyed now. The reason which obliges me to write to you briefly this time also, my dear Raffaelina, is the extreme weakness from which I have been suffering for the past few days. God alone knows the effort I have to make to put down these few items on paper.

I am passing through a dreadful crisis and I have no idea what is before me. The crisis I am undergoing is more spiritual than corporal, but it is none the less true that my entire body feels and participates in an extraordinary way in all my spiritual sufferings. Both body and soul combine to make me waste away with pain.

Alas! Who is to save me from this dark prison? Who will set me free from this body of death? But praise be to God in the highest heavens! He is my strength, He is the salvation of my soul, He is my portion for ever. In Him I hope, in Him I trust and I will fear no evil.

Don't let your fervent prayers be lacking before God's throne, Raffaelina, for my departure which I see not far off. This sight overwhelms me. I feel I am dying at every moment of life at the mere thought of not dying. Pray, because your prayer will be more acceptable to God, since it comes from a contrite, mortified and suffering heart. May all those souls who say they love me in the Lord's presence keep you company. I assure you that my gratitude to all of you who do me such a kindness is immense and that I'll remember you all continually before Jesus.

Do not say that you are all alone in climbing Calvary and that you are all alone as you struggle and weep, for Jesus is with you and will never abandon you. You would like to see Him, you would like to hear Him, but believe me this would be the worst thing for you and it would cost you too much if Jesus were to reveal Himself to you.

I beg you, for heaven's sake, to calm your anxiety and apprehension on this score. Remain at peace, continue to go forward and don't let your swift course be stopped when I assure you in our most tender Lord that you are already half way to the summit of Calvary. It is true that this is the darkest hour of the night for you, but may the thought of a bright dawn and a more brillant noontime sustain you, cheer you up and induce you to keep on moving forward. Do not doubt that the One who has sustained you so far will continue with ever greater patience and divine kindness to support you on the remainder of your difficult and trying journey.

Unless you want to increase my distress beyond what I can bear, do not tell me any more that I am indifferent to your suffering. God knows whether I have ever remained indifferent in this respect. And if I did not desire your improvement I could not put into words what I would do for you with the Lord.

You always object that these are just fine words, but God who reads men's hearts knows if I am lying. The day will come when the truth of what I am saying will be revealed to you.

I offer warmest thanks to the goodness of the heavenly Father for the reconciliation with your brother and his wife. I ask you now to put aside your pessimistic judgment on this situation. May the Lord continue to use mercy towards you all and grant you the grace of holy perseverance. Get rid of the diabolical thought that you have been the cause of the disagreement which has existed up to the present with your brother. Have we understood one another?

I don't know who suggested that expression to you: that I find your letters tiresome. I hope it is the last time this is mentioned and I should be inclined to impose on you a rigorous precept to write to me every time you can, were I not aware that such an order would upset you. Don't give me another chance to have recourse to this harsh measure.

I await your news before you go to Casamicciola.

Fra Pio.

77

Foggia, 21 July 1915.

Departure from Foggia. Trip to Casamicciola.

Jesus alone! Most Holy Spirit, help me.

Father,

Just a few lines in haste. Tomorrow, if Jesus wills, we leave for Naples by the morning train at 6 o'clock. On Friday we'll begin our Way of the Cross: several visits to stomach specialists and a radioscopic examination by Professor Piccinino. We'll hear the sentence. You keep silence all the time about Giovina's condition. I myself am in deep darkness and am extremely desolate. May Jesus, Mary and Joseph guide, protect and defend us.

After a few days in Naples (as we hope and trust) we'll embark for Casamicciola on Monday morning at 9 o'clock. May Jesus help us all the time. You do not approve of this trip. Our own doctor ordered this when he had examined Giovina carefully. What frightens everyone is the way she is losing weight continually and rapidly. What will happen when winter comes? I am leaving with death in my soul. I say no more. As a disciple and daughter of the cross I have not yet made up my mind to be a lover, a sweetheart and a spouse.

As we pass Benevento my thoughts will fly to Pietrelcina where there is a holy father who is praying for two unfortunates who are all alone and deprived of human comfort.

As soon as we are settled at Casamicciola I'll write to you and send you the address. For the moment I'll save you the trouble of answering me. I still have to reply to your last brief letter. Poor Father, how are you? Always fastened to the cross along with Jesus.

In a further letter I'll have to confide a great secret to you.

Pray continually for Giovina and for the conversion of this great sinner who is writing to you. Will Jesus pardon all my offences?

Father, help me. May all dangers and temptations be far from me and all that distracts me from Him, the Supreme Good.

Bless at every moment

Your poor tertiary.

78

Casamicciola, 31 July 1915.

Her sister's health. Description of the health resort. The state of her soul. "Answer me at once". Their lodgings.

Jesus alone! Most Holy Spirit, help me!

Father,

We have been fixed up, praise be to God, since the 26th. The trip from Foggia to Naples went very well for my Giovina. The Way of the Cross which took us to the three doctors was very painful. The specialist, Professor Tedesco, had doubts about the diagnosis: acute gastritis, followed by a large question mark which arouses great fear in my mind. He needed the X-rays in order to explain the ailment to us properly.

Professor Piccinino wanted to keep my dear invalid in his nursing-home at Capodimonte to have her undergo a long course of treatment, apart from the radioscopic examination, but Giovina refused this very decidedly. At the third station, Professor Matoni, a good fellow-townsman of ours who lives in Naples and who had examined Giovina several times, approved of Casamicciola for a change of air and prescribed some injections which are to be started at once.

Here Giovina had two attacks of pain. The first time the pains were slight, but the second time so acute that she had to have recourse to the doctor for a morphine injection at midnight. While Giovina was very well during the sea crossing, I myself was rather sick.

Her food consists of soups, pigeon's meat and nothing else. She suffers from hunger and thirst and is always at the same point, but getting thinner and thinner.

The great peace of these splendid natural surroundings ought to fill us completely in soul and body. This intense yet most eloquent silence ought to pervade our whole being. This ever beautiful and inspiring island of Ischia (which it always pleases and touches us to see again) invariably gave us days of great peace during the many tempests we experienced in the course of 21 years. But at present I believe there is nothing that will relieve the sorrow of that martyred soul. Nothing will serve to give back strength and energy to that weak and suffering body, although I hope I am deceived in thinking so. You are aware of everything yet you are silent and continue to keep silence. Is it charity that makes you keep the curtain lowered to hide the grim and terrifying future from me? Am I perhaps mistaken? Oh, if only I were!

What am I to tell you about myself? I am all the time in agony in face of this harrowing scene. Nothing whatsoever distracts me from this enormous, torturing nightmare. What upsets me at times is that these sufferings of mine are not acceptable to Jesus, because they have a human motive which concerns Giovina's bodily well-being, although I am convinced that her soul acquires merit when she suffers in this way, with resignation and in a Christian spirit. Is this a fact? Answer me on this point.

I am always looking at and thinking of the things of this earth, of transitory and deceptive things. O my Jesus, if it is possible, take this bitter chalice away from me, but may your will always be done! I feel your hand coming down more heavily on me. You are right, I deserve much worse treatment, but have mercy on me. This is the only invocation I continue to repeat. My dear Father, I don't know how to say anything else. I feel disheartened and I act like an automaton. I am amazed at what I did in preparation for our trip to Naples, etc., etc. (I felt I had neither strength nor common sense). It is all Jesus' doing. Thank Him very much for me.

I hope to be calmer when I write again. Answer me at once, for pity's sake. Don't abandon me, for my lamp is flickering and about to go out. It needs the fuel of your holy words and your ardent prayers. I have given you a little time to rest, a little holiday from writing to me. How are you? Good Rosa whom we left at home with the maid, and good Francesca who goes to see her every evening, are following us step by step in these painful events. We are counting on and trusting very much in the prayers of these two alone who are so attached to us, and on your own prayers, holy Father.

These good souls take a real interest in us, who are tossed about like leaves by the wind of every tribulation, and they are praying for us. I'll get Giovina to write to good Padre Agostino. We are surrounded here by the care and affection of this good and pious family. Giuseppina[1], who is angelic and of whom I told you in my last letter, is praying and praying to Jesus her Spouse for Giovina. The window (all plain glass) of St. Paschal's church which adjoins this house where we are staying, looks onto our terrace, from which we can see the high altar. Yesterday evening, as I didn't want to leave Giovina, I assisted from our terrace at Benediction.

Until late at night, from our room opening onto this terrace which is surrounded by vast gardens, we can see the dim light of the tabernacle lamp which tells us that the Spouse

[1] Giuseppina Morgera. See Letters 72 and 96.

is there, watching and suffering. And I myself? I don't want to suffer... shame on me!

I kiss your right hand.

Your poor unworthy tertiary.

P.S. I said I was going to tell you when I wrote, of a great big secret of mine that is known only to Rosa and Francesca, my faithful confidantes. In a further letter I'll tell you all, because you must hear everything from me.

Has Jesus revealed it to you already? Tell me without any reticence.

My new address: Raffaela Cerase, c/o Morgera a San Pasquale, Naples for Casamicciola.

79

Pietrelcina, 4 August 1915[1].

Good wishes. How to face up to suffering. The trial will still be hard. "Give me your heart." Her sister's health. "My strength is failing." Prayers.

J.M.J.D.F.C.

Beloved daughter of the heavenly Father,

May the grace of the divine Spirit comfort your soul with that consolation which can come from God alone. May Jesus make you ever dearer to Him and ever more like Him on the path of suffering. May Mary, the Mother of Jesus and our Mother, enable you to understand all that is contained in the great secret of suffering borne with a Christian spirit. May she obtain for you all the strength you require to climb to the summit of Calvary loaded with your own cross.

Great strength is needed, unfortunately, to follow this path, but take heart, for the Saviour will never leave you alone or without His help. Let us make haste, then, to join and mingle with all those pious and faithful souls who follow the divine Master. Let us hasten, I say, and not remain far behind this holy company. Let us always be united with them and

[1] From the postmark.

never lose sight of them. Let us never take our eyes off them or we shall never be able to reach them, we shall be deprived of those secret treasures which they alone possess and shall be excluded from the eternal joy which is only obtained through them and in their company.

Be consoled, Raffaelina, by this thought which should be exceedingly sweet for you, namely, that you are very dear to the heart of the divine Father who has deigned to make you similar to His divine Son. He intends to lead you to great holiness and hence He has subjected and will subject you again to uncommon trials.

Be docile in shouldering these crosses with humility. Seek comfort in the sacrament of the Eucharist. In the midst of great desolation let your soul never cease to sing to God the hymn of gratitude and praise. Keep far away from the corruption of the carnal Jerusalem, from profane assemblies, from corrupt and corrupting entertainment, from all ungodly company.

Prepare your lips, as the divine Redeemer did, and drink along with Him from the black waters of the Cedron by accepting tribulation and penance with holy resignation. Cross this torrent with Jesus by enduring the world's contempt for love of Him perseveringly and courageously. Recollect yourself continually and may your whole life be hidden in Jesus and with Jesus in the Garden of Gethsemane, that is to say, in the silence of meditation and prayer. Don't be frightened by the dark night of humiliation and solitude or the floodtide of mortifications. Go forward all the time, go forward, Raffaelina, and don't let the torrent of mortification stop you. Do not let the persecution of worldlings and of all those who live without the spirit of Jesus Christ deter you from following the road trodden by the saints. Continue to run up the steep slope of the mountain of holiness and don't let the rough path dismay you. Continue to walk close to Jesus, and if following Him means protection against every mishap, you will most certainly win through in all things as you have always done.

I cannot conceal from you, Raffaelina, that the trial to which you are still to be subjected will again be a very harsh one. Before breathing your last on the cross you still have to agonize in the olive-grove with Jesus Christ. Don't be frightened, however, by this fresh announcement. Remember the goodness with which the Lord has treated you up to the present. He will continue His work of perfecting you which will be to your advantage. He will continue to pour out upon you to the full not only the oil of His gladdening mercy but the oil of His virtue which will strengthen you and make you successful in the combat. We all know well that wrestlers rub oil on their limbs to make them more agile, more supple and more robust.

Carry on tranquilly, for the divine mercy will not be lacking and much less will it be lacking in your case if you show docility beneath the Lord's divine action. Ah, Raffaelina, don't be stingy with this heavenly physician. For pity's sake, don't keep Him waiting any longer. To you, too, He is saying: *Give me your heart*[2], my daughter, so that I may pour my oil into it. For pity's sake, let the invitation of such a tender father not be wasted. Open the door of your heart to Him with trustful abandonment. Don't hold up the precious stream of His oil as it is poured upon you, lest you have to go in search of this oil of His mercy at the hour of death[3] like the foolish virgins of the Gospel, for you will then find nobody willing to give it to you. Yes, during life always remain united with Jesus in the olive-grove as He suffers his agony. By sharing thus in the anointing of His grace and the comfort of His strength you will find yourself after death among the same olive trees to share in the joy of His Ascension and His glory.

---

[2] Prov. 23:26.
[3] Cf. Mt 25:1ff.

I urge you, then, not to lose heart in face of all the trials which your very dear sister is undergoing. May the Lord have pity not so much on her physical as on her moral state. Don't hold it against me and tell me I am to blame for hardly ever speaking to you about your poor invalid. God knows my reason for this! I myself keep silence, however, as I have no words to justify myself in this matter.

May it please Jesus to grant the ardent prayers I send up to Him for Giovina. Oh, would you ever believe it? Her cure means more to me than it does to yourself. You certainly won't believe it and you'll start to laugh when you read this statement, but God knows how much truth there is in it.

You must learn how to suffer in a Christian manner. Don't be afraid, for no suffering no matter how low the motive on which it rests will go unrewarded in eternal life. Trust and hope in the merits of Jesus and in this way even poor clay will become finest gold which will shine in the palace of the king of heaven.

I would like to continue, but my strength is failing me and I can no longer control myself. I am very ill and a few nights ago those who remained at my bedside expected the final catastrophe. But the Lord did not want that. He wants my martyrdom to continue still and may His will be done. And although I am more prepared to go than to live on, I desire nothing except what the Lord wants.

Do not cease to present me to Jesus continually, for I have extreme need of it. My soul is about to be crushed beneath His powerful hand and for me to die would be a great relief.

I would like to ask you, if this is not too much trouble, to do me the kindness of making a novena of Communions for my needs, or rather according to my intentions. I also presume you will be so good as to get other souls dear to Jesus to pray for the same purpose.

My respectful regards to your excellent sister.

May Jesus be always with you and with all those souls who love Him. I leave you all in the Lord's holy embrace and always remain,

Your most humble servant,
Fra Pio, Capuchin.

P.S. Write to me very often to give me a present of invariably good news about Giovina's state and your own.

80

Casamicciola, 22 August 1915.

Their correspondence. Half way up Calvary. Departure from Casamicciola. Symptoms of a disease (cancer). Postscript. Various news items.

Jesus alone! Most Holy Spirit, help me!

Father,

I delayed in replying to you in order to let you rest. There are two reasons why I don't write to you often. In the first place, I repeat, in order not to tire you; in the second place, because I realize that you are in need of comfort, since your own letters are full of desolation of soul and body.

You tell me in your second-last letter that I am "about half way to the summit of Calvary". I still have a long way to go and the path will become very much rougher. May Thy will be done! I would like to feel within me the sentiments of dear Sister Thérèse of the Holy Face, that is, to become a plaything in Jesus' hands[1]. Instead, my feelings are very different... how many sins! How do I stand before Jesus? It's a mystery!

---

[1] St. Thérèse of the Child Jesus, *Writings*, Letter 51, Rome, 1970, pp. 403ff.

The day after tomorrow, Wednesday, if Jesus so wills (if the sea, which is very rough this morning, permits) we'll be leaving Casamicciola and shall go on to Rome, Florence and Bologna for further medical examinations. The Way of the Cross has not yet ended. A month here has yielded no results. Through Jesus' infinite goodness we have a cousin with us, an engineer Cerase (married and with a family) who is more than a brother to us[2]. He lives in Syracuse (Sicily) and during one of her bad attacks Giovina asked him to accompany us on this journey of exploration.

Lord, have mercy on us. At all events, we place ourselves in Jesus' arms with trust. May an invisible hand, His most holy hand guide us in all that happens. Pray very hard. Pray also for a fresh gift Jesus has given me (this is the secret that I have to disclose to you). In the region of my heart Jesus has given me a certain internal ailment which is becoming most painful. If my poor martyr were to know about it she would die before her time from fright and grief. Only Rosa and Francesca know and as they are alarmed about it they are compelling me to have a medical examination. Unknown to Giovina, therefore, if Jesus permits it, I shall have to go through with his examination to avoid facing surgery if the disease gets worse as I feel it is doing.

Imagine how I am tortured by all this. I would prefer to die rather than expose my body. But they are obliging me to take care of myself and I don't think it is a sin. I must do it unknown to Giovina, for if I were to reveal everything to her it would be the same as killing her. She is already suffering very much herself in soul and body. In what a dreadful dilemma Jesus has placed me! May He be blessed for ever! What do you advise me to do? Do you know everything already? Speak to Jesus about it and inform me of His most holy will.

---

[1] All we know about this engineer cousin is that his name was Antonio.

I tremble as I look to the future, solely on account of my poor unfortunate sister. Darkness and desolation. Pray.

Don't write to me until I send you my new address (I am giving you a long rest). Pray and continue to bless,

Your poor tertiary.

P.S. We sent picture postcards to Very Reverend Father Provincial and he replied at once from Morcone (where he is carrying out a holy visitation). We also wrote to good Padre Agostino, but up to the present there has been no reply. Why? Do you know anything about him? Please send us some news about him as I am very anxious.

I am sorry to be obliged to leave and your reply would not reach me in time, even though it is pouring rain and the sea is very rough. Until the day after tomorrow we shan't know what is happening. At all events you alone know what line to take, as you know all by other channels, even from far away.

Answer me clearly and fully about my precious ailment. I beg you not to forget or fail to pay attention to this. Forgive me.

I was forgetting to tell you something that will please you very much, namely, that Giovina received Holy Communion on the feast of the Assumption and continues to do so at intervals. Thanks be to Jesus, she is now fairly well as she keeps rigidly to a light and very limited diet: a little soup, a little chicken and a little milk. Whenever she increases or changes this very slightly, there is trouble. May His will be done!

Pray that dangers, temptations and distractions may be far from us on this fresh trip. I am afraid of sinning and have a great fear of my own wickedness and weakness. Pray that Jesus may come absolutely every morning to pay me a visit, that He may enable me to find ways and means not to miss daily Mass and Communion, that He may facilitate these practices in all circumstances and in all places.

I regret very much that we are leaving this heavenly peace. May His will always be done!

81

Bologna, 4 September 1915.

Arrival in Bologna. Course of Giovina's illness. She is very dispirited. "Write to me at once." A tranquil conscience.

Jesus alone alone! Most Holy Spirit, help me!

Father,

A little respite at last; continual alternation of disappointments, fears, dismay, despondency; an occasional fleeting glimmer of calm, then back to the starting-point.

We have now been here in this Villa Rosa, a nursing-home for stomach cases[1], for five days. Giovina has started her massage treatment but has continual ups and downs.

As I have told you already, we left Casamicciola on the morning of the 25th. We disembarked in Naples, where we found our cousin at once, and were in time for the Rome train. We reached the Eternal City at 2 p.m. and remained there just one night. Next morning, the 26th, we went on to

[1] Taken from the envelope and letterhead: Villa Rosa, Via Castiglione 103, Consultant: Professor Augusto Murri; Director: Professor Giovanni Vitali. Establishment for the treatment of disorders of the stomach and nervous system, for morphine addicts and alcoholics. Radioscopy and radiotherapy.

Bologna, where we arrived at 6 p.m. The following day we went out to arrange for the medical examination by Doctor Murri, which took place four days later. There is a good deal of difficulty in getting to see him and people wait as long as two weeks for a hearing. We ourselves were fairly lucky, praise be to God.

Doctor Murri found nothing wrong with Giovina's stomach (and the same applies to the well-known surgeon Monari and Professor Vitali, Director of this nursing-home), except for severe contractions of the nerves which must be controlled, while her nourishment needs to be regulated by being gradually increased, as the patient is very run-down.

This is the judgment of the Italian doctors of science, but I myself have very little faith in their pronouncements. God alone knows the truth. There will either be an improvement and a complete cure, which I expect from Jesus alone, or else the precipice. There is no way out of it. I greatly desire the end of this very harsh trial (tell me, Father, is this a sin?). It is a nightmare that tortures me continually and does not allow me to find peace and quiet anywhere. In Casamicciola, in that corner of Eden, walking around holy Rome, later in Bologna, and now up here in this very beautiful villa where many people laugh and amuse themselves (there are very few real sufferers), where there are magnificent walks and excellent company, I myself remain indifferent, listless, disgusted and irritated. I would like to see my dear invalid improving, relieved and comforted in soul and body like many other ladies. The poor martyr spends hours, entire days and whole nights in pain, discouragement and terror which would move even the stones to compassion.

Can you obtain nothing from Jesus for this poor victim? Have you become powerless only where I am concerned? Forgive me, Father, if I reason in this way. Make allowances for me, for the rope is too tight and has bound me too long. When will the bottom of this most bitter chalice appear? This is my only hope, the one thing that brings me comfort.

With my spirit crushed, on this painful road, on these various sorrowful journeys I am doing what I can. In Rome I had to fast; in Bologna, through the mercy of Jesus our hotel was only a short distance from the cathedral, dedicated to St. Petronius, and I went there quite easily every morning. Here in this villa, by another supreme act of kindness on Jesus' part, we are also quite near a church, the parish of Our Lady of Mercy. When Giovina is well in the mornings I hurry out, as I have to be back before eight o'clock, at which time the nurse comes for massaging.

What is to become of my freedom, my quiet, my way of life? We seem to be living like gypsies. I can't make out what is happening. May His will be done!

How long shall we remain up here? It's a mystery! And afterwards, for the winter, where are we to go? A mystery! All the doctors have forbidden Giovina, who is very weak, to face the severe cold in Foggia, so where are we to pitch our tents? In Naples or the environs? A mystery, a distressing mystery all the time! Eventually we'll go where Jesus leads us. In His great goodness He has advised us so far. He led us to where we are now and He will continue to do so, as we have nobody but Himself, always and everywhere.

With joined hands I beg you to write me a long letter immediately after you receive this. I have given you a rest for a while and now you must make up for it to me. For some time I have been deprived of your light and your consolation; since 4 August, a whole month which to me seems a year.

You will have received my last letter from Casamicciola, dated 21 August. You will have the patience to read it over again very carefully and to answer me about everything in it. I want your advice about the very delicate question of my ailment. I wish to have news of your own holy father about whom we have heard nothing further. Living far away from my own environment, I feel lonely and depressed. I am afraid of dangers all the time; I am afraid of sinning and I am still waiting to go to confession. Pray that some priest according to the Most Sacred Heart of Jesus may convert me.

Write to me at once, holy Father. Tell me how you are. Pluck up courage and comfort my soul. May Jesus always reward you. May Jesus comfort my Giovina, enlighten the doctors and arrange everything for His own glory.

I don't know how to pray. I pray very little and in fits and starts. I am not really the mistress of my own time but must adapt myself whether I like it or not. On the rare occasions on which I have a little time to myself I feel listless, I repeat, and in my profound apathy I continue to say: "If it is possible let this chalice pass from me, may this combat be ended, but act as you will, have pity on these two poor unfortunates who are buffeted by a non-stop storm." Am I right in speaking like this? Speak to me frankly about it.

In spite of everything my conscience is at rest, comparatively speaking. Tell me, then, good Father, what is my state of conscience and tell me without holding anything back. Thank Jesus on my behalf for all the favours He has bestowed on me who by no means deserve them. Thank Him for all the good people I have met, for all the protecting angels He has sent us every time we were in such great distress. Pray that He may continue to send them to us, for we are in great need of them. We need to be comforted with Him, in Him and through Him all the time.

Give your blessing to,

Your poor tertiary.

P.S. My new address: Villa Rosa, Via Castiglione 103, Bologna.

82

Pietrelcina, 7 September 1915[1].

Trust in God: a twofold basis; two biblical narratives. The victory obtained by humility, tears and prayers. The secret of the Christian life. Never to despair of receiving divine assistance. "Embracing and kissing Jesus." Effects of this kiss. A most fortunate state. An exhortation. A reproof. Her sister's illness. Requests.

J.M.J.D.F.C.

Beloved daughter of Jesus,

May the grace of the divine Spirit be always with you to console you in all your trials.

I am more than a little consoled to hear that you continue to trust in the Lord. Well, then, always place your confidence in Jesus and He will know how to comfort your soul even when it is tossed about in a stormy sea. Never be afraid of the enemy's enticements, for no matter how strong they may be they will never avail to sweep you into his nets, as long as you remain faithful to the Lord and on your guard, while you build up your strength by prayer and holy humility. God has promised that He *opposes the proud but gives*

[1] From the postmark.

grace to the humble[2]; that those who *watch and pray* will not *enter into temptation*[3].

What are you afraid of, then? Is our God not faithful to His promises? We read in the Old Testament that when the patriarch Jacob returned to Mesopotamia[4], fearing for his own safety and that of his family because of the inveterate hatred of his brother Esau who lived there with great forces behind him, he crossed a stream with his eleven children, then withdrew from his family to pray for them to the Lord who had given him this family. And while Jacob was praying for his posterity and for the entire Jewish nation of which his family there on the spot was a figure, an angel appeared to him in the form of a man to wrestle with him and prevent his prayer from succeeding.

This angel assured Jacob of his blessing for himself alone. As for his descendants, the deicide Jewish nation, he showed him that it would be cursed and destroyed for it would one day repudiate the Messiah and put him to death.

The holy patriarch was horrified by this revelation of what the future held in store for his people. But full of faith he seized the heavenly messenger at very close quarters, clasped him in his arms and wrestled with him all through the night, telling him that he would not let him go until he had obtained his promise that the Jewish people, even though guilty of deicide, would be cherished and would one day be blessed and saved.

Then in order to overcome Jacob's resistance the angel struck him on the thigh, so that his thigh-bone was put out of joint and the sinew of his hip which gives athletes their strength was numbed. Then he made him powerless, crippled him and knocked him down. But who would believe it?

---

[2] Jas 4:6; 1 Pet 5:5.
[3] Cf. Mt 26:41; Mk 14:38.
[4] Gen 32:22 ff.

Weakened though Jacob was, he became even stronger. He clasped his heavenly adversary even closer and finally obtained his blessing. He asked for his people that they too might reap the benefit of the Messiah's blood, unworthily shed by their forefathers and that by the end of the world they too would have become Christians and would be sanctified and saved: All Israel will be saved[5].

A similar account is found in the New Testament with regard to the body of our Redeemer. When Jesus entered the Garden of Gethsemane and went apart from his disciples in order to pray to his Father[6], after the first hour of prayer and after the second, according to the Fathers of the Church the same angel who had appeared to Jacob many centuries earlier also appeared to Jesus Christ in the Garden.

This was the comfort the angel brought him. At this announcement by the angel, Jesus' love for us received a new cy towards the sons of men. He made known that to remove the curse which hung over the heads of the sons of Adam, to allow His merits to be applied to sinners and their ignominy to fall on the head of the Saint of saints, to permit innocence to be punished while crime was spared, was such an excessive act of mercy that He would be unable to obtain it unless by immense prayers and a most difficult combat.

This was the comfort the angel brought him. At this announcement by the angel, Jesus' love for us received a new stimulus, while His fears and apprehensions lest we should be lost were redoubled. Redoubled also was His strength to enter into combat with the justice of God, so that He continued his prayer with greater force and spiritual power. So great was the agony and the struggle which the Redeemer endured against God's justice that He then began to sweat blood from His entire holy body. This sweat was so heavy that ac-

[5] Cf. Rom 11:26.
[6] Cf. Lk 22:43.

cording to the sacred historian, not only was His whole body bathed in it and, as it were, baptized in His own blood, but all around Him the vegetation of that garden was so fortunate as to be sprinkled with it also[7].

Meanwhile God's justice, severe and unyielding, the first and second time Jesus prayed, seemed to say to Him: "separate your cause from that of sinners. Allow me to vent my anger on the proscribed posterity of a guilty father." At this third prayer of the Redeemer in which He wrestled with God's justice and continued to pray at greater length and more intensely, combining petitions of deepest humility with His prayers of most fervent love, tears of the heart with those which fell from His eyes, the shriller cries of the blood with those which His voice sent up, He obtained what He asked for us, namely, the divine blessing.

By this completely new prayer He obtained miraculous deliverance for the Jews also and ensured that they too would one day profit by His blood unworthily shed by His forefathers and that by becoming Christians themselves they would be sanctified and saved just as the apostle tells us: *All Israel will be saved*[8].

Now who could ever have imagined, Raffaelina, in the combat between Jacob and the angel, between God and mankind represented by our Redeemer, that God and the angel would not have been the victors? Yet this did not happen. Through Jacob, man vanquished an angel and in Jesus Christ the whole of mankind vanquished God: *You have striven with God and with men, and have prevailed*[9].

What was the secret of such an immense triumph by which the patriarch Jacob overcame an angel? One of the prophets has told us: humility, tears and prayer: *She besought*

---

[7] Cf. Lk 22:44.
[8] Rom 11:26.
[9] Gen 32:38.

him with tears[10]. St. Paul has also disclosed to us the secret of the strength by which Jesus Christ who took on Himself our miserable human flesh, vanquished God in all His glory, that is, by humbling Himself, by prayer, weeping and loud cries: *With loud cries and tears and he was heard for his godly fear*[11].

Here, then, Raffaelina, we are faced with a twofold scriptural fact. Here we find disclosed to us a great mystery in his own person and in what he stood for. When a man engages in a fight with another man, the one who is afraid of his adversary, the one who is wounded, who falls to the ground and sheds his blood is considered to have lost the fight, to have been defeated. However, in the battles of life, he who trembles before this same God against whose strength nothing is of any avail, for everything yields to His word, everything vanishes at a mere sign of His will, he, I say, who is bowed beneath the weight of tribulation, who is crushed by the sight of the wounds produced by his own failings and drags himself along face downwards in the dust, who humbles himself, weeps, sighs and prays, this man triumphs over God's justice and obliges God to show him mercy: *She besought him with tears and was powerful*[12].

No matter how great the trial to which the Lord is to subject you, no matter how unbearable your spiritual desolation at certain moments of your life, never lose heart. Have recourse with more childlike trust to Jesus who will never be able to resist bestowing on you some little solace and comfort. Turn to Him at all times even when the devil tries to cast a pall over your life by showing you your sins. Lift up your voice loudly to Him and let it express your spiritual humility, your heartfelt contrition and your vocal prayer.

---

[10] Est 8:3.
[11] Heb 5:7.
[12] Est 8:3; Gen 32:28.

It is impossible, Raffaelina, for God not to welcome these demonstrations of goodwill and not to give way and surrender to you. It is true that God's power triumphs over everything, but humble and suffering prayer prevails over God Himself. It stops His hand, extinguishes His lightning, disarms Him, vanquishes and placates Him and makes Him almost a dependant and a friend.

Oh, if all men who share this great secret of the Christian life which Jesus taught us by words and deeds were to imitate the publican in the temple, Zaccheus, Mary Magdalen, St. Peter and many illustrious penitents and pious Christians and were to go through this same experience, what abundant fruits of holiness would be theirs! They would very soon come to understand this secret and by this means would very soon be able to overcome God's justice, to appease Him when He was more angry with them, to change His justice into loving mercy and obtain everything they needed, forgiveness of their sins, grace and holiness, eternal salvation and the power to fight and overcome themselves and all their enemies.

Why, then, Raffaelina, should you get lost in vain fears which steal our time, upset our peace of mind and make us almost diffident of God himself? For pity's sake, let us flee from these useless fears the moment they rise up in us. Let us never despair of the divine assistance. Would this not be an offence against the divine mercy? When these fears well up in you, remember the true Jacob who prayed in the garden, remember that he discovered there the true ladder that connects earth with heaven[13]; he showed us that humility, contrition and prayer abolish the distance between man and God, bring God down to our level and raise man up to God by causing the immense distance of which the royal prophet sang to disappear: *Because you have made the Lord your*

---

[13] Cf. Gen 28:12.

refuge, you have made the Most High your habitation[14]. So, in the end, we arrive at mutual understanding, love and possession.

Take heart, then, my beloved daughter, even when you feel oppressed by the great number and the atrocity of your offences. Then more than ever should you come to the feet of Jesus Christ who is fighting and enduring agony for us in the Garden. Humble yourself, weep, entreat with Him and like Him. Ask with loud cries for God's mercy, His forgiveness of your faults, for help to walk all the time in His sight. Do this and have no doubt that this merciful and clement God will stretch out a compassionate hand as He has always done, to lift you up out of your poverty and spiritual desolation.

I would be glad, Raffaelina, if you would believe me just for once that everything that is happening in and around you has been arranged by Jesus because of His most ardent love for you. I would like you, moreover, to believe that you are still most dear to His divine Heart and that you are trying to love Him more and more.

Ah, what I am asking you as a favour is that you listen to me and put into practice all that I have been explaining to you in the Lord up to this moment, ever since the Lord has entrusted you to my care. Meanwhile I urge you to unite with me and draw near to Jesus with me to receive His embrace and a kiss that sanctifies and saves us. For this purpose let us listen to the holy king David who invites us to kiss the Son devoutly: *Deal gently with the son*[15], for this son of whom the royal prophet speaks is none other than the one of whom the prophet Isaiah said: *For to us a child is born, to us a son is given*[16].

This child, Raffaelina, is the affectionate brother, the

---

[14] Ps 91:9.
[15] 2 Sam 18:5.
[16] Is 9:6.

most loving Spouse of our souls, of whom the sacred spouse of the Song, prefiguring the faithful soul, sought the company and yearned for the divine kisses: *O that you were like a brother to me! If I met you outside, I would kiss you! O that you would kiss me with the kisses of your mouth*[17]*!* This son is Jesus and we can kiss Him without betraying Him, give Him the kiss and the embrace of grace and love He expects from us and which He promises to return. We can do all this, St. Bernard tells us, by serving Him with genuine affection, by carrying out in holy works His heavenly doctrine which we profess by our words[18].

Let us not cease, then, to kiss this divine Son in this way, for if these are the kisses we give Him now, He Himself will come as He has promised, full of mercy and love. He will come to take us in His arms and give us the kiss of peace in the last sacraments at the hour of death. Thus we shall end our life in the holy kiss of the Lord, an admirable kiss of divine condescension by which, according to St. Bernard[19], it is not a matter of approaching face to face and mouth to mouth. Rather does it mean that the Creator draws close to His creature and man and God are united for all eternity.

My daughter, I beg you in our most tender Lord not to become weary of asking the divine Bridegroom, with the spouse of the sacred Song, for this kiss of peace which is a truly delightful paradise. By this kiss you will defy all the vain fears of this world, the devil's promptings, the enticements of the flesh and without losing an iota of your calm you will overcome all these things and win a full victory over them. For pity's sake, do not refrain from asking Jesus for this blessed kiss through a feeling of false humility which would in reality be a most refined form of pride. By the wise ones

---

[17] Song 1:1; 8:1.

[18] Cf. St Bernard, *Sermones in Cantica*, Sermo IV:PL, Vol. 183, col. 796-798.

[19] *Ibid*.

of this world, unfortunately, to ask for this blissful kiss is considered to be folly, but, dear God, what more deplorable folly can there be, I wonder, than that which leads one to the brink of the grave with this show of wisdom which belongs entirely to the flesh?

May God protect us as He has always done from identifying ourselves with these foolish ones, according to heavenly wisdom. I grant you, moreover, that you belong all the time to the goodly number of those who have known how to make continual progress at the school of divine love. I am also convinced that in order to arrive at such a heroic degree of love which enables us to ask Jesus to favour us with a kiss of His divine mouth, God's powerful assistance is required and we can ask and desire this powerful help by seeking God continually with the spouse in the Song.

Let us approach to receive the bread of angels with great faith and with a great flame of love in our hearts. Let us await this most tender lover of our souls in order to be consoled in this life with the kiss of His mouth. Happy are we, Raffaelina, if we succeed in receiving from the Lord the consolation of this kiss in the present life! Then indeed will we feel our will inseparably bound at all times to Jesus' will and nothing in the world can prevent us from willing what our divine Master wills. O my God and my glory, then alone can we say: Yes, O divine lover, O Lord of our life, *your love is better than wine, your anointing oils are fragrant*[20].

O my daughter, who can tell what admirable secrets are hidden beneath the veil of these words of the spouse of the Song? I should be trying in vain if I sought to explain these admirable secrets to you. What I can say about them is that when our most tender Lord enables one to pronounce these words as the spouse in the Song pronounced them, one feels such a sweetness that one is well aware that Jesus is very near.

---

[20] Song 1:3.

All the faculties of the soul are then invaded by such perfect peace that one seems to possess God as much as one can desire. One comes almost to the point of being able to touch physically the nothingness of all the things of this ignoble world.

The divine Bridegroom continues to reveal to the soul most important truths in a completely new way. The soul, however, does not perceive this divine Lover who is manifesting Himself. There is a mere awareness that He is there close at hand and the soul can have no doubts on this point. It finds itself in an atmosphere of such dazzling light, it experiences such wonderful effects of this union with the Bridegroom and feels so strong in virtue that it is hardly aware of being what it was before. It is plunged so deeply in a completely heavenly ocean of consolation and so inebriated with joy that it no longer knows what to desire or ask from God.

To put it briefly, in that torrent of light and blessedness the soul does not know what has happened to it. It feels carried completely out of itself and is aware of being embraced by the Bridegroom in such a close embrace that the floodtide of joy causes the poor thing to experience a fainting sensation. It is precisely at this point that it appears to be carried lovingly in those divine arms. It feels Him pressing it to His side and to that divine breast and the heavenly rapture is so intense that the soul is bewildered and almost out of its mind, so that in a transport of holy madness it seems to me that it can well say to its dear conqueror: *Your love is better than wine, your anointing oils are fragrant*[21].

My dear Raffaelina, may it please the divine Master to give you an understanding of the great bliss of a soul that God has deigned to raise up to such a height, or rather may He enable you to feel this, for if one does not feel this bliss it would be useless to hope to understand it. It is the greatest

---

[21] Song 1:3.

happiness that it is possible to enjoy on this earth. By comparison with it, all worldly pleasure and satisfactions combined are nothing but filthy mud. Happy are those whose names are written in that book of bliss! You, Raffaelina, belong to this numerous company, so why are you so sad, why do you worry and torment yourself so much when you see yourself loaded more and more heavily with the cross.

Rejoice, for I shall have the happiness to see the Lord making known to the world His mercies towards you and then, wherever I am, I will raise my voice with ardent yearning in a song of praise to my Saviour and Redeemer. Let us be glad, for one day we shall sing more joyful hymns to our most tender Lover who is the sweetest repose of our hearts, enamoured of His beauty. Let us rejoice, I say, for the day will come, as I hope, on which our hearts will no longer be torn by cruel remorse for not loving our sweet Lord sufficiently.

In the meantime let us prepare ourselves for this great day and if we love Jesus let us now stir ourselves up and keep far from all that smacks of worldliness. Let us reflect well that all the sufferings of this world, according to St. Paul, are not worth comparing with the glory that awaits us[22]. Let us consider that the divine Bridegroom, not satisfied with the immense reward He has reserved in the next life in return for our love, intends to let us taste it even in this life. May the Lord enable us to understand how fortunate anyone is to be able to abandon himself in His arms and make a pact with Him in these terms: *My Beloved is mine and I am His*[23]; let Him think of me and I will think of Him.

Raffaelina, my daughter, let us love Jesus more and more. Let us remain united with Him always by constant and humble prayer and let us implore Him unceasingly to con-

---

[22] Cf. Rom 8:18.
[23] Song 2:16.

sole us with a kiss of His mouth and make us worthy to draw close to His divine breast. Happy shall we be if we succeed in snatching this further token of love from the divine lover! These words, however, must not seem too bold to you. Let us always speak these words to Jesus and even more so must we utter them at the supreme moment when we approach to receive Him into our hearts. Jesus will not be offended if we speak to Him in this way, because, Raffaelina, if a kiss means peace and friendship, why should Jesus take it in bad part? Why should we not ask Jesus for this kiss of peace? What more precious gift could we desire from such an illustrious monarch?

Away with the fears we have in our minds, then. Let us open our hearts to trust and ask Jesus continually for this peace with a kiss of His divine mouth.

Let us now come to ourselves. Your behaviour up to the present with regard to this new illness to which the Lord has been pleased to subject you hurts me more than a little. Do you mean to say you don't know that anyone who refuses human remedies exposes himself to the danger of offending the Lord? And do you not know that God tells us through the sacred Scriptures to love the physician for love of Himself[24]?

I don't intend to rebuke you, but I am certainly displeased with you. Please take note that I want you to have a medical examination without delay. In conscience you have a serious obligation to do this. If you refuse to obey it will be very painful for me to be obliged to deal with you and I won't know how to do so any longer. Obey me, then, and be at peace, for it is only the obedient man who cries victory[25]. Have yourself examined and let me know what the doctor says about it.

Don't worry too much about Giovina's illness and always

---

[24] Cf. Sir 38:1.
[25] Cf. Prov 21:28.

bear in mind that everything is willed by God. Ask by all means for the grace of a cure for her, but be resigned all the time to do whatever God wants. Moreover, you have already consulted too many doctors without waiting for the consent and opinion of the one to whom God has entrusted you. May the Lord continue to show you mercy!

Padre Agostino continues to be quite well, with heaven's help. From you he only received a picture postcard from Naples without any address. Perhaps this is the reason why he has deprived you of his news. However, he has asked me many times for news of yourself and Giovina and I always complied with his request.

I end by asking you very earnestly not to forget me in the Lord's presence, since you know the anguished state of my soul. I certainly don't mean to dispense you from writing to me frequently and at length, for the simple reason of my spiritual desolation, for this would mean a further torment for me and would add suffering to suffering.

Let us thank Jesus very warmly for giving me the strength which has enabled me to write a rather long letter to you. I would have liked to continue, but I have come to the end of my strength. Praise be to God!

My best wishes to Giovina.

May Jesus be with you always.

Fra Pio.

83

Bologna, 23 September 1915.

"I find you severe." Conversion. Doubts and queries. "The days slip by unnoticed." She replies to his reproof. "Write me a long letter soon." Her coming operation.

Jesus alone! Most Holy Spirit, help me!

Father,

I received your most precious letter in due course and thank you very much for it. However, I cannot but confess to you a judgment of mine (a rash one?). For some time past I have found your attitude very changed towards me. I find you severe, almost rough and at times quite harsh.

Forgive my frankness. It's a habit of mine, especially when dealing with you from whom I must not and cannot hide anything. Perhaps I may be mistaken, but to me, accustomed to your gentleness, what is merely justice appears to be strictness. On the other hand, you are quite right, for I am growing worse and worse, and I myself am aware of it. You see perfectly well that I am not reaping any benefit from your continual teachings and you become discouraged, irritated and weary. You are perfectly right and indeed you ought to use the whip on me.

Jesus is certainly raining blows on me, but never as much

as I deserve, yet I have not yet given in. What am I to do? Tell me, good Father, what I must do in order to be converted. Only by being converted shall I receive the grace of which you know. It is all very well for you to say that Jacob defeated the angel, but Jacob was righteous. In my case, you ought to and you could fight and defeat the angel for me. Like the new Jacob, our loving Redeemer, by your worthy and efficacious prayers you could and must win and triumph on my behalf and for my good. Do you agree?

Wretched nonentity that I am, what am I capable of doing? All I am capable of desiring is the end of this chalice. Is this a sin? (This is the second time I put this question to you, so please answer me). I feel that my conscience has become indifferent and apathetic. In spite of everything I am at peace. Is this a sin? I ask you this for the second time. Have patience and answer me. In this new environment (which I find most unpleasant—is this a sin? I thank Jesus for letting me experience sharp pain and disgust on all sides), I am losing count of time and of things. Even the feast of our Seraphic Father's Stigmata escaped my notice, and this tells you all.

I am so engrossed in the sufferings of my dear invalid (who, may Jesus be thanked, is picking up, although at a snail's pace), in my own physical sufferings and in thoughts of what is to happen to me, that the days slip by unnoticed. I ought to be thinking, instead, of the Eucharistic Gethsemane and the wound in Jesus' most holy side. How much subject matter for concentration, for tears and suffering! But instead? The Eucharistic Calvary where Jesus is perpetually receiving lance-thrusts in His Most Sacred Heart ought to be for me a school, a rebuke, an incitement to suffer, but very weak creature that I am, I am in great fear, never for myself but all the time for Giovina.

You rebuke me harshly. I honour the physicians, but in my case I could not question them immediately without letting Giovina know about it and I had to and still have to avoid that. For the moment I must conceal this new ailment at all costs from my poor martyr. She already has enough to cope with herself and she is already very worried as she sees me drooping more and more each day. This is only natural with the continual heartbreak I have on her account and in view of everything else.

You reproach me, but up to the present Jesus has not allowed me to have a doctor examine me unknown to Giovina—and what fault of mine is this? You intend to hold me responsible for something I could not and should not do for the sake of my poor sick sister. You must agree with me here. The saints sometimes argue with heaven.

A second reproof: "Moreover, you have already consulted too many doctors without waiting for the consent and opinion of the one to whom God has entrusted you" (your own words). The true physician is Jesus as I have told you before, but my conscience, our family doctor and all my relatives obliged me to act as I did. So then, what? I am not concerned about the money which is being poured out abundantly, since there is question of my sister's health which is very precious to me. Yet when I consider (from the human point of view) that our enemies will think of justice and punishment when they see us spending on doctors and medicines this money taken from our brother (as he says) who was put out of our home so that we two (the owners) should occupy it, then I can no longer think clearly and blows are added to blows. Enough.

I would like to have the happiness of seeing you and opening the infinite recesses of my wretched conscience to you in the confessional. Answer me fully on this point. By comparison with others, I see my only sister so very good yet constantly humiliated, and I feel I am very, very bad. Will Jesus forgive me? Answer me, Father, and do not forget it.

Pray hard for me and for my conversion. Write me a

long letter soon; tell me everything quite frankly and openly; don't be unwilling to manifest your feelings. May Jesus reward you. My weak prayers are always for you and with you.

I kiss your right hand respectfully. Continue to bless,

Your poor tertiary.

P.S. I am reopening this letter to tell you that in the end, after many attempts and dreadful emotion (which I'll describe to you in another letter) all of which I endured for the sake of holy obedience, Jesus allowed me to be examined by a doctor.

Unknown all the time to Giovina, I was examined yesterday afternoon in the home of a holy lady whose acquaintance I made in church and to whom I am now very united spiritually (our merciful Jesus sometimes sends the good angels in times of anguish and in certain horrible phases of our lives).

You want to know the verdict, so here it is: as soon as possible the left hand part is to be cut away and entirely removed. What have you to say about it? Imagine the state I am in. I am far from my own home, in a nursing-home where they don't perform surgical operations, with Giovina just beginning to improve but still in need of treatment and care. Where am I to find shelter?

The doctor has reassured me that this serious operation will be a success, but it is still an operation and I have no illusions about it. I must therefore think seriously about my affairs, first preparing my soul and then settling my financial business by making a will. I must put everything in order. I desire, in a word, to be in my own home. I desire to have whatever help is possible and I want to see Giovina well enough to bear this fresh trial.

What is to be done when Giovina finds the winter in Foggia deadly? My Jesus, what darkness! With great confidence

I expect all from the adorable Heart of Jesus. I am waiting until Giovina finishes her treatment so that I may tell her everything and decide what to do. If I were to speak at present I should obtain nothing. Giovina, who is very weak, would have a relapse. All the sacrifices of every kind which have been made up to the present time would be scattered to the four winds and my sister who must act for me and with me would be of no use to me because of her illness.

What is to become of me? Let Jesus decide, for I am in His most holy hands. He sees my very sad and horrible condition and He must provide for me. He is so good and He abandons no one. I want to suffer in my own home, if it pleases Him. Pray, Father, pray. Recite for me the three novenas to the powerful Queen of Pompeii. Mine is a really desperate case. May Jesus straighten out this very knotty problem and may He give me the key to it. I am waiting for light from Him. Pray a great deal.

For pity's sake, answer me at once.

84

Pietrelcina, 28 September 1915.

Why he did not reply sooner. Bewildered by her complaints against him. Means for conversion. "Jesus is with you and you are with Jesus." He replies to her doubts and queries.

J.M.J.D.F.C.

Beloved daughter of the heavenly Father,

May Jesus be in your heart, may He bless you, console you and smile upon you! Amen.

I received your last letter a few days ago and with an anguished heart I must inform you that I was unable to reply to you at once on account of my illness which has tormented me for several days and kept me immobilized in bed. Just this morning, thanks be to God, I was able to get on my feet, but all my strength has left me and my head is going round like a windmill. May it please Jesus to come to my aid so that I may stay with you for a little while by means of this letter.

I cannot hide from you, Raffaelina, my great bewilderment at your complaints that I have been very different in my attitude towards you for some time past, that you have found me severe, almost rough and sometimes quite harsh. On the other hand, I admire and appreciate your frankness, but for the sake of truth I cannot refrain from raising my voice to inform you that you are mistaken this time as always. What you attribute to the light is merely due to your own eyes.

Unfortunately, by this time I ought to have made you begin to feel what you attribute to me, but this is not necessary for the moment. We'll meet in Foggia and settle our accounts there. Meanwhile be at peace, for with the divine assistance all will work out for your own good, for God's glory, the salvation of souls and Lucifer's confusion.

You now come to ask me what you are to do in order to surrender to Jesus' tender love. I have nothing more to add, daughter. I refer you to what I have been suggesting to you up to the present in my poor writings. Put these things into practice and go on living tranquilly in our most sweet Jesus. In this way, without wearying yourself too much, you will be assured of the crown reserved for strong souls.

Pray constantly and you will thus win the victory over our enemies. Humble yourself beneath the powerful hand of the heavenly physician and thus, when the heavenly nuptials are celebrated, Jesus will have you sit in the first place at the banquet-table, for God has promised that whoever humbles himself will be exalted[1].

Always give most fervent thanks to God through Jesus Christ. By so doing you will prepare yourself very well to receive other favours from heaven. On the other hand, whoever does not appreciate the favours he has already received is very naturally unworthy of further favours.

As regards your spiritual state, be reassured in the Lord about what I have always told you. It is God's will and that is enough. If nature feels it and suffers, the spirit must utter its assent to God's will. Jesus is with you and you are with Jesus. You have chosen Him for your only portion, so everything will combine to strengthen your union with Him.

Your new bodily infirmity distresses me more than a lit-

[1] Cf. Mt 23:12.

tle, but as I know this to be precisely God's will I am resigned to it and give Him thanks. I ask you therefore to be comforted also by this divine thought, namely, that your spiritual and physical sufferings are proof of the will of God, who wants to bring you by this path to greater conformity to the divine prototype, Jesus Christ.

O my daughter, you ought then to humble yourself before God rather than being dejected if the heavenly Father reserves for you, as for a chosen victim, the sufferings of His Son. You should send up to Him a prayer of resignation and hope and thank Him for such a great benefit.

Rest assured that it is Jesus who wants so much suffering from you and I would ask you to be reassured within your soul, as far as possible, in accordance with the counsels and admonitions of your confessor and of all other enlightened souls. Although your counsellors do not all succeed in understanding what you are suffering, they are enlightened by God to guide and advise you. You should therefore be reassured by what they tell you.

If you want to go on wishing for the end of this chalice of which you speak, you may do so, as long as this is not an immoderate desire and disjoined from God's will. In that case I would consider it better for you to place the whole matter in the Lord's hands and peacefully await the fulfilment of all the divine plans.

When one who hopes in the Lord feels his conscience at ease, this cannot come from any one but God himself. Let this serve as the answer to your other question.

The fact of feeling in no way attracted to any place whatsoever in this ignoble world cannot have its origin in any one but God, who wants in this way to detach the soul from everything but Himself.

I end here as I am unable to continue for the reasons well known to you. Meanwhile I ask you not to keep me waiting a long time for news from you.

My warm regards to Giovina, with the earnest wish to see her regaining her former health as soon as possible.

Let me know if you have any further needs and pray for me all the time.

I bless you with fatherly tenderness.

Fra Pio.

85

Bologna, Feast of the Holy Rosary,
3 October 1915.

Reply to the last letter. She is preparing for the operation which is inevitable. Requests. "Write to me all the time, long letters."

Jesus alone! Most Holy Spirit, help me!

Father,

I am replying at once to your most precious letter. I am very sorry to hear of your illness and want to have news from you without delay.

With fatherly kindness you ask me not to keep you waiting for my own news. How good you are and so good to me who do not deserve it.

You tell me, and rightly so, that for some time past you ought to have made me feel the effects of your severity. Why is this? I beg you, Father, to tell me frankly. You intend to settle accounts with me in Foggia, but what accounts, holy Father? Don't be reluctant to tell me, I implore you.

By this you lead me to hope that I shall see my own birthplace, my home, those dear to me, after all that is to be done to me. May Jesus be infinitely blessed for ever! I am in His most holy hands and may He do as He pleases with me. It is all His doing that a wretched being like myself should have so much strength and be so calm in these critical circumstances. I always say this out loud to everyone. Am I right or wrong in this? Tell me.

However, I suffer a lot when eyes and hands rest on me: up to the present two doctors and a surgeon who is to operate on me in a few days' time. Some things they say frighten me and then the whole thing causes me distress, distress, distress of conscience. What am I to do? Is it not true that Jesus permits everything except sin?

After an initial Way of the Cross unknown to Giovina, I went along with her on the feast of St. Michael (poor martyr, this was just what was needed to complete her cure!) to make a second one. The first time I was accompanied by that holy lady to whom I had confided all as though to my good Guardian Angel, and we went to see Professor Monari who is the father of surgeons. We did not find him at his own home, for he was out at his nursing-home to perform an operation (see what God permitted) on a lady who was suffering from the same disease as mine. We remained in the waiting-room (again permitted by God, where I spoke with the patient's sister who was very upset and wept as she awaited the result of the operation). After a little while the stretcher bearing the poor patient passed by. She was still asleep, breathing heavily and her face was flushed.

The sight of her made me tremble! But this was not all. A little later I saw the Professor in his surgeon's smock all stained with human blood and with his sleeves rolled up (to me he looked like a butcher). In a brusque way he told us he could not examine me there and then but that he would see me at one o'clock on the following afternoon. I was convulsed as I went down the stairs and my knees were knocking. Our good Jesus permitted that just then a hackney cab should pass along that dismal and lonely road. I jumped into it along with my good friend Giustina, who was just as upset as I was, and we went on to pay a visit to the discalced

Capuchin nuns. (This was the excuse I had given Giovina for my outing with the good lady).

First of all, we went into the beautiful chapel attached to the convent, so spotless and so isolated from the world. I bowed down and offered everything to Jesus. I was unable to do anything else. We then went to the parlour and from behind a double grille and a closed door the voice of an angel in the person of a sister sent by Jesus spoke to me at length, comforted me and cheered me up. I confided all my worries to her and she wept with me, then promised her prayers together with those of the community and the superior, who is a saint and has been confined to her bed for the past six years.

As a guest from elsewhere I asked her to obtain permission to open the door of the grille and this she did with the superior's consent. Despite the darkness and the double iron grille plus a black veil drawn over her face, I could make out the beautiful countenance of a young woman. I presented her with my small offering and the voice of that angel thanked me humbly. But it was I who had to thank her for the great spiritual consolation she had given me at the critical moment. She told me her name was Sister Teresa of the Sacred Heart and I left her with the prayer that she might become a perfect copy of St. Teresa of Jesus. Oh, that holy angel! I'll remember her all my life, just as I'll never forget that horrible sight at Monari's place. I swore I'd never return there. Then that good lady, Giustina, suggested that I go to be examined by her own doctor. This was the first examination of which I told you in my last letter.

After a week I was obliged to decide on confessing everything to Giovina. You can imagine her painful surprise and distress. In order to have advice in this difficult matter we went to a friend of ours, a married lady from our own city who has been living here for 17 years. Next day, which was the feast of St. Michael (the second Way of the Cross) she brought us to her doctor, a very trustworthy man, to get some impartial advice. This doctor sent us and put in a good word for us (after he had examined me) to a good and clever surgeon who had studied under Monari.

All were of the same opinion, that the tumor which they say I have had for a year should be removed at once. This surgeon, Musini, has a nursing-home, and as we have no good surgeons in Foggia everyone persuaded me to go into this place as soon as my cousin arrived, to whom we had sent a telegram in Syracuse (Sicily). An operation is always a serious thing and nobody wants to take the responsibility, so the presence of one of the family is indispensable.

Musini assured us that after 12 or 15 days I'd be able to leave perfectly cured and with the wound healed. God alone knows what the future holds and I have no illusions. Our cousin is due to arrive on Tuesday. After a further examination, if I am in a fit condition, I'll go into this nursing-home at once. Meanwhile I'll go to confession tomorrow and receive Holy Communion as Viaticum.

In my new painful abode I shall not have Jesus' visit in the mornings and this grieves me very much, especially in my present very sad state. I would like to hear at least the voice of a priest (Oh, if only I were at home!). May His will be done! I hope our good Jesus will send me a priest. With your usual kindness you yourself will certainly not fail to send me your holy word even if I do not write to you, which I shall not be able to do on my bed of suffering. Write to me all the time and always use the present address until I give you the new one.

I'll send you a telegram to let you know the morning of my operation, so that you may pray at that time. Please write on my behalf to good Padre Agostino (I enclose the postage stamp) and tell him everything. However, I ask you to do this in the greatest secrecy, for we don't intend to let anything of all this be known in Foggia[1]. Tell him that I count very much on his worthy and efficacious prayers. I ask his pardon and beg him to pray for my wretched soul.

And what am I to say to you? Similarly, on my knees I bow down and ask your forgiveness for everything. I thank you for all the kindness you have shown me. May Jesus reward you. I urge you to take care of my poor letters and ask you to pray for my wretched soul. Follow me all the time with your prayers at this difficult and most painful juncture. May His will be done! Follow me with your blessing in life and in death. Implore strength, resignation and detachment for me. Implore for me a worthy preparation for death.

Write to me continually and at length. Don't be stingy with your spiritual help now that I have greater need of it. I'll write to you as soon as I can, and if I can't, I'll get Giovina to write.

I enclose five lire for a Mass for my agony. Jesus! Father! Into your hands I commit my spirit.

As ever,

Your poor tertiary.

---

[1] Padre Pio to Padre Agostino, Pietrelcina, 10 October 1915: "Raffaelina and her sister are not yet returning home. Pray more assiduously for both of these distressed souls, especially for Raffaelina who has greater need of the divine assistance than her sister has. In a further letter I intend to give you a surprise as regards Raffaelina. In the meantime, pray that all may work out according to the Heart of God" (*Letters*, Vol. I, No. 291).

86

Pietrelcina, 8 October 1915.

He shares in her suffering. Encouragement. This cross is willed by God. It is not a punishment for her past life. "Let us love Jesus." Communication with pious souls. Accounts to be settled! "Write to me more often."

J.M.J.D.F.C.

Beloved daughter of the heavenly Father,

May the grace of the divine Spirit always be in your heart and make you strong with the strength of chosen souls. Amen.

Blessed be the Lord who consoles us in all our afflictions[1], exclaimed the apostle of the nations. May Jesus, then, also console your spirit which is buffeted by storms. Have no fear, for you will not be submerged. The little vessel which is your soul always possesses the strong anchor of trust in the divine goodness. This mystical vessel will always have Jesus as helmsman and Mary as its beacon. Hence there is no room for fear.

Lift up your heart all the time and let us pray with a pure heart, a contrite and humble heart, so that the enemy may be quite unable to touch your soul in this extreme trial by

[1] Cf. 2 Cor 1:4.

fire to which God in His mercy has been pleased to subject you. For my own part I cannot but share with you willingly the suffering that weighs upon you, while praying more diligently to the good God for you and wishing you from our most sweet Jesus the spiritual and material strength to pass through the final trial of His fatherly love for you. This trial, moreover, will turn out to be for God's glory, your own merit and the good of many souls.

Courage, then, Raffaelina, I repeat. Rest assured that God is with you, so what are you to fear? Has He not let you know many times, through me, that He will be glorified in you? I would like very much to be with you at this time in order to relieve you in some way of the pain which is crushing us! But I will be beside you in spirit. I will make all your sufferings my own and will offer them as a holocaust to the Lord for you. He who has opened the wound in your heart will close it up before long, when it pleases Him to do so.

It seems to me, in the meantime, that I can read in the depths of your heart a doubt expressed in the following words: but is this new cross really the divine will? Am I perhaps mistaken? My daughter, be consoled in the Lord. The trial to which you are being subjected can leave no room for doubt. If it were not willed expressly by God for you there would be nothing left but despair. Who has sustained you up to the present in all your sufferings, spiritual and corporal? I was Jesus, and He will therefore be with you still and always. When a person is resigned to suffering, it can be said that he suffers with Jesus or rather that it is Jesus who suffers in him.

Now, haven't you always been resigned to God's will? I understand perfectly well that the conflict you feel between the spirit and the flesh is terrible. Very well, but it is not sinful and this should be sufficient to buoy up your poor spirit which is afflicted so extremely. This is willed by God as a testing-time for you and that thought that has served as the weapon of all those who love Jesus must inspire you with trust in His holy assistance.

Here again I seem to see in your mind another atrocious thought, no less distressing than the other of which I have just spoken. You consider that this trial is not a loving one but a punishment for your past life. Well, then, even granted that things are as you imagine, there would be no reason to despair or to be upset about it, for the divine mercy is infinite and well able to forgive a contrite and humble heart.

When the enemy wants to open a breach in your heart, then, in order to take it by force by means of this fear of the past, reflect that it is lost in the ocean of heavenly goodness, then think of the present, when Jesus is with you and loves you. Think of the future, when Jesus will reward your faithfulness and resignation, or better still, of all those graces which He has lavished and continues to lavish on you all the time and which you certainly have not maliciously misused. I would therefore ask you to get rid as far as possible (for nobody is asked to do what is impossible) of all fear and always to practise confidence, faith and love.

The virgin Sister Thérèse of the Child Jesus used to say: "We shall be judged on love!" So then[2]? Let us love Jesus. Let us allow Him to act in us as He likes best, knowing that His action is always aimed at His own greater glory and our greater sanctification.

Don't be reluctant, or rather don't fear that there is anything wrong in letting others know that what is going on

---

[2] Several paragraphs in this letter reproduce almost exactly what Padre Agostino wrote to Padre Pio on 17 August 1915. Cf. *Letters*, Vol. I, No. 276. The phrase used by St. Thérèse of the Child Jesus is similar to the doctrine of St. John of the Cross, who says: "At the end you will be examined on love. Learn to love as God wants to be loved and according to your state" (translated directly from the original Spanish of the works of St. John of the Cross, 6th ed. (BAC), Madrid 1972, p. 421).

in you is all the work of the divine Bridegroom. For as I have told you on a previous occasion, while *it is good to guard the secret of a king* (the king of heaven), it is also good, according to the words of sacred Scripture, *gloriously to reveal the works of God*[3].

May it please heaven, my good daughter, that these souls who announce the wondrous works of the Lord may be multiplied like the sands on the seashore and the atoms which make up all heavenly and earthly bodies! Do you perhaps think that these generous souls inflamed with divine love have not achieved much good by recounting the marvellous works which the Lord has done in themselves? If this is what you think, you are greatly mistaken.

Very many tepid souls have become fervent, very many fervent souls have become even more fervent and very many sinful ones have repented when they heard these souls in love with heaven telling of the marvellous things done within them by the Lord. Do not cease, therefore, you too, to proclaim in a loud voice that what is going on within you is entirely the Lord's work.

Please calm your anxiety as to the nature of the accounts to be settled when you return home (which will certainly be the case in spite of your vain fears), for these accounts are not based on any personal faults. Offer this further curiosity on your part to Jesus and don't worry. As far as you yourself are concerned, try to get well as soon as possible.

I beseech you, moreover, to relieve all anxiety on my part with regard to your health by writing to me more frequently during these days. If you cannot do it yourself, then arrange to have the news reach me through others of whom the Lord will not deprive you.

I would like to continue, Raffaelina, but you know the

---

[3] Tob 12:7.

state I am in at present. Give my very warm regards to your most worthy and respected sister.

May Jesus be with you always.

I leave you in the Lord's holy embrace.

Your servant,
Fra Pio, Capuchin.

P.S. Padre Agostino and others too are praying to Jesus for you continually. Do not forget in your prayers the humble writer of this letter, who feels greatly in need of the divine assistance at present.

87

Pietrelcina, 14 October 1915.

Greetings and good wishes. He thanks her for her news. Suffering with Jesus. "Never so near to Jesus as when we are suffering." He exhorts her to suffer with Jesus. The example of the Midianites. He awaits news.

J.M.J.D.F.C.

Beloved daughter of Jesus,

May the peace of the heavenly Father which surpasses all understanding[1] keep your heart from all stain of sin and enable you to grow more and more in mutual love and charity with your neighbour, in harmony of mind. May the Holy Spirit who is the spirit of light and strength guard your intellect, preserve doctrinal unity and prevent division or schism. May the most holy Virgin assist you and obtain for you all those heavenly aids which will enable you to follow out our vocation in a worthy manner with all humility, meekness and patience. May your Guardian angel make you prompt in preserving the unity and peace of your soul.

The letter which reached me from Giovina at such a solemn moment has comforted me more than a little[2]. I

---

[1] Cf. Phil 4:7.

[2] Her sister Giovina's letter was dated 11 October from Bologna. Padre Pio replied on the 14th. These letters will be published in a future volume of his correspondence.

don't know how to express my gratitude and thanks to God, in the first place, and then to yourself and your excellent sister. May Jesus bless you and enable my letters to bring you the divine consolation that I ardently desire for you.

Ah yes, I know that you will unfortunately go on suffering as long as you live. Job said: *Has not man a hard service upon earth*[3]*?* But trust and love, my dear Raffaelina, put your trust and love in the goodness of our God. You are suffering, but take heart, because this is the lot that falls to those who have chosen the better part in God's service, which is the cross. May the heavenly Father be thanked, therefore, for His infinite mercy in making you so dear to Him by treating you as a chosen soul who is to follow Jesus closely up the steep slopes of Calvary. I behold with joy and deep emotion that grace is treating you like this, beloved daughter of my heart.

Console yourself, I beg of you, in your very affliction, because the Lord's mercy will not be withdrawn from you. If He permits you to be subjected to all kinds of sufferings He does so in order that you may resemble Him in the anguish He endured in the desert, in the Garden and on the Cross. You are suffering, but it is with Jesus and for Jesus. Be convinced, moreover, for I assure you of this and ask you in the name of the good God to calm yourself. In your sufferings you have Jesus Himself at the very centre of your heart and you are not separated or far from the love of this God who is so good.

You who desire to follow Jesus closely, put fear out of your mind and calm your heartbeats, for you are never so close to this most tender Spouse as you are when in the midst of afflictions. Continue to live in the company of this picked militia, remain merged with this noble band and invariably repeat, as ought every good soldier of Christ: *Though a host*

---

[3] Job 7:1.

encamp against me, my heart shall not fear; *though war arise against me, yet will I be confident*[4]. We must not be afraid, Raffaelina, for in this militia of ours there is nothing difficult or arduous, nothing that is impossible. Have we not perhaps read with our own eyes in history how women and even young virgins such as St. Lucy, St. Agnes, St. Agatha, St. Cecilia and very many others suffered the most cruel torments of martyrdom for love of their divine Bridegroom?

To the weakness of their sex was added their tender age, yet they gained the victory in Christ. Lift up, lift up your hearts, let us rise up to the throne of God. Here it is not a matter of fighting with bodily strength, but with the power of the soul. Here one moves forward to victory, not with weapons of steel, but with prayers. Here our faith enables us to endure to the end of the trial.

When the enemy attacks us in life's trials, let us rise up and pray to the Lord to remove and always keep far from us the enemy's kingdom and give us the grace to be received into His own kingdom whenever this is pleasing to Him. May it be pleasing to Him as soon as possible.

Let us not be bewildered, my dear Raffaelina, in the hour of trial. By our perseverance in good works, by our patience in fighting the good fight we shall overcome the insolence of all our enemies. As the divine Master has said, *by your endurance you will gain your lives*,[5] for *trials produce patience and patience brings testing and from the testing springs hope*[6]. Let us follow Jesus along the path of suffering. Let us keep our gaze invariably fixed on the heavenly Jerusalem, and all difficulties that crop up on our journey towards the possession of it will be happily overcome.

Let us stir up our faith to a greater degree, bearing in

---

[4] Ps 27:3.
[5] Lk 21:19.
[6] Jas 1:3.

mind the outstanding victory of the Israelites over the Midianites as placed on record in the sacred writings. In the depth of the night, as we read, while the immense enemy host had come out of their trenches and were encamped on the plain without a suspicion[7], they were silently surrounded by a mere 300 of Gideon's warriors, each holding a trumpet in one hand and a torch enclosed in a water-jar in the other hand. At a sign from the leader the water-jars were smashed and the trumpets blared, while after every trumpet-blast the war-cry went up: "For the Lord and for Gideon."

At this tremendous shout, at the deafening noise of the trumpets and the immense glare of the torches, great terror invaded the enemy camp and all began running wildly around, still drunk with sleep. While the trumpets continued to send forth their dismal sound and the enemy fled headlong in wild confusion, many of them killed each other so that piles of dead were left on the field.

As we have seen, this victory was not gained by the use of arms, but by a singular stratagem of war.

Well, then, we too have to sustain a very hard fight as long as we live. Let us win this war by that unusual stratagem used by Gideon. Let the light of good works go before us in this battle, the strength of the knowledge of God, the ardent desire of God's word. Let us, too, fight to the sound of hymns and psalms and spiritual canticles, by singing and raising our voices loudly to the Lord. Thus will our Lord Jesus make us deserving of the victory, in Him to whom is all glory and power for ever and ever.

I must end here for reasons that are unfortunately well known to you. I urge you to keep calm, for before long, with God's help, you will have passed triumphantly through this present trial. Although I feel a keen desire to have news from you very frequently, I don't want you to sacrifice yourself

[7] Cf. Judg 7:4ff.

for this purpose. I hope your excellent sister, who is so very good, will be willing to continue to send me news.

Thank her most sincerely on my behalf for this.

May Jesus be with you always.

Fra Pio, Capuchin.

88

Bologna, 19 October 1915.

She gives thanks for the success of her operation. On the way to recovery. Consolations. She asks for prayers for her conversion. Her sister also thanks him. Postscript. A visit to the shrine of Our Lady of the Guard.

Jesus alone! Most Holy Spirit, help me!

Father,

We praise thee, O God! On my return to life, I give infinite thanks to our good Jesus who has helped and consoled me lavishly in this painful period. Although I do not by any means deserve it, Jesus makes His love and His infinite mercy shine forth more strongly upon me, His wretched creature.

How am I ever to thank Him? In what way am I to try to repay His kindness? This distresses, torments and discourages me. In addition it obliges me to make reparation for past faults. Just as the able surgeon's knife cut, extracted and got rid of the tumour in my body, so too will the heavenly physician, I hope, root out and remedy the corruption of my heart. My idea is precisely this, that Jesus wanted to reveal to me by my bodily disease the more horrible corruption of my soul. Is that right? What have you to say about it? Speak to me frankly and at length in this regard.

I am in bed as I write. Yesterday I got up for the fourth time, but in the afternoon I went back to bed as the thermometer always shows about one line of fever. The surgeon is not worried about the wound which is healing quickly. Two days ago he took out ten or twelve stitches and this morning he is to remove almost all of them, about twenty. All that remains is a small wound which will close up who knows when and Giovina is worried about this.

We intended to go home this week but it will certainly be next week before we leave. We are hoping in our good Jesus. If only I could face the journey without unfavourable results. Pray. At my first medication, fully conscious for the first time, I wanted to look at the wound and I fainted (how brave I should be if I had to help our poor brothers wounded on the battlefield, cowardly, useless, selfish creature that I am!)

Oh, those medications! I suffer much more from the moral point of view than under the surgeon's instruments. How many humiliations Jesus has permitted! But may his will be done! However, He has given me so very much light and strength and consolation.

First of all, a worthy minister of his came twice to speak to me on my bed of suffering, to speak at great length to me of Jesus, of His sufferings and His love, to bring me His blessing and absolution for my sins. Thank Him very much for me. Tell my good Guardian Angel and the angel whose name I bear to stand in for me.

Then there is a particular nurse who takes care of me (a real angel of goodness, Elisa by name, sent to me certainly by my patron, St. Elizabeth, a grace I do not deserve). She is with me day and night, kind and patient, assisting me with scrupulous attention. We should like to take her home with us to serve us. She would really be the right person for us and for our home, especially now that I am no longer able to do what I have been doing up to the present and must be very careful for fear of reproduction of the growth. However, Elisa does not want to come as she is very attached to Bologna, her city, and to her nursing career. Pray that Jesus may inspire and counsel her to satisfy us. He has granted us so very many graces during this storm, but, poor Jesus, how badly He has been repaid!

I still have a great many things to tell you, but for the moment I cannot do this as I feel very tired. I am tied up and swathed in bandages and am very intolerant of all this. I can bear nothing at all, I'm always complaining and am unwilling to suffer. The burning thirst I endured for two days and two nights, the slight pain in my left side and shoulder and all my small sufferings ought to have made me think of Jesus' indescribable pains and made me endure my own with resignation and love, but instead... Pray all the time for my conversion.

Giovina thanks you for everything, always grateful to you, good Father, for the holy words you wrote to her. She is really quite well. Pray, pray hard for her stomach trouble, that Jesus may rid her of it permanently.

Write me a long letter at the usual address: Via Dante, 16.

I kiss your hand while asking your holy blessing.

Your poor tertiary.

P.S. My Giovina has just returned from the church of the friars Minor where she went for confession and Communion, which she had promised in thanksgiving for the success of my operation. On the Saturday previous to my entry to the nursing-home we went together, accompanied by that good lady Giustina, to the famous shrine of Our Lady of the Guard and St. Luke. There at Our Lady's feet, Giovina promised to return and to receive Holy Communion as soon as I was on the road to recovery. She has decided to go tomorrow morning to carry out her promise, again with good Giustina, with our cousin and our friend from Modena (in whose house we stayed last year) who had come to see us. She'll send you a postcard from the shrine.

Pray to Jesus that He may inspire us where to go this winter, as we have received a letter of refusal from the good nuns in San Remo. May Jesus arrange things for our spiritual good and also for the good of our very unfortunate bodies. Pray.

89

Pietrelcina, 21 October 1915.

Good wishes. He exhorts her to spiritual calm. The example of St. Thérèse of the Child Jesus. The trial must be accepted. Greetings for her name-day.

J.M.J.D.F.C

Beloved daughter of the heavenly Father,

May Jesus continue with His divine charism, may He increase more and more your thirst for His heavenly love to the point of complete satiation. May He enable it to be shared by all those whose names, through His divine mercy and their own response, are written in the book of eternal life! Amen.

I am replying at once to your last letter, which I have awaited anxiously with indescribable emotion. I thank you, my child, on Jesus' behalf, for the sacrifice you have made in giving me news of yourself. And since you see that Jesus is so good as to allow you all this, I would like to ask you and I greatly desire you not to torment your soul so much.

I know you have reasons for doing so. But tell me, is it possible that Jesus is far away when you are calling and praying and seeking Him and, let us even say, when you possess Him? Is it possible that one who is with Him on the cross, can it be possible, I say, that God is not present in that soul, when He has committed Himself by His infallible word to be with that soul in the time of tribulation? *I will be with him in trouble*[1]. How is it possible that the fountain of living water which issues from the divine Heart should be far from a soul that rushes to it like a thirsty hart? It is true that this soul may also fail to believe it because it feels continually consumed by an unquenchable and insatiable thirst. But what of that? Does this, perhaps, go to show that the soul does not possess God? Quite the opposite.

This happens because the soul has not yet reached the end of its journey and is not yet totally immersed in the eternal fountain of His divine love, which will happen in the kingdom of glory. Let us therefore love to quench our thirst at this fountain of living water and go forward all the time along the way of divine love. But let us also be convinced, my daughter, that our souls will never be satisfied here below. In fact it would be disastrous for us if, at a certain stage of our journey, we were to feel satisfied, for it would be a sign that we thought we had reached our goal and in this we would be deceived.

I therefore urge you in the charity of Christ to make sure you calm your anxiety by drinking at the fountain of divine love, which you must do by faith and trust, by humility and submission to God's will. The Venerable Sister Thérèse of the Child Jesus says: "I am a little soul. I choose neither to live nor to die, but may Jesus do as He pleases with me"[2]. Here, daughter, is the example of a soul completely stripped of self and filled with God! This is precisely what you also must strive to become with the divine assistance.

Don't be distrustful in this respect, for Jesus is in your soul and if you show yourself docile to His action you will certainly achieve it. I understand, however, that the anxiety of a soul all on fire for its divine Lover often becomes uncon-

---

[1] Ps 91:15.

[2] The last two paragraphs, with the quotation from Sister Thérèse of the Child Jesus, are found almost exactly in the letter written by Padre Agostino to Padre Pio on 13 October 1915. Cf. *Letters*, Vol. I, No. 292.

trollable, but don't be scared by this. Just give free vent to this longing for Jesus and let yourself be guided by His love.

I give warmest thanks to the divine Father for having given me the grace to receive news from you, news that was most gratifying. May infinite praise be rendered to this most tender Father of ours who distresses us by sending us fresh crosses, whether to test us or to purify us more and more. He is very quick to make us feel His fatherly tenderness even in the midst of suffering! Rejoice, then, when you find yourself in the midst of sufferings, because you are never so pleasing to God as you are when surrounded by tribulation. Moreover, ought a follower of the Nazarene perhaps desire a better lot on earth?

I am persuaded and convinced that what has happened to you in this latest trial has all been for God's glory and the spiritual benefit of yourself and others. Yes, my daughter, the present trial is for me a guarantee that the Lord has wanted, so to speak, to exhibit His love for you. Wasn't it He who endowed you with the strength and patience to bear cheerfully this very harsh trial? Have courage, I tell you once more, for there is one who is watching over you and protecting you. You have climbed the steep hill with the cross on your shoulders. Just one more step and you will have planted it on the summit.

I would like to go on, but my strength fails me, so I am reluctantly compelled to stop. Before ending, though, I wish you every happiness in the Lord on your beautiful name-day. May our good Jesus accept the prayers which I will offer with great fervour during these days. Meanwhile, do not forget me in Jesus' presence, knowing as you do how much my soul needs His assistance in such a spiritual combat.

Give my most respectful regards to your excellent sister and in the meantime don't be stingy with news about yourself.

May Jesus be always with you.

Fra Pio.

90

Foggia, 2 November 1915.

Padre Pio is called up to the army. News of her health. She thanks him for name-day greetings.

Jesus alone! Most Holy Spirit, help me!

Father,

This morning good Francesca brought me a piece of bad news, namely, that our holy Padre Pio has to report on the 6th for a medical examination for the army.

I got a very great shock but calmed myself immediately when I thought of the assurance your own holy father gave me last March, when he told me it would be impossible for them to accept you in view of your obviously serious illness. Hence I am tranquil and quite reassured in view of what Padre Agostino, so wise and learned a person, has told me. Do you agree?

I have also calmed Francesca, but we have not ceased praying for this intention, for yourself and all the other good fathers.

Don't worry, for you are a soldier of Christ and you are serving your country by your prayers, your tears and your sacrifices. Be at peace, for Jesus will ward off every threat and all evil from the head of His minister and friend. Write to me soon and tell me the result of the medical examination.

What am I to say of my own poor health? Last Monday, the 25th, we returned home after a ten-hour journey which went fairly well for me. Imagine the sad surprise of Rosinella and all my relatives and friends when they saw me in this state and heard the unpleasant story.

I am still suffering slightly, but this is of no importance as long as my Giovina is no longer suffering from her stomach trouble. Some time ago I asked Jesus for an exchange. Has He granted it to me? If only this were a fact! Is that a sin? Tell me and do not forget it.

I thank you for your good wishes. Your precious letter reached me in Bologna shortly before we went to the station. Among the many good wishes which reached me here I found a really beautiful letter from good Padre Agostino. He tells me that he will come here on the 8th or 9th of this month, so I am expecting him next week. I have so many things to tell him! If I could only speak to you in this way! But Jesus will not grant me this grace because I am so very wicked! What must I do to move Jesus to consent to this? Advise me what to do and do not forget it.

I'll write you a long letter later. I am waiting until you are quiet and free from all worry.

Please reply to me without delay at the usual address: Via Manzoni, Foggia.

Pray for Giovina, Rosinella and Francesca all the time. Continue to be concerned about my conversion.

I kiss your right hand with profound respect.

Your poor tertiary.

91

Pietrelcina, 4 November 1915.

The medical examination for the army. Relations between the two sisters.

J.M.J.D.F.C.

Beloved daughter of Jesus,

May the grace of the heavenly Father fashion your soul continually and make it worthy of ever greater charisms. Amen.

I give infinite thanks to the Lord for your very happy return home. May it please him to enable you to live many holy days for His glory and the sanctification of yourself and others. My departure is now only two days off and I feel quite strong spiritually as I face up to this fresh trial to which Jesus through His sheer goodness intends to subject me. I do not know what awaits me, for Jesus wants to keep me in the dark about this. It is a sign that this is best for me, and may He be ever blessed of it!

You have said some beautiful things about this examination. May our most sweet Jesus in His infinite mercy grant the prayers you and others are sending up for this intention. When I look into my heart in all truth I can almost tell you already that the enemy of salvation is plotting a grievous and painful surprise for me. Among the army doctors, especially in my recruiting centre, there is little or no humanity. My illness is evident enough to everybody and is generally recognized, but I repeat that I am afraid and perhaps a painful surprise awaits me. May the most merciful God shield me from this thunderbolt, not so much for my own sake but for the sake of my poor parents who would precede me and go down into the grave before me and before their time.

I am expecting favourable results of the matter in question through the fervent prayers of yourself and others. Pray, then, implore and—I was about to add—pester the divine Heart and the most holy Virgin of Pompeii so that all may be well and may lead to a holy conclusion. And in order to be certain to make God in His divine mercy propitious towards us, make some promise or vow to Him with the firm resolution of fulfilling it when all has ended happily.

This is all I ask you to do in return for the fatherly affection I have for you before God and for all I am doing, unworthily, to lead you to perfection. I understand quite well that I am now asking you too much in the name of the love which binds both of us to Him, but do not doubt, daughter, that if I myself am unable to reward you adequately, there is one who will repay you two hundredfold for each holy act you perform.

I ask you not to worry about what you have done in God's sight with regard to your excellent sister, Giovina. The Lord has accepted the joint offerings we made Him and in a very different manner from what we intended. What pains me, however, is the fact that you only thought of informing me on this matter when you had already acted. In order to avoid being deceived in actions which appear holy, you ought, on the contrary, to seek the opinion of the one who has charge of you. Do you understand? Hence what you have not done in the past you must do now and thus make up for all the rest.

Don't tell me this time also that I am too demanding in a matter which to an ignorant person would appear negligible. Jesus who reads the depths of the heart knows whether of not I am too pretentious in this.

Wait for the result of my medical examination.

Give my respects to your excellent sister and to our common father, Padre Agostino.

I take leave of you all in the Lord's embrace. Remind them of my need and let them not cease praying.

Fra Pio, Capuchin.

92

Pietrelcina, 5 December 1915.

Military service in Naples. "A most harsh trial." A request for prayers.

J.M.J.D.F.C.

Beloved daughter of the heavenly Father,

May the grace of the divine Spirit always reign supreme in your soul and may it guide you to greater Christian perfection. Amen.

I refrain from telling you about my situation, both because I lack the strength to do it and because you have already heard all from our very dear Padre Agostino. Tomorrow, 6 December, I have to leave for Naples as I have been assigned to the Tenth Medical Corps.

My daugther, I cannot stand up to this very harsh trial to which I am being subjected. By a pure miracle I have been sustained up to this moment, but for the future? Alas, I can no longer lay claim to this! I yearn for the moment when I shall be released from this extremely dark prison, and may it be as soon as possible.

All I ask from the divine mercy of the Lord is that He may not allow His servant to depart for a better land with this two-edged sword piercing his heart, by which I mean my twofold exile.

Together with all those who are united with me in the bond of Christ's charity, my daughter, keep me company by asking insistently for what I myself am asking. In the meantime I want you and good Francesca, Annita and all the others who are dear to me to start at once for me the three novenas to the Virgin of Pompeii, by reciting daily the entire Rosary and by frequent Communion, which I earnestly hope will be every morning.

Thank your beloved sister on my behalf for the news she sent me. I appreciate immensely the picture of your own beautiful Virgin which you sent me. May Jesus reward you.

I end here, my dear Raffaelina, because I can go on no longer. May Jesus always console you.

Give my greetings to all.

Fra Pio.

P.S. I'll write to you as soon as I can from Naples.

93

Naples, 13 December 1915.

In the army. His first news from Naples. Physical and moral sufferings. A request for prayers.

J.M.J.D.F.C.

Beloved daughter of the heavenly Father,

May your heart always be the living temple of the Holy Spirit. Amen.

Since the 6th of this month I have been here in Naples for the reasons of which you are aware. From the very first day I applied for a medical examination. The request was granted and on the day which is sacred to Mary Immaculate I reported to the commanding lieutenant for this purpose. He questioned me as to my ailments and when I told him, he was very sympathetic about my most unfortunate state of health. Then, either to avoid taking responsibility or for other reasons, he sent me back for a second examination to the captain-doctor. But by bad luck or good, this doctor has not yet examined me and he keeps putting me off from one day to the next.

What is to become of me? My daughter, I feel I am dying. There are moments when it seems to me that my life is coming to a standstill. You could never have even the remotest idea of what I am suffering physically and morally. I just don't feel I have the strength to go on living. My stomach will retain no food. It refuses everything except the sacred species. Blessed be Jesus who in the midst of so much torment and suffering remains alone in me and rules me.

I point out to you that they have not yet made me put on a military uniform and I thank heaven that until I have had the medical examination I am allowed to eat out and to sleep in a hotel on my own. The fact remains, though, that in these sad times no amount of money is sufficient to carry on, especially in this big city of Naples.

Pray more insistently, daughter, to the most compassionate Heart of Jesus that He may be pleased to put an end to this most harsh trial. I expect to be treated with this same charity, through the benevolent influence of yourself, of excellent Francesca, of most pious Annita and of all those others who love Jesus and whose names are written in my heart. Pray, all of you, and don't fail to do in charity what I asked you in my last letter, dated the 5th of this month. I promise you that if the Lord grants me this grace it won't be long before we meet.

Carry on in all tranquillity yourself, for Jesus is with you and you love Him. Write me a long letter and tell me everything you want. This will give me immense pleasure.

My regards to Giovina, Francesca, Rosina, Annita and all those who love Jesus.

I leave you in the Lord's holy embrace.

Fra Pio, Capuchin.

P.S. Here is the address: Francesco Forgione, c/o Maria Vallillo, Via Cappuccinelle, 18, Naples.

94

Foggia, 15 December 1915.

Influence to have him declared unfit. One of her household is ill.

Most Holy Spirit, help me! Jesus alone!

Good Father,

Just a couple of lines in haste to let you know about an idea that came to me last night, the idea of writing about your pitiful situation to the daughter of my landlady in Casamicciola, a close and faithful friend of mine, Giuseppina Morgera. She may perhaps be in Naples at her aunt's home, at the Conservatory of San Nicola a Nilo.

She is a kind soul, a spouse of Jesus, of whom I told you in one of my letters. Her confessor is the Vicar of Cardinal Prisco, Father Antonio Lavano. The high position he covers can give him great influence if he puts in a strong word for you and takes a bit of trouble to have you declared unfit by your superiors without delay. In a word, he can be of the greatest possible use to you. However, I have asked Giuseppina to go to see you first in Via Cappuccinelle and to speak to you in order to come to an agreement as to how to go about the matter. With her great zeal for the benefit of her neighbour, she will get busy with her confessor to have you obtain the freedom you desire. Do you approve of my plan?

I am writing to you in haste so that you may know in advance about her visit. I hope my letter, sent off this morning, will find Giuseppina in good health and that it will reach her without fail at the Conservatory in Naples. If she has returned home nothing can be done and all my efforts will have been in vain.

Since you failed the first time, I hope you will be more fortunate the second time. I have had no news from you since October, when you wrote for my name-day. Let's hope for the best, trusting always in the merciful Heart of our good Father.

What a storm I am going through! Good Francesca is dying, the only person who understood me and to whom I confided all my thoughts, my worries, my tears. I am left spiritually alone. There is a boundless void in and around me, great desolation in my soul and I have begun again to have troubled sleepless nights which seem eternal.

Wrench this grace from the Most Sacred Heart of Jesus. He can do all things. I commend very earnestly to your prayers this beautiful holy soul... I no longer feel capable of reasoning. After only two weeks of sickness and not to see her even at the last. Pray for me.

St. Francis has sent me, moreover, a nice caress. Jesus permits everything. May He be blessed and loved for ever!

I kiss your right hand and ask you to pray all the time for,

Your poor tertiary.

P.S. You will have received by now a very long letter from me. Answer me when you can. I want to know the result of this new effort of mine.

95

Naples, 17 December 1915[1].

Convalescent leave. He gives thanks. He is very weak. His return home.

J.M.J.D.F.C.

My dear Raffaelina,

Thanks be to God. This very morning I had the collegial medical examination and since they recognized my illness, infection of the lungs, I have been granted a year's convalescent leave.

Let us therefore thank the goodness of the heavenly Father. Yesterday evening I received your most kind letter and God alone knows what balm it brought to my very dejected soul.

Forgive me if I write very briefly, as I am feeling extremely weak. Don't be afraid of anything in the meantime, for Jesus is with you. Write me a long letter at home if you want to do something I'll deeply appreciate.

I am more than a little grieved to hear of Francesca's illness, but let us be consoled, for it is an illness which leads to well-being.

---

[1] A picture postcard showing a pretty spray of ivy.

Please convey my respects and my thanks to all for what they have done for me.

May Jesus be with you always.

Fra Pio, Capuchin.

96

Pietrelcina, 21 December 1915.

He thanks Raffaelina and others. "Be imitators of me." It was impossible to reach Foggia on his return journey. He meets Giuseppina Morgera. It was God alone who solved his problem.

J.M.J.D.F.C.

Beloved daughter of the heavenly Father,

May Jesus be always with you, may He sustain you in all the trials which He sends you out of sheer goodness and may He fulfil in you His holy will for your salvation and for the salvation of all the other souls He wants to save! Amen.

At last we can sing the *Te Deum*. Our most compassionate Lord has shown me mercy and I am deeply convinced that He has been compelled to do all this because you and the others have pestered Him too much with your prayers. I therefore return infinite thanks in the first place to the Father of mercies and then to yourself and all the others who have obtained such a grace for me.

I don't intend to waste words in thanking you, both because you do not want it and because it might appear to be excessive flattery. However, in the sight of God I feel greatly obliged to you and to others and I can therefore do nothing else but work in the Lord's vineyard with greater ardour for your perfection and for that of all those whom the Lord is pleased to send me. What better occupation could there be than this, my daughter? I know of nothing better.

Accompany me continually, then, by your prayers that the divine Shepherd may give me what is lacking to me. Ask Him to give me the holiness of life that I lack. Oh, if only I could say at least once with the apostle of the nations, raising my voice to tell everybody: *Be imitators of me as I am of Christ*[1]. But alas, everything is lacking to me and I expect all things from your insistent prayers and those of others to the Heart of God.

Every minister of the Lord ought to work continually for the good of souls. He ought never admit weariness and never say: "I have worked too hard for the souls of others." This is the image of the genuine Catholic priest. Can I say that I am like this without fear of lying? Alas, I know myself only too well. I occupy a place in the Lord's house which is of no benefit to others and may God forbid that I should even be the ruin of other souls. It is true that in my own little way I do my best for the good of those souls whom the Lord enables me to meet, but I am convinced that I am of little or no use to them. May the Lord assist me in the fulfilment of my duty.

After quite a long apprenticeship, which I found very hard, I got back here at last on Saturday night, more dead than alive. But may the Lord be thanked for ever! It was my intention, Raffaelina, on my return trip from Naples to travel as far as Foggia in order to see you personally and to thank you all. But the Lord arranged things differently. I should undoubtedly have been unable to reach Foggia without endangering my life. Let us hope in the Lord, then, that He will keep this fresh consolation for me until a more suitable occasion presents itself before I am called to His embrace.

---

[1] 1 Cor 4:16; 11:1.

On Saturday itself, when I returned to the hotel (from the hospital to which I had gone that morning to have my permit signed), I learned from the owner of the place that poor Giuseppina had just left after a long wait[2]. The lady also told me she had left word that we could meet the following day at a certain hour. But I was due to leave that same evening. I was quite sorry not to have been able to make her acquaintance and from the few things the hotel-keeper told me in a rather confused way, I understood that poor Giuseppina also needed some spiritual food.

I should have been remorseful if I had left without going to see her, but where was I to look for her? The address Giuseppina had given orally to the hotel-keeper was by no means exact, but conscience told me not to leave without bringing some spiritual relief to that soul. So I took a guide with me and after I had done a lot of walking and questioning, thank heaven I was able to see her. What an innocent soul! We remained together for quite a while, speaking of spiritual things. Then I was reluctantly obliged to leave her as I had to catch my train. I went away happy, however, knowing I had left her in a much happier state of mind.

Jesus had willed to take up my problem all on His own and to bring it to a happy conclusion without the intervention of any human being. But this does not set a limit to my gratitude to your excellent sister and indeed I am only too greatly obliged to her. You have lost no merit on this account.

I desire very much to have immediate news of our very dear Francesca[3].

---

[2] Giuseppina Morgera, born in Casamiccicla 1 January 1885 and deceased in Genoa (Don Orione Institute) 27 July 1974. Some letters written by Padre Pio to this lady have been kept and will be published in a future volume. See Letters 72 and 78.

[3] On 20 December Padre Agostino wrote to Padre Pio: "Some days ago I learned that Francesca of Foggia, that good soul, was at death's door. I don't know how she is at present. Have you heard anything? May Jesus

I end by wishing you every happiness for the feasts of the heavenly Child.

Fra Pio.

---

help and bless that poor soul. May he also console Raffaelina, who has nobody who understands her so well and with whom she can speak so freely" (*Letter*, Vol. I, No. 306. In his letter of 23 December (*ibid*. No. 307) he speaks of Francesca's death.

97

Pietrelcina, 30 December 1915.

Good wishes. "Too rash in passing judgment." A moral picture of her servant Francesca. The meaning of holiness. He disapproves of her plan for a trip to Naples. His stay in Pietrelcina.

J.M.J.D.F.C.

Beloved daughter of Jesus,

May the most sweet Child Jesus bring you every grace and blessing, all the favours that are pleasing to His infinite goodness. May His most holy Mother also load you with every good thing and make you ever more worthy of eternal glory. Amen.

With trembling hand I hasten to pen these very few lines so as to avoid being accused once more of forgetting you, which is equivalent to neglecting your perfection and sanctification. You are unequalled and too rash in passing judgment! But I have no intention of complaining about this to you and God knows if I am telling the truth.

I heard of our very dear Francesca's departure for the heavenly homeland before you told me about it[1]. I shed a

[1] There is frequent mention of this Francesca in the correspondence. We intend to deal with this in a future volume of Padre Pio's letters.

lot of tears at the loss of such a precious, not to say rare existence. These tears were and are being shed solely because of the not inconsiderable loss the Church militant has suffered by her death. An immense sense of veneration surges over me at the thought of this departed one and almost without my being aware of it I feel induced to kneel down as if before a sacred image. Holiness shone forth from her and made her the most perfect and most lovable image of God.

You whose enviable lot it was to draw near to this truly holy soul will agree with what I have said about her. How many times when you were close to her, when you heard her speak and considered the way she acted and all that she was, have you not forgotten all about yourself, felt small and wretched and experienced a strange sense of admiration, veneration and joy which cannot be put into words? How often, I say, when you were beside her have you not felt closer to God and an indefinable need to become better?

She has now disappeared from our bodily sight but let us make her live on within us by imitating her in the practice of virtue and holiness. Let us remember or rather let us keep before our minds what goes to make up real holiness. Holiness means getting above ourselves, it means perfect mastery of all our passions. It means having real and continual contempt for ourselves and for the things of the world to the point of preferring poverty rather than wealth, humiliation rather than glory, suffering rather than pleasure. Holiness means loving our neighbour as ourself for love of God. In this connection holiness means loving those who curse us, who hate and persecute us, and even doing good to them. Holiness means living humbly, being disinterested, prudent, just, patient, kind, chaste, meek, diligent, carrying out one's duties for no other reason than that of pleasing God and receiving from Him alone the reward we deserve.

Briefly, Raffaelina, holiness contains in itself the power

to transform a man into God, according to the language of the holy books.

The person we loved so much and who has now disappeared holds up to us the finest example of holiness.

As regards the plan you conceived of going to Naples for the purposes of which you informed me, I want to tell you quite clearly that I cannot approve of it. I decline to take any responsibility for it before God and my conscience. Think well before you carry out this plan.

I want you to tell me how you can say that it is the will of Jesus for me to settle in Foggia. Please be quite sincere in this regard and tell me everything. I want you to know, moreover, that the fact of being obliged to live outside the cloister saddens my whole life. In this matter I have never relied on my own judgment. I have explained my case to learned persons who are enlightened as to God's ways and they have replied that in view of my exceptional situation and taking everything into consideration, I cannot venture to live in the cloister without directly attempting suicide.

Raffaelina, I am anxious to leave this exile without delay, but I do not want to go even a second before it pleases God, much less depart with sin and remorse in my soul.

Let us pray fervently to the Lord to change my situation.

I wrote a long time ago to Annita[2] but so far there has been no reply. What has become of her?

I end here as I feel I am dying.

May Jesus be with you always.

Fra Pio.

P.S. In order to set my conscience at rest I want to tell you that I said Mass for you on the 22nd of November. Has the prayer been answered?

---

[2] The orphan from Foggia, the Cerase sisters' seamstress.

98

Consoling counsels from Jesus to a holy and privileged soul[1].

"She must never neglect to satiate herself with the food of the angels.

"The temptations she will receive from the enemy will be many, for he is not unaware of the benefit her soul receives from this food. But she must not be frightened by any means. Jesus promises that He will not cease to assist her.

"Let her despise the snares of those impure apostates and with boundless trust sit down in the shadow of the divine Bridegroom, fearing nothing. Lucifer's burning rays will not penetrate the shade of such a tree. Her soul must not fear to be browned by those rays which want to wither it up, for they will make her proceed on her way with ever greater respect and love. Thus, where the devil would like to harm her, he causes her, instead, to earn new treasures for paradise.

"Jesus wants her all for Himself. Let her stir up her faith, then, and throw herself with sublime abandonment into the arms of God and God will carry out the plans He has for her.

---

[1] These "counsels", copied by Padre Agostino, were delivered by hand to Raffaelina in an envelope. We reproduce them here because we believe Padre Pio gave them to her for the good of her soul.

"Let her also drive far from her mind those useless fears she has that her frequent confession is not pleasing to God, for these fears are a sheer waste of time. Do your very best, then Jesus will perfect this work and be glorified by it.

"The interior pains she is enduring at present are many.

"Let her also drive far from her mind those useless fears she has that her frequent confession is not pleasing to God, for these fears are a sheer waste of time. Do your very best, then Jesus will perfect this work and be glorified by it.
to raise her up.

"This is the path by which Jesus leads strong souls. Here she will gain a better knowledge of our true homeland and will come to see the present life as a brief pilgrimage. Here she will learn to rise above all created things and to put the world beneath her feet. She will acquire admirable strength to carry a cross that is very heavy for a soul that belongs to God alone, that is, the boredom and extreme tediousness caused by everything here below.

"However, our sweet Jesus will not leave her in this state without consoling her.

"Praise and blessing to this God of goodness!"

A special prayer is asked for the one who gave these counsels and for the one who wrote them.

INDEX

ANALYTICAL INDEX

CHRONOLOGICAL INDEX OF LETTERS

For additional copies of this book write to:

Editions
"Padre Pio da Pietrelcina"
Our Lady of Grace Capuchin Friary
71013 San Giovanni Rotondo (FG) Italy
Tel. 0882.417294 - Tel./Fax 0882.457584
Internet: www.vocedipadrepio.com
padre.gerardo@vocedipadrepio.com
postulazione@vocedipadrepio.com

Australia Padre Pio Centre of Australia Bro. Michael O'Dwyer, OFMCap., Capuchin Friary, Po Box 153, Leichhardt, N.S.W. 2040

Mr. and Mrs. Paul MacLeod, 2 Hawthorn Ave, Belmont, Geelong, Victoria 3216 - Tel. (0352) 438304 Fax (0352) 438105.

Canada Padre Pio Capuchin Centre A/S Joseph Lancia Grilli, 8964, Place de Louresse, Anjou (Quebec) H1j-1V8 Tel. (514) 352-1077.

England Padre Pio Information Centre Stella Lilley, Kingsdown Park House, Tankerton, Whitstable, Kent CT5 2DF Tel. (01227) 274050 - Fax (01227) 276136. Website: www.cnt.co.uk/padrepio

Padre Pio Bookshop - Mrs. Kathy Kelly, 264 Vauxhall Bridge Rd., Victoria, London SWIV 1EJ Tel. (0171) 834-5363.

Please note that cheques and postal orders sent to the Padre Pio Centres in the U.K. (Kent or Glasgow) must be made payable to "Padre Pio Information Centre" or P.P.I.C.

North India Padre Pio Capuchin Centre - Krist Jyoti, C-2/36-A, Yamuna Vihar, Delhi 110053 - Tel. (011) 2266760.

South India Padre Pio Capuchin Information Centre S.F.O. Office, Capuchin Social Centre, 3 William's Rd, Tiruchi 620001 - Tel. (0431) 415812 - Fax (0431) 414071 - E-mail: udhayam@eth.net

Ireland Irish Office for Padre Pio Mrs. Eileen Maguire, 58 Dufferin Ave., S.C. Rd., Dublin 8 - Tel. (01) 4536359 Fax (01) 4546503 - Website: www.padrepio.ie

Padre Pio Repository - Mr. and Mrs. Sean Mulrine, 101 Templegrove, Derry Tel. (2871) 265926.

Malta Padre Pio Information Centre Mrs. Tessie Scerri, 25 Pietro Floriani St., Floriana - Tel. (00356) 231446 - Fax (00356) 245528.

Philippines Philippines Centre for Padre Pio - 188 E. Rodriquez Jr. Avenue - Libis, Quezon City, Metro Manila 1110 - Tel. (632) 6343668 - Fax (632) 6343669.

Scotland Scottish Centre for Padre Pio Kay & Eric Dick - 10 Sutherland Ave., Bearsden G61 3JR - Tel. (0141) 947771 E-mail: alvijopio@netscapeonline.co.uk.
Mr. and Mrs. Wm. Davidson - 75 Lamington Road, Glasgow G52 2SE Tel. 883-9297.

USA National Centre for Padre Pio, Inc. - Mrs. Vera M. Calandra, 2213 Old Route 100, Barto, Pa 19504 - Tel. (610) 845-3000 - Fax (610) 845-2666.
E-mail: ncfpp@earthlink.net - Website: www.ncfpp.com.
Please note that this office in Barto, PA, is a Federal tax exempt organization for residents of the USA.

BOOKS, BOOKLETS AND VIDEOS

BIOGRAPHIES

Everybody's Cyrenean
by Fr. Alessandro of Ripabottoni, OFMCap. The Cause biography.
€ 16.00 - $ 15.00 - £ 10.00

His Early Years
by Fr. Augustine Mc Gregor, O.C.S.O. A documented study of the Padre.
€ 5.00 - $ 4.60 - £ 3.00

A Biographical Sketch
by Edward White. A synthesis of Padre Pio's life with testimonials.
€ 2.00 - $ 1.85 - £ 1.20

A View of Padre Pio from Mary Pyle's House
by Geraldine Nolan. Recollections connected with Mary Pyle.
€ 6.00 - $ 5.50 - £ 3.70

Mary Pyle
by Bonaventura Massa, OFMCap. A more complete study of the Franciscan tertiary.
€ 7.00 - $ 6.50 - £ 4.30

WRITINGS

Padre Pio of Pietrelcina, Letters I
The correspondence between Padre Pio and his spiritual directors.
€ 16.00 - $ 15.00 - £ 10.00

Letters II
Padre Pio's direction of a Spiritual daughter (direction suitable to everyone).
€ 13.00 - $ 12.00 - £ 8.00

Letters III
Padre Pio's direction to different spiritual children.
€ 16.00 - $ 15.00 - £ 10.00

Padre Pio Counsels
Collection of maxims, words of wisdom and advice.
€ 2.00 - $ 1.85 - £ 1.20

Have a Good Day
A thought of Padre Pio for every day.
€ 6.00 - $ 5.50 - £ 3.70

DEVOTIONAL

Way of the Cross
Meditations with excerpts from Padre Pio's writings on the Cross.
€ 3.00 - $ 2.75 - £ 1.90
The Prayer Book
A collection of favourite prayers, the Way of the Cross and prayers at Mass.
€ 8.00 - $ 7.50 - £ 5.00

FOR CHILDREN

A Child's Story
by Paul Mandina . A pocket-size edition with drawings in colour.
€ 3.00 - $ 2.75 - £ 1.90
Francesco Forgione Becomes Padre Pio
His life up to 1918 (with cartoon illustrations).
€ 8.00 - $ 7.50 - £ 5.00

MISCELLANEOUS

The Great Sufferer
by Fr. Alessandro da Ripabottoni, OFMCap. A small booklet on the big theme of suffering in our lives.
€ 3.00 - $ 2.75 - £ 1.90
God's Grace Through Padre Pio's Intercession
A collection of graces granted through Padre Pio's intercession.
€ 13.00 - $ 12.00 - £ 8.00
Padre Pio's Mass
by Fr. Tarcisio of Cervinara, OFMCap. Many things Padre Pio said about his Mass.
€ 3.00 - $ 2.75 - £ 1.90

The Mysteries of the Rosary and Padre Pio
by Fr. Pietro Tartaglia, OFMCap. Homilies on the mysteries of the Rosary with thoughts of Padre Pio.
€ 6.00 - $ 5.50 - £ 3.70

The Mystery of the Cross in Padre Pio
by Fr. Gerardo Di Flumeri, OFMCap. A glimpse into the mystery of the Cross that was the centre of the Padre's life.
€ 3.00 - $ 2.75 - £ 1.90

On the Road with Padre Pio
by Stella Maris Lilley. The experiences of 25 years, travelling around England, Scotland, Wales and Ireland, talking about Padre Pio.
€ 11.00 - $ 10.00 - £ 6.75

Padre Pio of Pietrelcina
by Fr. Alberto D'Apolito, OFMCap. Memories, experiences and testimonies gathered by a local Capuchin over many years.
€ 13.00 - $ 12.00 - £ 8.00

Jack of All Trades
by Padre Pellegrino Funicelli, OFMCap. Enjoyable reading of personal experiences shared with Padre Pio.
€ 13.00 - $ 12.00 - £ 8.00

Homage to padre Pio
Based on Pope Paul's words. With many photos in colour.
€ 3.00 - $ 2.75 - £ 1.90

"Send Me Your Guardian Angel"
by Fr. Alessio Parente, OFMCap. A book on P. Pio and Guardian Angels.
€ 8.00 - $ 7.50 - £ 5.00

The Holy Souls
by Fr. Alessio Parente, OFMCap. About the holy souls in Purgatory and Padre Pio.
€ 8.00 - $ 7.50 - £ 5.00

Guides to Pietrelcina and S. Giovanni Rotondo
Handy, pocket-size booklets, with colour photos.
(each) **€ 2.00 - $ 1.85 - £ 1.20**

The Devil in Padre's Life
by Fr. Tarcisio of Cervinara OFMCap. Documented examples from the Padre's writings.
€ 5.00 - $ 4.60 - £ 3.00
Padre Pio's Prayer Life
by Fr. Gerardo di Flumeri - Gennaro Preziuso. Insight into the Padre's prayer life.
€ 5.00 - $ 4.60 - £ 3.00

VIDEOS

The Marked Man
An introduction to the life of Padre Pio.
€ 16.00 - $ 15.00 - £ 10.00
At Heaven's Gates
Ceremony of canonization process. Testimonies of healing. Padre Alessio celebrates Mass.
€ 16.00 - $ 15.00 - £ 10.00
Way of the Cross
Father Alessio guides us along the Way of the Cross of the Shrine.
€ 16.00 - $ 15.00 - £ 10.00
Pray, Hope & Don't Worry
Summary of Padre Pio's life and includes Pope John Paul II's visit to the shrine.
€ 16.00 - $ 15.00 - £ 10.00
I Can Refuse No One
Padre Pio's life, development around his tomb and testimonies.
€ 16.00 - $ 15.00 - £ 10.00
Beatification video
The video of the Pope's Eucharist. Includes the miracle, Padre Pio's Mass, Pietrelcina, the Padre's stigmata, comments of friars and devotees. (30 minutes).
€ 16.00 - $ 15.00 - £ 10.00

THE VOICE OF PADRE PIO

"The Voice of Padre Pio" is published by OUR LADY OF GRACE CAPUCHIN FRIARY, San Giovanni Rotondo.

The journal is published in five languages. The English language edition is bimonthly and costs $ 14.00 USA; $ 21.00 Canada; € 15.00 Ireland; £ 9.00 England and $ 25.00 Australia.

Finished printing
in October 2002
by GERCAP Printers, S.r.l.
Foggia, Italy

1. Padre Pio of Pietrelcina at his desk.

2. Padre Pio in 1911.

3. The servant of God in 1919.

4. Pietrelcina, Padre Pio's birthplace.

5. Foggia, St. Anne's Capuchin church and friary.

6. Pietrelcina: the Castle zone, where the house of Padre Pio's birth is located.

7. Raffaelina Cerase (1868-1916).

8. Padre Pio of Pietrelcina (1887-1968).

MARE ADRIATICO
MAR LIGURE
Golfo di Genova
MARE TIRRENO
MEDITERRANEO
MAR JONIO
CORSICA
SARDEGNA
SICILIA
BASILICATA
TOSCANA
UMBRIA
LOMBARDIA
EMILIA ROMAGNA
MILANO
TORINO
GENOVA
LA SPEZIA
LIVORNO
FIRENZE
BOLOGNA
VENEZIA
PADOVA
ROMA
NAPOLI
TARANTO
PALERMO
CATANIA
CAGLIARI
Golfo di Taranto
I.e Eolie o Lipari
I.e Egadi
I.e Tremiti
I.e Maltesi

S. GIOVANNI
ROTONDO
Rodi
Garganico
S. Menaio
Peschici
Manacore
Vico
del Gargano
Carpino
Vieste
Testa d. Gargano
682
Mattinata
Scavi di
Monte Saraceno
Manfredonia
Lido di Siponto
Golfo di
Manfredonia
Zapponeta
Carapelle
Saline
Margherita
di Savoia
Trinitapoli
Ofanto
Barletta
Trani
Bisceglie
Cerignola
CANNE
Canosa
Andria
Corato
Ruvo
di Puglia
Terlizzi
Minervino
Murge
540
Castel
del Monte
Lavello
Spinazzola
Venosa
Maschito
Palazzo
S. Gervasio
Grumo

S. ELIA
A PIANISI
SERRACAPRIOLA
CAMPOBASSO
VENAFRO
S. MARCO
LA CATOLA
MORCONE
PIETRELCINA
BENEVENTO
MONTEFUSCO
GESUALDO